Russia's Foreign Energy Policy

This book examines Russia's multidimensional foreign energy policy and the emerging and ongoing conflicts with energy-consuming and transit countries.

Russia's Foreign Energy Policy examines whether the interdependence patterns shaped through various channels (such as foreign trade, investment, finance, technology, and social interactions) between Russia and energy-importing countries could prevent energy-based conflict. Drawing on semi-structured expert interviews, Kenan Aslanli challenges the one-sided conventional wisdom that focusses on foreign policy ambitions and overlooks the peculiarities of the energy dimension. Instead, Aslanli highlights the complexity of contemporary energy affairs using a holistic approach that goes beyond geopolitics. He examines various energy types such as crude oil, natural gas, and nuclear and considers a diverse range of actors which include energy companies and international organizations. Using examples from Europe, Asia, and the Middle East, Aslanli demonstrates how the Russian strategy of using energy resources as a tool or energy weapon for foreign policy goals has a diminishing return in the long run.

This book will be of great interest to students and scholars of energy policy, foreign policy, and Russian studies more broadly.

Kenan Aslanli is a faculty member at Ankara Yıldırım Beyazıt University (AYBU), Department of International Relations. He works as an expert on the energy and political economy of the wider Eurasian powers at the Center for Iranian Studies (IRAM) in Turkey. He graduated from the doctorate programme at Ankara Yıldırım Beyazıt University, Department of International Relations (English), in 2022. He was a project partner and researcher at the Center for Eastern European Studies at the University of Bremen (Forschungsstelle Osteuropa) and a visiting lecturer at the Vienna BFI University of Applied Sciences (Austria).

Routledge Studies in Energy Policy

Ethics in Danish Energy Policy
Edited by Finn Arler, Mogens Rüdiger, Karl Sperling, Kristian Høyer Toft and Bo Poulsen

Mainstreaming Solar Energy in Small, Tropical Islands
Cultural and Policy Implications
Kiron C. Neale

Appraising the Economics of Smart Meters
Costs and Benefits
Jacopo Torriti

Wind Power and Public Engagement
Co-operatives and Community Ownership
Giuseppe Pellegrini-Masini

Social Movements against Wind Power in Canada and Germany
Energy Policy and Contention
Andrea Bues

Nuclear Power in Stagnation
A Cultural Approach to Failed Expansion
David Toke, Geoffrey Chun-Fung Chen, Antony Froggatt and Richard Connolly

Russia's Foreign Energy Policy
Resources, Actors, Conflicts
Kenan Aslanli

For further details please visit the series page on the Routledge website: http://www.routledge.com/books/series/RSIEP/

Russia's Foreign Energy Policy

Resources, Actors, Conflicts

Kenan Aslanli

Routledge
Taylor & Francis Group
LONDON AND NEW YORK

earthscan
from Routledge

First published 2024
by Routledge
4 Park Square, Milton Park, Abingdon, Oxon OX14 4RN

and by Routledge
605 Third Avenue, New York, NY 10158

Routledge is an imprint of the Taylor & Francis Group, an informa business

British Library Cataloguing-in-Publication Data
A catalogue record for this book is available from the British Library

ISBN: 978-1-032-52808-3 (hbk)
ISBN: 978-1-032-52809-0 (pbk)
ISBN: 978-1-003-40848-2 (ebk)

DOI: 10.4324/9781003408482

Typeset in Times New Roman
by codeMantra

Contents

Abbreviations

APEC	Asia-Pacific Economic Cooperation
ASEAN	The Association of Southeast Asian Nations
BPS	Baltic Pipeline System
BRICS	Brazil, Russia, India, China, South Africa
CEE	Central and Eastern European
CEO	Chief Executive Officer
CIS	Commonwealth of Independent States
CNG	Compressed Natural Gas
CSTO	Collective Security Treaty Organization
EEU	Eurasian Economic Union
ESPO	Eastern Siberia–Pacific Ocean
EU	European Union
FDI	Foreign Direct Investment
FEP	Foreign Energy Policy
GDP	Gross Domestic Product
GTS	Gas Transmission System
IPE	International Political Economy
ITC	International Trade Centre
LNG	Liquefied Natural Gas
MW	Megawatt
NATO	North Atlantic Treaty Organization
NPP	Nuclear Power Plant
OPEC	Organization of the Petroleum Exporting Countries
PSA	Production Sharing Agreement
SOCAR	State Oil Company of the Azerbaijan Republic
RECSID	Russia's Energy Conflicts and Supply Interruptions Dataset
REM	Rare Earth Metals
TPP	Thermal Power Plant
UGS	Underground Gas Storage
UGSS	Unified Gas Supply System
UNSC	United Nations Security Council
USSR	Union of Soviet Socialist Republics

Figures and Tables

Figures

Tables

1 Introduction

1.1 Research Rationale, Problematization, and Theoretical Framework

Russia's energy reserves (oil, gas, coal, and electricity), energy exports to European, Asian, and post-Soviet markets, nuclear energy capabilities, and active position in the regional and international energy settings have transformative power over the country's domestic and foreign policies. Energy resources, energy infrastructure, and energy export volumes could be considered a component of the holistic national state power of Russia. Also, the energy factor is part of the geopolitical struggle strategies over energy-rich territories considering that energy (e.g., crude oil, natural gas, coal, and uranium) resources are depletable and finite. Energy resources have often been considered a source, objective, and means in inter-state conflicts between Russia and counterpart entities (states, non-state actors, etc.). But the existing energy studies literature considers mostly inter-state militarized conflicts, border disputes, and wars, ignoring the potential role of energy resources and energy infrastructure (e.g., oil-gas pipelines) in the facts about the non-militarized inter-state conflicts. Especially, there is no systematic formal and empirical analysis of the Russian attempts to use energy factors (i) to link energy conflicts with foreign energy policy (FEP) considering the pattern of interdependence over a longer time horizon, and (ii) to examine foreign energy policy under the context of foreign policy and grand strategy aims. Russia's foreign policy ambitions or goals towards Europe and post-Soviet geography create strong narratives for its foreign energy policy towards the same regions, including using the "energy power" with political motivations. This feature distinguishes Russia's systematic energy conflicts from the misuse of energy by other oil-gas countries such as the USA, Saudi Arabia, Turkmenistan, and Iran.

Why is it important to academically study Russia's foreign energy policy and energy conflicts? The first major factor is the *scale* of Russia's energy conflicts in terms of harmful repercussions for the world energy markets. As Bogaturov (2017, p. 264) argued, Russia is the only "nuclear-oil great power" in the world that we can modify as the largest "nuclear-fossil great power" globally. Because Russia owns the largest gas reserves and is the largest gas exporter in the world, it is the second-largest gas producer and third-largest crude oil producer in the world (IEA,

DOI: 10.4324/9781003408482-1

2022a). Russia's oil and gas export plays a crucial role in the energy markets of the EU, CIS countries, and selected Asian markets. The second major factor is the *intensity* and tools of the Russian energy conflicts. "*Russia's Energy Conflicts and Supply Interruptions Dataset*" (RECSID) identified 813 energy conflicts and supply interruption cases of Russia (or with the country's direct involvement) with a total of 60 states (or their energy companies), "quasi-states", and various organizations between 1991 and 2021. Russia as a critical player in the energy landscape of the Eurasia region has an attitude to misuse its energy resources as a tool in foreign policy intensely with large-scale effects where it exploits sets of tools. But it suffers from profound constraints in the foreign energy policy such as crude oil and gas prices, technological dependence, gradual energy transition reputational decay, or capacity-ambition mismatch. As one of the largest energy producers and exporters in the world, Russia's aggressive foreign energy policy and energy conflicts have large-scale regional and global repercussions. There is a need to go beyond the existing narratives on the Russian foreign energy policy to unlock the predictive determinants and limitations with a verifiable data-based approach via the unique RECSID, and semi-structured interviews.

This book based on the extended and updated version of the author's doctoral dissertation attempts to fill the gap in the literature on the causal role of energy (oil, gas, nuclear, coal, electricity, and transit) in inter-state conflicts in Russia and valid tools and mechanisms for the "energy-conflict" nexus under the framework of foreign energy policy. The research intends to challenge one-sided conventional wisdom in the existing literature on Russia's foreign energy policy that concentrates on foreign policy ambitions and overlooks the peculiarities of the energy dimension. There is a need to examine and disclose the complexity of contemporary energy affairs with a holistic approach that cannot be explained only by geopolitical considerations ignoring multiple interacting actors. The book's ontological approach to the foreign energy policy is the interplay of the integrative phenomenon where the Russian foreign policy accommodates the energy dimension more dynamically with reciprocal interaction. The book investigates the pattern of interdependence in Russia's foreign energy policy as a determinant of the tools and constraints through quantification of the energy conflicts under the hierarchical structure of constant foreign policy aims such as hegemonic expansionism. The book aims to take the more dynamic view (identifying changes in tools, significant constraints, conditions, and policy patterns over time) and more comprehensive view in terms of energy types (gas, oil, nuclear, coal, electricity) to the long-term misemploying of energy resources as a foreign policy tool by Russia and its energy conflicts. The current book earmarks to illustrate the possible determinants, dynamics, motivations, and limits of the conflictual nature of Russia's foreign energy policy and its tools under the context of changing and constant foreign policy and grand strategy goals. The conceptual framework, dimensions, scopes, tools, and constraints of the Russian foreign energy policy illuminate specific patterns for energy conflicts that have substantial policy implications for energy-importing countries.

The theoretical background of Russia's foreign energy policy and energy conflicts is highly debatable. Existing literature correlates Russia's foreign energy policy with energy types, the level of interdependence, the personality of statesmen, and growing external risks. Some authors (Baldwin, 2016; Bogaturov, 2017; Dannreuther & Ostrowski, 2013; Pirani, 2010) argue that gas is less conflictual than oil or minerals on the international level. Another group of authors (Balmaceda, 2021; Gustafson, 2020; Keohane & Nye, 2011; Yergin, 2011) underlined the role of energy interdependence in global and regional energy affairs as a constraining factor that alleviates the level of conflicts. Also, there are scholars (Buzan & Waever, 2004; Larsson, 2006; Marange, 2019; Mironov, 2003; Shaffer, 2009) emphasizing the personality and professional background of rulers (e.g., Putin), and the growing regional securitization of energy. Theoretical frameworks containing the power-centric neorealist approach and multi-actor complex interdependence approach are contesting to construe Russia's foreign energy policy.

Why does the theory of complex interdependence deserve to be tested in Russian foreign energy policy studies? Complex interdependence as a theory emerged in the 1970s after the energy crises (it is worthwhile to apply this theory almost 50 years after the 1973 oil crisis) and it has relevant examples from the energy sector to reveal the vulnerability and sensitivity of the countries. Complex interdependence takes into account the complexities of modern and globalized energy affairs and energy markets. States aren't the only actors in the energy sphere and the corporate interests of the energy companies partly determine the foreign energy policy. The stable international organizations and regional platforms ensure multiple channels of communication among Russia and other state and non-state actors. For example, Russia successfully cooperates with OPEC member oil producers under the framework of the "OPEC Plus" format till 2016 to influence the global oil market through commitments related to the oil production level (OPEC, 2022). This cooperation platform endured serious challenges in the global oil market including demand contraction during the global COVID-19 pandemic in 2020–2021 or an oil supply crunch during the war in Ukraine in 2022. Despite the energy market crises, Russia and other "OPEC Plus" actors stick to their commitments to oil production and export. Energy trade and energy investment flow to ensure the interconnections of the actor under the framework of multiple channels and multiple agenda formation of the energy affairs based on complex interdependence.

The weakest point of the complex interdependence theory in the case of Russia's foreign energy policy is the postulate about the irrelevance of the military factor in interstate relations. The Russian state has a special history of militarization, therefore, it is inclined to connect energy policy with militarization and securitization of interstate affairs and the functioning of the state. Russian and Soviet militarized strategic culture connected energy policy with grand strategy ambitions and militarism. For example, the state's military structure was responsible to build domestic pipeline systems in the USSR. Also, the USSR started gas export to Europe (Austria) almost simultaneously with the military intervention in Czechoslovakia in 1968 (Moravcsik, 2019). Russia's military doctrine related nuclear energy to security and nuclear weapon indirectly after the well-known speech at the Munich Security Conference by the President Putin in 2007. But the economic interdependence acted as a relative limiter in the foreign energy policy (e.g., the "gas for pipes" program in the 1970s or the "energy export in return of petrodollars" approach concerning the EU after 2000). Russia's energy trade with the Western partners developed the interdependence pattern via various channels: (a) to receive fiscal revenues that could boost economic growth in Russia; (b) to import high technology and equipment in return for raw material export; (c) to supply fossil fuel to the European market that drives industrial production in the continent; and (d) to increase interactions between various state and non-state actors.

Even Russia was forced to take into consideration the pattern of energy interdependence before the severe phases of the political and military conflicts. In the case of the Russia-Ukraine complex political and military conflict, Russia firstly made an attempt to change the pattern of interdependence with Ukraine and the EU establishing asymmetric dependence (shifting oil-gas export from Europe to Asia, bypassing the Ukrainian route in the gas transit using TurkStream and Nord Stream-2) before military intervention in 2014 and 2022. Russia continued stable energy flows during the military intervention in Ukraine in order to proceed "petrodollar" inflow smoothly. Russia could intend to use an energy factor as a foreign policy tool ("energy weapon"), but the multi-actor structure and interdependent realities of the energy market dictate adjustments in the foreign energy policy. Russia applied "energy weapon" against target countries, but the pattern of interdependence and rebalancing factors such as diversification and sanctions could partly make it obsolete. Energy geopolitics isn't sufficient to elucidate Russia's foreign energy policy under the interdependent and highly globalized energy market environment (despite the risks of "geoeconomic fragmentation") with the permanent evolution of instruments and technologies.

The main argument of the book is that although the level of symmetry in the pattern of interdependence between Russia and counterparts shaped by various channels (such as foreign trade, investment, finance, technology, and interactions) isn't a "valid preventer" of the energy conflicts, it is a "confined mitigator" in terms of the tool selection of both Russia and partners in the foreign energy policy. Also, interdependence with counterparts can be asymmetric, providing additional "bargaining power" to Russia in conflictual interstate political affairs when we could employ "timing" and "correlation" as criteria to differentiate energy conflicts with (geo)political and economic motivations. The research put forward some initial hypotheses (H) for testing in the data analysis and empirical part of the current research based on the argument of the research, the theoretical assumptions representing interdependence theory on Russia's foreign energy policy and foreign policy dimension:

H-1: *Russia cannot "weaponize" all types of energy including gas, oil, electricity, uranium, and coal for grand strategy and foreign policy goals considering the fact that the energy type is globally traded shaping interdependence pattern.*

H-2: *Complex interdependence in energy trade and economic parameters (energy domain of the FEP) can partly limit Russia's aggressive FEP and diminish the "returns" of energy conflicts and FEP's applied and evolved tools.*

H-3: *Under the pattern of interdependence, Russia's relatively aggressive foreign energy policy and energy conflicts don't depend on the political personality of President Putin and had a similar behavioural pattern in the pre-Putin period, as well.*

H-4: *Foreign policy domain of the FEP determines the growing external threat perceptions and "securitization of energy" that raise the geographical coverage of the energy conflicts of Russia in alignment with foreign policy goals.*

1.2 Research Design and Methodology

The book applies deductive reasoning of the theory/concept testing perspective proposed by De Vaus (2001, pp. 5–8) and Bernard (2013, pp. 12–13) as an epistemological slant. It is based on the concepts of foreign energy policy and appropriate IR theories (it applies complex interdependence theory from liberal school with the limited combination of the "state-market interaction" concept from the IPE position) to explain Russia's conflictual energy interactions with partner countries using a unique dataset and complementary qualitative observations. From the research methodology perspective, the study applies a hypothesis-testing framework based on the relevant components of interdependence theory. In addition to the hypothetico-deductive approach, the research possesses the elements of inductive generalization of empirical observations and facts about Russia's foreign energy policy and energy conflicts with a holistic approach. Hypotheses have been derived from theory, but also some patterns based on observations, facts, and cases on the energy conflicts contributed to the (re)formulation and the testing of the initial suppositions. The current research could be qualified as explanatory research based on deduction-based epistemology and hypothesis-testing (Rich et al., 2018, p. 70). But it contains some elements of exploratory research from the research design perspective where the research produces unique postulations (Neuman, 2014, p. 38), applies qualitative methods, and generates distinctive dataset that contradict conventional wisdom on Russia's foreign energy policy to a certain extent. Exploratory research is mostly applied to the less-researched areas. The author underpins the argument that components of the Russian foreign energy policy in terms of energy types aren't researched broadly and deeply for a long-term time horizon.

It is an empiricist scientific inquiry (rather than interpretative and normative) partly based on the positivist paradigm (Kauppi & Viotti, 2020, p. 2). The study attempts to translate the findings based on empirical evidence and collected facts to describe Russia's foreign energy policy ambitions (including expansionist nuclear energy strategy) by establishing the mechanisms of a causal linkage under the theoretical frames. The research design constitutes arguments from the theoretical and conceptual framework for testing via data. It starts from the contextual and theoretical frameworks and then analyses collected data/observations. Qualitative and quantitative data are employed independently to examine the same phenomenon under a "triangulation" basis. Major dimensions of energy conflicts (oil, gas, nuclear, electricity, coal, and energy transit), the evolution of available tools of Russia's conflictual foreign energy policy between 1991 and 2021 (energy conflict tracker or dataset covers from 1991 to 2019), constraints for foreign energy policy under the pattern of interdependence, external conditions, and domestic "political economy" dynamics, and a foreign policy based on grand strategy will be building blocks of the theoretical construction and analysis of quantitative and qualitative data. The conceptional substructure and the theoretical framework presented by existing literature on the topic and the researcher's prior knowledge and assumptions will define precise hypotheses for testing.

From a methodological standpoint, the book intends to identify determinants, tools, and constraints of Russia's energy conflicts and foreign energy policy attitudes by examining a uniquely generated dataset (*Russia's Energy Conflicts and Supply Interruptions Dataset – RECSID*), the results of expert interviews, the basic content analysis of official documents and official statements. The research examines Russia's foreign energy policy and energy conflict in the connection with the peculiarities of the energy sector and broader foreign policy purposes. The research exploited a dataset on Russia's energy conflicts and the supply disruptions that energy factor is a source and tool. The current research's findings can pave the way towards a better understanding of the Russian energy conflicts and foreign energy policy in relation to the topical theoretical foundation and practical decision-making process of the energy importing countries.

1.3 Research Methods

The research based on the extended and updated version of the author's doctoral dissertation applies the combination of *qualitative* (semi-structured expert interviews and basic content analysis[1]) and *quantitative* (data analysis based on energy statistics and findings of RECSID as energy conflicts tracker, correlation matrix to reveal the sensitivity of Russia's energy conflicts to diverse variables/indicators) research methods to describe and quantify the phenomena. The author attempts to incorporate three methodological techniques in the current research: *expert interviews* to reveal limitations and driving factors of the Russian foreign energy policy and its available toolset; *statistical analysis* to disclose the significant trends in Russia's foreign energy conflicts and supply interruptions; and *basic content analysis* to monitor the changing discourse and context on energy factor in the official statements and documents. Qualitative analysis (some elements of grounded theory based on induction) and quantitative analysis (basic content analysis based on word counts) of qualitative data were applied in the research.

1.3.1 Semi-Structured Expert Interviews

Semi-structured interviews are a relevant tool for elite and expert interviews where the interviewer applies preprepared questions and instruction but also allows the emanation of new content during the interview process. Ahlin (2019) underlined that semi-structured interviews, as a qualitative data collection method, combine prearranged questions with new non-standardized and open-ended questions that are emerged during the interview process. The semi-structured expert interviews present in-depth and publicly unavailable knowledge on the selected topics from manifold viewpoints. The semi-structured expert interviews assisted to comprehend the real drivers and the tendencies of the phenomenon of Russia's energy conflicts and narrating the data analysis (RECSID).

This research is supported by semi-structured expert interviews that were conducted in Moscow (Russia), Kyiv (Ukraine), Tbilisi (Georgia), Baku (Azerbaijan), Albena (Bulgaria), and Telč (Czech Republic) in 2018–2019. Masaryk University's (Brno, Czech Republic) Center for Energy Studies organized "Energy in Europe: Sources and Politics" summer school during August 3–10, 2019, in Telč, the Czech Republic where regional and global energy settings, energy geopolitics, and energy security issues were discussed covering oil, gas, coal, nuclear, and renewables. The author of the book took part in the summer school to learn more insights into energy policy, take interviews with prominent energy and foreign policy experts, and present the initial findings of the current book in an informal format. Also, the author visited Moscow in October 2019 to take part in the "Russian Energy Week" International Forum, where representatives of the Russian Ministry of Energy and energy companies presented the updated status of the country's energy sector. Several expert interviews have been conducted in Moscow during the visit in October 2019 with key energy and IR experts.

Ten leading experts in energy and international politics, who represented both Russia and the energy-importing countries of the post-Soviet space and the EU that have intense energy conflicts with Russia, took part in the semi-structured expert interviews. Additionally, the author addressed the relevant questions to the three practiced energy experts during question-and-answer (Q&A) sessions of the various workshops on energy issues to get opinions about Russia's foreign energy policy and energy conflicts. The interviewees include a range of current and former government officials from energy and foreign ministers, academicians, public policy analysts, leading energy experts, and foreign policy experts. As most of the interviews were conducted individually, the names of interviewees are indicated in Table 1.1 and their contributions were decrypted using text analysis techniques.

In addition to the expert interviews, the author participated in the focus group discussion on the energy sectors of post-Soviet countries and the external role of Russia that was initiated by the World Experience for Georgia (WEG) on July 17, 2018, in Tbilisi, Georgia. Energy experts from Georgia, Ukraine, Moldova, Armenia, Azerbaijan, Belarus, and Uzbekistan participated in the focus group discussion where the author benefitted from getting practical knowledge on the energy sector

1.3.2 The Methodology of RECSID and Statistical Data Analysis

"*Russia's Energy Conflicts and Supply Interruptions Dataset*" (RECSID) covers the energy conflicts between Russia and its main foreign energy partners, and multipurpose (geopolitical, political, economic, commercial, technical) energy supply interruptions by Russia from 1991 to 2021. The database was formed from primary (in-depth interviews and focus group discussions with experts and former officials on the energy sector from Russia and conflicting counterparts) and secondary (study of media reports, energy, and foreign policy news, books, magazines, official statements, think-tank reports, and non-official records) sources information. The author has used the electronic archives of well-known, relevant, and professional Russian and Western media (e.g., *Kommersant*, *Vedomosti*, *Nezavisimaya Gazeta*,

Table 1.1 List of interviewed experts for the current research

Name	*Position*	*Date*	*Place*	*Method*
Giorgi Mukhigulishvili	The lead researcher in energy studies at World Experience for Georgia (WEG)	17.07.2018	Tbilisi, Georgia	Semi-structured interviews
Ilham Shaban	Director of the Oil Research Center in Baku, Chief editor of the Caspian Barrel	19.08.2018	Baku, Azerbaijan	Semi-structured interviews
Andrii Chubyk	Energy expert at the Center for Global Studies Strategy XXI (Ukraine) and Minister of Energy and Coal Industry	22.10.2018	Kyiv, Ukraine	Semi-structured interviews
Prof. Dr Eckart Stratenschulte	Acting Chairman of the Board, German National Foundation (Berlin), professor and lecturer at the Free University of Berlin on European foreign affairs and EU-Russia relations	04.06.2019	Albena, Bulgaria	Semi-structured interviews
Dr Stanislav Pritchin	Analyst on energy policy of the Eurasian region at the Institute of Oriental Studies of Russian Academy of Science; Director of the Expert Center for Eurasian Development	03/10/2019	Moscow, Russia	Semi-structured interviews
Dr Alexey Belogoryev	Deputy Executive Director on Energy Studies, Institute for Energy and Finance	04/10/2019	Moscow, Russia	Semi-structured interviews
Dr Marcel Salikhov	Head of Economic Department, Institute for Energy and Finance	04/10/2019	Moscow, Russia	Semi-structured interviews
Dr Olga Bogdanova	Department Director of Energy Market and Infrastructure, Ministry of Economic Affairs of Latvia	04/08/2019	Telč, Czech Republic	Semi-structured interviews
Dr Andras Deak	Senior Research Fellow, Institute of World Economics, Hungarian Academy of Sciences	05/08/2019	Telč, Czech Republic	Semi-structured interviews
Dr Martin Jirusek	Assistant Professor, International Institute of Political Science, Masaryk University	08/08/2019	Telč, Czech Republic	Semi-structured interviews
Dr James Henderson	Director of the Energy Transition Research Initiative at the Oxford Institute for Energy Studies (OIES)	08/08/2019	Telč, Czech Republic	Discussion in the Q&A session of the workshop
Vaclav Bartushka	Special Envoy for Energy Security, Ministry of Foreign Affairs, Czech Republic	04/08/2019	Telč, Czech Republic	Discussion in the Q&A session of the workshop

Novaya Gazeta, İzvestiya, RBK, Expert, Reuters, The Economist, The Financial Times, The New York Times, and *Oil & Gas Journal*) for the data collection on complex energy conflicts of Russia.

The time interval of the data collection in the current study covers the period between 1991 and 2021 except for a few determinative cases from 1990. A huge misconception in the Western scholar community and media is to associate Russia's energy geopolitics with Putin's political rule, his unique type of governance, and the role of the political "inner circle". But also, RECSID sheds light on the pre-Putin era to prove deeper roots in the foreign energy policy and energy conflicts of Russia. *One of the central questions that RECSID attempts to answer is, "does Russia's conflictual foreign energy policy depends on the energy type, or the nature of this energy actor is intrinsically conflictual, and contradictious that reflected in all energy types under the pattern of interdependence?".*

For this research's definition, energy conflicts are contradictious incidents that could be realized and revealed between energy partner countries (nation-states), unrecognized "quasi-states" or separatist units, state-owned or private energy companies, and even international organizations that have interconnections in terms of energy supply, energy demand, energy assets acquisition, energy transit routes, energy infrastructure, and energy policy. Also, we can interpret the energy conflict concept as energy interventions and disputes that are partly the result of Russia's "exploitation" of energy resources as a foreign policy tool. The current study uses a broad definition of the "energy conflict" concept that goes beyond the facts of supply disruptions. Also, Russia's indirect conflicts with third parties related to the country's direct energy affairs with the main energy partner could be included in the list of energy conflicts. At first glance, some energy conflicts seem to have been initiated by the partner countries, not Russia. However, these conflicts externalize and mirror the reactions, fears, concerns, and active countermeasures of the counterpart countries towards Russia's foreign energy policy.

When we research Russia's energy conflicts, it is important to count not only actual and already completed facts but also energy threats and intimidations that Russian officials openly stated towards consumer and transit countries. Because those officials' statements about the "energy weaponizing" by Russia create fear and a negative conception of the reliability and durability of the country's oil-gas supply.

Russia's energy conflicts not only indicate the country's behaviour against energy partners and other institutions but also reflect the conflictual nature of its foreign energy policy. Russia's energy conflicts often did not occur among governments but between private or state-owned energy companies. In addition to the energy conflict concept, the current research broadens the concept of "energy weapon" (even though this concept was criticized as an over-politicized approach) adding a domestic dimension to the energy conflicts of Russia with partner countries. In certain cases, Russia's internal clashes within ruling elites or among Moscow and federal regions triggered an energy conflict with foreign partner countries. Russia's foreign energy policy towards any counterpart country sometimes could lead to a domestic political crisis in the target country. This study classifies this type of domestic political scandal as the energy conflict associated with Russia.

Besides the energy supply interruptions, disrupted transactions related to the energy assets, explosions, and sabotage attempts against energy infrastructure and energy assets including oil-gas export pipelines, terminated energy deals, and failed energy negotiations were included in the Russian energy conflict categories. The database covers all major energy types such as crude oil, oil products, natural gas, nuclear energy, electricity, and coal. Existing literature on the "Russian energy weapon" and energy conflicts mostly commences with a theoretical foundation and then justifies it by using some well-known cases such as the energy conflicts with Ukraine, Georgia, and Belarus. Additionally, RECSID also aims to contribute to the partial application of inductive reasoning shaping generalizations based on the dataset and building linkage with the foreign policy based on the concrete evidence of Russia's foreign energy policy incidents, energy conflicts, and energy supply interruption cases. Also, some indicators of RECSID could be considered as an operationalization of theory meaning converting theoretical framework to quantitative data and indicators (Haucke, Hoekstra, & Ravenzwaaij, 2021, pp. 191–354). In summary, the current study generated its unique dataset on Russian energy conflicts and energy supply interruptions. The dataset has undergone various statistical analysis including correlation analysis to reveal relations among different variables.

1.3.3 Basic Content Analysis

One of the methods in the research (partly qualitative method) was a *basic content analysis* based on deductive reasoning when the researcher firstly develops the hypothesis and then tests this premise through text-based analysis. In this research, the basic content analysis was partly based on the deductive reasoning approach, as well, when the author developed categories beforehand the analysis was based on initial knowledge and presupposition of the research findings. Lamont (2015) argued that keyword counting is a basic form of content analysis. But the results of the keyword counting provide quantitative data that can be analysed to reveal correlation among different concepts. The output of the word count was the correlation matrix that was based on the "case-by-variable matrix" or "key-word-in-context" (KWIC) matrix which is also the tool of grounded theory (Bernard, 2013, pp. 524–539).

In the book, the text-based content analysis covers the Russian President's annual messages to the Federal Assembly (Parliament) of Russia, foreign policy concepts, and NATO Summits' final declarations. The President's annual message to the Parliament is an operational document that summarizes the internal policy, foreign policy, and economic (including energy) developments of the last year and sets a goal for the new year. Foreign policy concepts are more fundamental, conceptual, and strategic documents that are adopted in key milestones in terms of the electoral or geopolitical cycles related to the Russian ruling elite's foreign policy preferences. NATO's final declarations were examined in terms of growing emphasis on energy security in parallel to the negative connotations of the relations with

Russia. The level of analysis is keywords and their context on the level of sentences and paragraphs as the bigger volume of content. The research doesn't fully apply the discourse analysis method to reveal geopolitical narratives and the political economy context of the Russian foreign energy policy towards CIS and European countries. But the analysis based on the study of Russia's official programmes and strategies, newspaper and magazine articles, analytical reports, regular bulletins, and interview materials, identified opposing representations ("energy as a source of cooperation", "energy resources as an instrument of geopolitical hegemony") on the energy (oil, gas, nuclear) interactions between Russia and energy partners.

1.4 Research's Limitations and Challenges

The current research has content-related thematic and methodological limitations. First, we can briefly review the thematic boundaries of the study. The transformative power of technology and efficient energy systems make it nearly impossible for resource-rich nations to fully concentrate power and build a monopoly over the energy value chain. Even though it describes the role of access to technology in Russia's dependence on the developed world, including the western countries, the current study doesn't shed much light on the technological features of the energy sectors. The author argues that linking the entire energy sector of the country to the "great power" aspirations of the Russian state is a relatively simplified approach that neglects the economic, financial, technological, environmental complexity, and consequent limitations of the sector that compelled the Soviet Union and Russian states to cooperate with external state and non-state actors. This complexity limits Russia's realization of "energy superpower" and "energy weapon" techniques. But this argument that envisages "complexity-led cooperation" demands rational thinking from decision-makers in the state, irrationality dimension of the decision-making process in the puzzling Russian state is out of the scope of the current research. Decision-making models that are suitable for Russia's foreign policy haven't been analysed lengthily. A hedging strategy could be applied to find out the foreign energy strategies of the small-scale post-Soviet and European countries to diminish energy dependence on Russia's hydrocarbon exports. The book's level of analysis covers the state and international levels with particular emphasis on energy companies with group logic. Still, it focused less on the individual level based on the political leader's psychology.

The current research also has methodological limitations. Applying the game theory and the comparative case study method for Russia's energy conflicts with concrete countries could be feasible. Although the thesis includes country cases (e.g., Georgia) in terms of Russia's energy conflicts based on RECSID findings and it applies the case study method to scrutinize Russia's energy conflicts, case study analysis doesn't include dimensions such as internal politics. It didn't focus on Russia's interstate energy conflicts with Ukraine as a post-Soviet "toxic" neighbour or Turkey as an emerging market neighbour from a domestic political viewpoint. An in-depth case study analysis could reveal the targeted countries' domestic political and economic settings. Detailed and software-supported discourse analysis hasn't been conducted parallel to content analysis of the Russian foreign policy concepts, energy strategies, and other critical official documents. But the book has analysed the discourse and context of the domestic political system of Russia that was related to the energy sector's influence. The scope of content and number of participants could be extended in the expert interviews to cover Russia's energy partner countries with dissimilar economic, (geo)political, and energy dependency peculiarities (e.g., China). But material and time constraints didn't allow the author to accomplish this task. Regression analysis didn't produce meaningful output on the relationship between a dependent variable (number of Russia's energy conflicts and supply interruptions based on RECSID) and various independent variables (oil price, oil rents, GDP per capita, etc.).

There are certain "traps" for the research on the Russian foreign energy policy: (a) exaggerated outcry or "noise" in the Western public opinion (media, think tanks, etc.) about the non-reliability of Russia as an energy supplier; and (b) Russian state-sponsored propaganda about the country's "energy superpower" and reliable energy supplies towards the EU (starting from the 1960s) and other energy markets. The Western decision-makers labelled Russian energy (oil and gas resources) as "toxic assets", "assets with high-risk premium", or "conflict commodity". To avoid the "noises, labels, and propaganda", we need an evidence-based approach through dataset and quantification of Russia's energy conflicts (RECSID). Prof. Indra Overland from Nord University (Norway), one of the pioneers in this field, led the research team to collect shreds of evidence on the Russian energy conflict for the period of 2000–2010. RECSID covers the period of 1991–2021 with a more comprehensive approach in terms of energy types, actors, and conflict classification (geopolitically motivated and commercially motivated conflicts). Generally, Russia's foreign energy policy was examined from 1991 to 2022 in the book. But also, there is room to extend the timeframe of RECSID as an energy tracker from 2022 to 2023 when Russia had a series of energy conflicts with the EU member states, other developed countries and Ukraine. Also, continual attempts should be made to renew independent variables in the regression analysis.

1.5 Contribution to the Existing Literature and Future Studies

The book contributes to the existing literature on the Russian foreign energy policy and energy conflicts. Firstly, existing literature mainly concentrates on linking Russia's foreign energy policy and energy conflicts with the (geo)political realm via the "energy weapon" concept, while this research deconstructs the foreign energy policy into the two domains (foreign and energy policy), demonstrating the role of the multi-actor structure of the energy affairs that installs the pattern of interdependence. The study's data collection period covers an unprecedentedly long-run time interval from 1991 to 2021. Analogical studies (e.g., Orttung & Overland, 2011) comprised shorter time intervals between 2000 and 2010. The study's comprehensiveness encompasses all energy sectors (oil, gas, coal, nuclear, electricity, transit), relevant actors, and broader geographical coverage. The book applied "identification and classification of energy conflicts" techniques as a unique contribution to the literature. The predictability of the energy conflicts using analytical techniques such as "weak early warning signals" was proved by dataset. RECSID revealed that Russia had highest number of oil-related energy conflicts with Azerbaijan which is new finding in related literature. Another contribution of the research to the existing literature on Russia's foreign and energy policy is that it uncovered the valuable opinions of less-known (at least, in English sources) Russian authors (economy and IR) such as Bogaturov, Inozemtsev, Degterev, Shevtsova, and Zubarevich.

The study applies a combination of different research methods and theoretical perspectives. In addition to academia, the research findings could be relevant for decision-makers of partner countries of Russia on energy issues (e.g., Turkey, EU states, and CIS states) to have a proper and conjecturable understanding of Russia's strategic pattern in the foreign energy policy. The current study applied the basic content analysis to reveal the intensity of energy and threat/cooperation connotations in official and annual Presidential messages and foreign policy documents. This approach can be further deepened in future research to develop Energy Aggression Index or Energy Aggression Matrix with predictive capability. Also, separate vulnerability and sensitivity indexes could be framed and developed to analyse the pattern of interdependence. The examination of the misconduct factor in the foreign energy policy that was touched upon in the book to reveal the energy sector's actual interconnection mechanism can be deepened further in future theoretical and applied studies.

1.6 Short Outline of the Following Chapters of the Book

Chapter 1 described the research rationale and the tenets of problematization, research design, research methodology, and applied research methods. The research's limitations and contribution to the existing literature and future studies were elucidated. Chapter 2 frames the theoretical framework of Russia's foreign energy policy consisting of complex interdependence theory and a review of the alternative theories and concepts on Russia's FEP. Theoretical framework and overview of the literature on Russia's foreign energy policy and holistic energy conflicts from complex interdependence and alternative perspectives pave the way for the analysis of the conceptual framework of the research. Russia's foreign policy, domestic factors, and applied aspects of foreign energy policy (e.g., objectives, tools, concepts, dimensions) can be reviewed as the conceptual framework of the book. Chapter 3 defines a conceptual framework including Russia's foreign policy, grand strategy, domestic factors, and foreign energy policy (tools, objectives, and conflicts).

Chapter 4 covers the role of energy in the Russian economy, economic performance, and energy reserves as empirical content of the research. Chapter 5 covers major actors of the foreign energy policy of Russia including state-owned and foreign energy firms, the government, and adopted strategic documents by the governments. Chapter 6 describes "Russia's Energy Conflicts and Supply Interruptions Dataset" (RECSID) in terms of energy conflicts, energy type, and economic interdependence. Chapter 7 describes the geopolitical and commercial motivations, constraints, determinants, metrics of foreign energy policy, and "balancers" of interdependence (energy diversification and sanctions) based on RECSID, expert interviews, and content analysis. Chapter 8 narrates the finding-based conclusions of the book and significant policy implications.

Note

1 Content analysis based on word counts also can be characterized as a quantitative research method.

2 Theoretical Framework

2.1 Overview of Basic Literature on Russia's Foreign Energy Policy

The theoretical background of the foreign policy, grand strategy, foreign energy policy (FEP), and energy conflicts of Russia is contentious. Also, various theoretical frameworks weren't supported by convincing and fully explanatory case studies and evidence on the Russian foreign energy policy to reveal the conditions under which their supported cause-effect relations were realized by the actors. Tsygankov (2018) argued that Russia is a complex case to comprehend and examine, considering the extensive territory, broad geographic engagement, the multi-actor structure of the state, and the diverse society (p. 15). Graaf et al. (2016) noticed that energy politics hasn't a well-grounded theoretical foundation, because of the technical knowledge that energy studies require and the multidimensional feature of the energy sector (pp. 3–44). Therefore, we could apply complex theoretical frameworks and analytical instruments to interpret Russia's foreign energy policy. Acharya and Buzan (2019) argued that the existing major IR theories (realism, liberalism, Marxism, English school, constructivism) reflect peculiarities of the West's political history and related theory-formation process that disregard non-Western theoretical perspectives (pp. 2–3). Prominent Russian IR scholars (Bogaturov, 2017; Dugin, 2015; Karaganov, 2018; Kortunov, 2010; Lukin, 2020; Tsygankov, 2016) emphasized the uniqueness of the Russian case, but it cannot be considered as an adequate effort to develop a relevant and perceptible theoretical framework for the Russian foreign and energy policy. Different components of Russia's foreign energy policy such as major propositions of foreign policy and energy strategies, energy conflicts, and energy diplomacy can be explained by different theoretical frameworks.

Various international relations theories have arguments about the energy resources and energy power of Russia, but two streams come forward: state-centric and conflict-based neorealist theoretical framework; market-based and cooperative neoliberal theoretical framework. Graaf et al. (2016) stressed that two intellectual and theoretical streams exist in the literature on international energy affairs: the realist stream refers to the geopolitical narrative, politicization, and securitization of energy; the liberal stream adverts complex interdependence,

DOI: 10.4324/9781003408482-2

cross-border cooperation, market rules, and global institutions. Many authors including Lomagin (2015) think that there is a clash between two different perspectives on Russia's foreign energy policy that reflect geopolitical/strategic (realist) and market/commercial (liberal) approaches (p. 6). Realist scholars underline that large energy companies are instrumentalized ("weaponized") by the state. Market, commercial or liberal perspective argues that foreign energy policy is determined by strong state-owned (e.g., Gazprom, Rosneft) and private (e.g., Lukoil) energy companies that follow market-based commercial incentives.

Keohane and Nye (2011) pointed out that international politics can be well explained by the combination of liberal's complex interdependence theory and realism expressing that global political-economy situations are often located between these two theoretical edges (pp. 20–29). The offensive and defensive realist perspective can explain the foreign policy dimension of Russia's energy policy that considers energy power as a complementary component of national power. But when we examine the real application of the so-called "energy weapon" or realization of "energy power" (through certain parameters such as duration and timing of energy conflicts, real outcomes of energy conflicts, mutual concessions, etc.), the liberal "complex interdependence" theory has a quite adequate level of relevance and explanatory power considering the complexity of the energy sector. The empirical part of this research also demonstrates that combining diverse components and arguments of different theories could be relevant to explaining the complex foreign energy policy and energy conflicts of Russia. But complex interdependence theory has the relative appropriateness to address the complexity of global politics and the world economy including global energy markets, energy policies, and energy geopolitics that influence the interstate and inter-actor energy conflicts.

Thorun (2009) deeply analysed the shortcomings of different IR theories in the process of understanding Russian foreign policy and its energy dimension (pp. 1–12; 137–151). The realist approach argues that Russia's cooperative and aggressive foreign policy towards the West was related to the actor's relative power in the global system. He underlined that realist theory cannot properly explain Russia's confrontation with the West over Yugoslavia in the 1990s (using its gas supply) when Russia had a very fragile position and clash with the West was contrary to the power-maximization strategy. Russia used energy (gas supply) leverage against Serbia and threatened some Western countries with energy supply cuts. Structuralist theories (e.g., neorealism) that focus on Waltz's third-image or international system analysis cannot elaborate on the decision-making mechanisms of the Russian foreign energy policy. Neorealist theory cannot explain Russia's domestic economic, technological, and institutional incompetence and backwardness that found the dependence on Europe.

Balmaceda (2013) also analysis the energy dependence of the post-USSR republics on Russia from the perspectives of IR theories (pp. 3–36). She argues that the state-centric realist approach could explain Russia's exploitation of energy as political leverage. Still, it cannot elaborate on dependent countries' acquiescent stances on the changes in energy dependence patterns. For (neo)realist theory that neglects domestic interest groups' role, energy-dependent countries should strive for energy independence from Russia. Still, these states (Belarus, Ukraine, Lithuania) do few steps towards energy diversification. She believes that ignoring diverse domestic interests made a constructivist approach also non-adequate to explain energy dependence patterns. She points out that the international political economy (especially, the liberal stream) approach has relatively upper explanatory power for patterns of energy dependence combining political dynamics with domestic interest groups' attitudes. Ziegler (2016) underlined that the set of interdependent patterns conditions the Russian foreign policy partly based on domestic preferences from the liberal perspective (pp. 230–234). The liberal interdependent theory relies on a multi-actor structure of the energy sector and an energy market that relieves the state's central role where it could be argued that the Russian state as a coherent unit isn't the only actor in the foreign energy policy.

2.2 The Relevance and Operationalization of Complex Interdependence Theory

Russia's energy sector and energy policy are interrelated with foreign policy ambitions to a certain extent. But also, it is interconnected to the global energy markets and global energy affairs. For Borovskiy (2018), liberal theory affirmed that geopolitical and power collision contexts don't allow adequate analysis of global energy affairs that were complicated after the energy crises in the 1970s (pp. 110–134). Liberal scholars believe that the increasing role of non-state actors in the global energy market deprives the state-controlled actors to dominate the energy markets, applying "energy weapon", and dictating energy prices anymore. Fettweis (2009) argued that international energy market actors and the diminished number of conflicts worldwide made a "resource war" and sharper energy conflicts more outdated and irrelevant (pp. 66–77). Mironov (2003) argued that globalization, liberalization, privatization, and other economic processes increased the influences of non-state actors and transborder corporations in the energy sector (p. 165). Esakova (2012) investigated the energy security concept from a complex interdependence perspective, arguing that cooperation will be inevitable when the costs of any distortions in the energy supply will lead to reciprocal consequences for all energy market participants (pp. 16–53). The third-party effect will be higher in the regional gas market than in the global oil market. Also, she asserted that the energy sector's supremacy couldn't give energy-rich countries additional power to dictate their stipulations in other policy areas and sectors under an interdependence pattern. Russia's interdependence pattern with the "target" countries of the foreign energy policy could consist of the below-mentioned energy-related components (Table 2.1).

Yergin (2011) affirmed that interdependence in the energy sector isn't a new phenomenon. It was a case even before the dominance of crude oil and coal in the early industrialized countries (e.g., wood production contributed to the rapprochement between some European countries) (pp. 508–528). Bilgin (2011) argued that even though the state rules over the Russian energy sector, the country used and continues to use advantages of free-market conditions such as free trade

Table 2.1 The components of energy interdependence pattern

Mutual dependence components	
Russia	*"Target"*
1 Energy sales revenues	1 Russian energy (oil, gas, coal) resources
2 Foreign investments	2 Russian nuclear fuel
3 Foreign technologies	3 Russian REM resources
4 Export without restrictions	4 Russian internal market
5 Participation in international platforms	5 Russia's contribution to "OPEC Plus"

and foreign investment flows (pp. 119–127). The Russian oil-gas sector needs further investments for modernization to maintain production levels. Thus, a complete rupture from market principles and isolation in foreign energy policy would counter the economic interests of the Russian government and energy companies. Liberals assume that international energy trade engenders advantageous interdependence that puts down energy conflict probabilities.

Keohane and Nye (2011) developed a *complex interdependence theory* that envisages three categories: (1) "*multiple channels*" that are tied to states and societies in the form of "interstate" communication (realist stance), "transgovernmental" communication (states aren't coherent units), and "transnational" communication (states aren't only units in the international system); (2) *the lack of "hierarchy among issues"* – the distinction between the domestic and foreign realm gradually disappear with multiple agendas for debates; (3) *unsuitability of military power* – military factor isn't relevant in the intra-regional issues having higher costs without vivid long-term outcome (pp. 3–31). Trade, investment, technology, and market-level interconnectedness can be considered as a component of multiple channels and multiple agendas under the complex interdependence patterns.

Keohane and Nye (2011) argued that complex interdependence is a mutually costly and mutually beneficial result of foreign operations where "power is elusive". The costs and benefits of interdependence determine the sensitivity and vulnerability that contain economic, social, and political dimensions. The vulnerability concept is related to the political economy of foreign relations having a strategic aspect. Vulnerability depends on the government's capacity, political will, and availability of various resources. Manipulating sensitivity interdependence without considering the availability of alternatives and capabilities that determine vulnerability interdependence, will be relatively less effective. Manipulation of sensitivity interdependence can be seen as an instrument of power with certain restrictions.

The complex interdependence in the foreign energy policy envisages the cost of vulnerability and sensitivity of the interdependent actors, the complex interconnected elements of the energy market, the peculiarities of the energy types (oil, gas, nuclear, coal, electricity) and energy infrastructure (pipeline, LNG, etc.), domestic political preferences in the target states towards energy import sources, and the level of energy dependence through trade and investments. Multiple channels under complex interdependency in the foreign energy policy are ensured by multiple actors including state-owned energy companies who control more energy resources and private energy companies who control more energy technologies and know-how. Maybe, the complex interdependence theory's argument about the diminishing role of military factors cannot be considered an adequate approach considering Russia's traditional imperialism and modern militarization trends that especially re-appeared after the 2008 Georgian and 2014/2022 Ukrainian military aggression (these interventions had energy dimensions). But the outcome of both aggressions was indeed high-priced and uncertain for Russia, considering the international sanctions on finance, energy, and technology.

Complex interdependence doesn't reject military factors or use military force to resolve interstate matters. States can use power to protect vital interests about sovereignty and territorial integrity. Still, the modern interconnected world makes military factors more complex for decision-making variables. Imperial expansion with military presence is an ontological extent of studying Russia's state behaviour, statehood, foreign policy, and grand strategy. But the energy dimension of the broad state policy and foreign energy policy is a particular tool and the source of power that can be flexible, reflecting the multi-actor energy sector's technical specificities and almost indispensable interdependence pattern. Mingst, Mckibben, and Arreguín-Toft (2019) explained that "commercial peace theory" defends the argument about the vital link between economic interdependence and leaning towards war (p. 210). The higher economic interdependence between states via mutual trade and mutual investments decreases the inclination towards a war that can potentially break the commercial benefits. The absence of interdependence can lead to more aggressive resolutions of interstate conflicts.

Keohane and Nye (2011) affirmed that complex interdependence drives up the complexity and limits states in the goal-setting, tool selection for state policy, agenda-settings, and ensuring interlinks between "low politics" and "high politics". Complex interdependence obstructs governments from running after coherent and specific goals (we can include the same approach to the Russian foreign energy policy) Manipulation of economic interdependence can be pushed forward under the environment of complex interdependence as an important tool of state policy with some severe limitations. Complex interdependence circumstances reflecting congruent and incompatible interests of different transboundary groups compel governments to modify and limit the toolset of state policies, including foreign energy policy. The elements of complex interdependence such as multiple channels of interstate communications and multiple agenda issues in interstate affairs can limit states' one-sided decisions and actions. Complex interdependence and the manoeuvre opportunities of small states may avert the negative consequences of asymmetric interdependence on the benefit of "great power". If all countries theoretically would be self-sufficient and the equilibrium of this self-sufficiency will dissipate for technological, political, economic, or military reasons, then the newly created asymmetric interdependence would allow employing energy as a geopolitical lever.

We could distinguish between two types of interdependence: *classic interdependence* and *complex interdependence* (Keohane & Nye, 2011). Applying to the energy context, classic interdependence means outstanding "goods in return for revenues" dichotomy when country A provides strategic commodities (oil, gas, coal, electricity, uranium, and other minerals) to country B and obtains revenues in exchange. Both countries are mutually vulnerable to each other's steps regarding the flows of energy resources and financial resources (two one-sided flows or connections consisting of two agendas: energy issues vs. financial issues). The concept of complex interdependence means the existence of multiple connection channels that bring forward various agendas such as commodity (e.g., energy carrier) flows, financial flows, technological capacity issues, environmental issues, human rights issues, corporate issues, social policy, procedural issues, and individual preference. The framework of interconnectedness complicates mutual sensitivity and vulnerability leading to more complex relationships and interdependence that force the parties to avoid major breaking conflicts (Figure 2.1).

Keohane and Nye (2011) propose two measurements of interdependence patterns in terms of power influence over outcomes of policy decisions: "*sensitivity*" and "*vulnerability*" (pp. 10–12). We can operationalize "sensitivity" in terms of deducting measurable units from the theory in the example of Russia's foreign energy policy as the total cost of the gas supply disruption for the target country (e.g., Ukraine) without any change in the energy diversification or energy transition framework of the country exposed to influence. Suppose the target country or Ukraine intends to switch from Russian gas to nuclear or solar energy. In that case, this shift will create new financial and political costs for the country, reflecting the level of "vulnerability".

However, there are no precise measurement tools for complex interdependence; for current research purposes, we could operationalize economic interdependence (e.g., the share of the EU, Asian, or CIS countries in the Russian foreign trade, the volume of mutual trade turnover, and foreign investment flow, technological interdependence) and energy interdependence (e.g., the share of Russian energy export in the target country's total energy import) as a direct reverberation of complex interdependence. We could assume that the level of complex interdependence between Russia and the target country can be considered a function of economic interdependence and energy interdependence. The multiple-channel dialogue and multiple-issues agenda may potentially exist mainly between Russia and the target states that have higher economic and energy interdependence. For

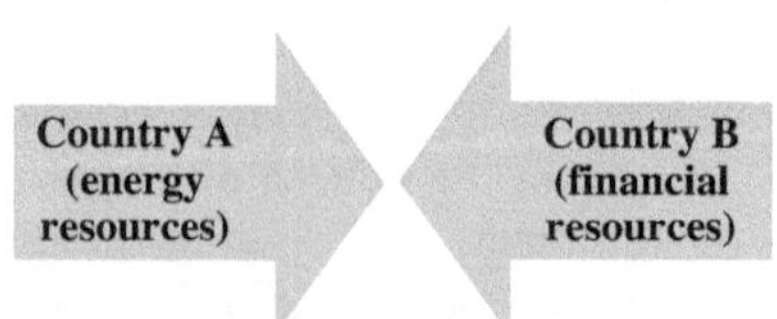

Figure 2.1 Classic interdependence pattern.

operationalization of the complex interdependence theory for the research aims, we could use the following categorization:

1 *Multiple channels of interaction*: trade negotiations; foreign investment negotiations; interactions within the framework of the regional and international energy organizations such as OPEC and GECF; communications within formal platforms and informal networks on foreign and energy policy.
2 *Multiple agendas of interaction without hierarchy*: trade, investment, technology transfer, environment, institutional issues, technical assistance, etc.
3 *Irrelevance of military dimension* (complex interdependence theory doesn't fully disregard the military factor but argues about its high cost for the "initiator").

Also, we have to take into account the complex structure of contemporary and global energy affairs where corporations (not only private but also state-owned: in the example of Gazprom),[1] bureaucrats' non-formal meetings (Russian energy minister's non-formal communication with "OPEC+" states), interest groups (representatives of oil-gas companies and oil traders), various domestic and interlinked external networks (e.g., Rosneft's foreign shareholders), business associations (Russian Industry and Trade Chamber), organized and non-organized civil society entities (e.g., energy-oriented think tanks), and active citizens (e.g., ex-deputy minister of energy Vladimir Milov through social media) play a more critical role in the agenda-setting, decision-making, and decision implementation processes (maybe, not in goal-setting strategy). There are influential state-owned enterprises and "pseudo" private energy companies that pursue divergent profit-based purposes from Kremlin's geopolitical considerations. For example, gas supply to politically loyal states such as Serbia and non-state entities such as South Ossetia were opposed by Gazprom based on commercial considerations. Profit-driven actors such as Gazprom and Rosneft could influence foreign energy policy to maximize profit. Their influences on Kremlin's policies were contestable under Putin's rule when top managers of these companies (e.g., Igor Sechin and Alexei Miller) represented the "inner circle" of Putin's close personal friends. The self-interested behaviours of influential energy sector representatives may complicate the state's accomplishments in the foreign energy markets.

Based on the complex interdependence theory, we can enlist a broader list of participants in international energy affairs: transnational energy-finance companies, intergovernmental organizations, influential individuals, and non-governmental organizations. Configuration of material interests and power capabilities of state and non-state actors formulate the foreign energy policy and increase global interconnections and growing interdependence for a liberal perspective proposed by Keohane and Nye (2011). If we look at the liberals' "state isn't coherent unit" argument in reverse, energy-importing states, and blocks such as the EU are not coherent actors, as well. Lack of coherence is an obstacle and limitation for Russia's foreign energy policy and its partner states' countermeasures (e.g., lack of consensus in the EU on energy import diversification and nuclear energy production).

Waltz (1979) underlined that interdependence, meaning that the states are mutually dependent, leads to shared vulnerability. But asymmetric interdependence envisages not mutually dependent states but the states that unequally influence each other. When we study interdependence from the theory's operationalization perspective, he points out that we must consider two indicators: "the aggregate gains and losses states experience through their interactions; the equality with which those gains and losses are distributed" (pp. 143–144). In interdependence, the ratio of supply of tradable goods in the total imports of counterpart countries plays an important role. Waltz (1979) touched on the interactions between states (units) and the international political systems or structure (pp. 99–100). Still, he provides only state-centric and macro-level interpretations about the nature of this interaction process.

Waltz (1979) correctly disagrees with the argument that economic, military, and political capacities can be investigated and considered separately to understand distinct actions of the state (p. 152). But on another hand, Keohane and Nye (2011) underline that the distribution of power (e.g., in energy flows) cannot guarantee for the state to ensure that it can control the political outcome through military power (pp. 25–26). The number of full-scale *interstate wars* has fundamentally declined, and it was replaced by "hybrid warfare" including energy-related manipulations and direct attacks on energy infrastructure. Under complex interdependence conditions, less powerful states as rational actors also gain and utilize available tools to deactivate dominant powers' actions, contrary to Waltz's (1979) justification that more dependent state concentrates on access to the resources (e.g., access to uninterrupted energy supply) that is the basic condition for survival under one-sided dependence domain (p. 153).

For example, Russia supported the separatist Transnistria region of Moldova in the geopolitically significant border area with Ukraine positioning a "peacekeeping" military contingent in the region. To complement the military component of influence with energy power, Russia used natural gas supply and price against Moldova's political will to distance geopolitically from Russia towards the EU and specifically Romania. But Russia's energy conflicts and supply cuts with geopolitical motivation towards Moldova as the smallest post-Soviet country didn't prevent this country from consistently moving towards EU and European security architecture, or towards deeper integration with Romania. Moldova didn't hesitate to sign the Association Agreement with the EU based on the "Deep and Comprehensive Free Trade Area" to access the European goods and services market. Also, Romania became Moldova's top trade partner in import operations outpacing Russia after 2014 (Trade Map, 2021). So, Russia couldn't control the geopolitical and geo-economic outcome of "hard power" (military) influence or "energy weapon" against small-scale actors such as Moldova. Relatively small-scale and less powerful (militarily and economically) states such as Kuwait, Qatar or Ecuador combined their efforts under OPEC during the 1973–1974 oil crises and made a vigorous decision to embargo leading western countries (Office of the Historian, 2021; OPEC, 2021). This was against the realist IR theory that relied on great powers and ignored the effect of thematic organizations. Mearsheimer (2014) firmly acknowledges that the interlink between military power capabilities and economic wealth cannot be constant and unidirectional (p. 81). Military power can be influenced by the economic wealth that is open for liberal multiple channels and multiple agenda approaches of complex interdependence patterns.

Regarding the disputable linkage between complex interdependence and cooperation, we could argue that there are specific areas such as the oil and gas industry where growing economic interdependence ("*raw material in exchange for technology and finance*") compels even ambitious nation-states, including Russia, to cooperate with various external actors. The nature of the Russian state can be centralist, militarist, and imperial expansionist. But the complexity, interconnection, and interdependence of real-world affairs could potentially limit the real expansionist intentions of the Russian state, forcing it to cooperate and compromise at least in the energy sphere (even during the Soviet era).

Completely asymmetric or symmetric interdependence is impossible in natural political and economic systems. We could use "fuzzy logic" (variable's value can vary between 0 and 1 illimitably) instead of "binary logic" (variable's value can be only 0 and 1) when we examine the actual level and long-term outcomes of complex interdependence (for "fuzzy logic" concept's definition: Stanford Encyclopedia of Philosophy, 2021). This varying degree of interdependence formulates the bargaining power of different states or actors independent from their place in the world in terms of power capabilities. With the complexity of world affairs and states' external relations, interdependence cannot always boost cooperation but also trigger conflicts (realists (e.g., Waltz) and liberals (e.g., Keohane and Nye) have almost identical opinions on this "cooperation-conflict" nexus). Repyeuskaya (2010) argued that interdependence in gas trade between Russia and the EU had shaped joint interests. But Russia intends to alter equipoise in the energy interdependence for strategic purposes. The EU couldn't propound energy policies regarding alternative options congruently to reduce energy dependence on Russia. But the EU has the technological and financial advantage that could materialize against Russia in energy affairs. The technological dimension plays an important role in multiple agendas promoting cooperation. Kurdin (2020) argued that the Soviet Union's domestic pipeline deficits in the 1970s compelled it to start the "natural gas in return for pipes" initiative with Western Europe (pp. 152–159). In addition to technological deficiency, Russia encounters a profound transformation in the significant energy export market – the EU. Diversification, energy market liberalization reforms, energy transition, new pricing mechanisms, and ecologic sustainability shape new mutual vulnerabilities, and new items for multiple agendas between Russia and the EU under complex interdependence.

Dannreuther (2013) argued that the major liberal thesis on energy issues is the positive function of international energy markets to prevent or alleviate energy conflicts (pp. 79–97). They argue that the integrated and multifactor global oil market made any oil sanctions or oil embargoes almost impossible. But natural gas hasn't yet a functional global market (it emerges gradually), therefore, it is still possible to use gas trade as political leverage on the regional level (especially by Russia). Högselius (2019) described the complexity of energy relations and dependence, focusing on energy systems, energy internationalization, energy technologies, and energy economics. He found out that uranium and oil (around 70 exporter countries) have a higher ratio of internationalization that is measured by the percentage of energy export from the country of production (energy export/domestic production). This indicator reveals the difficulty of transforming energy dependence into energy interdependence. The level of internationalization in natural gas (around 30 exporter countries) and coal is medium, while it is lower in electricity (RECSID examines the linkage between energy conflicts and the level of internationalization of energy types). The level of internationalization of energy-related commodities is inversely proportional to the number of Russia's energy conflicts in that field (except for electricity: "low interstate conflicts and lower level of internationalization"). The drivers of energy's internationalization are stable energy production and export and the financial and ecological results of energy export. Meta considerations on foreign policy can be left unnoticed by energy companies and related bureaucrats which could lead to interagency disharmony. Högselius (2019) proposed the "system approach" on the energy dependence when we must look at the fuel import dependence of consumer countries, but also the dependencies of energy exporting countries on energy technologies, energy services, human resources, and various production processes (pp. 68–154). Also, energy consumption in the energy-exporting countries influences the energy importing countries' energy dependence. These mutual dependences shape the pattern for complex energy interdependences. Energy interdependence patterns can be easily shaped by gas (high number of conflicts) and electricity (low number of conflicts) rather than oil (medium number of conflicts), coal (low number of conflicts), and uranium-based nuclear energy (low number of conflicts).

Russian presidents, prime ministers, and ministers of foreign affairs often reiterate the concept of interdependence from the "compulsory cooperation" perspective. The former President of Russia Medvedev underlined that the global financial crisis in 2008–2009 demonstrated the total and unprecedented interdependence of world economies (Kremlin, 2009a), through the linkage between financial and energy markets. President Putin (2021) characterized the "deal of the century" between the USSR and the Federal Republic of Germany in the 1970s, and the Nord Stream gas pipeline projects between Russia and Germany nowadays laid the foundation for "constructive interdependence" on long-term supplies of natural gas to European countries. Russia's interdependence and interaction discourse used for manifold European and Asian countries included the energy cooperation dimension. Putin argued in 2014 that the division of "spheres of influence" cannot be based on the total domination of single power. Still, it should rely on the interdependence principle as an optimal tool for coordinating positions. Under the multipolar world, interstate and regional affairs in various regions or geopolitical poles should be institutionalized through integration projects, regional organizations, and the rules for interactions without external intervention. These complimentary regional power poles should cooperate on global security, politics, economics, and energy in the next stage.

Putin underlined that political and economic interdependence is crucial for Russia's foreign affairs and global outlook in the multipolar world: "it is impossible to control the world from one point" in the growing uncontrollability of global threats (power diffusion approach) (Kremlin, 2014a). Putin argued that Europe's one-sided energy dependence on Russia isn't possible; the supply of energy resources always creates interdependence (Kremlin, 2014b). Interdependence exists in various areas, including energy, and only closed countries can disconnect from this interdependence pattern. Putin also stated the risks and threats of interdependence in different speeches. Putin argued that the high interdependence and interconnectedness of economies could be evaluated as a risk factor for negatively affecting the entire system of world economic relations. He has underlined that interconnectedness and interdependence cannot totally prevent global chaos (chaos and interconnection coexist in the world). Globalists' assumption that economic interdependence would be a guarantee against conflicts and geopolitical rivalry did not happen. On the contrary, the nature of global confrontations has become more complicated, multi-layered, and non-linear (Kremlin, 2017). Russia's political elites could use the emphasis on interdependence as a tactic to hide real geopolitical intention (realist approach), exhibit straight confidence in the power of interconnection together with its high risks ("*contagion effect*"), and express an attitude to construct cooperative foreign affairs based on mutual interests (liberal approach). But also, oil, gas, and overall energy affairs between Russia, former-USSR republics, and the EU members are highly politicized because of "path dependency" based on previous practices and lack of trust stemming from the Russian government and parliament representatives' statements acknowledging "energy weapon". Trust-building and a serious cooperative manner are an antidote to politicization and securitization of energy in the context of foreign policy.

In parallel to Putin's "frustration" about the role of interdependence in the alleviation of global conflicts, also, Keohane and Nye (2011) underlined that economic interdependence and even multiple communication channels with non-hierarchical agendas might increase competition and conflict probabilities parallel to cooperation opportunities and influence options. But complex interdependence may increase foreign policy alternatives without large restrictions and raise the complexity of foreign policy cases. It isn't fully excluded that various transnational actors may create challenges, destructive influences, and negative results for the government's foreign energy policy under complex interdependence.

The liberal school focuses on the function of domestic actors in foreign and energy policy that is interconnected to complex interdependence theory. The target country's domestic settings (e.g., Ukraine's domestic confrontation among the political and economic elite) play an essential role in the Russian energy conflicts in the framework of the interdependence pattern. The domestic politics perspective of the liberal school envisages that group dynamics and group interests, structures/ideas/values of domestic politics in the host country such as Russia interact and influence foreign economic policy (e.g., energy and finance) and its outputs (Frieden, 1991, pp. 31–71). The marginal interests of Putin and his "inner circle", misconducts, and lack of competition, directly and indirectly, affect Russia's foreign energy policy. In Russia, the power is concentrated on small groups of influential rulers and elite representatives who can plan and realize energy policy through various methods, including energy supply disruption, price manipulation, open and hidden subsidies, and misconduct mechanisms in the energy sector (Nemtsov & Milov, 2008, pp. 11–14). Russia's oil-gas and nuclear energy specialists and experts formulate a moderate "epistemic community" with similar energy policy approaches, views, and understandings (Haas, 1992, pp. 187–224). Balmaceda (2013) argued that the post-Soviet countries (representing CIS and the EU) with high energy dependence on Russia possess powerful domestic political and economic groups that benefit from dependency patterns (pp. 3–36). Countries aiming to break energy dependence on Russia should struggle with Russian energy power and domestic interest groups.

Moravcsik (1997) presumed that individuals and various private groups, including NGOs, companies, and trade unions, as crucial actors in the global political system shape states' domestic preferences that are directly reverberated in the foreign (energy) policy preferences (pp. 513–553). He argued that the state's foreign policy preferences represent the interests and attitudes of the active individuals and private groups as innermost domestic political and societal actors. Increasing oil-gas revenues changed the domestic power configuration of Russia towards the consolidation of a small and closed elite group that made critical foreign policy decisions. The Russian political scientist Kirill Rogov (2020) points out that, the foreign policy of Russia (FPR) is a function of its domestic politics (DP), but also Russia's domestic politics is a function of foreign policy conditions (FPC) or the external environment. We can formulate that interlink with the following function:

$$^{*}\mathbf{FPR} = \mathbf{f}\left(\mathbf{DP}\right); \mathbf{DP} = \mathbf{f}\left(\mathbf{FPC}\right)^{*}$$

Ziegler (2018) pointed out that Putin centralized policy-making of foreign policy in his hand, and the Ministry of Foreign Affairs only implemented that policy (including the energy dimension of foreign policy) in coordination with the Kremlin (p. 126). Still, this fact doesn't purport to ignore the corporate profit-driven interests of Russian state-owned and private energy companies and the bureaucratic group interests of the potent elite fractions in domestic politics. As a reflection on the nexus between foreign and domestic factors, Kandiyoti (2015) juxtaposed significant factors that led to the gas supply conflicts between the EU and Russia: (a) power rivalry between NATO, the EU, and Russia over Eastern Europe and Ukraine; (b) Ukraine's domestic political configuration that created antagonism in terms of gas transit to Europe (pp. 2–9). The domestic political system's attitude towards authoritarianism decays the cooperative foundation of foreign energy policy. The spoils system and decay started from a domestic political setting and diffuses to the international political-economic system's energy domain for liberals. In this context, there are claims that Russia's energy companies operate as "spoilers" in regional and international energy markets in terms of distortion of market basis and politicization.

The main findings of the Focus Group Discussion (2018, Georgia) were about the "export" of market distortion techniques including corruption by Russia to the energy sectors of neighbour states (Ukraine, Georgia, Belarus, Armenia, Azerbaijan, Moldova, Turkey) and the political exploitation of market powers by Russia's state-owned oil-gas companies ("antidote": better energy regulation and diversification). Market distortion techniques were an integral part of Russia's behaviour in foreign energy policy towards targeted countries. For example, there were misconduct assertions on (a) Rosatom's and Russian officials' negotiations in Bulgaria on Belene NPP (Jirušek et al., 2015, p. 424); (b) Gazprom's subsidiaries and local natural gas intermediaries' operations in Romania; (c) privatization of "*Naftna Industrija Srbije*" (NIS) formerly state-owned oil-gas company in Serbia when Gazprom Neft obtained ownership (Jirušek, 2017, pp. 177–188). There was a misconduct scandal in Slovakia taking part of Gazprom in the privatization of the local natural gas monopolist, "Slovensky Plynarensky Priemysel" (SPP) in 2004.

James Henderson (UK) expressed in a presentation in the Czech Republic in August 2019 that Russia's energy sector and energy companies such as Gazprom carry on Soviet legacies including huge bureaucracy, misconduct, lack of efficiencies, and huge public assets. These energy companies gained huge assets as a heritage from the USSR and operated under an ineffective and "controlled competition" environment. Nemtsov and Milov (2008) argued that Gazprom became the first large business entity that Putin began to systematically seize the leading position. Gazprom was deliberately diverted from its core energy business functions focusing on domestic political manipulations and aggressive gas conflicts against Ukraine, Belarus, Georgia, Armenia, and Azerbaijan. The official reason was to protect the country's economic interests, but corporate and group interests prevailed.

The representatives of sociological liberalism (e.g., Burton, 1972; Cerny, 2010; Rosenau, 1990) underlined the growing role and appearance of transnational webs of peoples, groups, and organizations in world politics and the global economy (Jackson & Sorensen, 2013, p. 105). Burton (1972, pp. 35–45) developed a "cobweb model" that describes the international system as entangled transnational exchanges between various interest groups. Doubling group affiliation in transboundary thematic networks (including energy) and communicative transactions may alleviate conflicts and promote cooperation (Burton, 1972, pp. 35–45). Cerny (2010) underlined that growing transnational operations gradually transform states from coherent units or subjects to multilevel networks of power politics (pp. 22–85). The transformation happens through powerful coalitions of international political and economic actors that aim to fill a global political and economic gap, establish new power chains, and penetrate perceptions of global affairs. "Interaction effects" of the intensive contacts and communications between states' bureaucrats, businessmen, non-state actors, and subnational units or regions create more exhaustive alternatives for political economy influence among actors. It isn't feasible to claim that nation-states, including Russia, are coherent units in complex and modern international politics and a global economy characterized by deep economic integration and profound globalization trends (despite some regionalization and fragmentation tendencies in global supply chain during 2020–2022). Globalization (indicator in the energy sector can be global oil-gas trade transactions) and technological changes are possible preconditions for the complex interdependence that doesn't exclude competition.

Transnationalism offers a rather wide range of alternatives, options, and choices that increase the complexity of world political and economic affairs, complicate power equilibrium among states by changing the bargaining potential of relatively small actors and constrain the manoeuvring capacity of great powers. Farrell and Newman (2019) assert that newly emerging networks that operate under the complex interdependence environment could formulate new power arrangements or power settings that are "weaponized" by the networks' prerogative controller or the nodes of the networks (e.g., globalized financial transactions have unearthed SWIFT system that the USA misemploys against Russia) (pp. 42–79). It can be relevant in the global energy markets, by empowering energy companies to dominate in international energy affairs. Rosenau (1990) proposed a "multi-centric world" model based on cooperative and integrative, but more situational and temporary networks of transnational firms, bureaucrats, subnational entities, global and regional organizations, and various political groups (pp. 36–250). A "multi-centric world" focusing on outcomes was developed as an alternative to a self-restrained and static "state-centric world" concentrating on process.

The neoliberal institutionalist perspective postulates that incessant interactions among states can lead to accumulated cooperation based on absolute gains and collective interests (e.g., in the areas such as trade and ecology). Dialogue-based, cooperative, and rational energy regimes (e.g., "OPEC+") that consist of norms and procedures could gradually institutionalize the pattern of interdependence. The global energy regime as a set of norms and rules, partly implemented by OPEC, had limited and transformed Russia's foreign energy policy from a conflictual mood to cooperation ("OPEC+" format). In the early 2000s, higher oil prices motivated Russia to raise oil export, and the country refused to cut oil production under the OPEC deal. But the collapse of oil prices in the global oil market forced Russia to cooperate with OPEC led by Saudi Arabia under the "OPEC Plus" agreement in 2016 where even small oil producers had an important margin of influence via collective bargaining (Soldatkin, Gamal, & Lawler, 2016). The compelling dialogue and network-building activities between the former energy minister of Russia Alexander Novak with the energy ministers of other OPEC and non-OPEC oil producer countries played an essential role in the cooperation among Russia and cartel members over the global oil production agenda. Changing economic conditions, the growing role of cross-border actors, and the international energy regime partly influenced on agenda-setting process and pattern of foreign energy policy reflecting the partial relevance of complex interdependence and cooperation.

2.3 Review of the Alternative Theories on Russia's FEP

The central ontological status of the alternative theories on Russia's foreign and energy policy varied from economic, security, and military power to institutional quality discourse.

Realist theory on Russia's FEP. The current study applies a theory of interdependence, but it is also worth describing the relevant and irrelevant aspects of the alternative theories of IR (and IPE) for the Russian foreign energy policy. Dannreuther (2013) argued that certain factors condition realist and geopolitical approaches to energy resources: (a) natural resources and energy resources are finite; (b) natural and energy resources are unequally dispersed around the globe; (c) natural resources and energy resources are subjects for global competition because they are contributors to national interests (pp. 79–97). He underlined that the strategic competition over natural resources and energy resources made a realist theory a more relevant framework to analyse and understand global energy systems and energy affairs. Borovskiy (2018) argued that the neorealist perspective approaches energy resources from the context of national interests and energy security through expansionist hegemony ("offensive") or a more "defensive" minimalist stance in terms of vital interests (pp. 110–134). Defensive neorealism would argue that Russia's foreign energy policy doesn't aim to thrust into the EU or post-Soviet countries' domestic political and economic arrangements. But it seeks to defend Russia's national interests with an energy dimension in the critical regions, including Eastern Europe, Ukraine, the Balkans, South Caucasus, Central Asia, and the Middle East.

Waltz (1979) underlined that energy independence is an overpriced option for nation-states and this fact reveals the influence of the international system (structure) on units or states (p. 157). This approach considers interdependence as sensitivity when the probability of conflictual situations increases. Waltz (1979) described the global political system as an interaction of "structure" (international political system) and "units" (nation-states) where "structure" is determined by systemic order, states' functions, and dispersion of capabilities (pp. 100–101). But, as it was investigated in the previous sub-chapter, it is contestable to describe federal and multi-actor Russia as a coherent unit in the world political system. Different lobby or interest groups, liberal bureaucrats, representatives of security structures ("*siloviki*"), the leadership of state-owned energy companies (oil, gas, nuclear, energy transit, coal, electricity), and the political leadership of the resource-rich federal regions (e.g., Tatarstan) disrupt the state's behaviour as a Waltzian "coherent unit" and ensure "multiple channels and multiple agenda" conditions of.

Mearsheimer (2014) underlined that the states realized that the optimal way for survival in the anarchic system is to maximize relative power including offensive tools and resources to reach the regional (rather than global) hegemon position. From an offensive realist perspective, the current multipolar world order triggers more international tension including inter-actor energy conflicts. Offensive neorealism hypothesizes that energy is a tool for Russia to accomplish regional hegemonic expansion through power maximization and manipulations. Mearsheimer (2014) believes that NATO's eastward expansion is an existential threat for Russia triggering its energy power exercises towards Eastern Europe and the post-Soviet countries such as Georgia and Ukraine (pp. 21–139).

Mearsheimer (2014) underlines that nation-states can follow non-military objectives in the international system such as economic welfare but ignore the growing roles of non-state actors in the process of reaching non-security aims (p. 30). This reality is against of argument of Mearsheimer (2013) that economic components of national power serve the military power only (p. 78). He categorizes non-military components of national power as a "latent power" that contradicts the reality of foreign energy policy that accumulated energy power. Even if the liberal hypothesis on the diminishing role of military power will not be acceptable for Russia by realist scholars, the lack of human, financial, and technological capacity could lead to gradual regression in the country's relative military power. As a first scenario, this will increase the role of non-military groups and various non-state actors within political elites that will (a) equalize the social-economic agenda with deep-seated military agenda and (b) increase the active communication channels for global affairs. Mearsheimer (2014) posits that great powers aspire to reach four major goals: achieving regional hegemony, controlling wealth, gaining land power, and pursuing nuclear supremacy (pp. 140–146). We can match Russia's hypothetical great power goals with its foreign energy policy (Table 2.2).

Russia's active manoeuvres in the Arctic and the Mediterranean Sea demonstrate that it seeks more than regional hegemony over "near abroad". An alternative hegemon such as the USA could enter the vital interest zone of Russia from a far distance to fully support (military, security, political, diplomatic, economic, and indirect energy supply assistance), as Mearsheimer (2014) expressed, an "upstart state" (p. 142) or local challenger against Russia. The "upstart state" of the post-Soviet region against Russia can be Ukraine, not from an economic but a sovereignty perspective considering the unique history and geographical position. The strategic calculation and power projection angles of the USA-Russia rivalry over Ukraine have a strong energy dimension (transit power of Ukraine, Russia's energy manipulation, the USA's sanctions against Russia's energy projects such as Nord

Table 2.2 Great powers' goals and Russian foreign energy policy actions

Great powers' goals	*Russian foreign energy policy actions*
Propensity to regional hegemony	Domination in the energy markets of post-Soviet and the European region; controlling and manipulation of energy prices and supply volumes; gaining strategic energy partnerships and alliances in Europe.
Propensity to wealth maximization	Domination in the crude oil and natural gas extraction sectors of the Caspian Basin, Central Asia, the Middle East, Africa, Latin America, and the Arctic; entering oil products' markets in Europe and North America.
The propensity of land power	Domination in energy geopolitics of the Eastern and Central Europe, Central Asia ("heartland"); the strong network of oil-gas pipelines and energy infrastructure.
Propensity to nuclear dominance	Expanding nuclear power plants in the post-Soviet, MENA, and Eastern European regions; domination in the uranium and plutonium extraction business; transferring nuclear energy capacities.

Source: Great power goals were modified from Mearsheimer (2014), but the matching with foreign energy policy was developed by the author.

Stream-2 pipeline or state-owned energy companies) can be through the lens of Mearsheimer's "regional hegemony" viewpoint. But we could observe the repercussions of economic or complex interdependence that limit the capabilities of actors[2] up to February 2022 and socially (re)constructed "great power" – "upstart state" – "global hegemon" identities of Russia, Ukraine, and the USA, respectively. From Mearsheimer's offensive realist perspective, Russia's "hybrid threat" towards Ukraine and other key post-Soviet states such as Baltic states, Georgia, or Moldova that combine military and non-military tools (including "energy weapon" measures such as gas supply disruption) is typical great power behaviour to itch to regional hegemony.

Molnar (2014) argued that neoclassical realism theory based on materialist ontology and national/state power components could adequately explain Russia's foreign energy policy (pp. 77–90). The different interest groups partly reshape the country's foreign energy policy goals within the state apparatus and state-owned oil-gas companies. Lobell, Ripsman, and Taliaferro (2009) argued that the influences of the international system determine a state's foreign policy behaviour. There is an intervening variable in this transmission process from a neoclassical realism perspective: the domestic political elite's strategic estimates, expectations, restrictions, and perceptions. The nature of a state's (relative) power defines its reaction to external challenges by mobilizing domestic resources, including energy resources. The USSR and Russian states' centralized and autocratic nature facilitated quick mobilization and decision-making in the strategic rivalry with the collective West. The USSR's and Russia's state structure and state-society relations could temporarily enable the building of a sphere of influence in Eastern Europe to obtain nuclear capability. "Imperial overstretch", poor economic growth, technological backwardness, and unproductive investments in army-building decayed the state's domestic and foreign energy policies.

Another realist approach to the Russian foreign energy policy could be the hegemonic stability theory (developed by Kindleberger (1973) and Gilpin (1975)) meaning the existence of the strongest global power that distributes, balances, and regulate world order supporting open economic regimes. Hegemonic power would support an open and transparent system for the regional energy transactions and punish the "game-changers" at least in the European and CIS markets. From this perspective, the lack of global hegemonic power encouraged Russia to follow a very assertive foreign economic and energy policy in the 2000s rather than in the 1990s or during the USSR's era. Krasner (1996) points out that "economic transactions" including energy operations between the USSR and Western Europe were broadly politicized during the Cold War (p. 109).

IPE Perspective on Russia's FEP. The theoretical foundations of the Russian foreign energy policy could be analysed from an international political economy (IPE) perspective. IPE analysis the interaction between politics and the economy at the global level when different sides of the economic transactions enter the political struggle based on divergent interests and expectations (Oatley, 2019, p. 25). IPE offers a relevant theoretical framework to analyse and understand international energy relations that homogenize political and economic drivers through state-market interactions. IPE explores political determinants and major consequences of economic and energy decisions, and the mutual effect between power (state) and wealth (market).

Methodological and epistemological debates continue between positivist and post-positivist schools within the IPE that affects global energy studies. The interpretative post-positivist methods of the IPE and IR link the energy factor with civilization, environment, poverty, and justice. The rationalist methodology and epistemology based on empiricism and positivism in the IPE and IR always seek rational ground for any energy policy and energy strategy. The IPE scholar researched mostly the international oil market and oil-related global and regional affairs rather than gas, coal, nuclear, renewables, and electricity. The nexus between energy policy and foreign policy of leading energy-exporting and energy-importing countries are also attractive topics in the IPE community.

Liberal IPE school envisages the supremacy of the energy market in the economy-politics interactions of the FEP while realist IPE underpins the prevalence of political decisions on the energy policy. Ostrowski (2013) argued that when we analyse the global natural resource management issues and "*resource wars*" from the IPE perspective, we must include the new tide of state capitalism initiated by the state-controlled natural resources and energy companies in this analytical framework (pp. 98–115). Putin's administration transformed the Russian economy from crony capitalism to state capitalism when (a) the state started to dominate in vital economic sectors, including the energy sector, and (b) energy export was utilized as a foreign policy tool. Mercantilist/realist theory within IPE that supports strong state concepts approaches an energy factor as a component of the state's power. Mercantilist and realist theories argue that state command over energy resources is a strategic necessity to defend national interests under the "energy conflicts" circumstances. Goldthau and Witte (2010) argued that contemporary global energy affairs conceptions were framed by two major approaches: "*geopolitics and mercantilism*" (pp. 2–12). They argue that these theoretical frameworks approach energy issues as state-centric and antagonistic, disregarding the energy market, regional and international institutions (OPEC, IEA), and complex developments in the global energy systems such as new actors (China and India) and new regulatory acts affecting energy sales. Orban (2008) argued that Russia used its state-controlled oil-gas and other energy companies as a tool of neo-mercantilist and neo-imperial foreign policy and power competition with the USA over Central and Eastern Europe.

Akçapa (2020) argued that the realist paradigm of the international political economy that is based on state-centric economic interventionism and economic nationalism could be considered an adequate theoretical framework to analyse the Russian foreign energy policy (in the case of Gazprom-led energy affairs between Russia and Serbia under Putin) (pp. 38–54). From the realist and nationalist perspectives of IPE, energy resources and energy infrastructure shape the power of the Russian state to achieve national interests in interactions with other countries. For the countries such as Russia, the export of energy resources is a crucial way to accumulate national power. Energy export transactions, energy infrastructure, and energy projects could be used as political leverage with economic and technological constraints.

Russia's foreign energy policy could partly be explained by Susan Strange's (1988) "state-market interactions" approach when nation-states' various measures influence energy markets and global oil-gas markets have influence reciprocally on states' active energy policies, economic development, and national security (pp. 195–197). She underlined that energy is an essential condition to realize the power in the world system. Structural power based on state-market interlink could be the basis for understanding global energy as a secondary structure of power. Strange (1988) differentiated governments, oil companies, and global oil markets as three major players or actors in the oil industry. Strange (1992) underlined the growing bargaining power of companies in the face of governments altering classical foreign policy goals with industry-based economic priorities. Sometimes governments and companies' particular actions could have unintended power influence over other actors, in addition to the intentional power measures. It means state-owned oil companies could be considered more crucial actors in the oil market rather than the Ministry of Energy or the national government in terms of potently managing the oil sector.

Unintentional power can be attributed to the "structural power" concept that Strange (1988) defined as a power that forms global frameworks under which the states and non-state actors will function. The "structural power" has four crucial control-based bases: security, production, finance, and knowledge. These four components have a reciprocal and complex influence on the global energy (e.g., oil) sector shaping its power in the interactor relationships. Strange (2000) argues that the role of corporations had a growing role in the international political economy, international diplomacy, and interstate affairs with huge bargaining power (p. 60). The global changes in high technologies, capital movements, widening transportation, and communication rise to the transformative power of energy companies. Also, Putin has several times emphasized the role of companies in the official decision-making process (Kremlin, 2014c). Strange (1988) affirmed that power is diffused and decentralized in the international political economy and nation-states should balance wealth creation and security concerns in this system. The power diffusion concept enables us to include non-state actors ("multi-actor approach") including energy companies in the decision-making process on foreign energy policy and "energy games" where actors exploit energy supply as leverage for the pursuit of power. Belyi and Locatelli (2015) argued that the commercial interests of market players such as public or private energy companies don't always coincide with the overarching national interests of nation-states (p. 3). States are inclined to employ actors of energy markets to underpin foreign energy policy to control resource-rich areas or to guarantee energy security. Positive and negative energy interdependencies that can be emerged during the interactions among state-centred political actors and market-centred economic actors may bolster regional integration efforts. Nation-states have certain limitations in the state-market interaction in terms of the effective inducement of energy market actors towards their national interests.

Stoddard (2013) asserted an intellectual clash between "realist-pessimistic and liberal-rationalist ontologies" to explain global energy relations where companies benefit from globalization while governments have more nationalistic moods in recent decades (pp. 437–463). He suggested a "two-forked" political economy ontology to describe international energy relations as an alternative to liberals' rational/progressive ontology (Devetak, George, and Percy, 2017, pp. 92–93) and realists' confrontational regressive ontology. Therefore, IPE could offer a relevant perspective to explain these contrasting economic and political structures' inclinations in the global energy configuration. Stoddard (2013) argues that the Eurasian energy landscape or "geo-energy space" has the "energy interdependence" pattern (pp. 437–463). Strange's (1995) pluralist multiple actors approach containing power diffusion (pp. 55–74), Cox's (1996) relevant ontological proposition about three facets of global affairs ("transnational social forces, the state's structure, and world order") (pp. 174–188) and complex interdependence theory of Keohane and Nye (2011) combine the intersected perspective of IPE, neoclassic realism, and interdependence liberalism. In addition to the powerful and leading functions-capacities of the states and the "economy-politics" nexus, the constraining role of markets determines the intrinsically complex ontology of energy affairs and foreign energy policy.

The Constructivist Theory of Russia's FEP. Constructivism is one of the important IR theories that represent idealist and holistic ontological foundations using positivist epistemology together with interpretive methodology (Küçük, 2019, p. 365). Constructivist theory underpins the argument that major concepts of regional and global energy affairs including energy security and related energy conflicts are not static but are shaped via constant social interaction and subjective interpretation. Constructivism theory puts the state's identity, interests, and ideas at the centre of the global stage that is shaped through intersubjective social interactions among actors (Jackson & Jones, 2017, pp. 256–258). Wendt (1999) argued that ideas determine interests, interests determine material conditions, and material conditions determine reality in international politics (p. 139). It means energy-rich states' national interests based on an ideational basis make of the strategic sense of the energy resources. Energy-exporting states may develop and apply various approaches to "friend" and "enemy" states in terms of the energy export volumes and prices (Russia demanded from "unfriendly countries" to make a gas payment with rubles in 2022).

If we will attempt to apply a constructivist approach to the Russian foreign energy policy, firstly, we should accept that the Russian state has manifold (historical) identities about itself and its relations with the external world such as "great power" ("*velikaya derzhava*"), the leader of "Slavic world", the protector of the Russians in the world, safeguard of the "near abroad" region, "sovereign democracy", "unique federation", etc. Each of these layers of the multilayer identity could play a potential role in the domestic policymaking of the energy sector and foreign energy policy towards the target or consumer countries. Wendt (1999) describes the social interaction between states that shapes their identity as a causative action of "mutual adjustment" or the arrangement of "desires, beliefs, strategies, and capabilities" (pp. 82–148). But these explanations are not sufficient to illustrate the *complexity* of modern global political, economic, and energy affairs, including interstate relations stemming from growing interchanges through varied channels with multiple agendas. The relative appropriateness of complex interdependence relies on its contributions to addressing the complexity of global politics and economics, including world energy markets, energy policies, and energy geopolitics.

Russian constructivist IR scholar Tsygankov (2012) argued that Russia historically had three behavioural patterns concerning the West (cooperative, defensive, and aggressive) and all these scenarios were determined by the "sense of honour" as an emotional category having two dimensions (external (the Western) and domestic) (pp. 2–4). This approach links Russia's aggressive and defensive policies using energy power to the recognition by the West that is significantly narrowing down the scope of the complex and mutual energy interdependence. Tsygankov (2016) argued that the energy dimension combining conflicting and cooperating behaviours was always a constant and independent variable in this strategic interaction between Russia and the West under the context of national identity and national interest. Energy played a strategic role in Putin's "pragmatic cooperation" and "assertive" foreign policy paradigms. Energy power was a tool for Russia's "great power assertiveness" and modernization under Putin's rule (pp. 1–28; 193; 261–269).

Constructivists may argue that Russia's foreign energy policy was mitigated when the collective West recognized Russia's great power status and took into consideration Russia's threat perceptions towards the geopolitical fate of the "near abroad". Deviated foreign energy policy in alignment with the more cooperative foreign policy could be reflected in the intensity and scope of the Russian energy conflicts. We can examine the relevance of one exemplary case. The President of the USA Barack Obama started to "reset" the complex affairs with Russia in 2009 launching a multidimensional and comprehensive dialogue on various regional and global issues (on arms reduction treaty, Russia's WTO membership, nuclear non-proliferation, a global energy, Iran, North Korea, Afghanistan, Georgia, Kyrgyzstan, etc.) (The White House, 2010). This mutual dialogue and recognition environment partly affected Russia's foreign and energy policy. But relations started deeply deteriorating after 2011 because of a series of domestic (mass protests in Russia; death of well-known lawyer Sergei Magnitsky) and regional (Syria, Ukraine) developments (Taylor, 2014). As a result, the number of Russia's foreign energy conflicts and supply interruptions increased again after 2012 reaching a new peak in 2014.

Generally, it is questionable to believe that short-term improvement in the USA-Russia relations and short-term (non-systematic) social interactions between Obama, Medvedev, and Putin could fundamentally shift the mutual distrust and clash of interests among the historical antagonists. Relatively pro-reform Russian President Dmitry Medvedev instructed the Government to develop an Energy Security Doctrine at a meeting of the Security Council in December 2010.

Medvedev expressed that: "Energy security is seen as a guarantee of the nation's sovereign development. Russia is not interested in monopolistic high prices for energy resources, but their predictable boundaries" (Security Council of the Russian Federation, 2010). He acknowledged decreasing proven oil-gas reserves, weak technological progress in the Russian energy sector, the deterioration of the energy sector's capacities especially in the electric power industry, and disruptions in power and heat supply. So, there are objective and material determinants of Russian foreign energy policy and foreign economic policy that are not related to the social construction of world political affairs. The crucial determinants are the technological and economic backwardness of Russia that consubstantiate with the peripheral stance of Russia in front of the West (Feklyunina, 2018, pp. 5–21). The intersubjective connotation of Russia's foreign energy policy also will be insufferable and inappropriate for the West and the post-Soviet countries. Even though the constructivist theory can explain the Russian sensitivity to the Western perception and recognition of its "great power" status and related overarching identity, generally, this concept could not elucidate the domestic and global dynamics of Russian foreign energy policy towards global powers and post-Soviet countries.

Neo-Marxist Perspective on Russia's FEP. Marxist perspective on the FEP focuses on the exploitation of energy resources and raw materials of developing countries (in collaboration with the local elites of resource-rich countries) by the multinational energy companies of the core states creating imbalances and injustice (imperial/colonial patrimony, dependency, and world-system theories). Marxist perspective, which is absent in the current literature on Russia's foreign energy policy, emphasizes the concentration and accumulation of capital in the hands of small groups and transnational corporations (Gilpin, 1987, p. 36). Marxist perspective also recognizes the interdependent pattern, but in the context of exploitation of economic and energy resources. "Dependency Theory" (developed by H. Singer, R. Prebisch, P. Baran, A. G. Frank, and other authors) distinguishes two different types of states in the world system: dependent and dominant states (Ferraro, 2008, pp. 58–64).

The dependent states export cheaper raw materials to the dominant states. The dominant states process these raw materials adding value and exporting them to the dependent states as a more expensive final product. This helical pattern of interstate interactions that transnational corporations reinforce increases global economic and technological inequality. When we apply the Marxist perspective to the Russian foreign energy policy, the Kremlin should be seen as an agent of energy and finance "oligarchs" who control the energy and financial resources of the country. From the neo-Marxist "dependency theory" perspective, the reliance on raw materials such as oil, gas, metals, and wood in the Russian export to the Western countries and China resembles the pattern of the global economic system where the West and China allegedly "colonizes" Russia by exploiting its natural resources. Russian neo-Marxist scholars argue that Russia has already been transformed to function as a "raw material appendage" of the West and China, therefore, couldn't prepare and implement an independent foreign energy policy to achieve national interests (Tumakova, 2021).

Wallerstein (1974) separated three major blocks of a world system based on labour division: *core, periphery, and semi-periphery*. The economically and technologically developed core states exploit less developed periphery states where semi-peripheries function as a "buffer zone" between these two groups of states with blended institutions (Martinez-Vela, 2001, p. 4). From the perspective of the "world system" theory, Russia's economic, political, and technological position partly fits a semi-peripheral state between resource-rich former-soviet republics and more advanced Western or Asian states or economies. Russia imports some portion of the post-Soviet countries' primary products and surplus wealth. It processes and re-exports these products (including petroleum products) back to peripheral and core countries. Russia tries to generate regulatory and integrative institutions (e.g., EAEU and CSTO) for peripheries to maintain imperialist and exploitative economic and political order. At the same time, some Russian politicians and scholars criticize developed Western states for acting against Russia as a peripheral zone with a resource-based surplus. Also, post-Soviet countries denounce Russia to attempt to function as a core state against former "colonial" regions trying to control their energy and natural resources. But Russia has gradually lost the post-Soviet countries' energy resources exploitation to the Western and Chinese companies because of a lack of technology and financial resources. The continuous alterations and improvements in the world energy system and cross-border supplies interchange the geopolitical positions of energy centres and energy peripheries.

Balockaite (2012) defined "energy imperialism" as the exploitation of energy resources for foreign policy, as an interchangeable concept with "energy colonialism" (pp. 85–96). She differentiates (a) the state level of "energy imperialism" when the oil-gas shape the foundations of the state's basic mechanisms and institutions; (b) the international level when energy-rich countries create energy dependency in all directions encircling the target country or region. In energy imperialism, energy-rich countries use oil-gas supply to control the territory or politics of the target country. In "energy colonialism", an energy-dependent country partly relinquishes its state sovereignty to the energy-exporting country in place of an uninterrupted energy supply. Balockaite (2012) argued that Russia, as an energy-exporting country, employs oil-gas resources to stiffen its domestic power and global influence. In the foreign realm, energy dependency is the primary channel for Russia to expand or preserve its geopolitical influence in the post-colonial countries as a way of "(neo)energy imperialism". Lin (2009) underlined that Russia exploits energy resources and energy policy to urge its imperial status and global hegemonic greed. Russia's "energy imperialism" strategy covers its immediate neighbourhood, Europe, Asia, and the Middle East. The history of Russia's "energy imperialism" could be traced back to the Cold War when Moscow planned to construct an interconnected network of gas-exporting pipelines connecting the Western Siberia's gas basin with the Western European energy market with geopolitical considerations (p. 2).

Morozov (2018) argued that Russia is a "subaltern empire" meaning that, on the one hand, Russia is an exploitable semi-periphery of the capitalist core (the West). On the other hand, Russia functions as the capitalist core in a relationship with peripheral states in the wider Eurasian region ("near abroad") (pp. 22–42). A "subaltern empire" identity is shaped by the country's imperial legacy, the current complex (with the military, security, economic, political, social, and energy dimensions) hegemony in the "near abroad", and economic and qualitative dependence on the EU. Gradually diversifying external trade and foreign investment patterns of the post-Soviet and EU countries don't fully support the argument to characterize Russia as a "second-tier power" between different regional domains. The theory of "subaltern empire" identity cannot elucidate the complex and multi-actor relationships between domestic and external agents and institutions that influence Russian FEP to a certain extent.

Institutionalist perspective on the Russian FEP. The institutional quality of an energy-rich state such as Russia is a crucial determinant of the policy outcomes of the foreign energy policy. The "*resource curse*" and "*rentier state*" phenomena increased the level of misconduct among the actors of global energy markets (energy companies, governments of resource importing/exporting states, and global organizations) and gradually made the globalized market-based affairs more illiberal. Obviously, illiberal energy markets cannot function as a cooperation-based institution. Ahmadov, Mammadov, and Aslanli (2013) affirmed that energy resource incomes hurt government effectiveness and institutional quality in energy-rich post-Soviet countries including Russia. Natural resource extraction and management under the weak institutional framework erode the quality of the foreign policy-making process and foreign policy institutions, as well. The "resource curse" that led to the gradual degradation of institutions based on oil and gas revenues controlled by the political elite's core group ("*the siloviki*") would undermine the effective economic activities in all economic sectors, including oil-gas and mining. Consequently, "extractive institutions" and institutional "path dependence" would gradually weaken Russia's energy production, energy export potential, and foreign energy policy (Acemoglu & Robinson, 2012; Hedlund, 2005; Travin, Gelman, & Zaostrovtsev, 2018).

Some authors argue that Russia promotes state capitalism, resource nationalism, oligarchic capitalism, crony capitalism, state corporatism in the energy sector, and energy policy (Aslund, 2019; Rutland, 2016; Sikri, 2010). State capitalism and resource nationalism changed the owners of energy resources and reinforced that state-owned companies could play a more active role in foreign policy and shift energy geopolitics from the multinational actors to the national actors. The primary motivation was the consolidation of economic power through state control over natural resources for foreign policy goals as the "political leverage". Shevtsova (2009) argued that Russia's "petrostate" model could expose the domestic political instability and long-term economic stagnation and lead to a systemic crisis when central administration emaciates, and centrifugal drifts may expedite in the country (pp. 61–65). Latynina (2009) argues that Russian foreign and domestic politics can be characterized by the concept of "petrocracy" that envisages monopolized ownership over oil-gas resources by the ruling class and total reliance on oil-gas revenues in internal and external issues without serious technological advancement. Cooperation with the West guaranteed foreign investments and energy technologies for

Russia's energy sector, but the political regime relinquished pragmatism in favour of geopolitical motives. Putin always believed in and supported the supremacy of national interests in regulating the national economy, the appropriateness of state intervention in the economy (especially in the oil-gas sector), and the concentration of economic wealth in the hands of a small group.

In his Ph.D. thesis, Putin (1997) argued that it is impossible to compete with the transnational corporations of the West on equal terms without the support of the state and the creation of large financial and industrial corporations in Russia. He supposed that the strategic factor of Russia's economic growth should be the restructuring of the national economy based on the available oil-gas resources. Putin justified effective government intervention in long-term national projects to develop natural resources. Since 2000, higher oil prices have contributed to the nationalization of the oil-gas companies and assets, and the trend towards re-nationalization has strengthened Russia's global aspirations for great power. Domjan and Stone (2010) argued that resource nationalism under a higher energy prices environment is an apparatus for Russia to reaffirm its great power status by employing oil and gas output, oil and gas export infrastructure, and alternative geographical routes for energy transport (pp. 35–62). Bremmer and Johnston (2009) emphasized that resource nationalism and "energy weapon" are linked to oil-gas prices (pp. 149–158). Persistently low prices could obligate the Russian state to revise its approach towards foreign companies' participation in the energy sector to increase the oil-gas production output. Russia arising as a "petrostate" in the domestic domain with a potent "energy weapon" (via energy price and energy supply) in the foreign domain also could not succeed in forming high-quality state institutions and a diversified economy.

2.4 "Energy Weapon" and "Energy Superpower" Concepts

From an analytical perspective, Russian foreign energy policy can be examined from different angles including energy power (incorporating "energy superpower", energy security, and energy geopolitics concepts) and "energy weapon". The research elaborates on these concepts from a complex interdependence perspective that is related to foreign energy policy and energy conflicts.

Russia's energy power and "energy superpower" concept. Power is a central phenomenon in the complex interdependence theory. Sascha (2008) defined energy power as a "strategy of utilizing the control over important energy resources or central elements of international energy infrastructure as a weapon" (pp. 25–26). A sum of material (including energy) and non-material resources of Russia can be titled "*potential power*".[3] For example, Russia's vast energy resources (oil, gas, coal, nuclear, electricity, and transit power) can be considered as "potential power" or "property concept". But the "real power" is revealed in relationship with other states or actors when a resource-owner country (e.g., Russia) would realize its power over the resource-scarce country (e.g., Eastern European or CIS countries). If the power concept is examined in the context of interstate or interactor relations, this can be categorized as "relational power". The relational power concept is partly related to the asymmetric pattern of complex interdependence developed by Keohane and Nye (2011) where *sensitivity* (initial cost of influencer's action for the target) and *vulnerability* (final cost of the influencer's action for the target when it changed the policy to improve the situation) of the target country is revealed against influencer country's energy policy action in the mutual relationship (pp. 11–15). In an asymmetrical interdependence context, less dependent actors have a more powerful influence over more dependent actors (e.g., Russia's influence over the EU states that have more energy dependence on the energy import from this country).

Dellecker and Gomart (2011) argued that Russia only could exploit energy power under precise *time* and *space* considerations (pp. 206–208). This feature of temporariness is an essential limitation of the foreign energy policy of the country. Sari (2021) argues that if the state aims to convert its resources and material assets into power (from potential power to relational power), it depends on some qualities or characteristics that will be attached to the resources that could be assessed as power in the relation with other states or actors (p. 118). Baldwin (2016) underlined that relational power is a multidimensional concept that includes the "scope, domain, weight, base, means, costs, time, and place" of the power-affiliated influence in social relations with other states or actors (p. 50). The operationalization of Russia's multidimensional energy power indicates that costs of energy power for Russia include gradual losing energy markets, discrediting reliable energy partner reputation, and devaluation of energy power means overtime when energy importing countries develop countermeasures (Table 2.3).

Russian IR scholars, energy experts, and officials often prefer to express that Russia is a global "energy superpower" ("*energeticeskoy sverxderjava*") in terms of energy resources, energy production, and energy export. Great power attitudes, state-centric structure, and "energy superpower" rhetoric can be part of the Russian strategic narrative that political elites formulate and interpret to accomplish geopolitical goals combined with national interests. The Russian political elites agreed to return the country to the vague status of an "energy superpower" fully dependent on extracting and redistributing natural resources or assets including the oil-gas rent in the lucrative territories. The idea of President Putin and his presidential aide Surkov to turn Russia into an "energy superpower" had become a debated concept in 2005–2006 (Neftianka, 2020). Surkov argued that "the fuel and energy complex should remain predominantly Russian". He pointed to the need to use Russia's competitive advantages in the energy sector and "the energy superpower is quite consistent with this approach" (Grivach & Denisov, 2008). But Russia needs to get access to high technologies in gas, crude oil, and oil products production.

Alksnis (2019) defined the "energy superpower" concept as the availability of large proven energy reserves (oil, gas, coal, uranium, or renewables) and enormous energy export potential, using the energy "leverage" as a foreign policy instrument and influence the world energy market prices. Examples of "energy superpowers" could be Russia (for natural gas) and Saudi Arabia (for crude oil). Marcinkevich (2020) defined an "energy superpower" state as an entity that has large proven reserves of at least one energy resource on its territory (oil, gas, coal, uranium); the

Table 2.3 Operationalization of Russia's multidimensional energy power

Power dimension	*Content*
Scope	Energy resources (oil, gas, coal, nuclear, electricity, energy transit infrastructure, energy assets abroad); energy balance and crucial energy decisions of the target countries; energy geopolitics.
Domain	Energy-importing countries from the post-Soviet and European regions, emerging Asian energy markets (e.g., China, Japan, South Korea); energy-exporting states from the former USSR and the Middle East region.
Weight	Several political and economic concessions that Russia obtained from the target countries; the share of the Russian energy resources in the target countries' energy balance.
Power bases	Oil and gas reserves and production, coal reserves and production, nuclear energy capacity and nuclear technology, electricity output and exports, energy diplomacy experience, and skills.
Means	Energy supply disruptions, threats with supply cuts, sudden and rapid energy price changes, price differentiation based on target countries' political loyalty in front of Russia, energy assets direct nationalization, and energy assets acquisitions in the target markets.
Costs (A = B) (A > B) (A < B)	*Costs of energy power for Russia (A)*: to gradually lose energy markets; discrediting reliable energy partner reputation; devaluation of energy power means overtime when energy importing countries develop countermeasures. *Costs of energy power for target countries (B)*: energy shortages during the winter seasons; financial costs of the energy transition to decrease the energy dependence on Russia; political discords on substitution of Russia with alternative energy suppliers.
Time	Putin's ruling era after 2000 had more conflictual than Yeltsin's ruling period between 1992 and 2000; periods when Russia had a geopolitical power struggle with the collective West over the post-Soviet region; periods of the "coloured revolution" in the "near abroad" region; energy transition period may accelerate conflicts.
Place	Key oil-gas pipeline routes, key oil-gas hubs, key oil-gas basins, strategic areas of the "near abroad" countries under the "sphere of influence" concept, crude oil/LNG export terminals, and nuclear plants.

Source: The names of power dimensions modified from Baldwin (2016); the content developed by the author.

largest exporter of at least one of the above-listed energy resources. He pointed out that Russia as the "energy superpower" has double challenges: (a) reindustrialization based on new technologies; (b) the implementation of the Fourth Industrial Revolution. He argued that if Russia will not succeed to respond to these double challenges, the "energy superpower" status will end and the country will be a raw material supplement of the Western countries. Critics raised the voice that the prioritization of the "energy superpower" concept only reinforces Russia's specialization in depletable raw materials such as oil and natural gas (Simonov, 2006, p. 272).

Kurdin (2018) argued that there isn't a consensus among Russian public opinion on the role of Russia's energy sector in global affairs that range from "energy superpower" to "commodity appendage" (pp. 135–159). Cohen (2009) qualified Russia as a "revisionist" energy superpower that uses an instrument against Europe and adjacent neighbourhoods successfully connecting economic and political factors (pp. 92–105). Kroenig (2020) argues that Russia's economic power and "energy superpower" position revived by Putin is challenged by its mismanagement of resources based on political autocracy and kleptocracy, ineffective state-owned enterprises, shrinking gross domestic product (GDP) and national wealth, oil-gas prices huge volatility, EU countries energy diversification plans, and the US's global energy dominance including the growing LNG supply to Europe (pp. 162–163). But Saradzhyan and Abdullaev (2018) approached energy resources and energy consumption as a part of Russia's global power vis-à-vis Western powers, BRICS countries, natural resource-dependent countries, and former USSR countries using different techniques (GDP Index, Revised Geometric Index of Traditional National Capabilities, Experimental Index of National Power). Their measurements indicated that Russia performed relatively well in the energy-based economic output indicators against the Western countries, but it lags behind the emerging powers such as China and India.

Inozemtsev (2015) pointed out that Russia's "energy superpower" is deeply diminished, but alternative sources for domestic economic development have not been proposed. Russia pursued the "sovereign democracy" policy in the domestic policy, "energy superpower" strategy based on the oil-gas industry in the foreign energy policy that envisages large investments in oil-gas pipelines, which are regarded as an instrument of geopolitical expansion. The Russian concept "*derjava*" (independent and powerful state) means the self-sufficient state to ensure the independence of Russia from the leading global powers. In the mid-2000s, Putin declared that Russia intended to be an "energy superpower" that emboldened the geopolitical and strategic dimension of the country's foreign energy policy. Policy concepts such as "energy diplomacy" and "energy superpower" envisage the application of the energy reserves as a tool in the foreign policy towards Europe, Asia, and CIS that overlaps with the realist approach (Milov, 2006). Barkanov (2018) summarized almost all leading sources in the existing literature on the theoretical framework for Russia's foreign policy and its energy dimension. He listed the factor in the related literature about the determinants of Russia's "energy superpower" (pp. 138–152):

a asymmetrical interdependence;
b the EU's energy market reforms and NATO's expansion;
c the world power order and the US supremacy;
d domestic and international limitations;
e complexities of the energy (gas) market and energy (gas) prices;
f state's dominant role in the economy;
g balance of power and great power aspirations;
h securitization of energy and institutional issues.

The author applies the political economy approach from a realist perspective connecting geoeconomics to geopolitics under the unipolar order. Russian state's broad strategic aims overlapped with energy companies' corporate strategies about incorporating the global energy markets. Russia intends to monopolize control over energy export pipelines and control domestic energy distribution networks of energy-importing countries to reinforce energy power.

Energy power determines economic wealth and states' security. Growing global concerns about *energy security* raised Russia's significance as an energy power. The security dimension partly shaped the dynamics that drove Russia's foreign and energy policy. Securitization is a concept that could be related to energy affairs as a crucial component of the English School and constructivist theoretical frameworks. Buzan and Waever (2004) developed a "regional security complex theory" that was built upon the English school's international society approach, materialist approach, and the constructivist argument about the social construction of securitization (pp. 3–4). The theory means that the interaction between global and regional players overlaps in the regional domains where all regional affairs are prone to be securitized. In this context, the growing securitization of energy mainly occurs at the regional level as a reflection of a new pattern of interdependence-based interactions among Russia, the EU, and "near abroad" countries. In the context of the securitization of energy, NATO also declared that energy security was an issue of direct relevance to the alliance considering the energy confrontation between Russia and Europe NATO (2021). NATO determined to protect the energy security of member states such as Poland, or Latvia turning into a military-energy bloc in the mid-2000s. Some authors declare that Russia's new gas export pipelines projects such as Nord Stream-2 and the growing perception in the EU political leaders of Russia's "energy weapon" accelerated the "securitization" of bilateral and regional energy affairs (Kurze, 2010; Zelensky, 2009).

Güney and Korkmaz (2014) argue that complex interdependence doesn't envisage a conflict-free environment, but the limitations in the energy actors' mutual behaviour based on a full understanding of the costs of the changes in the balance of interdependence (pp. 35–59). They consubstantiate politicization and securitization of the energy affairs between Russia and the EU with sensitivity and vulnerability patterns of interdependence. Securitization of energy affairs could emerge as a natural and expected consequence of interdependence. When actors realize that changes in the balance of interdependence could weaken their economic roles, they can securitize their foreign energy affairs. Also, Keohane and Nye (2011) argued that manipulating economic vulnerabilities cause reactional strategies by the "targets" including even military responses based on energy security concerns. Mironov (2003) argued that the global energy security concept has six different dimensions: military, political, economic, financial, technology, and ecology (p. 165).

Shaffer (2009) defined energy security as a concept having three elements: unbroken access to energy supply (*trustability*); optimal prices of the energy resources (*affordability*); balancing energy production with the ecosystem in a sustainable way (*ecology*) (p. 93). Larsson (2006) argues that the security dimension is a key aspect of Russia's foreign energy policy (p. 5). Russia intends on one hand to expand geopolitical influence and on another hand to prevent geopolitical threats through energy policy. Securitization of energy-related issues based on

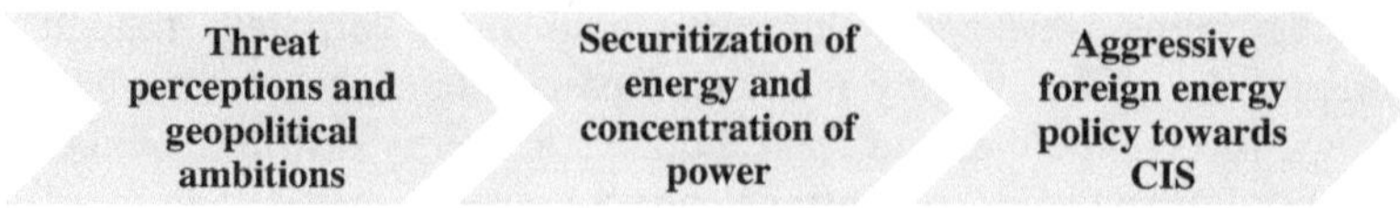

Figure 2.2 Larsson's foreign energy model for Russia.
Source: Modified from Larsson (2006).

threat perceptions and geopolitical ambitions indirectly legitimizes assertive foreign energy policy using various tools (Figure 2.2).

In the case of Russia, the doctrine of energy security was a continuation of the "energy superpower" concept put forward by Putin. Energy security implied by Putin was the political agreement between energy consumers (e.g., the EU) and Russia supplemented by long-term commercial contracts for the supply of energy resources. Long-term agreements would ensure suppliers against price and energy demand volatilities and provide Russia with a relatively long period of guaranteed high oil and gas revenues (Kommersant, 2006). Russia as an energy-exporting country had a different interpretation of energy security than energy-consuming countries.

Dyer and Trombetta (2013) argued that it isn't complicated to identify the threats to energy supply or energy demand in terms of energy security (pp. 3–18). But objective energy threats (e.g., physical disruption of oil-gas supply) can be undergone a subjective social construction process through adequate expectations, scales of the threat, and a real driver of the danger. Therefore, regular power cuts in the EU members stemming from energy transmission problems in the underinvested areas were perceived as less problematic than Russia's natural gas supply disruptions that actively started after 2004–2006. Russia's used its G8 presidency in 2006 to declare energy security at the top of the agenda at the energy ministers' meeting in March 2006 and the G8 leaders' summit in Russia in July 2006. The tightening of the energy market conditions after the Russia-Ukraine gas dispute has forced many European countries to re-focus on energy security issues. The main implementing actors of Russia's energy security agenda in 2006 were President Putin and Gazprom CEO Miller.

The central thesis of the Putin-Miller energy doctrine explaining Russia's gas disputes with Europe envisaged that energy security must be considered from three sides: *security of supply, security of demand, and reliable transit* (G8, 2006). Putin proposed to establish an "energy axis" between Russia and Germany to guarantee energy security instead of energy isolationism. Putin always emphasized that there are no geopolitical overtones in Russia's oil-gas and energy projects, and they serve regional energy security. For example, Nord Stream-2 pipeline diversifies gas supply routes, removes transit risks, and strengthens the energy security of Europe. Sakhalin-2 oil-gas exploration project could solve the problem of energy security in Japan and reduce the country's dependence on Middle Eastern oil. But Russia's energy security doctrine that emerged in 2006 was designed to guarantee relatively high prices for energy suppliers and control over the pricing process via a strategic advantage in energy geopolitics.

Jiznin (2013) proposed that *energy geopolitics* can be viewed as the impact of territorial-spatial features of the energy resources of states or the energy position of alliances on regional and global processes (pp. 7–42). Russia's energy geopolitics taken shaped by oil-gas export pipelines, state control over the energy resources, and using energy determinants to increase strategic influence on the various Eurasian countries overlapped with the country's geopolitical fault lines. Also, geographical location conditions the energy geopolitics of Russia. Dugin (2011) argued that the geo-economic map of Eurasia overlaps with the geopolitical maps consisting of strategic "sea" and strategic "land" with the economic and energy components including energy pipeline routes and energy-rich regions (p. 583). Savin (2012) accentuated that the energy geopolitics of Russia has two goals: to create an energy geopolitics alliance with other energy producers of Eurasia and ensure direct access to the energy consumers of Eurasia. Goldthau and Witte (2009) argued that over-concentration on energy security and energy geopolitics refuse to acknowledge the significant role of the energy market actors such as private and state-owned energy companies and thematic regional and international energy agencies (pp. 373–390).

Energy Weapon. Russia allegedly deployed energy resources as an instrument or "energy weapon" for solving national, regional, and global political, military, and economic tasks. "Energy weapon" can be defined as a capability to employ an energy factor against a target country to obtain commercial (paying high prices, paying energy debts, having asset acquisition, controlling energy assets and infrastructure) and political (preventing the target country from joining alternative economic unions and military unions, domestic power change, political misconduct) benefits. It was not only Russia that used "energy weapon" for foreign policy and economic purposes. In the austere winter of 2007/2008, Turkmenistan halted gas supply to Iran which led to a serious heat shortage in various provinces of Iran. After the supply cut-off, Turkmenistan increased gas prices almost nine times and demanded payback of Iran's accumulated energy debts (Pannier, 2017). Chinese state decided to stop coal import from Australia in November 2020 due to bilateral political tension and Australia's request to investigate China's role in the spread of coronavirus (Lkhaajav, 2021). In parallel with that prohibition, Russia increased coal export to China by more than 40% in 2021 to fill the gap in the coal market (The Coal Hub, 2022)

Russia's difference from other oil-gas exporting countries is the quantity, methods, and the scale of the energy supply disruptions and intense energy conflicts in terms of immediate and long-term results. In other words, the number of energy conflicts and supply interruptions are exceptionally high and politically very "sonorous" on the global level in the case of Russia. But also, the claims regarding the "energy weapon" that Russia allegedly uses should be empirically researched by removing Western media's excessive fuss and noise in global public opinion. One of the most prominent scholars researching "energy weapon" in the Russian case, Stegen (2011) described the "energy weapon" or "oil weapon" model as a process consisting of different stages (pp. 6505–6513):

a consolidation of oil-gas resources in the hand of small elites.
b controlling energy export and energy transit infrastructure and roots.

c implementation of "energy weapon" (energy price increases, supply energy interruptions, energy blackmailing or threatening).
d target state's consent or other types of behavioural reaction.

If the resource state succeeds in all these stages, we can claim that energy resources have already been converted to political tools or influential leverage. But Weber (2018) argued that growing oil-gas incomes are not automatically transformed into the assertive foreign policy of "petrostate"[4] in interstate conflicts. Rising energy incomes created foreign policy alternatives for Russia, but the realization of a more aggressive foreign policy and foreign energy policy depends on the Russian elite's political power. The preparation and completion of Russia's foreign policy much more depend on domestic political power and previous foreign policy priorities than on "energy weapon" or "energy power" (pp. 99–113). Russia's assertive foreign policy with a robust foreign energy dimension under Putin's rule was based on Primakov's statist stance in the foreign policy seeking great power status for Russia in a preferable multipolar system. Domestic political power concentration and authoritarian attitude interlinked with growing oil-gas incomes were other determinants of Russian ambitious foreign policy and decisive energy policy. However, the absolute concentration of power isn't feasible under the rising complexity of contemporary domestic governance and international political-economic systems (Figure 2.3).

Weber (2018) argued that the petrostate's assertive foreign policy doesn't necessarily correlate with global energy prices. Some highly aggressive foreign policy manoeuvres of Russia have occurred under the lower oil price conditions. Growing oil-gas revenues can indeed (a) decrease the quality of institutions through "rent-seeking" mechanisms; (b) strengthen military capacity; and (c) recall historical ambitions of the "petrostate" against rivals or neighbours. But crucial determinants for Russia are domestic politics and reactions to the emerging threats to great power

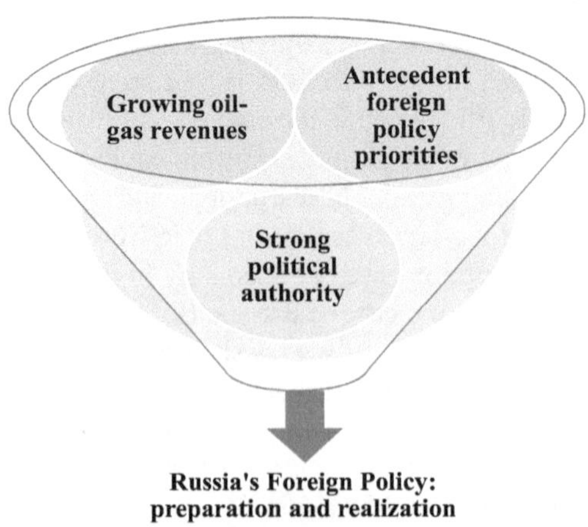

Figure 2.3 Weber's "Petropolitics Theory".
Source: Modified from Weber (2018, pp. 99–113).

aspirations. He underlined that Russia prioritized domestic economic performance using energy diplomacy as an instrument and sought to ensure its stable position among great powers with regional concentration. Gonchar, Chubyk, and Ishchuk (2015) argued that an "energy weapon" is a complex system of using the energy and infrastructure potentials of the state to achieve the economic and political defeat of the potential opponent (pp. 9–13). They proposed to categorize the "energy weapon" concept as "resources and infrastructure weapon". *Resources weapon* is a systematic use of hydrocarbon resources (oil, gas, coal) and other energy sources (nuclear, electricity) supply with the aim of the economic and political setback of the potential opponent country to ensure political and economic concessions and preferences from this targeted country. *Infrastructure weapon* is the systematic use of energy infrastructure by energy-rich countries to reorient energy flows, bypassing the other countries to implement economic and political pressure and obtain concessions and subsequent preferences.

Graaf and Sovacool (2020) characterized Russia's energy relations with post-Soviet countries such as Ukraine as an "energy weapon", but the energy affairs with the larger consumers led by the EU and China as a "foreign energy policy" (pp. 284–286). In reality, Russia applied a "weaponization" of energy resources (crude oil, gas, coal, electricity) and infrastructure against *the post-Soviet* (e.g., Ukraine, Belarus, Georgia) and *the EU states* (e.g., Poland, Lithuania, and long-run partner Germany). Russia's target countries present the cases that can be considered as examples to demonstrate using energy resources as a foreign policy instrument:

1 Unilateral disruption of Russian oil transit via Latvia in 2003.
2 Reduction of Gazprom's gas supply to Belarus during wintertime in 2004–2006.
3 Blockade by Transneft of Kazakh oil transit to Lithuania via Russia in 2006.
4 Crude oil supply cut off by Transneft to Lithuania in 2006.

Pravosudov (2017) emphasized the "oil weapon" to characterize energy as leverage. He argued that transit countries such as Turkey also used their regional transit capacities as commercial and political pressure (e.g., Bosporus strait) (pp. 17–144). Varol (2013) pointed out that Russia's foreign energy policy aimed to achieve regional dominance and outlined its foreign policy concepts based on its "energy weapon" capabilities under multipolar order patterns (pp. 20–397). The author points out that even though Russia used the elements of the liberal paradigm such as cooperation and positive integration in the early 1990s and early 2000s, Russian foreign policy and its energy dimension were generally based on realist assumptions seeking great power status. "Energy weapon" can generate fragility depending on the dynamics of global energy trade and strict commercial reactions by the target countries and alliances. Some authors ascribe negative connotations to the potential of "energy weapon".

Lo (2015) asserted that Kremlin sees energy resources and minerals as strategic assets that warrant great power status and global influence via "energy weapon" practice. He argues that "energy weapon" declined Russia's geopolitical domination in the "near abroad", the EU, and Asian markets (pp. 19–213). Russia has been criticized for employing oil-gas resources to restore geopolitical power in the "near abroad" that the country mislaid after the USSR's decadence. Russia officially denied accusations about the use of energy resources as a "weapon". Especially, Putin consistently ignored the claims that Russia is using energy as a weapon. He insisted that Russia didn't use any economic activities as a weapon. Putin expressed that Russia's use of energy as a weapon is "the politically motivated chatter" (Bobylev, 2021).

Putin argued that Russia regularly and entirely fulfilled its contractual obligations in the gas supply to Europe even during the most challenging periods of the Cold War. But Russia functions under the power transition period that brings out the competition with the collective West and China over the former-Soviet countries simultaneously. The competitive international environment forced Russia to use "energy weapon" (in the form of energy price and supply volume manipulation) more intense than the USSR against not directly to large energy partners such as Germany and China, but against smaller CIS states that have more profound one-sided energy dependence on Russia under the liberal interdependence pattern. Even though Russia cannot outface the West in terms of economic and technological power under the pattern of interdependence, a military power that recovered thanks to energy revenues and "energy weapon" challenged the West to deactivate NATO's and the EU's enlargement. But Russia's strategic goal to obstruct NATO's and the EU's eastward enlargement using energy power didn't fructify showing the impotence of the "energy weapon".

Shevtsova (2010) claims that Russia cannot use energy resources as a political weapon and contend to be developed states simultaneously. Russia's "gas war" and Gazprom's desire to consolidate its monopoly were both a function of the Russian system and a mode of its existence (p. 67). O'Sullivan (2013) argued that energy-producing countries may realize the "energy weapon" strategy meaning to attain political tasks using energy manipulation (pp. 30–47). Realists believe that the Russian state may attempt to manipulate oil-gas export flow to change the foreign policy behaviour of the counterpart countries. Krasner (1996) argues that economic (and energy) intimidation could formulate a "credible threat" if these will create asymmetric and relative opportunity costs in foreign economic relations (p. 116). Asymmetrical opportunity costs mean that cutting-off natural gas supply to Europe would potentially bear the smaller cost to Russia and a relatively larger cost to EU members as a target country. In another word, the asymmetrical opportunity costs of the Russian "energy weapon" could be a part of Russia's national power. But in reality, the relative opportunity costs of the "energy war" between Russia with the European countries are not fully asymmetrical taking into account the role of oil-gas revenues in the Russian economy and the reputational damages.

Decreasing the fossil fuel intensity of the world economy also atrophies Russia's applied "energy weapon". IMF's calculations revealed that the oil intensity (barrels of crude oil required to manufacture USD 1 million of GDP) of the global economy is 3.5 times lesser in 2022 than in the 1973–1974 oil crises (Valckx, 2022). Global oil intensity dropped from around 850 barrels in the early 1970s to around 250 barrels in 2022. In addition to energy intensity, the effect of the "energy weapon" depends on the global market of the energy type, and the capability of the energy-producing country to encounter negative repercussions (e.g., economic sanctions, diversification, and reduction in the energy import) by the targeted consumer countries under the patter of interdependence, the readiness of the consumer country to present political and economic concessions to the producing country.

Energy interdependence is an antidote to "energy weapon". Russia has an interdependence pattern of relations with energy-importing and transit countries ("double function"). Transit states' strategic significance increased as the energy (gas) hub in Europe in terms of energy geopolitics. Gustafson (2020, p. 9) and Moravcsik (2019, pp. 30–31) argued that despite the realistic geopolitical threats such as the Russia-Ukraine conflict in the Donbas region that shrink profit-driven energy communication, generally, profound commercial motivation prevails political uncertainties in the EU-Russia energy affairs. Guillet (2011) argued that macro-level or geopolitical narratives on Russian foreign energy policy are irrelevant because they ignore oil-gas export pipelines' extensive interdependence (pp. 58–73). He underpins that the "energy weapon" rationale is unsuitable with market realities, and no side can be victorious in the "energy war". "Energy weapon" can be applied only in the case of complete asymmetrical energy connections (e.g., Russia's total dominance in the Armenian gas and electricity markets), and these cases are very rare. But when there isn't one-sided energy dependence, but an interdependence pattern prevails (such as Russia-EU relations), an "energy weapon" can be evaluated as a "nuclear weapon" with a mutual dissuasion effect. "Energy weapon" is a kind of "suicide" for an energy-rich country with a "self-destruction" effect.

The construction of oil-gas export pipelines is a complex, multistakeholder, multifactor process where bureaucrats or politicians cannot dictate the sole geopolitical agenda. The author distinguished 11 components of pipeline building that finance, markets, technology, design, project and risk management, and reserve management play a key role in addition to politics. We can conclude from Guillet's contributions that Russia's "energy weapon" could be occasionally exaggerated ignoring the deep interdependence that oil-gas pipelines and energy trades shape. The only exception is asymmetrical dependence when all energy exporters that have a monopolistic position could desire to exploit this energy dependence setting for their benefit. It isn't only characteristic of Russia, there are other examples of the asymmetric "energy weapon", as well (e.g., Turkmenistan's natural gas cut to Iran in 2017 (AA Energy, 2017); OPEC's oil embargo in 1973).

Henderson (2016) underlined that globalized and interconnected commodity markets are an antidote against the "energy weapon" or "gas weapon" of Russia aiming to achieve foreign policy objectives (pp. 461–483). Pascual and Elkind (2009) argued that pipeline infrastructure had shaped interdependence between the EU and Russia and decreased energy conflicts among exporters, importers, and transit states (pp. 2–23). O'Sullivan (2013) believes that interdependence between oil-gas exporters and importers limits the ability of the producer countries to exploit oil and gas as an "energy weapon" in foreign policy (pp. 30–47). Even though oil and energy are often viewed by political scientists as "energy weapons", the practice of the last decades had shown to what extent these weapons were ineffective even as an idea. The threat of interruptions in energy supplies would immediately lead to a reduction in forecasts for the growth of the world economy. Russia's oil revenues directly depend on the growth of the world economy. The threat of a crisis in the financial markets is immediately transformed into the threat of a decrease in the rates of economic growth in the largest economies, and a reduction in the discrepancy between demand and supply for energy resources. Therefore, he argues that the long-run efficiency of the "energy weapon" for Russia is quite controversial. Transparency, reliability, and open communication could unravel energy conflicts between the EU and Russia forming the interdependence. Lack of communication strengthened geopolitics-based foreign policy behaviour and interest-based power rivalry in the EU-Russia energy affairs.

Balmaceda (2021) revisits the "energy weapon" concept arguing that this concept is based on the *realist* concept of "power" which means geopolitical and one-sided influence (pp. 25–27). This concept of energy power isn't adequate in the energy sector, with multiple stakeholders throughout the uninterrupted "value chain" process from energy producers to the final consumer. The manifold stakeholders that are mostly ignored in the existing literature on "energy weapon" or energy power include local gas and electricity distribution companies, oil-gas refineries, natural gas storage centres, and intermediary energy trading companies. Balmaceda (2021) argued that private actors and individuals are more powerful in the Russian energy system than state-owned energy companies' formal structures. These actors shape social and political interactions with the energy-importing countries multiple actors (sometimes, based on misconduct patterns) with the aim of alliance-building. These interest-based and misconduct -based networks can prolong the life of energy dependence on Russia and mitigate Russia's great power ambitions to the level of private interests. Balmaceda (2021) proposed the "techno-politics" concept to reflect the *complexity* of the energy factor in Russia's foreign energy policy (pp. 25–27). She argues that there is an oversimplified approach to Russian energy:

1 Analyzing it from an "energy power" standpoint only and ignoring financial and technological aspects.
2 Concentrating on oil (maybe also natural gas) and neglecting other energy sources such as coal and nuclear energy.
3 Focusing mainly on the supply-side and disregarding the constant changes in the energy demand side.

Neglected technological and financial aspects of the Russian foreign energy policy present additional bargaining power to the energy actor on the demand-side by diminishing the energy-exporting country's energy power. Balmaceda's "techno-politics" or "global value chain" approaches to energy power are deconstructionist and aim to dismember energy power into the various components ("upstream-midstream-downstream" or "producer-transit-consumer") and reveal sub-structures that diffuse the power from the producer to multiple actors (political, technological, financial, social, etc.). The necessity of various energy types (oil, gas, coal, nuclear), the surroundings of the governance process, and actors' preferences on the energy system play an essential role in the energy power of Russia. Belarus' "midstream power" or Germany's "downstream power" could relatively offset Russia's "upstream power".

Yergin (2006) argues that Russia intends to command strategic energy resources and oil-gas export pipelines to secure the energy demand (p. 2). But he also pointed out that political risks and challenges related to the government regulatory mechanisms and hard geological conditions will cut back Russia's oil-gas production. Therefore, the reliance on the oil-gas reserves in the foreign and domestic policy can be risky in the long term. Rising energy interdependence via the globalized world energy market demands a multilateral partnership between energy exporters such as Russia and importers such as the EU countries. Bogaturov (2017) argued that the states are not the only actors in solving global economic and energy issues. In addition to states, various non-state actors including TNCs, international movements, interest groups, and various networks have a great influence on global economic and energy issues. International energy corporations including oil-gas corporations have been influencing the changes in the price and volume in the global energy market. The stability of the world economy largely depends on the actions of the transnational energy business (Bogaturov, 2017).

Some authors have demonstrated a slightly different position on the role of energy interdependence to avert the "energy weapon" of Russia. Busygina and Filippov (2013) examine the role of energy interdependence as a constraining factor in the Russian foreign energy policy. They concluded that energy interdependence via growing energy trade didn't prevent political disagreements between Russia and the EU that were related to the energy disputes ("energy curse" concept) (pp. 91–109). They underline that the reason for the dysfunctionality of the energy interdependence is that "manageable" energy conflicts with the EU and CIS countries were the rational strategic preference of Russia based on domestic and international power accumulation motives. Kofman (2019) asserts that Russia intends to carve out durable and asymmetric energy dependencies with the European countries through energy pipelines and energy export (i) to exterminate the EU's capability to act collectively against Russia and (ii) to fulfil deliberate and opportunistic plans of the grand strategy. Complex energy dependence on Russia, geographic proximity to this country, and conducting "pipeline diplomacy" to decrease Russia's aggressive foreign policy were the arguments that dominated Western policies towards Russia.

Braterskiy (2018) affirmed that Russia's foreign economic policy, foreign policy, and national security goals and tasks are intermingled (pp. 106–109). But the main principle should be to avoid asymmetric interdependence patterns to reduce vulnerability in front of rival great powers. He has underlined that Russia should use energy exports to set up more beneficial asymmetric interdependencies in favour of its geopolitical interests. Graaf and Sovacool (2020) predicted that the future of global energy politics will have four predictable features: (a) *interdependence* based on the global exchange of technical expertise, foreign trade, and foreign direct investments; (b) *interconnections* between energy and other cross-cutting issues such as ecology, infrastructure, finance, and security; (c) *competition* between domestic lobby groups and stakeholders; and among growing powers and emerging economies globally; and (d) *uncertainty* based on risks of transition from traditional to renewable energy (pp. 349–359). All these possible trends for the prospective period will have severe implications for Russia's foreign energy policy and tools/effects of its "energy weapon" as a dominant energy power in the EU and former-USSR region.

Notes

1 Kremlin demanded Gazprom to realize asset purchase policies towards owning shares of Eastern and Central European energy companies with political motivations and geo-political considerations. But Gazprom preferred to conduct the economic feasibility and convince the Kremlin about the potential losses when purchasing gas assets in Central Europe. It means there is a divergence of interests even between the Kremlin and the state's energy corporations (there is no one-sided influence).

2 Russia's "back and forth tactics", Ukraine's concessions on the Donbas, and the US waiver of sanctions on the energy project revealed the mutual vulnerabilities of the actors preventing them from deepening the conflict.

3 Russia's national power components and foreign policy resources include energy and natural resources, transport infrastructure, permanent membership in the UNSC, largest nuclear arsenal globally, armed forces, scientific and intellectual potential, global diplomatic apparatus, global intelligence networks, cyber potential, religious network, media propaganda, and other "soft power" resources.

4 Weber proposed that any state that exports more than 2 million barrels of oil daily that accounts for at least 5% of GDP can be considered as "petrostate".

3 Conceptual Framework

Foreign Policy, Foreign Energy Policy and Energy Conflicts

3.1 Russia's Foreign Energy Policy and Grand Strategy

Russia's foreign energy policy moves can be examined in parallel to the country's foreign policy doctrines based on grand strategy. Grand strategy is a consistent declaration of the state's utmost strategic intents to be sustained internationally in the long-run period. Grand strategy cut across major domains regarding the protection of national interests and promoting the state's position in the global system including political, military, diplomatic, economic, energy, and technological aspects. Russian foreign policy has written and unwritten strategic goals that could be characterized as "*grand strategy*" such as attempting to establish a multipolar order instead of a unipolar world order, strengthening the integration with the countries of the former Soviet Union defined as "near abroad", building an area of influence extending from Eastern Europe to the interior of the continent, protecting economic independence, protecting interests in certain economic areas including energy markets, establishing global and regional alliances, descending to "warm seas", and consolidating its military presence in key regions. There is the strategic dimension of the Russian foreign policy that aims to achieve the strategically autonomous great power status.

Protopopov et al. (2018) concluded that the minimum threshold for Russia's grand strategy is to be a great power ("*velikaya derjava*") in the Eurasian region (p. 448). Marsh (2019) argues that the Russian state is possessed of a two-pillar grand strategy: (a) Russia's strategic influence on the "near abroad" or post-Soviet countries; (b) to build a strategic alliance with China to challenge the US's global hegemony and to pave a way to multipolar world order. Charap et al. (2021) identified six components of Russia's grand strategy that were officially stated in the official documents and strategies: integration of internal and external threats for statehood (vulnerability dimension); geopolitical supremacy, and influence in the "near abroad" ("sphere of influence" dimension); Russia's preparedness for instability at the regional level and owning limited military presence on its periphery (military dimension); the selective collaboration while restricting aspirations of the West (Western dimension); and building strong ties with the new global power centres such as China (multipolarity dimension).

DOI: 10.4324/9781003408482-3

Clark (2019) believes that the ultimate goals of the Russian grand strategy are to regain the great power status with domestic social-political support and to secure its uncontested "sphere of influence" in the perimeter of the border. Russia's geopolitical aspirations to construct a "sphere of influence" with the military, political, economic, and energy dimensions throughout the border perimeter in the "near abroad" region can be explained by Ikenberry's "hierarchical relations" concept. Ikenberry (2004) argued that the USSR set up a forcible "sphere of influence" in Eastern Europe to institutionalize hierarchical relations (we could incorporate the pattern of asymmetric energy interdependence) with the unequally smaller powers of the region (pp. 609–630). Topol (2019) assumes that Russia reacts to the opportunities offered by the USA to fill the regional power gaps or vacuums in the various parts of the globe (e.g., the Eurasian region and the Middle East), rather than implementing a clear-cut grand strategy.

Person (2019) argues that the ultimate ends of the Russian grand strategy are to set up the "sphere of influence" in the post-Soviet area; to be among "great powers" in the various key geopolitically important regions such as the Middle East and the Arctic; to contain the USA's unilateralism and unipolar system around the globe. Russia's grand strategy under Putin's ruling era targets to neutralize the domestic centrifugal groups through the solidification of the country's position in the key regions including Caucasus, Central Asia, and the Middle East. The asymmetric balancing strategy implemented after 2007 against the West uses low-cost asymmetric means (including energy-related means) to gain a higher level of influence on the targeted countries or regions.

Grand strategy is accomplished using various tools with the inclusion of military, political, diplomatic, economic, technical, and energy means that should match the objectives. There are ongoing debates about Russia's possession of adequate economic, energy, technical, political, military, and diplomatic resources to reach the strategic ends of the grand strategy. Brzezinski (2000) argued that Russia's main objective under Putin's ruling is to reinstate a strong state with geopolitical ambitions recalling great power status. But the country couldn't maintain even regional hegemony because of (a) political and economic backwardness; and (b) a mismatch between ends and means. Tsygankov (2011) argues that despite the growing pragmatism in the official decision-makers towards foreign policy's strategic objectives, the "goals-means mismatch" and resource scarceness is a serious problem for Russia's grand strategy (pp. 28–44). The major debates on Russia's grand strategy and foreign policy from identity, vulnerability, militarization, imperial expansion, "sphere of influence", "Greater Eurasia", the relations with the West, and multipolarity perspectives are accompanied by energy dimension. Therefore, we must examine the role of the foreign energy policy in the Russian grand strategy and foreign policy separately.

When countries map out a grand strategy, they assess internal and external strengths and fragilities, including access to and realization of energy resources. The grand strategy envisages assuring national security, and the national security strategy should safeguard energy security by exploiting soft and hard power elements. The countries can use political, economic, diplomatic, and even military instruments to achieve the energy component of the grand strategy. Various Russian and foreign IR and foreign policy scholars relate Russian grand strategy and foreign policy principles and ideas (e.g., territorial expansionism towards the Greater Eurasia edge, multipolarity, and identity) with the energy dimension. Brzezinski (1998) affirmed Russia's vital geopolitical interests, including energy interests to control energy export infrastructure and energy basins in the post-Soviet region as a part of the post-imperial grand strategy (p. 64). The energy imperative is crucial in the great-power competition in the Eurasian region among Russia and other critical regional and global actors. Dugin (2015) argues that Russia needs territorial expansion towards the natural borders thanks to energy resources as a land-based power.

Kaplan (2013) argues that Putin realized "neo-czarist expansionism" (Russia as a land power without "natural borders" aspiring towards access to the seas and oceans) based on natural resource revenues that will be challenged by world oil-gas prices and the rising power of China, especially in the "near abroad" and Siberia region. Russia tries to adopt the grand strategy to the new realities: e.g., to strengthen the country's position in the Arctic to control energy resources and transport corridors in the wider Eurasian region. Lo (2019) underlined that Russia used the "Greater Eurasia" initiative to create new export markets for Russian oil-gas resources and nuclear energy, rather than geopolitical expansionism (p. 19). But also, this regional rapprochement paved the way for China to enter the Russian energy infrastructure in the Arctic region, establishing complex energy interdependence between the two powers. Karaganov (2018) argued that Russia became an appendage of China in terms of energy and economic parameters (pp. 15–29). Russia can be converted into a raw material "colony" of China after the energy embargo of the Western countries in 2022. Belogoryev (2014) believes that setting up Russia-China complex energy cooperation would allow official Beijing to improve energy security and Russia is going to become the energy rear of China. Milov (2021) argued that Putin chose the "one-sided raw material model" of relations with China despite the huge economic and ecological costs for Russia for the geopolitical alliance against the West.

Auzan (2021) emphasized that "space" ("*prostranstvo*") is a strategically and vitally crucial concept and substance in the Russian state mentality. But it isn't feasible to assimilate these massive and vast lands economically and demographically. The long-term economic development of Russia as a united and integrated territorial entity will be impossible because of unintegrated and scattered areas, and domestic fragilities. As an economically underdeveloped country, Russia will not be able to pursue the "great power" aspiration that is the value of the ruling elites together with global recognition and controlling vast lands. Russian scholar and former prime minister representing the "liberal stream" Yegor Gaidar (1997) believed that the Russian state permanently generates internal and external "enemies" in the "statist" social environment, mobilizing the productive economic resources for unproductive imperialist or expansionist grand strategy objectives (Figure 3.1). Russia has the cult of a "strong state" carrying out territorial expansion with the permanent mode to catch up with Europe technologically and economically (p. 46).

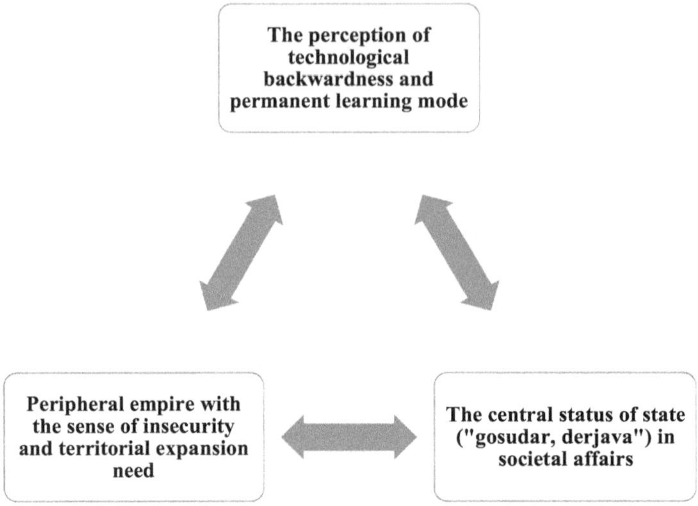

Figure 3.1 Russia's national identity triangle.
Source: Modified from Inozemtsev (2019).

Rumer and Wallander (2003) claimed that Russia's geography with rich natural resources is a source of vulnerability than great power resources in the present-day world (pp. 57–73). The lack of economic and military reforms, lack of foreign investment, and technological innovations would limit Russia's influence on the former imperial peripheries. The technological backwardness of Russia strengthens the interdependence pattern with the developed countries weakening grand strategy ambitions. Inozemtsev (2019) argues that Russia's national *identity* that determines its grand strategy was shaped as a consequence of these three factors: (a) the perception of technological backwardness and permanent learning mode; (b) the central status of state ("*gosudar*", "*derjava*") in societal affairs; (c) the peripheral empire with the sense of insecurity and territorial expansion (Scheme 3.1) (pp. 54–55).

Graham (2021) argued that the main patterns of the foreign and security policies are matching the aim to protect large and undefended territories of Russia via zones of influence, destabilizing the neighbourhood, and manoeuvring among big powers. The only factor of the uncertainty in this pattern of grand strategy and foreign policy would be the disruptive role of technological development. One of the central principles of Russian foreign policy under the framework of the grand strategy is to achieve recognition and affirmation by foreign actors as a "strong state" with large territories and rich energy resources. An effort to introduce itself as a powerful state and get recognition is part of Russia's state identity, and this identity cannot be considered apart from its rich energy resources. Being an "energy superpower" could reinforce Russia's "strong state" identity. Bouzarovski and Bassin (2011) argue that the "energy superpower" image is a part of the national identity of Russia and its global status as a "great power" via related discourses (policy narratives) and material base (energy infrastructure) (pp. 783–794). Regional energy domination and asymmetric dependence of post-Soviet neighbours ("near abroad") on Russia's oil, gas, refining, and transit hegemony found grounds for the energy component of national identity.

Trenin (2011) argues that both Russia and post-Soviet countries experience "post-imperial syndrome" and an energy factor is a crucial element of the Russian economy to establish itself as a post-imperial power suffering from "territorial losses" in this transformation process. Russia recognizes that all post-Soviet countries attempt to put distance from Russia and pursue multidimensional and balanced foreign policy including autonomous foreign energy policy (such as the contracts with the Western oil-gas companies by Azerbaijan, Kazakhstan, Turkmenistan, and Uzbekistan). Primakov (2009) argues that the dialectic between the emerging multipolarity and the interdependence of the emerging power centres of the world system is a prominent feature of the current world order (pp. 23–141). He believes that Russia's vast energy resources and geographical position could breach any global powers' attempts to isolate Russia. Shafranik (2005) argued that multipolarity exists in world politics and the world energy markets. Russia competes with the USA, OPEC, Norway, and other energy producers to form "energy poles" and obtain a share in the energy consumption markets such as India and China. Degterev (2020) argued that Russia with its weaker economy is situated between two huge economic gravity zones – China and the EU, despite having the largest territories in the world and rich energy resources. This reality weakens the perspective of solid political-economic integration of the post-Soviet counties around Russia and forces it to fulfil multi-dimensional foreign economic and energy policy towards both Eurasian "edge powers".

The energy factor should be evaluated as a means, tool, and strategic end of the Russian grand strategy that will include its domestic energy resources and geopolitical interests in the critical energy-rich territories, energy export routes, and energy chokepoints primarily in the Eurasian region. Energy resources including oil, gas, and nuclear can be considered as means of Russia's grand strategy. Tsygankov (2011) included the energy factor to the list of the Russian foreign policy and grand strategy tools together with military, diplomacy, culture, and technology that function under the framework of certain geopolitical circumference (p. 35). Energy is an instrument to strengthen domestic power and to realize a "defensive strategy" of maintaining global and regional domination. He advocates the argument that the capacity of Russia in the energy sphere partly subscribed to the recognition of the country by global powers, at least in the Eurasian region. But Russia's hard position in the energy conflicts with the neighbour and EU countries damaged the country's reputation as a reliable energy partner and revealed Russia's regional and global political ambitions that utilized the energy factor to reach at. Tsygankov (2011) asserted that the energy factor persists to be Russia's strategic comparative advantage in the grand strategy implementation (p. 41). The oil-gas reserve is an architect of the national power of Russia, enabling only short-term triumphs towards the grand strategy goals.

Marsh (2019) argues that the energy resources in Russia contribute to the country's political ambitions in Europe. Russia aims to invest in the downstream sectors in the oil-gas markets of the post-Soviet and the EU states to strengthen the economic and political control over the energy supply chain. O'Sullivan (2013) argues that the energy factor could be evaluated as a part of all major elements of grand strategy. Energy could be the end or objective of the grand strategy in terms of (a) energy security of the energy-scarce countries (e.g., Japan aims to secure its energy independence as a part of the grand strategy) or (b) dominance in the energy basins by energy-rich countries (e.g., Russia aims to dominate in the energy basins of the Caspian Sea, Middle East or Arctics). The energy factor could contribute to the alliance-building of the energy producer countries in the form of energy subsidies to the politically loyal countries (e.g., Russia's energy subsidies to Belarus and Armenia). If we match the grand strategy goals with the foreign energy policy of Russia, major components of the grand strategy have corresponding goals and actions in the foreign energy policy (Table 3.1).

O'Sullivan (2013) underlined that energy factors and oil-gas revenues can also play the role of means (resources) or ways (tools) to attain grand strategy objectives (pp. 30–47). For energy-rich countries such as Russia, their energy resources

Table 3.1 The grand strategy goals and foreign energy policy of Russia

The grand strategy goals of Russia's foreign policy	*Related issues in the foreign energy policy*
The transformation from the "land power" to "sea power" by gaining permanent access to the seas from the Baltics to the Mediterranean.	Launching LNG projects in the Northern Route through the Arctic and being actively engaged in the energy projects in the Mediterranean.
Strategic control zones from the Black Sea to the Far East to secure domestic stability in Russia.	Energy and electricity integration of neighbour countries to the relevant systems of Russia.
Establishing buffer zones in the Western, Southern, and Eastern borders.	To support loyal governments via cheap oil (Belarus), energy infrastructure, and credits.
Supporting various secessionist movements (domestic actors) in the strategic zones.	Providing cheap natural gas to secessionist Transnistria region in Moldova.
Playing the central role in the European security settings/order and preserving the interests of Slavs and orthodoxies in Europe.	Gas export to Europe (e.g., Germany) from the 1960s; complex energy relationships with Serbia and Bulgaria ("South Stream").
Presence in the various key geopolitically important regions such as the Middle East and the Arctic.	Control energy assets (pipeline infrastructure, gas hubs, oil terminals) in the Middle East.
To maintain "great power" status through "spheres of influence" in the "near abroad" or post-Soviet region.	Energy dominance in the region (e.g., Belarus) via Gazprom, RAO UES, Rosneft, and Rosatom.
To contain the US-led unipolar system and promote multipolarity in the world order.	Building strong energy ties with the new global power centres such as China and India.

Source: Protopopov et al. (2018, p. 448); RECSID.

and energy exports are mostly a tool to achieve the grand strategy. Russia used energy resources as a political and economic pressure tool violating an acceptable market competition to reach the strategic ends of the grand strategy. Russia's abundant natural resources including oil-gas reserves function as a tool to reach the strategic objectives of the grand strategy. But also, this tool could be converted to the strategic goal of the grand strategy that requires protection from any foreign take-over or capture (Katz, 2006). In other words, the energy factor has a double function for the Russian grand strategy as a mean and end simultaneously. The tactics that Russia has used to realize the grand strategy combine militarism and energy dimensions.

3.2 Russia's Militarist Strategic Culture and Foreign Energy Policy

The third criteria of complex interdependence are the level of relevance of the military factor in interstate affairs. Russia has militarized strategic culture that is interlinked with grand strategy and foreign energy policy. Heikka (2000) highlights that Russia's grand strategy has been historically constructed through interactions with strategic culture (pp. 4–34). Baev (2020) analyses "*strategic culture*" as a mega concept determining and interacting with Russia's "great power" aspirations. The energy factor plays a role in the transformation of the Russian strategic culture together with the nuclear weapon arsenal, cyber dimension, widespread misconduct, and the pivot to China. Baev (2020) argues that oil-gas export to China plays a certain role in the changes in strategic culture, but the security factor prevails which means the military weakness of Russia in the Far East region in the neighbourhood of China. Analysing Russia's foreign policy and national security documents and doctrines, Marange (2019) underlines the impact of the "Soviet strategic culture" (prioritizing NATO's expansion as an ultimate threat, but not China's military rise) and the perception of prestige on the Russian grand strategy-building process. She points out that Russia's strategic goals are the restoration of the global power status and the protection of regional dominance in Europe and post-Soviet geography through establishing "buffer zones" of neutral states with "limited sovereignty" (e.g., diverting Ukraine and Georgia from NATO's expansion) (pp. 50–69). For Rudakov (2019), as a part of the Soviet Union's strategic culture, "the doctrine of limited sovereignty" or "Brezhnev doctrine" provided for the possibility of the USSR, if necessary, to intervene in the affairs of the satellite countries in Eastern Europe in the 1970s.

Marange (2019) underlines that Russia started to militarize its foreign policy against the "near abroad" after 2007 (Putin's well-known speech at the Munich Security Conference) and reached the peak of that policy in 2014 with the illegitimate annexation of Crimea from Ukraine. But this aggressive strategy could be unsustainable in terms of economic prosperity and the perception of the "Russian threat" in the "near abroad". To reach the strategic objectives, Russia actively used military intervention, hybrid warfare, nuclear deterrence, energy supply disruption threat, complex influence using soft power, cyberspace operations, and political and economic destabilization tools (Table 3.2).

Table 3.2 The military and non-military tools of Russia's grand strategy

Russia's grand strategy						
Objective 1				*Objective 2*		
The return to global power status				The protection of regional hegemony		
			Tools			
"Energy weapon"	Diplomacy	International organizations	Military threat	Trade and investment	Nuclear deterrence	Cultural dominance

Source: Modified from Marange (2019).

Shevtsova (2010) argued that high oil prices and the nuclear factor increased the Kremlin's perception of self-confidence and self-sufficiency against the West during Putin's power. Reliance on energy resources indirectly promoted militarism, imperialism, and geopolitical revisionism in the grand strategy, domestic policy ("sovereign democracy"), and foreign policy towards problematic post-Soviet countries (e.g., Ukraine) and the EU (p. 67). Before the conflict with Ukraine (2014), the "*Gerasimov Doctrine*" was disclosed by the Chief of the General Staff of the Armed Forces of Russia Valery Gerasimov (army general) in 2013. The doctrine was a foreign policy programme that rethinks the modern concept of interstate conflict and puts military action on a par with political, economic (including energy policy), informational, humanitarian, and other non-military measures. The doctrine became known after its publication in February 2013 and subsequent actions of Russia concerning Ukraine in 2014–2015, which fully coincide with the theses of this doctrine. Key elements of the "Gerasimov Doctrine" lie at the heart of the concept of a "new generation and non-linear hybrid warfare" including "energy war". Gerasimov (2013) argued that Russia should be in leading positions in the new interstate conflict techniques with preventive measures beyond the borders. The application of the "Gerasimov Doctrine" (2013) could be seen in the conflict with Ukraine in 2014–2015 and the militarization of the Arctics. Russia turns the Arctic zone that owns 20% of the undiscovered oil and gas reserve of the world (Smirnov, 2021), into a highly militarized zone to protect geopolitical and geo-economic (energy) interests.

The new wave of Russia's confrontation with the Western world (militarily with NATO, politically with the USA and EU) in August 2008 (intervention in Georgia) was accompanied by the "gas war" with Ukraine and other Western energy partners in January 2009. It was the turning point in Russia's military doctrine and security strategy that partly determined the foreign energy policy afterward. The secretary of the Russian Security Council, Nikolai Patrushev (KGB officer and army general), was one of the architects of the new security concept and military doctrine promoting the idea of nuclear deterrence capabilities of Russia. Piontkovsky (2020) argues that nuclear strike capacity and the possibility to use the nuclear weapon appear in contemporary national security strategy and military doctrine, reflecting the "*Patrushev Doctrine*" (Piontkovsky, 2020). This method of warfare can be interpreted as "*de-escalation through nuclear escalation*" (Brezkun, 2015).

The Kremlin didn't conceal the intention that nuclear weapon intimidation was essential to the hybrid war (including "gas war") that Russia declared on Ukraine and the West. Former President Medvedev signed a decree on the implementation of the "*National Security Strategy of Russia until 2020*" in 2009. The document predicts that the risk of an increase in the number of states possessing nuclear weapons will increase. The Strategy links security risks with energy goals underlining that "*the long-term attention of global politics will be focused on the possession of energy sources, including in the Middle East, on the shelf of the Barents Sea and in the Arctic, in the Caspian Sea basin and Central Asia*" (Kremlin, 2009b).

The doctrinal shift in Russia's foreign and military policy that accentuated the nuclear factor was supported by Rosastom's expansionist and politically motivated active policy in other geographical areas beyond the "near abroad" including the Middle East. Rosatom was deeply involved in the nuclear power and nuclear capacity-building projects around the Middle East where the Russian foreign policy, foreign energy policy, military vision, and long-run strategic interests were intertwined. Kremlin's nuclear-related foreign energy strategy aggregates nuclear energy expansion with nuclear weapon proliferation around the globe. Dynkin and Burrows (2016) point out that the broader use of nuclear energy occurs in many volatile and conflict-prone regions (p. 32). The line between military and peaceful employment of atomic energy is largely blurred, mainly due to nuclear fuel cycle technologies. Atomic energy has economic and political dimensions in terms of the status, prestige, and defence capabilities of countries. The risk accompanies the spread of nuclear power that nuclear energy countries could start atomic weapon programmes. The nuclear energy dimension plays a crucial role in the Russian foreign energy policy and nuclear-based military doctrine. Also, Russia's foreign energy policy is partly positioned in the juxtaposition of new military doctrine and more aggressive foreign policy under the grand strategy. Bogaturov (2017) argued that Russia is the only "*nuclear-oil great power*" in the world combining large fossil fuels export with nuclear energy potential. He believes that the nuclear factor is to reproduce the West's suspicions about Russia, but the oil factor increases constructive interest in Russia. But the military intervention in Ukraine in February 2022 seriously harmed the position of the Russian oil sector and oil supplies in the regional and global markets.

Energy factor combines considerations of national security, economic development, and ecological concerns. Russia's energy strategies, foreign policy concepts, President's annual messages to Parliament, official statements, and speeches relate foreign energy policy primarily to the security dimension based on external threat perception in parallel to the pattern of economic, energy, technological, and complex interdependence. Historically, Russia's energy resources and energy policy were related to the military and security issues based on the country's specific militarized history that strengthened the role of the "gas weapon" or "energy weapon" concept (Zygar & Panyushkin, 2008, pp. 2–3). After the hybrid military intervention in Georgia in 2008 and Ukraine in 2014, Russia demonstrated a more offensive strategy to solidify regional hegemonic power and to protect its sphere of influence in the "near abroad" using an aggressive foreign energy policy.

3.3 Periods of Foreign Policy, Energy Dimension, and Domestic Conditions

Russia's foreign policy is determined by the domestic political discourse and international context. Russian foreign policy is a function of the domestic political and economic elite's power configuration, interaction and geopolitical recognition by the West, NATO's enlargement and centrifugal trends, technological dependence, economic backwardness, demographic trends, historical identity, and regional expansionary ambitions. The energy factor ensures the multi-dimensional and multi-vector aspect of Russian foreign policy. Russia has used its energy resources to amplify its foreign policy and to reach the strategic objectives of the grand strategy to be an independent global power. Russian foreign policy and foreign energy policy followed a multidimensional approach in terms of priority regions (including the EU, post-Soviet, and China) and various tools that could multiply the real influence of Russia concerning its objective economic (including energy) or political capabilities. Russia's foreign energy policy moves are examined in parallel to the country's grand strategy and foreign policy doctrines. Russia's foreign energy policy is affiliated with the country's foreign and energy policy as subcategories of grand strategy.

Bogaturov (2007) argued that Russian foreign policy was a reflection and continuation of the domestic policy and political situation in the early 1990s (pp. 54–69). He distinguishes several stages of Russian foreign policy doctrines in relation to domestic developments. Russian foreign policy has passed through several stages after the collapse of the Soviet Union in 1991 when the conflict between the security ("*siloviki*") and liberal wings within the Russian state structure affected the country's foreign policy. For example, while Andrey Kozyrev, who was the country's foreign minister from 1992 to 1996, was the representative of the liberal stream (liberal imperialist), all three ministers (Yevgeny Primakov, Igor Ivanov, Sergey Lavrov) who have been serving since 1996 stand out with their "security-statist" identities, statements, and actions. In the early 1990s, Russia's foreign policy was under the influence of the Gorbachev era's value-based and liberal foreign policy rhetoric that envisaged deeper integration with the West. Russia's economic crises in the early 1990s and its huge foreign debts to Europe (inherited from USSR) constrained its foreign policy and energy policy manoeuvre capabilities of Russia.

Russian President Boris Yeltsin and Foreign Minister Kozyrev worked towards the direct integration of Russia into the main transatlantic and European institutions. On the one hand, appointing "pro-Western" and liberal Kozyrev as the minister of foreign affairs was a message to the West indicating new features of Russian foreign policy. On another hand, Russia never relinquished the national interests related to the sphere of influence, economic benefits, new energy markets, and basic security considerations. Contrary to Bogaturov's argument about the totally liberal foreign policy of Russia in the early 1990s, Kozyrev's speech at Organization for Security and Co-operation in Europe (OSCE) in 1992 revealed Russia's assertive foreign policy shift and using energy diplomacy as geopolitical leverage.

Kozyrev played role in the Russian *foreign energy policy*. We can describe two related cases:

a In September 1994, Kozyrev supported the idea to deny the Azeri-Chirag-Guneshli (ACG) agreement of Azerbaijan with the foreign oil-gas companies in the Caspian Sea, but former "oil-man" Prime Minister Chernomyrdin supported the idea to recognize the ACG contract and Lukoil's participation in the project. Kozyrev proposed to Chernomyrdin (the prime minister had an affiliation with the energy sector) to introduce economic sanctions against Azerbaijan. Kozyrev sent an ultimatum to both Azerbaijan and other parties to the ACG agreement that they shouldn't ignore Russia's energy interests (Presidential Library of the Office of the President of the Republic of Azerbaijan, 2020).
b In October 1995, Gazprom complemented Russia's diplomatic efforts to solve the Bosnia-Serbia conflict by supplying natural gas to Sarajevo via Belgrade (Zhikharev, 1995). Firstly, Gazprom stopped gas deliveries to Sarajevo, referring to accumulated gas debts that the Bosnian government refused to pay. A transit gas pipeline stretched to Sarajevo from Hungary through the territory of Serbia and the territories occupied by Bosnian Serbs. Russia promised to resume natural gas supplies to Bosnia as a political pre-condition for starting a ceasefire. Kozyrev noted that Yeltsin's initiative to set up a ceasefire in Bosnia was being implemented through the agreement between Gazprom and the Bosnian government. Also, Prime Minister Victor Chernomyrdin, affiliated with Gazprom, used his personal contacts with Milosevic to make pressure on Serbia for pursuing Russia's regional interests (Talbott, 2007, pp. 232–379). Kremlin created a tradition to intervene in military conflicts using energy diplomacy and strengthen its role in the strategic Balkans.

Bogaturov (2007) argued that the appointment of Yevgeny Primakov to the position of minister of foreign policy reflected more anti-Western and pro-China ("triple alliance") attitudes in Russia's foreign policy doctrine (pp. 54–69). In 1998, Primakov put forward a plan to develop trilateral cooperation between Russia, China, and India as a practical mechanism for promoting global multipolarity. He considered Moscow's strategic partnership with Beijing, Delhi, and Tehran as an attempt to deter NATO's military expansion. Primakov declared that establishing relations with the CIS countries or the "near abroad" was a priority task of Russian foreign policy. Primakov had backed the idea of multipolar world order and Russia's equal partnership with global powers. Primakov played an important role in Russian energy diplomacy in the Middle East (Iraq) during his active duty as a minister and after the official position. Russia took an increasing amount of Iraqi oil in 1997 thanks to the personal relations of the Minister of Foreign Affairs Primakov both with the political leadership of Iraq and with the largest figures in the Russian oil sector. It was an example of the interlink between the foreign policy of Russia and its benefits from the international energy market. Primakov as the President of the Russian Chamber of Commerce and Industry visited the Iraqi Kurdistan region in 2017 to discuss the referendum process and oil-gas business

(Kasaev, 2009). Primakov had confessed to the Gazprom's instrumentalization in the hand of the Kremlin for geopolitical purposes supplying gas to Bosnia, Belarus, Ukraine, and Georgia. But Gazprom also had institutional autonomy protecting its business interests. *Primakov's foreign policy doctrine* was based on pragmatism and realism, enabling Russia to accumulate economic resources and concentrate on strategic goals to become one of the poles of global power eventually.

The turning point in the domestic politics of Russia started in 1998 when the "statist wing" of the political and bureaucratic elite started to strengthen its position in the state and the government, in the example of the premiership of Primakov. But the conventional point of view is that President Putin started to concentrate the power in Russia suppress all alternative factions in the domestic realm and pursue more aggressive foreign policy abroad. Putin only continued the trend of authoritarianism that commenced before his regime and the oil price was one of the factors that played a role in the solidification of power in one's hand. Putin appointed Igor Ivanov minister of foreign policy (as a successor of Primakov) who continued the foreign policy doctrine that can be characterized as defending national interests and "selective cooperation" with the West (e.g., cooperation on international security with NATO, nuclear non-proliferation with the USA, and energy issues with the EU).

Former Foreign Policy Minister Ivanov (2002, pp. 8–72) argued that Russian foreign policy after the 2000s built upon the growing economic strength based on oil-gas revenues. Russia's integration into the world economic system should meet the national interests of the country meaning the "elimination of discriminatory restrictions" against Russian energy companies in world markets. Russia had successfully sophisticated energy diplomacy tools to create a reliable and credible energy partner image that abides by the market principles from the early 2000s until the series of geopolitical clashes with the West in 2014–2015 and 2021–2022. Ivanov (2002, pp. 8–72) examined Russian energy diplomacy as an integral part of economic diplomacy that has the following tasks: attracting foreign investment in the energy sector, protecting the interests of Russian energy exporters in global markets, finding new energy sales markets, optimization of the routes of energy transportation networks, and active participation in the world energy (oil) prices formation. He acknowledged that Russian *foreign energy policy* has strong political and diplomatic dimensions, but also the country shouldn't be converted only as a "raw material" reservoir for the world economy.

Ivanov underlined the interdependence and complementarity ("energy for finance") of Russia-EU energy relations. He believes that expanding oil-gas supplies to the EU on a long-term basis can prevent short-term "energy supply shocks". Ivanov (2002) argued that Russia should pay attention to the formation of the new energy infrastructure of the Asian-Pacific region; strengthen integration processes within the CIS; avoid a passive or isolationist foreign policy; pursue an interest-based pragmatic and realistic policy towards a system-forming role in international affairs (pp. 8–72). The basis of the Russian active foreign policy could be the country's growing economy thanks to oil-gas revenues. The appointment of highly experienced diplomat Sergey Lavrov as the minister of foreign affairs in

2004 strengthened the Russian state's active diplomatic stance on global affairs and foreign energy policy.

Yavlinsky (2015) points out that unprecedented high oil and gas prices in export markets in the 2000s, in absolute and relative terms, somehow forestall "authoritarian modernization" based on a "statist" approach and distrust of "market forces" in Russia (pp. 30–61). Yavlinsky (2015) argued that Russia experienced the fusion of power and property after the early 2000s (thanks to the export of raw materials and fossil fuels that enabled power consolidation) via the subordination of business to the state and the reduction of the private sector in the economy in the case of YUKOS in 2003 (p. 101). Lo (2002) argued that when Putin came to power in 2000, a significant shift in foreign policy was the securitization of external affairs (pp. 114–158). Trenin (2012) underlined that the integration-oriented foreign policy was unsuccessful in 2003–2004 for several domestic and international reasons including the US invasion of Iraq, YUKOS (a private oil company of Russia that built good relations with the Western countries) affair, the Beslan tragedy in North Ossetia, the "Orange Revolution" in Ukraine, changing image of Putin in the Western media and international organizations (p. 59). These internal and external factors changed the dimension of Russian foreign policy from integration into the West to strengthening its great power positions. The material foundation of the new foreign policy course was the rising crude oil prices that helped Russia to achieve financial independence from the West.

Bogaturov (2007) underlined that Putin's speech at a meeting with ambassadors and permanent representatives of Russia on 27 June 2006 was doctrinal in terms of content (pp. 54–69). Putin argued that Russia should bear responsibility for global and socio-economic development proportionate to its power position and economic capabilities. Russia's "*diplomatic efforts must be supported not only by successes in ensuring international stability but also by significant financial and economic levers*" (recognition of energy factor as foreign policy leverage). He acknowledged that Russia's competitors in global economic markets could be key partners in international politics. Such a pattern of contemporary international relations paves the way for elements of cooperation and competition to be closely intertwined (Kremlin, 2006). Primakov (2018) pointed out that the turning point in the Russian foreign energy policy in the direction of radicalization vis-à-vis foreign partners was 2006. In that year, the Russia-Ukraine gas conflict had culminated, and the crisis had occurred with the foreign operator of the Sakhalin-2 project. About 80% of the transit volumes of gas from Russia to Europe passed through Ukraine before the commissioning of the Nord Stream. Russia intended to deprive countries whose territories pipelines pass, including Ukraine, of its transit power against Russia. The crisis with Sakhalin Energy in 2006 demonstrated that economically more assertive Russia intended to revise the conditions of previously signed oil-gas contracts and nationalize the energy sector (Primakov: "*refuse the predatory practice of a foreign partner*") (pp. 319–341).

The tectonic shift in the Russian foreign policy was expressed by Putin in his speech at the Munich Security Conference in 2007 where Putin expressed that "*a unipolar model is not only unacceptable but generally impossible or the modern world*" in terms of military, political, economic resources and energy security of the EU (Kremlin, 2007). Stulberg (2008) asserted that Russia's energy leverage against European and CIS countries would have incentive or coercive functions depending on the "energy statecraft" under Putin or Yeltsin (p. 354). At the beginning of Putin's rule, the emphasis was on an alliance with the USA and NATO under the framework of fighting international terrorism and on rapprochement with the EU underpinned by energy cooperation. Under Putin's leadership after 2000, Russia attempted to regain its status as a major power using energy resources, which were degraded in the post-Soviet period. Russia intended to become (i) the dominant force in the former Soviet space; (ii) a reliable energy supplier and political partner of other major powers; (iii) the cornerstone of the European energy security system; (iv) a leading actor in the exploitation of Arctic resources; (v) an active member of main global and regional energy organizations; and (vi) a key actor in the global and regional energy systems. Russia aimed to be one of the world leaders in the oil and gas sector, nuclear energy, and the development of new technologies in these areas. The country tried to retain the role of leading energy supplier to Europe and the most important market for European goods and investments.

Russia-Georgia war and the global financial crisis in 2008 deepened the antagonist cliff between Russia and the external world (not only Western but also post-Soviet countries). The sharp drop in oil prices, reducing foreign investments, and deteriorating foreign affairs forced the Russian political elites to alleviate the confrontational foreign policy in 2008–2009. There were political changes in Russia in 2008 when Dmitry Medvedev replaced Vladimir Putin in the presidential position. In 2009, President Medvedev proclaimed a course of modernization for Russia gradually softening the relations with the external world under the collapse of the oil revenue boom. In the ruling period of Medvedev, on the one hand, Russia's conflictual foreign energy policy continued with partner countries (from "near abroad", Europe, and Asia), but on the other hand, the Russian energy companies built strategic alliances with the leading Western energy companies and Chinese institutions. In 2011, the state-owned company Rosneft entered into multi-billion agreements with BP and ExxonMobil on the exchange of assets and joint development of oil fields in the Arctic (Parfitt & Rushe, 2011). The first and second lines of the Nord Stream gas pipeline from Russia to Germany with a transport capacity of 27.5 billion cubic metres of natural gas per annum were inaugurated in 2011–2012 (Nord Stream Pipeline, 2020). State-owned oil production and oil transit companies Rosneft and Transneft obtained credits from Chinese state banks between 2009 and 2011. The Eastern Siberia-Pacific Ocean (ESPO) crude oil pipeline was launched in 2012. Discussions were activated with China on the "Power of Siberia" gas supply pipeline during Medvedev's presidency, and the construction started during the period of Putin's presidency in 2012.

Shevtsova (2015) argued that Russia adopted a more aggressive "*Putin Doctrine*" towards world affairs in 2011–2012 that was related to the domestic political protests as a survival policy (pp. 22–36). But Lipsky (2021) argues that the alteration to the foreign policy of Russia didn't occur in connection with the mass protests and integration efforts towards the EU/NATO in Ukraine in 2013–2014, and global reactions to Russia's intervention. Mass protests against Putin's presidency and elections ("*Bolotnaya*" process) in Russia in 2011–2012 only accelerated the foreign policy towards isolationism that had repercussions on the energy policy. The Ukraine war (occupation of the Donetsk and Luhansk regions by Russia in 2014 and the annexation of Crimea in 2015) has been a turning point for at least the "*near abroad*" countries' perception of Russian foreign policy. Even the members of the EEU (such as Belarus, Kazakhstan, and Armenia) and Russia's closest allies were seeking to distance themselves from Russia and reduce their political, military/security, economic, and energy dependence on Russia. This demonstrates the close linkage between foreign policy actions and the domestic political process in Russia that also contributes to the interdependence balance through domestic political, economic, and social fragilities.

Foreign and domestic policies are interconnected in the agenda-setting (hierarchy-free) process of complex interdependence. The formulation of formal and official agendas of governments depends on the complexity of domestic affairs, the level of interlinks among issue (policy) areas, and the level of interactions with foreign actors. Relatively strong states with alternative power resources can easier link various issue areas including military and non-military priorities (e.g., linking the country's military priorities with energy priorities in the Arctic region). Russian foreign policy depends on the political and economic context actively in responding to the emerging global and domestic challenges. Also, Russia's foreign energy policy hasn't only encountered systemic challenges of the international system but also has been affected by the domestic political and economic setting.

Kaczmarski (2014) argued that Russia's foreign and internal policies have "fluid" interconnections (pp. 383–409). Russia's foreign policy is shaped by the influences of various domestic and external factors with great power, compound identity, security, and economic/energy dimensions. The nexus between domestic economic policy and foreign policy can be examined separately. Russia's foreign policy strongly depends on the situation in the country's economy, society, and politics. Also, Russia's domestic politics and energy economics depend on Russia's foreign policy course, primarily on its relations with the West and the post-Soviet region. Primakov (2015) considered the country's domestic and foreign policy as complementary and interrelated issues. He argued that if Russia cannot solve the technological backwardness and lack of innovative components in the national economy, it will be challenging to preserve a "great power" status and positively contribute to global affairs (pp. 4–69).

Mankoff (2009) argued that domestic power consolidation and hegemonic expansion are unchanging principles of Russia's security-sensitive foreign policy (pp. 5–42). Energy revenues consolidated the Russian elite, who preferred to pursue foreign policy assertively and achieve great power positions ignoring norms, values, and institutions. But on the other hand, relying on oil-gas resources made the Russian economy and foreign policy more vulnerable to world oil-gas prices' oscillations and energy demand adjusting the asymmetric pattern of interdependence with the energy-consuming countries. The conflicts with the post-USSR countries such as Georgia and Ukraine demonstrated that the phase of domestic consolidation had already concluded, and the new more aggressive foreign policy stage has commenced (despite economic and technology shortcomings). Russia's shifting foreign energy policy from Europe to Asia overlaps with domestic public attitudes towards the EU and China. Russia's conflict with the EU over Ukraine which started in 2013 and continued in 2014 coincided with the declining positive attitude towards the EU in the Russian public. In parallel, the Russian public's positive attitudes towards China started to go up by the end of 2013 mutually interacting with the state propaganda.

The foreign policy depends on the state's structure, decision-makers, and federal arrangements. Yavlinsky (2020) argued that Russia's *hybrid political system* consists of (i) Soviet, national-Bolshevik political models and institutions; (ii) primitive, semi-market capitalism; (iii) large-scale misconduct relationships without independent justice and free media; and (iv) oligarchy – the big business merged with power. Nodia (2009) asserted that the concepts of "hybrid regime" ("grey zone" amidst democracy and autocracy) and "petrostate" (oil-gas resources ensure the stability of the political regime) are not enough to understand Russia's domestic and foreign policy (pp. 34–38). Petrov and Gelman (2019) argued that top managers of the state-owned companies (including powerful energy enterprises), officials representing the executive branch (ministries, state committees), and officials representing the military and security apparatus have a relatively higher influence on the Russian foreign policy than other sub-groups of the country's political and social elite (pp. 1–11). Belkovsky (2007, pp. 190–192) described Russia as an "*energy empire*" where a small group of bureaucrats and businessmen controlled about 40% of the economy and 65% of the country's industrial potential. Putin and his inner circle deprived the regional governors and local elites of influence on the political and economic processes in Russia between 2000 and 2003 (Belkovsky, 2007, pp. 190–192).

The economic problems and challenges related to the federal subjects seriously deepened the domestic fragilities of Russia weakening its position in front of external actors under the pattern of interdependence. Pain (2019) points out that Kremlin uses the energy resources and other lucrative sectors of the extractive economy to preserve the loyalty of the leaders of federal subjects and to protect the idea of federalism in Russia. Therefore, the energy sector isn't only a foreign policy tool, but also a cement to consolidate domestic power and maintain the federal state's unity. The vast employment of the natural resources for the cementing of national unity demonstrates that Russia's energy resources and even foreign energy policy are linked to domestic ethnopolitics. If we could deepen the analysis of Emil Pain (2013) on the Russian "imperial syndrome", it is feasible to find out the linkages with the country's foreign energy policy. The weak integration of the federal subjects and various nationalities into the administrative centre and united sociocultural environment create a permanent threat of centrifugal forces in Russia. Therefore, Russia aims to fortify its geostrategic position in the neighbour countries using the energy resources and energy dependence across the perimeters of the border to prevent domestic centrifugal trends.

Sergeeva (1996) argued that the *sub-national* dimension of Russian foreign policy was important in the early and mid-1990s. Atomization of foreign economic and international relations was necessary to avoid the inefficient governance system of the USSR. Federal authorities and regions started to build cross-border trade and investment cooperation in various sectors including the oil and gas sector. But Putin started to weaken the economic autonomy of federal regions by consolidating and centralizing the power in the early 2000s with a "pragmatic imperial" mindset. The weak regional development created a negative pattern of dependence on foreign investments and technology in the energy sector. Zubarevich (2021a) argued that small Russian towns in the periphery have underprivileged material conditions and the regional inequality pattern hasn't changed fundamentally from 1999 to 2018 in terms of the per capita regional gross product level in Russia. Poltoranin, Chelnokov, and Postavnin (2012) argued that the Far East region of Russia deeply depends on Chinese migration (p. 13). Russia tried to lay the ESPO pipeline on its own human resources but quickly realized that it would be difficult and expensive. Russia invited the Chinese labour force which was a highly productive, well-organized labour force, especially in the construction of complex energy projects. This is a piece of evidence indicating the pattern of interdependence between China and Russia in complex energy affairs.

Some authors linked Russia's foreign and energy policy with the domestic economic situation. Movchan (2019) argues that Russia could become internally unstable and a fragmented country that has completely left the technology market and the world labour distribution market if the country's current economic trends will continue based on an undiversified quasi-monopolized economy with the oil-gas production collapse (p. 495). Russia is too large geographically that it is challenging to be tied by a single economic core. Currently, oil-gas revenues bind the unity of the country through the distribution of oil-gas incomes to the regions to create dependence on the centre. But regional ties will disintegrate from the centre after the qualitative transition in Russia when energy resources will be depleted. Russia's foreign and energy policy confrontations with major partners and neighbouring countries are highly harmful because the economy cannot be developed in isolation in the interdependent world. Kortunov (2010) argued raw material and natural resource-dependent Russia couldn't restore the status of powerful economic power, confirming its position to be in the group of the world's largest and most powerful countries with innovative paradigms. Graham (2010) affirmed that domestic economic modernization is a matter of survival for Russia because the country is encircled by more dynamic economies that never occurred before, increasing Russia's vulnerability (pp. 55–74).

Imyarekov and Kevbrina (2017) argued that Russia has an impasse or paradoxical situation in terms of foreign policy and economy (pp. 17–18). Russia needs economic resources to pursue power-based foreign policy goals to balance both the West and the East. If the country only uses oil-gas resources to develop the economy and reach foreign policy goals, then the economy will be one-sided based on raw materials. The non-diversified energy-based economy will not be able to sustain the military power of hegemonic Russia. Rogov (2021) highlighted that the goals of economic development and the goals of Russian foreign policy are in direct conflict during Putin's era. Economic development requires openness, while the current foreign policy of Russia solidifies the geopolitical isolation. The current Russian model is a coexistence of isolationism, state control of economic affairs, expanded political constraints that ensure systemic stability, and a suboptimal equilibrium of stagnation. He argued that the economic isolationism and foreign policy confrontation were partly determined by the redistributive model in the Russian domestic economy based on the energy windfalls (wealth consolidation in the hand of the small elite). Russia faced a decline in the FDI inflows and an increase in targeted sanctions that impede the transfer of capital and technology (components shaping interdependence pattern) in the oil-gas industries since 2014.

Pastukhov (2021) underlines different phase transitions that mean a qualitative leap in the state of the political regime in Russia (that gained new characteristics after 2014), affecting all its main parameters including domestic politics, foreign policy, and economy including energy. Each phase transition periods overlap with the relevant reactions (supply cuts, price changes, etc.) and reflections on Russia's foreign energy policy. Dymarsky and Ryzhkov (2012) parallelize the domestic and foreign policy and economic model of the Putin era in Russia and the Brezhnev stagnation in the USSR comprising the "state capture" and misconduct in the energy sector, the conservative ideology, power centralization, bureaucratic hierarchy, social contract, and the energy-based economy. They argued that the quality of the Russian foreign policy is the USSR's "modernized" foreign policy "without ideology" and "predominance of economic interests".

3.4 USSR's FEP: Lesson Learnt for Russia

Russian decision-makers developed an argument against the "energy weapon" claims that the country started to contribute to the energy security of Europe from the period of the USSR without serious energy conflicts and oil-gas supply disruptions. Belyi and Locatelli (2015) highlighted that the Soviet legacy determined the predominant role of the state in the oil-gas industries in terms of reserve classification, inefficient energy infrastructure systems, vertical integration of energy companies, and domination of the Russian state over oil-gas companies (p. 3). Chernenko and Petrovich-Belkin (2019) argued that total control over energy resources including gas (exported mostly to Europe), oil, and coal are commonalities of the energy policy of the USSR and Russia (pp. 89–118). Molnar (2014) argued that the dualist roots of Russia's foreign energy policy stem from the USSR when the state aimed on the one hand to subsidize the economies of the socialist Eastern European countries in return for the political loyalty and on the other hand to acquire foreign currency and technology from the Western European countries (pp. 77–90). It means that interdependence formed the basis of the USSR-Europe energy affairs.

The first negotiations on gas supplies from the USSR to the Western European region started in 1966 with the Italian energy company Eni, but negotiations had failed due to political differences (Kommersant, 2018). It means the USSR's energy journey in Europe commenced with the conflict. Shaban (2018) argued that the natural gas from the Soviet Union began to flow to Eastern Europe in 1967 when the "Brotherhood" export pipeline dispatched the first gas supply to Czechoslovakia. The Brotherhood gas pipeline was a strategic step by the USSR to economically tie the Warsaw bloc countries. The Soviet Union signed the first natural gas supply agreement with Austria cooperating with a long-run partner company – OMV. The case of Austria was unique because the gas hub in Baumgarten was 1.5 km from the border with Czechoslovakia which inspired Austria to make a final decision to buy Soviet gas. Austria had a shared history and social mobility with Slovakia. Austria was not part of NATO as a military-political transatlantic alliance. Even USSR's military intervention in Czechoslovakia in August 1968 didn't prevent Austria (OMV) politically from cooperating with the USSR, and the first gas was delivered to Austria on 1 September 1968.

A similar agreement was signed with socialist East Germany or the German Democratic Republic (GDR) in 1968. Crude oil could be transported in tankers, but pipes were needed for the export of natural gas. As a result of the USA's political pressure, some European countries forbade the sale of large diameter pipes to the USSR during the 1960s (Zygar & Panyushkin, 2008, pp. 2–3). The USSR competed with the USA for the gas pipeline and "pipes for gas" programme to Germany and Western Europe (Kremlin.ru, 2021). The technological backwardness was a constraining factor for the USSR's foreign energy policy, as was the case for independent Russia after 1991. Also, existing technological backwardness was an interdependence factor that drove energy cooperation with Europe. The USSR concluded the "gas-pipes deal" with capitalist West Germany or the Federal Republic of Germany (FRG) to exchange gas pipes and equipment for gas supplies with natural gas in 1970. The USSR and West Germany agreed to exchange large-diameter pipes from Germany to supply 3 billion cubic metres of natural gas per year from the USSR as a new model of economic cooperation (Gazprom, 2013). The USSR's natural gas supplies began to FRG and GDR in 1973 when another long-run partner company of the USSR/Russia – Ruhrgas (Germany) – started to import gas. The USSR had signed gas supply contracts with Bulgaria, Hungary, Finland, Italy, and France in 1975, Yugoslavia in 1978, Romania in 1979, and Turkey in 1986 (the Trans Balkan gas pipeline). The total volume of the USSR's natural gas exports to Western European countries amounted to 55 billion cubic metres in 1980.

Simonov (2018) believed that the gas treaty between the USSR and Austria removed the psychological barrier in Europe and made it possible to conclude contracts with Western countries such as Italy, Germany, and France for the supply of gas from the USSR. He pointed out that the gas trade increased mutual trust between the USSR and Western Europe as trading partners, not political enemies. Certain factors mitigated the position of Austria and other European countries allowing them to sign gas import agreements with the USSR: the economic need for new volumes of gas; the opportunity to exchange pipes and equipment with natural gas; the chance to give a loan to the USSR; and positive experience of Eastern European countries to import gas from the USSR.

Högselius (2013) argued that existing concerns in the Western European states on the import of natural gas from the USSR in the 1960s and 1970s were related to the indirect use of "energy weapon", rather than direct supply disruption when export volumes hadn't shaped deep energy dependence on the Soviet regime (pp. 218–224). The potential spillover effects of the Soviet gas export to Western Europe that could potentially be considered as indirect mechanisms of the "energy weapon" were:

1 Subsidized relatively cheap natural gas prices that could harm vulnerable coal-producing regions in Germany.
2 To split the Western capitalist block into various fractions based on deeper energy cooperation with the USSR.
3 To stiffen the international and regional reputation of the USSR in the European region and the world.

Högselius (2013) underlined that the USSR's desultory and not intense exploit of the "energy weapon" (nevertheless, it had an intention to use it in a favourable environment) doesn't guarantee the same moderate pattern by Russia. Energy export infrastructure, including oil-gas pipelines, could be easily used for political purposes, despite commercial motivation to gain foreign currency as a vital and relevant factor for the Kremlin. European countries had divergent perceptions and country-specific motivations to import the Soviet gas, ranging from the hope of positive economic interdependence to domestic policy preferences.

The domestic dimension of the Russian foreign energy policy is based on the "state energy capitalism" concept through the centralization of the state power as in the USSR and the nationalization of the lucrative oil-gas companies. Because the enterprises of the USSR's entire oil complex belonged to three different state institutions. For instance, oil production and transportation were controlled by the Ministry of Oil Industry, oil refining – by the Ministry of Oil Refining and Petrochemical Industry, and the entire distribution network (from oil depots to gas stations) was part of the State Committee for Material and Technical Supply system. The production, transportation, and marketing of gas were wholly owned by the Ministry of Gas Industry of the USSR (Historical and Bibliographic Reference, 1999). The USSR had a small-scale, closed, but collective decision-making process in the energy sector that prevented the process from the individual interests' influences.

Gaydar and Chubais (2011) argued that the USSR supplied oil and oil products to Eastern Europe under barter contracts when oil prices fell by half between 1985 and 1986 (p. 32). But the USSR couldn't stop this supply and redirect it to countries that could pay for oil and oil products in convertible currency. Because this measure would mean the dissolution of Eastern Europe as part of the Soviet Union's zone of influence and the rejection of the geopolitical dominance in the region that cheap energy directly contributed to. During the USSR's energy supply to Europe, politically disloyal countries (for instance, Romania) were penalized for higher energy prices than subsidized prices. The USSR deepened the energy dependence of the socialist block's countries, increasing the share of the USSR's energy in the target countries' import basket to more than 90%. This colossal energy dependence intensified the target countries' vulnerability against the USSR's critical energy (primarily natural gas) supply decisions. Molnar (2014) underlined that Russia attempted to follow the same behavioural pattern of the USSR period, especially during Putin's ruling. Russia misused the extensive energy dependence of the post-Soviet states to obtain (geo)political leverage and to solidify its regional power (pp. 77–90).

The energy factor was transformed from the national power to a state power component to serve the USSR's foreign policy goals towards Western Europe and Russia's ultimate foreign policy goals in the Eurasian region. The USSR acted under the bipolar world order where it clashed with the USA over the socialist camp all over the world and the European continent. Even in the "cold war" period, the geopolitical tensions and deterioration in political relations negatively influenced the USSR-USA energy cooperation. For example, the Soviet military intervention in Afghanistan in December 1979 caused a negative response from the USA administration limiting the scope of scientific-technical cooperation in the oil industry. The USSR's and Russia's foreign energy affairs with the USA were more problematic than Europe.

Volchek (2020) argued that in addition to the Western dimension of the USSR's foreign energy policy, plans to build a large oil pipeline from Western Siberia to the East and the Pacific Ocean emerged in the early 1970s. Significant preconditions were the availability of oil-gas resources (based on the giant Samotlor), economic motivation to accelerate the development of the Far East region of the USSR, and growing energy demand in the Asian countries (Japan and "Asian tigers", not China). Even though the USSR's energy export plans towards the Asian region's rising markets had never been realized during the Soviet period, the energy cooperation established the foundation for the future mega-projects. Latin America, Africa, the Middle East, and South Asia were the regions where Russia continued Soviet economic affairs including the energy sector. The USSR supplied necessary resources and free crude oil to the socialist developing countries with ideological motivation. As a result, Russian energy companies (oil, gas, and even nuclear) had a global vision and global scope of activities where the economic and political affairs of the Soviet time also contributed. Almost all nuclear power plants in the former Soviet republics and countries of the socialist camp in the CIS and Eastern Europe were built using Rosatom technologies and are still dependent on the Russian-made nuclear fuel. These indicate that the primary motivations of the USSR's/Russia's foreign energy policy were to create a complex interdependence with crucial partner countries, to get advanced technologies for modernization, to receive financial resources for the national economy, and to fortify regional and international power hegemony. But both the USSR and Russia failed to utilize hydrocarbon incomes for the technological modernization of the national economy and pursue a sustainable policy towards power accumulation.

Slavkina (2016) argued that the inefficiency of the resource-based national economy created a vulnerable situation for the USSR. Ineffective use of the oil-gas revenues could not bring the country out of economic stagnation, leading to the century's "geopolitical catastrophe". The Soviet Union embarked on an unprecedented hydrocarbon exploration initiative to develop unique oil and gas fields in Western Siberia in the mid-1960s. The USSR annually produced 20% of world oil production during the 1960s and 1980s. The USSR didn't join OPEC in 1973 for the "energy blackmailing" of the European countries and the USA; therefore, it had a reliable partner status. After the 1973 energy crisis, the USSR rapidly increased the volume of oil exports to Western countries from 44 million tons in 1970 to 81 million tons in 1985. The amount of foreign exchange earnings of the USSR from oil exports increased from USD 1 billion in 1970 to USD 15 billion in 1980, coinciding with rapidly growing crude oil prices. The unexpected drop in world oil prices always had adverse consequences for the Soviet Union and Russia's economy. The share of revenues from the energy sales in the Soviet Union's foreign exchange earnings reached 55% in 1984.

Gelovani, Britkov, and Dubovskiy (2009) underlined that raw materials and energy resources accounted for almost 60% of the total annual export of the USSR in the mid-1980s (p. 169). The export of raw materials and energy resources increased 15 times from the 1970s to the 1980s in the USSR, while the export of machines and equipment increased only four times for the same period. The Soviet economy had huge sensitivity against global energy prices and the weakening economy accelerated the collapse of the Union (Zaslavsky, 2011).

The development of Western Siberia and the higher world oil price provided some potential opportunities for the domestic economy. The USSR had used oil and gas revenues for importing food and consumer goods from abroad instead of large-scale technological modernization. The USSR formed a resource economy, where the country's dependence on hydrocarbons and the global oil-gas price circumstances was consistently growing. The USSR hadn't a well-prepared foreign economic strategy, therefore, the collapse of the world fuel prices in the mid-1980s led to the USD 10 billion annual losses in the Soviet economy while maintaining the same volumes of oil and gas exports (Alekperov, 2011). Finally, lower oil prices in the global market are considered one of the factors that paved the way for the USSR's collapse. Hill and Gaddy (2013) argued that higher oil prices that lasted almost a decade after the 1973 oil crisis didn't contribute to the long-term development and production increase of the Soviet economy (p. 154). Just the opposite trend started in the economies of the Western countries after 1970s energy crises in terms of technological development and efficiency leap triggered by higher energy prices. As the USSR, higher energy (oil and gas) prices also didn't become the "development contributor" to the Russian economy paving the way for deep social inequality, economic inertia, power consolidation in domestic politics, solid authoritarianism in governance, and foreign policy conflicts.

The legacy of the USSR's central planning mechanism directly influenced Russia's natural resource management system. Shafranik (1996), the former Minister of Fuel and Energy of Russia, argued that the fuel and energy complex traditionally plays an important role in shaping state foreign policy in the USSR and Russia. Free access to the Soviet Union's cheap energy (oil and gas) resources was one of the drivers in the integration of the Council for Mutual Economic Assistance (CMEA) member countries and the formation of the world socialist system. Through the export of energy resources and the construction of the large electric power plants and oil industry facilities, the USSR had a tremendous impact not only on the policies of the socialist countries but also on many other countries of Asia, Africa, and Latin America, on the global energy situation. The USSR's energy resources formed the basis of the fuel and energy balance of most socialist countries in the late 1980s. The total export of fuel and energy resources (oil and gas) from the Soviet Union to the socialist countries increased from 170 million tons in 1970 to 450 million tons in 1988. The energy factor strengthened the USSR's political and economic influence on world politics through foreign policy in the 1970s–1980s. The impact of energy resources on foreign policy decreased after the collapse of the USSR in 1991. In the period from 1990 to 1991, oil exports fell by more than 40%, petroleum products by 18%, and coal by 12% (Shafranik, 1996). Global and regional energy markets have been lost weakening foreign economic relations of the USSR.

The foreign energy policy of the USSR has not been researched deeply as a consequence of the lack of access to information. Therefore, it is now challenging to link Russia's conflictual foreign energy policy with the same approach as its predecessor. The communist legacy of the USSR prevails in current Russia's energy policy through different decision-making models and property issues related to state capitalism and natural resource nationalization. Allegedly, Russia adopted the use of "*energy weapon*" as a legacy from the Soviet Union. The Kremlin's employment of the "energy weapon" began before the collapse of the USSR in December 1991. For example, Russia stopped crude oil and petroleum products supplies to the Baltic states in 1990 to weaken national independence movements. By combining the Soviet legacy of state control over natural resources and geopolitical ambitions, Russia started a new wave of nationalism in the oil-gas industry that had global repercussions. Russia's higher number of energy conflicts with partners can be inherited from the deep-seated revisionist Soviet strategic narratives about the state-centric global system and essential conflicts in interstate affairs.

The current strategic narratives of Russia that partly originate from the USSR premeditate (a) the multipolarity, (b) the decline of Western powers, and (c) the national interests based on security-related threats (also, against Russia's energy resources). Generally, the USSR had more symmetric energy affairs with Europe, but Russia's energy relations with some EU member states have an asymmetric interdependence pattern. The politicization of Russia-EU oil-gas relations could be considered as an inheritance of that antagonistic Cold War legacy that existed between the USSR and the West. After 1991, the national security concerns of Russia and the West started to drive foreign energy affairs between these powers at the regional level notwithstanding domestic political configuration. But even realist scholars argue that the militarization and politicization of energy-related issues and foreign energy policy have a limit in terms of application and outcome under complex circumstances of energy systems.

3.5 Overview and Objectives of Russia's FEP Pattern

Foreign energy policy is situated at the "junction" of foreign policy and energy policy of Russia. Russia's central strategy in foreign energy policy is (i) to continue its hegemony in the EU's and post-Soviet countries' energy markets considering market mechanisms as a "rule of the game"; and (ii) to generate "windfall profits" for sustaining economic growth and technology-based modernization in the domestic socio-economic domain. *The pattern of interdependence in the energy policy and hegemonic ambitions in the foreign policy had established a conflicting environment for the Russian foreign energy policy.* When we examine Russia's foreign energy policy, we could observe that Russia could enter into energy conflicts with any country unhesitatingly, regardless of its economic and political strength. But the tools of the energy policy could vary depending on the characteristics of the counterpart country. Russia didn't hesitate to employ oil-gas resources to accelerate political and economic integration in the CIS region through "energy leverage" in connection with the regional geopolitical issues from the early 1990s. In the early 1990s, Russia already started to instrumentalize an energy factor against CIS countries, especially Ukraine. Russia used the energy prices and oil-gas supplies as leverage to maintain the former USSR military bases in post-Soviet countries, especially in Belarus and Ukraine. Based on an imperial "mindset" and legacy, Russia officially demanded from Ukraine to hand over the Black Sea Fleet in return for writing off the gas debts and undisrupted gas supply in 1993. Oil export terminals in the Black Sea and Baltic Sea, and oil-gas export pipelines to Europe got out of the hand of Russia which was required to deal with "transit countries" such as Ukraine, Belarus, and Baltic states.

Geographical location, energy infrastructure, military infrastructure, and the ports developed in Soviet times turned out to be the strongest leverage for the post-Soviet countries (e.g., Baltic states, Ukraine, Belarus) to transport Russia's oil-gas resources to the world market as a "transit" country. After the collapse of the USSR, Russia lost control over the oil-gas resources and reserves of the post-Socialist countries, especially "near abroad" countries (Azerbaijan, Kazakhstan, and Turkmenistan). The resource-rich post-Soviet countries started to invite Western companies to invest in the oil-gas fields and energy infrastructure bypassing Russia. The long-term oil-gas conflicts of Russia with the post-Soviet states such as Ukraine, Belarus, Azerbaijan, Georgia, and Baltic states undermined the integration processes throughout the Eurasian space and led to the accelerated disintegration of the former Soviet geopolitical space (Mishchenko, 2020). But Russia made an enormous and continuous effort to restore the strategic role of the energy factor in foreign policy adjusting goals and tools to the new geopolitical and economic realities.

Orttung and Overland (2011) distinguished various operational *objectives* of Russia's foreign energy policy which are to control oil, gas, and transit price and the volume of energy sales on a regional and global scale; to increase asset ownership abroad; to build alternative transit pipeline. Russia's foreign energy policy has strategic political-military goals such as military presence in key regions, intervention in domestic politics and elections, and afflicting undesirable oil-gas pipelines (pp. 74–85). Orttung and Overland (2011) list the political goals of Russia's foreign energy policy as a political integration with neighbour countries, supporting politically loyal governments, and military positioning in the key geopolitical zones. The economic goals of Russia's foreign energy policy could be to increase oil-gas export revenues to the country's fiscal system, to get direct access to the lucrative European market with minimum transit countries, to get permanent ownership of the key energy assets abroad, the convergence of the energy prices between CIS and EU markets.

Orttung and Overland (2011) analysed Russia's conflictual foreign energy policy behaviour revealing certain patterns. They found that Russia entered energy conflicts mostly with post-Soviet countries such as Ukraine and Belarus that not only consume but also transit Russia's oil-gas resources to the European countries. Russia made pressure on the transit countries using alternative or diversified pipelines, and just cut off energy flows via oil-gas pipelines. Russia often made decisions to decrease energy subsidies to the former Soviet Union countries excepting politically loyal countries (pp. 74–85). Russia's state-owned energy companies pursued a strategic aim to get control over energy assets (e.g., pipelines or other key infrastructure) in various countries.

The compatibility and conflicting nature of political and economic aims of foreign energy policy would be offset by the available tools of Russia. The configuration of available tools in Russia's foreign energy policy formulates policy patterns of the country in relation to counterpart countries. Orttung and Overland (2011) argue that the policy pattern of Russia combines political, commercial, corruption-related, and opportunism motives (pp. 74–85). Russia followed political goals in the foreign energy policy only against Ukraine and Georgia, never having political motivation against the EU or the Western European developed countries where economic goals prevailed. Russia had a combination of political and economic purposes in the foreign energy policy having a restricted set of tools forcing the country to achieve trade-offs between different aims. Russia pursued a cyclical foreign energy policy consisting of de-politicization and re-politicization of energy affairs with its counterpart countries.

Shnyrov (2004) underlines that Russia's foreign energy policy pursues both purely economic and political goals (p. 62). On the one hand, the Russian state elaborates on achieving the optimal financial and material conditions for the extraction, transportation, and consumption of energy resources. Russia could employ "the oil factor to put pressure on other states, to obtain political concessions from them". Shnyrov (2004) points out that (i) the politicization of the problems of the oil and gas industry and (ii) the "oilization" of domestic and foreign policy occurred in Russia simultaneously (p. 4). Yanovsky (2018) underlined that the priority of Russia's foreign energy policy is to maintain the leading position of the country's energy sector in the global energy system in the face of rapid global changes and the continuous emergence of new challenges (pp. 4–6). He argues that the normative principles of Russia's foreign energy policy include openness, consistency, and unconditional conformity to the international law norms.

Former Prime Minister of Russia Y. Primakov (2009) refused that Russia uses its superiority in energy resources as an "*imperial weapon*" (pp. 23–141). He argued that Russia lacks the intention to use the energy resources for political purposes during the supply of its oil and gas resources to the EU market through diversification of routes to deliver primary energy resources. He tried to explain the "non-conflicting nature" and motivations of the Russian energy policy using various arguments on the prevalence of economic reasons over geopolitical ambitions: boosting economic growth and sustainable energy production; vulnerability and dependence on foreign investments and advanced technologies the development of new oil-gas fields in hard-to-reach places in Eastern Siberia, the Arctic, and the Caspian Sea; serious interdependence with the EU countries; the geographic location of the leading oil and gas fields; diversification towards alternative export markets such as Japan, Korea, China, and the USA; mutually beneficial cooperation with foreign energy companies and financial institutions; and breaking the economic isolation. But also, Primakov (2009) acknowledges that the growth in oil and gas production and the power concentration in the energy sector strengthen Russia's foreign policy positions. But the primary motive for building up the energy sector's potential is the economic development to "*remove Russia from the raw material needle*" (pp. 23–141).

Primakov (2018) argued that the reliability of Russian energy supplies is verified by historical evidence so that energy supplies towards Eastern and Western Europe were not interrupted even during the Cold War (pp. 319–341). He asserted that Western politicians and media have exaggerated Russia's energy manipulations against the EU arguing that the EU was a victim of Russia's energy conflicts with Ukraine when Naftogaz decided to purloin the gas from the supply intended for European consumers. Also, he acknowledged that there are political motives in Russia's foreign energy policy towards Europe and post-Soviet states in addition to the economic incentives through developing energy interdependence.

Legvold (2008) believes that Russia never had a coherent energy policy and relevant strategic vision. He argues that the role of energy in politics would emerge as "*a multiplier, not a cause*" (pp. 10–22). It means that the energy solidifies the existing trend in the foreign policy, rather than resulting in collaboration or serious conflict between countries. If political affairs between Russia and the counterpart country will deteriorate, then the foreign energy policy towards that country will reflect that deprecating environment, or on the contrary. Russia's behavioural pattern in the foreign energy policy is political "event-driven" rather than "goal-driven". Milov, Coburn, and Danchenko (2006) point out that Russia doesn't have a systematic energy policy and coherent future-oriented energy strategy. Russia's foreign energy policy is "*fragmentary and contradictory*" and "*insensitive to the market environment*" with serious limitations (pp. 285–313).

Leijonhielm and Larsson (2004) argued that Russia needs to control energy transport infrastructure (oil-gas pipelines, strategic ports, and pumping stations in the soul of transit states) as a necessity to apply energy leverage (pp. 12–30). Therefore, Russia aims to amalgamate critical energy infrastructure in the territory of the post-Soviet states with strategic thinking. Authors examine Russia's foreign energy policy and the state's approach to the strategic goods, including oil and gas, from two critical enablers: capacity to act and intention to act. They underlined that energy-importing countries' energy dependence on Russia or their vulnerable position in terms of any changes in Russia's policy is not enough to start the energy conflict. There is a need for a "*trigger*" for Russia to launch an energy conflict that could lead to supply disruption or other serious outcomes. These triggers could be a political revolution in the target country, economic nationalism towards Russian energy (oil, gas, nuclear) companies, new regulatory acts, etc.

Leijonhielm and Larsson (2004) predicted that the final output of the Russian foreign energy policy in the context of "energy weapon" or "energy power" will be a failure politically, economically, and worsening perception. But Russia is a persistent actor acting towards its strategic aim – to reintegrate post-USSR states into Russia (pp. 136–137). Larsson (2006) points out that the Kremlin accomplished the power concentration task in the energy sector, especially, during its ruling period of Putin (p. 6). Russia applied assertive energy policy tools including supply disruptions against former Soviet Union countries (rather than EU states) to preserve strategic aims in the "near abroad" territories. Market rules in the energy export or energy transit are applicable for Russia only if the political framework of bilateral affairs allows this approach. Russia built its affairs with CIS based on market prices of natural gas in the mid-2000s. Hydrocarbon prices started to form not only the state budget but also the foreign policy of Russia (Dorofeev, Solovev, & Bashkirova, 2018). This approach combines political and economic factors in Russia's foreign energy policy towards the CIS region.

In addition to the European and post-Soviet countries, there is a growing Asian dimension of Russia's foreign energy policy. Russia's statist IR scholars Karaganov (2020, pp. 1–22) and Lukin (2020, pp. 67–69) emphasized the existential confrontation between Russia and the West during the rise of China. Primakov's trilateral (Russia, China, India) cooperation format would include controlling the Central Asian energy resources. The strategic rivalry of the global and regional powers (the USA, the EU, Russia, Turkey, Iran, China, India) intensified competition over the oil-gas reserves of the Central Asian region and the network of oil-gas pipelines from Central Asia and the Caspian region to Europe through the Caucasus in the late 1990s. Dynkin and Burrows (2016) predict that the risk of conflict between major powers (the USA, China, and Russia) is increasing, and that trend triggers energy conflicts. Almost the entire post-Soviet space and adjacent regions and the western part of the Asia-Pacific region, the Middle East, and the northern part of the Indian Ocean become a platform for the serious geopolitical rivalry between the leading powers. Russia sees its energy future in Asia, and energy supply contracts with China are fuelling its unbalanced economy. Russia formulated a solid pivot to the Asian direction in the foreign energy policy in alignment with foreign policy and grand strategy.

Asian dimension includes joint projects in nuclear energy and unification of electricity supply and the oil-gas supply. China is a cornerstone country of the Asian dimension of the Russian foreign energy policy. China's growing economy deeply needs energy, and Russia is one of the five largest oil exporters to this country. But disagreements have arisen between Russian suppliers and Chinese buyers over the oil export price occasionally. Lukin (2015) argued long bargaining over the terms and costs of the oil and gas supply from Russia to China because both countries defended their national interests (pp. 377–548). China's primary interest in developing trade and economic cooperation with Russia is to access sources of raw materials, primarily oil and gas, metal ores, and timber resources. Russia aims to diversify energy export to the promising Asian market and create an alternative to the "problematic" EU market. Chatham House report (2021) claims that Russia's hegemony in the post-Soviet region gradually slides towards China which hasn't a monotonous dynamic in the complex (with growing tensional essence) relationship with Russia, including the energy sphere (pp. 7–10).

Lomagin (2015) argues that Russia's conflictual energy and security affairs with the West (especially, painful US and EU sanctions after the conflict with Ukraine) combined with the country's economic growth model and demands from state-owned energy companies to "conquer" new markets determined the Asian dimension of the Russian foreign energy policy (pp. 3–5). The political economy of Russia's new foreign energy policy ("pivot to Asia") reflects the elements of Putin's rational Eurasia-oriented strategies and "oligarchs-statists" coalition. Despite the Kremlin's influence on the key strategic decisions of the state-owned companies such as energy prices, energy assets ownership, and alliances with foreign energy companies, the swift shift from the lucrative and geographically proximate European market to the Asian markets generate logistical impediments (e.g., pipeline building challenges with China) would be only the long-term goal for Russia.

Lomagin (2015) underlines that the Asian pivot of the Russian foreign energy policy is just a safeguard mechanism (or "*hedging*" mechanism as Claes (2001, p. 81) pointed out) for the country to reduce risks and vulnerabilities in the European market that is still the largest destination of Russia's energy resources. The depletion of the oil-gas fields closer to the European market (the traditional Western Siberia areas) was another determinant of the Eastern dimension of the country's foreign energy policy (the exploitation of the oil-gas fields in the Far East and the Eastern Siberia regions). The growing energy demands in the Asian economies including China, South Korea, and India would be another determinant. The author draws the conclusion that Russia's foreign energy policy combines the elements of "*strategic and market*" ingredients. Lomagin believes that there is a consensus between state-owned companies that pursue profit-driven behaviour and "siloviki" who represents military/security decision-makers on new Asia-oriented foreign policy and energy policy. Russia had energy disputes with China over energy prices and logistical issues such as the construction of the energy supply pipelines. China's diversified gas import strategy ensured its bargaining power that differs China from European countries have a higher level of energy dependence on Russia.

In 2014, Russia had a successive gas conflict with Ukraine and the EU, but the country signed a new gas delivery contract with China against the West. Russia under Putin's rule used various networks and was perceived as a serious challenger for political fundaments of the Western-centric global order. As a response, the governments of Western powers had hesitations about the economic and energy transactions with Russia and its attempts to purchase economic and energy assets in Europe (Oatley, 2019, pp. 258–455). The Ukrainian crisis and subsequent sanctions by the US and EU countries rapidly accelerated Russia's energy integration towards Asia, most importantly China. China became the second-largest buyer of the Russian crude oil and oil products between 2013 and 2020 consuming almost 13% of the total Russian crude oil and oil products exports (Federal Customs Service of Russia, 2021). Oil-gas resources accounted for 70% of the Russian export to China in 2019 (Federal Customs Service of Russia, 2020a). The "Power of Siberia" gas pipeline was launched in 2020, and the volume of supplies through the pipeline was far from the declared peak of 38 billion cubic metres. Only 4.5 billion cubic metres of gas were exported from Russia to China till 2021 (Lyutova, 2021), while the key market for Gazprom's gas export about 200 billion cubic metres annually is still the EU. The evidence indicates that the political alliance with China has fiscal costs for the Russian economy, and the "pivot to Asia" against the Western powers cannot succeed in the short term for Russia. Also, the Russian foreign energy policy exploited various tools in the energy conflicts with the Asian and European partners.

3.6 Russia's Energy Conflicts and Tools of FEP

The nexus between energy factors and interstate conflicts is also a relevant topic to examine. Strüver and Wegenast (2018) argued that the abundance of natural resources (including oil-gas and other energy resources) enables political elites of resource-rich countries to disregard diplomacy and embrace the antagonistic and overbearing foreign policy (pp. 86–106). Oil-gas and mineral revenues can be employed to strengthen the state's capacity for any interstate conflicts. The politicians in energy-rich countries don't depend on tax revenues and any other domestic constituencies that can prevent foreign policy aggression. Large energy-importing and developed countries may demonstrate silence against the petrostate's foreign policy "hawkishness" not to harm stable energy inflows. Strüver and Wegenast (2018) assert that the cross-border implications of the civil war and any other types of domestic conflict in the resource-rich countries may be another mechanism for the ignition of interstate conflict. Caselli, Morelli, and Rohner (2013) study the effect of endowments and geographic distribution of oil-gas resources on the risk of inter-state conflict (p. 41). They specifically accentuate two important issues that increase the risk of inter-state conflicts: geographical proximity of oil-gas resources to the border and asymmetrical endowments of oil reserves between neighbour states. Colgan (2013) reveals that "revolutionary petrostates" demonstrate relatively higher proclivity towards the conflicts with other states than oil-poor countries.

Russian foreign policy analysts and IR scholars often underline the rising conflictual nature of world order and the intensity of the interstate conflicts (including energy conflicts). Bogaturov (2017) developed a concept envisaging that there is a difference between static stability and dynamic stability in terms of attitude towards interstate contradictions including energy conflicts. The principle of isolating potentially conflicting aspirations prevails in the static stability model, while the logic of multiplying coincident prevails in the dynamic stability. Different interstate contradictions including energy conflicts couldn't be isolated from each other, these conflicting areas may interact or intersect. Interstate energy conflicts could be balanced by common interests that bind the great powers to each other via the formation and expansion of the sphere of coinciding aspirations. Klare (2002) stressed from a realist perspective that "resource wars" over natural and energy resources will be the primary building block of the international security architecture (p. 208). Market dynamics and technological development may alleviate the interstate conflicts over natural resources, while globalization may toughen the situation. Klare (2008) predicted that increasing energy demand in emerging powers and decreasing available energy resources would intensify global competition over natural resources and conflicts in unprotected resource-rich countries (pp. 7–259). Great powers refrain from clashing directly over access to energy. Thus, they redirect the energy conflict to less powerful, energy-rich, and transit regions and states (e.g., Iraq, Ukraine).

Ridder (2013) argued that the politicization of natural resources, state intervention in business, and protectionism have already intensified, and this trend will likely continue (pp. 12–16). These restrictive measures and tendencies may incite interstate resource-related conflicts between resource-rich and resource-poor countries, and domestic similar conflicts within underdeveloped states. Also, the author has proclaimed that high prices for natural resources will encourage import-dependent countries to increase efficiency and decrease consumption. As a result, global competition over natural resources can be alleviated and force resource-rich countries to cooperate with importers to receive finance and technology ("*reverse dependence*"). Even though Ridder developed this approach for mineral resources, we could argue that the coexistence of cooperation and conflict will be feasible in all types of natural resources including energy resources such as oil, gas, coal, and uranium. Energy cooperation often alters oil-gas disputes between exporting and importing countries, preventing the conflict from lasting for a long-term period. Dannreuther and Ostrowski (2013) examine the link between global oil, gas, and mineral resources and conflict and cooperation between states (pp. 6–8). They listed seven major drivers of conflict and cooperation between various actors in the oil and gas sectors:

1 *The price and market value of oil, gas, and minerals*. When prices increase, the strategic asset value of natural resources soars up, attracting the strategic attention of rival global and regional powers to get control over the natural resources.
2 *Geographical distribution of oil, gas, and mineral resources*. For example, European Union countries have more concerns about the oil-gas import from the North African countries and the Soviet Union/Russia, than non-EU oil and gas-rich countries from the European continent such as Norway or the UK.
3 *Struggle for geopolitical hegemony*. The shift in the geopolitical dominance among powers could change the ideological approaches to oil, gas, and mineral resources. Also, new revisionist power can challenge existent power's

dominance over oil-gas resources or could "weaponize" oil-gas resources to outface the hegemon. The same conflictual behavioural pattern exists in the relationship between former colonial power such as Russia and newly independent states such as "near abroad" countries that verge on implementing independent energy export or energy import strategies.

4 *Interconnection between resource-rich countries and energy companies*. Some severe energy conflicts emerge from the difference in interests and positions between "host" states and "visitor" companies. Profit-maximization attitudes of oil and gas companies and the technological needs of the resource-owner states often lead to energy conflicts under asymmetric interdependence patterns.
5 *The domestic distribution system of resource rents*. Domestic revenue distribution systems can impact the domestic political system and the state's conflictual foreign policy via power consolidation or power diffusion.
6 *Technological transformation*. Technological development could contribute to the more effective exploration of the new unexplored oil and gas resources, accelerating of energy independence of previously energy importing countries. The technological factor can facilitate the energy transition that will set up a new landscape of energy geopolitics.
7 *Environmental factor*. The potential ecological damages of extraction, transit, and consumption of oil-gas extraction determine the conflict or cooperation among nation-states, energy companies, and other local and international actors.

Dannreuther and Ostrowski (2013) underline that energy conflicts are multidimensional, containing economic, commercial, ecological, institutional, political, and military dimensions (pp. 232–237). The concepts of "energy weapon" and energy security constantly evolve through technological changes and globalization. Dannreuther and Ostrowski (2013) underline that oil price fluctuations, oil and gas export infrastructure disputes, and extractive companies' local behaviour provoke oil-gas conflicts. Authors believe that the oil resources often led to international energy conflicts, while gas resources triggered regional energy conflicts. Not only Dannreuther and Ostrowski (2013) but also some other authors link energy types and the energy conflicts in Russia.

Lasswell and Kaplan (2013) argued Russia started to employ natural gas as a geopolitical "weapon" against Europe after 2000. They pointed out that the USSR never halted gas export to Western European states misusing different seasonal factors and political reasons (p. 97). Implementation of restrictions and cuts in its natural gas supply by Russia to Ukraine (2006–2007) and Georgia (2008–2009) began to be referred to as the "gas war". Crandall (2011) argued that the energy crises of Russia with European partners, Ukraine, Belarus, and Georgia in 2006 and 2009 were a decisive moment in Russia's harsh foreign energy policy pattern (pp. 74–86). O'Sullivan (2013) differs oil and natural gas in terms of the impact of an international market on "energy weapons". Oil has a globalized market that enables targeted consumer countries to switch from one producer to the alternative rapidly. The existence of a global oil transportation system and an almost stable level of available oil quantity ease the manoeuvre of the importing countries. He concludes that the framework for the efficient use of oil as a political "weapon" (foreign policy and national security tool) is comparably restricted. But he pointed out that natural gas can be better utilized for political purposes than crude oil because the international gas market is just emerging, and the transportation of natural gas is much more complicated than oil.

Baldwin (2016) argued that different energy resources have a varying power influence over time (p. 56). For example, crude oil and uranium resources as raw materials for nuclear energy have a rising power in the international politics of the 20th century. Oil is a more movable good, while gas depends on infrastructure that forms precise communication between host and destination countries. Natural gas and renewable energy will have higher power assets in global affairs in the 21st century. Russian "energy weapon" is almost synonymous with "gas weapon" because internationally traded oil, coal, and uranium cannot be "weaponized". Globalized gas markets and domestic energy regulations offer gas alternatives for the EU, which incapacitates the Russian "gas market" where the state-controlled Gazprom is a crucial tool. Bogaturov (2017) argued that Russia approaches oil supplies as a "politicized" means for the stabilization of the world economic situation and energy tension ("international energy security mission"). Russia perceived gas exports as a commercial instrument with a narrower task ("regional energy security mission").

Strange (1988) argued that the oil sector and oil industry with a high level of politicization have higher mobility currently transporting via tankers in addition to export pipelines. Pirani (2010) distinguishes oil and gas resources in terms of the "energy weapon" when the former has a globalized market with relatively easy transportation, while the latter has demanded long-term engagement based on the long-term contracts and pipeline infrastructure. He defends that Russia has gas conflicts mostly with former-Soviet Republics such as Georgia and Ukraine, rather than the EU countries. Pirani (2010) argues that Russia's gas conflicts with the post-Soviet countries have two motivations: (a) *commercial* – to end the Soviet practice about the cheap gas supply with price subsidies when the gas prices soared in the EU market; (b) *political* – to deter post-Soviet countries to realize "coloured revolutions", and integration to the NATO (pp. 84–86). He concludes that the reasons for the gas disputes were more about commercial motivation than grand politics; Russia's gas conflicts should be explained by market-based arguments than the "energy weapon" against the EU.

Empirical evidence demonstrates that Russia's energy (oil, gas, nuclear, coal, electricity) resources function as a means, tool, and goal of the foreign policy and grand strategy simultaneously. In addition to oil and gas, the nuclear energy partnership is also part of the Russian "hybrid strategy" to influence not only the Eastern European countries but also some Middle East countries. Strategic penetration into the territory of other countries and preserving the dominant position in that territory determine the aggressive foreign energy policy of Rosatom through building nuclear power plants and providing modern nuclear technologies. Rosatom controls very complex, critically important, and not-safe energy infrastructure abroad through NPPs. It is debatable whether this is the corporate policy of Rosatom, or it is the Russian state's strategic policy. The pattern of the conflictual energy policy can be revealed through evidence-based empirical studies taking into account the energy types.

Orttung and Overland (2011) pioneered collecting evidence on Russia's foreign energy conflicts and to analyse the factors that drive this conflictual behaviour (pp. 74–85). The authors identified 31 energy conflicts with 20 European and CIS countries from 2000 to 2010 using secondary literature and anonymous interviews. The research didn't include Russia's partner countries from Asia arguing that the country hadn't significant energy conflicts with Asian neighbours (RECSID covered Russia's energy conflicts with the Asian partners). Authors concentrated on European and former Soviet Union countries that had oil-gas conflicts with Russia. Another restriction of that article was the sectoral coverage of the energy conflicts. Orttung and Overland (2011) examined oil and gas sectors, without coverage of nuclear energy (RECSID covered nuclear energy, coal, and electricity). They argued that Russia's energy conflicts mostly were related to the exports of natural gas where the well-functioned international market is absent, unlike crude oil. Authors categorized "energy conflict" as a major controversial event between Russia and partner countries that attracted huge attention and was mainstreamed in the media or raised by experts in the interviews. For example, they included Russia-Ukraine energy conflicts in the study only from January 2006, January 2009, and April 2010. These two countries entered a high number of energy disputes after the collapse of the Soviet Union over natural gas prices, energy debts, non-payments, and disruption in the gas supply with commercial and political-military motivations (intervention in the elections or controlling naval base in the Black Sea). In addition to Ukraine, Belarus and Georgia were other countries where Russia had intense energy conflicts. Authors affirmed that Russia's energy conflicts accelerated after 2000 when Putin came to the power and controlled state-owned energy enterprises (Table 3.3).

Russia employs various tools in foreign energy policy that can be perceived as political and commercial leverage. In addition to being instrumentalized in the energy conflicts to accomplish economic and political goals, the tools of Russia's foreign energy policy themselves could also trigger new energy conflicts. The toolset of Russian foreign energy policy (based on existing literature and RECSID findings) includes total suspension of energy (oil, gas, coal, electricity, nuclear fuel) supply, warning to stop energy (oil and gas) deliveries, terminating subsidized gas price, and demanding higher prices, manipulating the volumes of energy supplies, reducing final and transit oil-gas supply volumes, filing a lawsuit on a gas deal with the partner country, foreign energy assets' acquisition problems, long negotiations on energy transit tariffs, etc. Orttung and Overland (2011) identified the most influential tools of the Russian energy conflicts that are energy price subsidies, oil and gas pipeline interceptions, oil-gas pipeline explosions, construction of alternative pipelines to bypass transit countries, blackmailing through a media campaign, import restrictions from the conflicted country, and cyber-attacks. They argued that the toolset that Russia used in the foreign energy policy had certain limitations in terms of their impacts on the partner countries that the Kremlin aimed to "scourge".

Table 3.3 Russia's energy conflicts by country (2000–2010)

Country	*2000*	*2001*	*2002*	*2003*	*2004*	*2005*	*2006*	*2007*	*2008*	*2009*	*2010*	*Total*
Finland										1		**1**
Norway										1		**1**
Estonia								1				**1**
Latvia		1										**1**
Lithuania							1					**1**
Belarus					1		1	1			1	**4**
Ukraine							1			2	1	**4**
Moldova					1		1					**2**
Poland						1						**1**
Czech Repub.									1			**1**
Turkey			1									**1**
Croatia				1								**1**
Germany								1				**1**
UK							1					**1**
Spain									1			**1**
Italy									1			**1**
Georgia	1					1	1					**3**
Azerbaijan								1				**1**
Turkmenistan					1					1		**2**
Kazakhstan			1					1				**2**
Total	**1**	**1**	**2**	**1**	**3**	**2**	**6**	**5**	**3**	**5**	**2**	**31**

Source: Orttung and Overland (2011, pp. 74–85).

Table 3.4 Russia's foreign energy policy tools

Tools	*Countries*	*Date*	*Content*	*Motives*
Energy price subsidies	The Baltic states, Ukraine, Georgia, Azerbaijan	2004–2006	Russia decided to cut energy price subsidies	Geopolitical and commercial considerations
Oil-gas flow disruptions	Ukraine, Belarus	2006, 2009	Gazprom cut gas supply	To punish final consumers or transit countries
Oil-gas pipeline explosions	Georgia, Turkmenistan	2006, 2009	Russia always argued that explosions were accidents	There were serious coincidences that proved Russia's presence in the explosions as a political pressure tool
Construction of the alternative pipelines	Belarus, Turkey, Poland	The 1990s, 2000s, 2010s	Russia intended to diversify oil-gas supply routes to the EU	Transit countries were not politically loyal to the Kremlin
Assets purchases in foreign countries	Armenia, Belarus, Ukraine, Hungary, Moldova	2007–2010	Russia used energy debts to acquire energy assets	EU countries accused that Russia's political motives prevailed its commercial motives

Source: Modified from Orttung and Overland (2011, pp. 74–85).

Orttung and Overland (2011) revealed that Russia's use of the construction of transit pipelines increased (Table 3.4). Russia's use of energy price subsidies, energy supply disruptions, and energy assets acquisitions reduced between 2000 and 2010 (pp. 74–85).

Larsson (2006) distinguished various policy tools of the Russian foreign energy policy such as real energy supply disruptions, publicly open and non-open threats towards oil-gas flow disruptions, using energy prices as intimidation or promotion of political and economic affairs, using accumulated gas debts and attempts towards the acquisition of energy companies or strategic energy infrastructure (p. 177). Starr and Cornell (2014) describe the tactics and tools that Russia has used to implement the grand strategy including acts of sabotage, diplomacy, information and propaganda, irregular fighting and cyber-attacks, ethnic conflicts, separatism, economic enforcement, and energy conflicts (pp. 59–81). They accentuate Russia's manipulation with the export of energy resources against the neighbour countries that try to pursue autonomous foreign policy as the tactics or tools of the grand strategy. Energy-related tools to achieve the hegemonic goals of foreign policy and to accomplish geopolitical objectives include energy supply interruptions, retributive price increases, manipulating the access to energy infrastructure, and swapping energy debts with lucrative energy assets against disloyal and even politically loyal countries. For example, Russia obtained power plants and a nuclear reactor from Armenia as compensation for the country's energy debts. As a result, Russia controlling 90% of the target country's energy market could adjoin Armenia in the EEU with geopolitical considerations (Danielyan, 2003).

The Russian government established a new procedure for pricing and payment for the supply of Russian energy resources to the former Soviet republics aiming the transition to world average prices in energy trade, eliminating the channel of their sales to the West through the territories of the former USSR, and making political pressure during the 1990s and 2000s. Primakov (2009) argued that the growth in energy prices against CIS countries resulted from switching to a market condition, not a political pressure (23–141). Russia artificially lowered prices for oil and gas supplies to the CIS countries to subsidize the economies of these countries. Gradually, Russia shifts to "market conditions/rules" in the sale of oil and gas and it swiftly abandons the subsidized and cheap energy provisions, especially for former Soviet republics or CIS countries.

Tsygankov (2016) listed the toolbox of the Russian foreign energy policy under the relatively aggressive foreign policy as a reaction to the lack of recognition by the West: controlling of the state-owned and private energy companies; diversified network of oil-gas export pipelines and other related; increasing energy prices for energy-importing post-Soviet countries terminating energy subsidies; controlling energy infrastructure in the post-Soviet countries; cooperating with anti-Western oil-gas exporter states. Högselius (2019) proposed five tools of energy leverage or various manipulations for foreign energy policy tasks: energy supply manipulation; energy prices manipulation; energy systems and oil-gas pipeline exploitation; possession/command of energy resources; and energy discourse fraud (pp. 68–154; Table 3.5).

Energy supply manipulation means changing the exported energy volume to accomplish political tasks. Högselius (2019) presented Russia's gas supply interruptions to Ukraine and other post-Soviet countries in 2006 and 2009 as an example (pp. 68–154). He argued that Russia never proclaimed that the major motive of

Table 3.5 Five tools employing energy as a foreign policy mean

No.	*Ways*	*Examples from Russia*
1	Energy supply manipulation	Natural gas supply disruptions to Georgia and Ukraine in 2006, 2009, and 2014.
2	Energy prices manipulation	Russia's 33% natural gas discount to Ukraine in 2013 for geopolitical motivation.
3	Energy systems and pipelines exploit	Russia's Arctic policy: military dominance vs. the depletion of onshore oil and gas deposits.
4	Possession and command of resources	Gazprom's foreign energy acquisitions in Eastern Europe and post-soviet countries
5	Energy discourse's manipulation	Russia's gas supply disruption to Estonia in 1993 overlapped with its restrictive citizenship law adoption.

Source: Högselius (2019, pp. 68–154) and RECSID.

those supply cuts was (geo)political. But Russia's energy strategy for the period up to 2020 which was adopted in 2003 openly stated that energy resource is a foreign policy instrument for Russia. He correctly pointed out that Russia and the EU have clashing views on the post-Soviet region that triggered the energy conflicts. Russian officials openly state that "near abroad" and Ukraine is a geopolitical influence zone for Russia. But the EU desires to see a more integrated Ukraine to the Western economic and military blocks. He argued that the Russia-Ukraine energy conflicts are a two-sided process when Ukraine decided to disconnect Crimea from the electricity network in 2014 in exchange for Russia's gas supply cuts. But he doesn't specify that Russia made a political decision to stop the electricity supply to Ukraine maintaining supply to the unrecognized/separatist Lugansk region violating the state sovereignty of Ukraine in 2017.

Shaffer (2009) argued that even though energy importers and energy exporters mutually blame each other for the cause and effect of "energy weapon", there was an insufficient number of deliberate energy supply interruptions in real life (pp. 28–29). She claimed that transit countries provoked most of the energy supply stoppages cases. Energy transit states (Belarus, Ukraine, Georgia, Poland) also have the power to use transit capacity to pressure energy-exporting country such as Russia. Transit countries' capacity to employ their energy infrastructure as political leverage is an additional factor that partly determines the effect of Russia's "energy weapon" or energy power. Högselius (2019) affirmed that the employment of energy for foreign policy objectives could have a local-level motivation (pp. 68–154). Finland experienced a rapid reduction in electricity imports from Russia from 2011 to 2012. He argued that the local Russian energy company initiated this supply reduction to sell that electricity in the Russian domestic electricity market for higher prices. Firstly, it is not realistic to believe that local electricity companies can reduce energy flows to the neighbouring EU country that has imported electricity from Russia since the 1980s. Secondly, the counterpart country (Finland) may easily construe the fact of supply drop as political leverage for Russia.

Energy price manipulation can be grasped as unexpected and unprecedented changes in energy prices against energy-importing and energy-transit countries. Högselius (2019) argued that price manipulation could be more easily applied to gas and electricity than more mobile and globalized crude oil, coal, and nuclear energy (pp. 68–154). He claimed that the Soviet legacy of monopolistic oil-gas pipeline infrastructure enabled Russia to manipulate energy prices (rapid increases and discounts) against the post-USSR countries. For instance, Ukraine's President Yanukovich could obtain more than a 30% discount on the gas prices from Russia in exchange for political loyalty (refusal to sign an association agreement with the EU) in 2013. Russia and the USSR also supplied very cheap energy to politically loyal countries throughout the second half of the 20th century. The energy-rich state's changing energy export volumes or energy prices towards the target country leads to foreign policy changes towards the influencer state (Russia and the USSR).

Misuse of energy systems and infrastructure (system-building approach) could cover the manipulating of strategic export routes (e.g., the export of the energy resources of the Caspian Basin through/bypassing Russia), the lack of access to technology (Western countries' export bans for energy technology), building energy infrastructure in the geopolitically sensitive border or offshore areas, organizational manoeuvres for foreign policy objectives. *Energy assets possession* and resource proprietorship also can be the object of foreign policy-related manipulation allegedly. Energy assets acquisitions of the Russian state-owned or private energy companies in the "near abroad" and the EU markets created concern in the target country as an asymmetric interdependence factor solidifying Russia's strategic presence in those regions. The purchases of strategic electricity and gas distribution networks can be accompanied by corrupt interpersonal relationships and domestic political consequences (e.g., it was the case in Armenia, Baltic states, Serbia, and Romania).

Högselius (2019) argued that politicization of the energy-related discourses also can be manipulative (68–154). Besides the governments' real actions, their rhetoric is important in the foreign energy policy. Discourses on the geopolitics of energy can act as powerful tools for foreign-policy makers. Energy discourse can be changed concerning political developments. Soviet Union's covert support of the communist government of Poland to exterminate political opposition in 1982 led to the stop of gas export negotiations with the Western European states. As a response to discriminatory citizenship law towards ethnic Russians, Moscow totally stopped gas supply to Estonia in 1993 which was dependent on Russia for energy imports. But at the same time, Russia made a similar supply disruption decision on Lithuania in 1993 that wasn't related to the policies against ethnic Russians. Estonia could encounter Russia's "energy sanction" even if its parliament wouldn't adopt citizenship law, but politicized energy discourse effectuated Russia's foreign policy towards the target.

Korteweg (2018) claimed that misusing energy factors for offensive and defensive foreign and domestic policy objectives is characteristic of authoritarian states (not only Russia) (pp. 4–6). Regime survival is a constant ingredient of authoritarian states' foreign energy policy. Russia can employ energy factors, both defensive and offensive goals combining economic (to increase market shares and revenues) and geopolitical (political oppression over post-Soviet and EU states) motivations. He highlighted several tools of Russia's foreign energy policy: exploiting hydrocarbon prices, halting energy exports, command over critical pipelines in the transit and consuming countries, building alternative energy export options, and manipulating energy contracts. Godzimirski (2021) examined all ground-breaking studies on the tools of Russian energy policy and systematized the following instruments: energy subsidies, shutdowns of pipeline gas flows, explosions in energy infrastructure including pipelines, building alternative transit infrastructure for the energy export, fervent political rhetoric against targeted energy import or energy transit country, prohibition of imports, cyberattacks to energy infrastructure, professional media campaigns, using private connections for energy politics purposes, recourse to courts and arbitration, creating a military threat (pp. 57–83). He classified the instruments into four categories (legal, economic, communicative, and structural related to physical energy infrastructure) based on the categorization proposed by Egmond, Jonkers, and Kok (2006).

Russia's foreign energy policy tools have evolved over time and the applied tools of the Russian aggressive foreign energy policy differed from the 1990s to the 2000s depending on the changes in the energy markets. Also, the tools used by Russia in realizing its "hybrid threat" strategy or "energy weapon" have developed over time. For example, Russia used gas price hikes mostly after the 2000s under a well-prepared geopolitical leverage strategy covering the "near abroad" and the EU, while it applied some combination of instruments under a relatively chaotic pattern. New price-setting mechanisms in the energy markets (transition from long-term contract prices to instant spot market prices) were designed to narrow down Russia's possibilities for control and manipulation over prices. But Gazprom advanced in spot market fundamentals by establishing an Electronic Sales Platform (ESP) in 2018 as an auction mechanism for gas trading where different European gas import companies take part in the electronic buying of gas (Gazprom, 2021a). In critical periods (especially, in the winter seasons), Gazprom books only a small portion of additional capacities that are submitted by European gas operator companies through the auction platform (Kobzeva & Soldatkin, 2021a). Gazprom traditionally advocated for long-term gas sales contracts with the pricing mechanism linked to the crude oil price. Spot gas market relatively lowered natural gas prices of Russia's exported gas to Europe, it created a new environment where "near abroad" countries such as Belarus and Armenia require more discounts from Russia.

The transition from contract prices to spot market prices via electronic trade platforms could allegedly weaken the position of Russia in the European gas market. But Gazprom sorted out the advantage of spot gas markets via its controlled auction mechanism as an additional tool for supplies of its surplus gas to Europe in addition to its long-term contracts (Elliott, 2021). The company even offered price concessions to European clients after 2010 to reinforce its market position. The auction system reinforced Gazprom's position in the EU market and led to record-high gas prices in 2021. Under an open auction system, when Gazprom doesn't book gas supplies to Europe via the Yamal-Europe route, Russia officially offers an excuse that German and French companies, who buy gas along this route, did not submit bids for purchase (Shaban, 2021). In the winter of 2021, Gazprom lowered gas supply to Germany via the Yamal-Europe pipeline (without violating basic contract commitments on gas supply) when the West disputed with Russia the fate of the Nord Stream-2 pipeline project and the Ukrainian crises (Kobzeva & Soldatkin, 2021b). The Executive Director of the International Energy Agency (IEA), Fatih Birol, accused Russia of deliberately causing the gas crisis in Europe in winter 2021 through high selling prices and underperformed storage (Sokolov & Meredith, 2022).

Russia effectively used the EU's gas market reforms to transform from long-term gas purchase contracts to short-term spot market transactions. Russia can easily manipulate open auctions by increasing or decreasing its gas offer to the free available volumes of the EU and triggering record-high gas prices in the EU market (Caspian Barrel, 2021). Open auctions on gas supply to Europe based on spot market prices (plus auction margin) can be considered as the peak of the evolution of Russia's foreign energy policy tools. The rise in gas-related energy prices revealed

Europe's dependence on Russia for gas which requires troublesome collective countermeasures. The challenges of the EU as a coalition of sovereign states to produce adequate energy policies to decrease the energy dependence on Russia strengthens the effect of the Russian foreign energy policy instruments.[1]

Russia's decision to sell pipeline gas to "unfriendly countries" for rubles, allowed a flexible transaction mechanism for euro and dollar payments of the European consumers from 1 April 2022, aimed to secure gas revenues from blocking (Dzyadko, 2022). Flexible gas export mechanism using the "double account" (ruble and euro/dollar) via Gazprombank in 2022 was a new and supple innovative tool of the Russian FEP towards the EU states partly based on market principles and it had contained domestic psychological dimensions to support the ruble's value. Russia applies the most sophisticated tool against the institutionally most developed partner – the EU. It shows the adaptability and rationality of the Russian foreign energy policy (but maybe with short and medium-term effects only) and its implementing actors such as Gazprom that bring corporate adjustability to the energy policy. Even though directly applied energy supply interruptions and export quota measures result in consumers turning to different energy import scenarios for ensuring energy security, these tools continue to be seen as more viable options by Russia. The evolution of foreign energy policy tools indicates that Russia's energy power accompanies the actor's foreign policy and foreign energy policy behaviour in the last 30 years. But we must also distinguish between empirical and objective studies of Russia's foreign energy policy and the "buzz" in Western and some post-Soviet media about Russian "energy weapons".

Note

1 Russia's occasional gas supply cuts in the Yamal-Europe pipeline, which delivers gas to Germany via Belarus and Poland, triggered higher gas prices in the EU market in 2021 (Gazprom, 2020). Although the Kremlin attributes the supply cuts solely to commercial motives, the assumption that Putin tried to use these gas disruptions to create pressure in the certification process of the Nord Stream-2 gas pipeline was prominent in European public opinion. Major EU member states such as Germany and France have different stances on the future of natural gas and nuclear energy in the European community (Coşkun, 2021).

4 Empirical Content

Economic Performance and Energy Resources

4.1 The Role of Energy in the Russian Economy and Economic Performance

4.1.1 Russia's Economic Growth and the Share of Oil-Gas in GDP

Russia's natural resources are the foundation of the national economy, domestic policy, and even foreign policy. The Russian economy is built on the export of natural resources and raw materials extracted from the subsoil of the country, primarily hydrocarbons: oil, gas, coal, and products of their primary processing. World Bank (2021a) assessed Russia's total wealth (sum of produced capital, human capital, natural capital, and net foreign assets) as USD 25 trillion for 2018 (World Bank, 2021b). The share of natural resources in the total wealth is 20%, produced capital 45%, and human capital 35% in Russia. Russia's GDP based on current market exchange rates was an estimated USD 1.7 trillion in 2019 and USD 1.5 trillion in 2020. Even though the Russian GDP doubled in 2019 in comparison with 2005, it is a still smaller amount than South Korea or Italy (USTR, 2021). The share of the oil and gas sector in the gross domestic product (GDP) of Russia was around 20% in 2018–2019 on average which declined to 15% in 2020 after the collapse of crude oil production (Rosstat, 2021). About 15%–20% overall economic dependence on the oil-gas sector is in alignment with the world average for oil-gas countries. In 2021, the Russian mining industry provided 13% of GDP in basic prices and 12% of GDP in market prices.

Oil price and oil production decline adversely impact the GDP growth in Russia. About 10% growth in the global oil price boosts the GDP of Russia from 0.6% to 2% as a long-term effect (Simola & Solanko, 2021, pp. 6–8). The increase in the added value of extractive industries (especially, natural gas, gas condensate, mining of ores, and non-ferrous metals) had the greatest impact on the GDP growth in 2019 (Interfax, 2020a). There was an increase in the share of mining or extractive industries (+1.4 percentage points) in the structure of GDP in terms of production in 2017–2019, but the share of manufacturing industries increased less significantly (+0.8 percentage points) (Analytical Center for the Government of the Russian Federation, 2020a). The oil and gas sector accounted for 40% of the industrial production in Russia in 2019. The mining sector makes a significant contribution to industrial growth. The current state of the resource-based Russian economy can be denominated as "long-term stagnation" that appeared after 2010. GDP growth

DOI: 10.4324/9781003408482-4

Figure 4.1 GDP growth (annual %): Russia versus upper middle-income countries.

Source: World Bank (2022).

was 2.8% in 2018, 2% in 2019, and (−3%) in 2020 (Figure 4.1). GDP growth was around 4.7% in 2021 as a post-pandemic recovery. It was predicted that GDP may fall by 6%–13% in 2022 due to sanctions (Interfax, 2022a), but in fact, Russia's GDP in 2022 decreased only by 2.1%.

Aslund (2021) pointed out that the Russian economy pass through deep and long stagnation after the 2008–2009 global financial crises that stiffened after 2014 (GDP dropped from USD 2.3 trillion in 2013 to USD 1.5 trillion in 2020). Russian economist Konstantin Sonin (2021) has argued that the Russian economy is not just stagnating during the last decade, it simply lacks any sound growth and development model. Russia's average *GDP growth* per annum was 7% between 2000 and 2008. The average GDP growth rate of the Russian economy from 2009 to 2019 amounted to 1%, and economic growth was only 0.8% annually over 5 years (2014–2019). The GDP per capita growth rate of the Russian economy from 2009 to 2019 was 0.9% (Federal State Statistics Service, 2021). On one hand, the Russian economy was negatively influenced by oil prices collapsing in 2008–2009, 2014–2015, and 2020. On another hand, Russia performed less successfully in terms of economic growth in comparison with an upper-middle-income group of countries that had an identical level of development (their average growth rate was 4.7% between 2009 and 2019). The average annual growth rate of the lower-middle-income countries from 2009 to 2019 was 5%.

GDP per capita of Russia varied around USD 10,000 without serious progress between 2010 and 2020 based on the current exchange rate (UNCTAD, 2021a). GDP per capita in purchasing power parity for Kazakhstan was 89% of Russia's same indicator in 2009, but it raised to 97% in 2019. The share of Russia in the global economy (1.3%) was decreasing and the gap between Russia and the developed world was increasing (Trading Economics, 2021). Russia's substantial oil-gas resources, nuclear power, and global influence legacy from the Soviet Union could convert the country into a "great power" despite the relatively smaller national economy compared to other global powers. But the state-controlled economy based on raw materials, an authoritarian government, and an obsession with imperial territorial expansion are interrelated factors that make Russia an inevitably outdated country. Orlova (2021) argued that the current economic model aims to extract the maximum profits from the natural resources including oil and gas and to form a financial cushion based on the resource export revenues that can be used by the government in the future. This model should be supported by external factors such as high global demand for energy resources or increasing trade ties with major trade partners. She predicts an "inertial scenario" for the Russian economy to keep low, but stable economic growth (1%–2% per year) thanks to import substitution, an increase in taxes, and stimulating public investments.

Rogov (2021) concluded that an unfavourable demographic trend, the shortage of labour force, problematic investment/business environment, an aging population, lack of competitiveness, and lack of diversification were the additional factors that determined Russia's economic stagnation in terms of growth. Aleksashenko (2021) underlined that political confrontation with the West, economic and technological self-sufficiency, nationalization and statism in the economy, lack of the rule of law, insecurity of property rights, unfavourable investment environment for private business, monopolistic attitudes, and lack of effective political institutions are components that restrict the growth in the Putin's economic model. He argues that the current economic system in Russia is ineffective, but this does not mean that it is unsustainable. Growing demand for raw materials in the world economy and control over the political system can maintain the current economic system or model by 2035–2040 when there will be a drop in the global oil demand causing a serious long-term crisis in Russia. Changes in the global energy balance can potentially lead to changes in the strategies of global energy market players and undermine the external source of financing for the Russian economy.

4.1.2 Oil-Gas Reliance of the Export and Fiscal System

In terms of the place of Russia in the foreign market, Russia ranks first place in the world for the total export of fuel and energy resources (first place in gas supplies, second place in oil supplies, third place in coal supplies). Russian energy supplies play a significant and leading role in the fuel and energy balance of many countries in Europe and Asia. Despite the Russian authorities' efforts to diversify the economy, the fuel and energy sector continues to play a key role in Russia's GDP, exports, and federal budget revenues. However, with the ongoing decline in oil and gas prices, the fuel and energy complex retains its importance for Russia's financial wealth and economic welfare. *The Russian fuel and energy complex share in GDP was almost 20%, the percentage in federal budget revenues was nearly 40%, and the share in exports was nearly 60% in 2019*. The mineral extraction tax amounted to 46% of revenues to the federal budget of Russia, with 98% of revenues provided by oil, condensate, and natural gas in 2021. The share of mineral products in Russian exports (in value terms) amounted to 56% in 2021, including 54% - the share

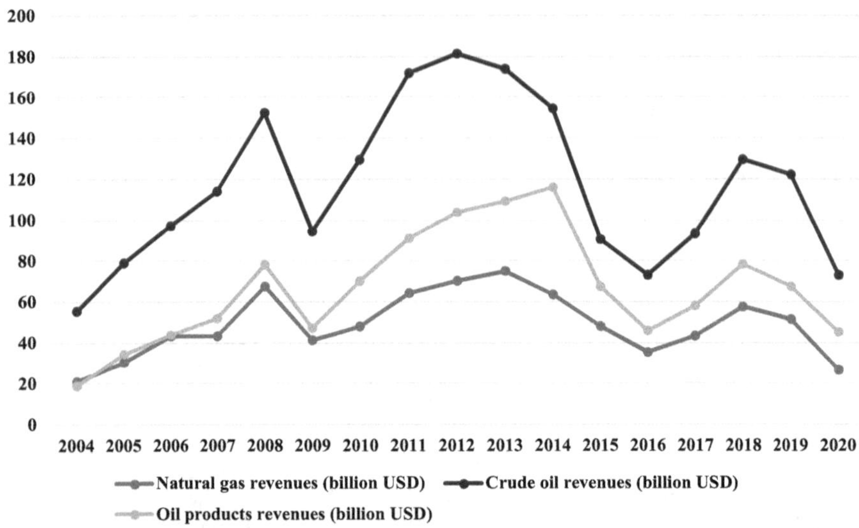

Figure 4.2 Russia's oil-gas revenues (2004–2020).
Source: Federal Customs Service of Russia (2020b).

of fuel and energy products. Russia has a relatively higher dependence on the oil-gas sector in export and fiscal revenues. Crude oil, oil products, gas condensate, and natural gas accounted for an average of 60% of commodity export between 2011 and 2020 (Simola & Solanko, 2021, pp. 6–8). If we will add metals, wood, and minerals, the share of raw materials and products of its processing in the total Russian exports was almost 80% in 2019 (Federal Customs Service of Russia, 2020b). The government uses the country's natural resources to acquire foreign currency, secure government revenues, maintain domestic subsidies, and exert political influence on foreign countries (Figure 4.2).

Natural resources revenues including oil and gas export sales provide a significant part of the federal budget of Russia (EIA, 2017). Revenues from the mineral resource complex accounted for 50%–60% of all budget revenues in Russia (Larchenko, 2015, pp. 2–12). The share of taxes, fees, and payments from the extraction, transportation, and use of oil-gas and minerals in the federal budget revenues was 70% in 2018. The share of the oil-gas sector was 56% of federal budget revenues in 2019 (Tkachev & Kotchenko, 2021). In 2020, 64% of federal budget revenues were covered by activities related to the extraction, transportation, and use of oil-gas and minerals (Accounts Chamber of Russia, 2020). The non-oil budget deficit accounted for almost 9% of the GDP between the 2011 and 2020 average in Russia. The federal budget non-oil primary deficit decreased to 5% of GDP, compared to 10% of GDP in 2013 (World Bank, 2021c). The federal regions that are rich in oil-gas resources receive a lesser portion of the oil-gas revenues leading to the tension between the centre (Moscow) and peripheries. For example, the annual revenues of the oil/gas-rich Nenets Okrug from the fuel and energy complex (mainly from oil production) are around USD 2 billion. Only 15% of revenues remain in the region's local budget, and the other 85% of the income is transferred to the budget of Russia (Federation Council, 2021, pp. 5–41). Russia's accumulated revenues from the export of crude oil, oil products, and natural gas were around USD 4 trillion from 2004 to 2020 (Federal Customs Service of Russia, 2020b). Revenues from the export of crude oil, petroleum products, and natural gas followed an identical trajectory depending on world oil and gas prices that collapsed in 2008–2009 and 2014–2016. This evidence revealed the reality that the Russian economy deeply depends on oil, gas, mineral, and various natural resources.

4.1.3 Forex Reserves, Debt, and FDI

Russia's economy is integrated into the global economy through financial (exchange rate, stock exchange, bank loans, debt transactions, financial asset management) and trade (wide range of imported and exported goods and services) channels. Russia has the minimum external debt among all large economies in the world – USD 489 billion, or 18% of GDP at the end of 2021 (in the USA – USD 28 trillion, or 108% of GDP). Russia's per capita external debt was more than USD 3,200 for 2019–2021 on average (an 80% increase between 2005 and 2020) and the share of foreign debt in GDP was around 30% between 2005 and 2020 (Bank of Russia, 2021; Figure 4.3).

Russia's foreign exchange and gold reserves reached USD 640 billion in early 2022 (Bank of Russia, 2022), but almost 50% of these reserves were frozen in 2022 by the USA and the EU (NBusiness, 2022). Despite sanctions and economic hardships, it hovered around 600 billion USD at the beginning of 2023. The country had a balanced budget and a surplus of the current account balance of payments

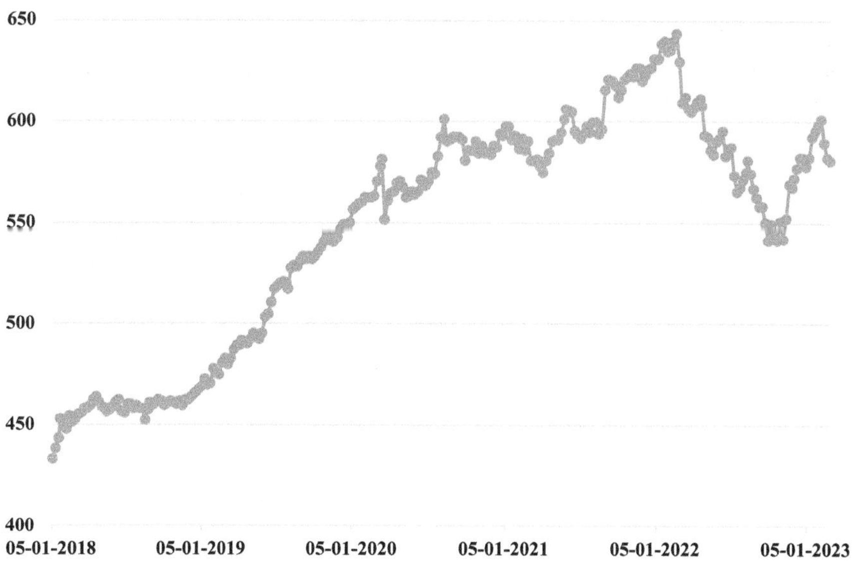

Figure 4.3 International forex and gold reserves of Russia (billion USD).

Source: Bank of Russia (2023).

exceeding USD 90 billion in 2021 (Litova, 2021). Considering the structure of the international foreign exchange (dominated by the dollar and euro) and the gold reserves of Russia, the sanctions on forex and gold reserves increase the sensitivity of Russia to the growth of external market risks under the pattern of interdependence.

Another transmission channel of economic interdependence is foreign direct investment. The mining sector had accounted for 23% of all accumulated foreign direct investments in the Russian economy, while the share of the manufacturing industry was 20% in 2020 (Ministry of Economic Development of Russia, 2020a, pp. 3–43). The share of Russia's oil, gas, and mineral industries in the net foreign direct investment (FDI) inflows was 25% in 2019. The ratio of annual FDI inflows to GDP was 2%, and FDI inward stock to GDP was more than 27%. There was a net outflow of FDI from the Russian economy from 2010 to 2019 (USD 23 billion in 2019). The ratio of annual FDI outflows to GDP was 1.3%, and the percentage of FDI outward stock to GDP was more than 23% in 2019 (UNCTAD, 2021b). Russia attracted USD 76 billion of foreign direct investment to the country, accounting for 5% of the global volume of foreign direct investment transactions in 2008. For this indicator, Russia was the fifth country globally after the USA, China, the UK, and Spain. But Russia has moved to 22nd place in the world for its position in the world ranking of FDI recipient countries in 2019 with USD 32 billion (2% of world FDI transactions). The lowest level of FDI inflows in the Russian economy was observed in 2015 (since 2004) because of the Ukrainian war and international sanctions. As a result of international sanctions and worsening external conditions, FDI inflows to Russia's economy decreased from nearly USD 70 billion in 2013 (before the illegal annexation of Crimea by Russia) to nearly USD 30 billion in 2019 (57% reduction) (UNCTAD, 2021c). Decrescent oil-gas export revenues, market fluctuations, and geopolitical risks triggered capital outflows from Russia that reached almost USD 50 billion in 2020 against USD 20 billion in 2019 (World Bank, 2021d). The most significant sources and destinations for the FDI inflows and outflows into/from Russia are offshore jurisdictions such as Cyprus because of the "*tax haven*" and special offshore zone regime (Table 4.1).

Table 4.1 The largest sources/destinations of the FDI inflows/outflows in Russia

Largest FDI sources	*FDI (billion USD)*	*Share of the total FDI (%)*
FDI inflows (2019)		
Cyprus	8.1	25.6
Netherlands	6	18.7
United Kingdom	4.8	15.2
Ireland	3.2	10.1
Hong Kong	2.7	8.5
FDI outflows (2019)		
Cyprus	14.5	64.4
United Kingdom	2.5	11.2
Singapore	1.9	8.5
Germany	1.54	6.4
USA	1.3	5.9

Source: Ministry of Economic Development of Russia (2020a, pp. 3–43).

4.1.4 Social Development Indicators and Regional Disparities

The economic growth and technological development of Russia are impacted by *demographic crises* that include the aging of the population, the decline in the number of women of reproductive age, and population decline without net migration (Ministry of Economic Development of Russia, 2019, p. 19). Russia's population almost didn't grow between 1988 and 2021 (it varied around 146 million) with a huge decline in natural growth despite the annexation of Crimea (Ukraine) in 2015 (Neskuchnaya Ekonomika, 2022). Social and economic indicators indicate severe inequality in Russian society. The first quintile (20% – with the lowest incomes) of the population controlled almost 10% of the country's total income in 1990, while its share decreased to about 5% in 2017. The fifth quintile (20% – with the highest income) of the population controlled 33% of the country's total income in 1990, while its share approached 50% in 2017 (Tikhonova et al., 2019).

Regarding the World Inequality Database, the share of the top 1% of the population with the highest income in the total income of the population increased from 7% in 1990 to 22% in 2018. The share of the bottom 50% of the population with the lowest income in the total income of the population decreased from 28% in 1990 to 17% in 2018 (WID, 2021). The GINI index increased from 0.37 in 2016 to 0.41 in 2020 (World Bank, 2020a). The poverty rate varied from around 13% from 2018 to 2020 (World Bank, 2021c). Real incomes of the population were constantly decreasing from 2013 until 2020 (10%) with a constant increase in average wages in Russia (Solovieva, 2021). The reasons for this negative dynamic of real income are associated with the lack of economic growth and the implementation of a constraining budget policy. Russia has a high level of social polarization in terms of the income of the population and poverty level across the country. Russian economist Zubarevich (2021b) revealed that Russia has a high proportion of an impoverished population in the regions.

In absolute terms, the highest rates of nominal wages (USD 1,250 per month) were expected in the Nenets, Chukotka, and Yamal-Nenets Autonomous Districts, Moscow, Magadan, Sakhalin, and Kamchatka in 2021. These regions are mainly rich in oil-gas and mineral resources. The smallest rates of nominal wages are in the republics of Ingushetia, North Ossetia, the Chechen Republic, and the Ivanovo region – which are poor regions in terms of energy and natural resources (Ministry of Economic Development of Russia, 2021, pp. 30–94). More than 50%–55% of the GDP was generated by 11 regions in 2019–2021: Moscow (city and adjacent region), St. Petersburg city, Sverdlovsk region, Samara region, Rostov and Sverdlovsk region, Khanty-Mansiysk Autonomous Region (Okrug), Yamalo-Nenets Autonomous Region, Krasnodar Territory, Krasnoyarsk Territory, Tatarstan Republic, and Bashkortostan Republic (their share will increase to 70% by 2024). These are either megacities with large economic bases or have enormous mining areas including oil, gas, coal, and gold (Ministry of Economic Development of Russia, 2020b, pp. 33–38). The largest contribution to GDP was made by the Tyumen Region and the Yamalo-Nenets Autonomous Region (regions in which the mining industry is specially developed), as well as financial and economic centres (Moscow and St. Petersburg) and the Moscow Region in 2018. Only 4 million people inhabit the energy-rich Tyumen Region and Yamalo-Nenets Autonomous Region (AC, 2020a, pp. 3–10). Underpopulated vast territories of energy-rich Siberia may increase the expansionist appetite of China to capture the natural resources. The decline in global oil prices leads to a decrease in the value of Russia's exports of crude oil, oil products, and natural gas as a negative external factor not only for big cities but also for distant regions of the country. Zubarevich predicted sanctions-related economic difficulties for Russian regions, where the share of enterprises in the fuel and energy complex and petrochemical sector is high (e.g., Tver, Sverdlovsk, Chelyabinsk, Tatarstan). The departure of foreign manufacturers, potential reduction in petrochemical sales, and sanctions on imported energy technologies will cause socioeconomic and political problems in the regions of Russia in 2022 and afterward (Degotkova, 2022).

4.1.5 Russia's Foreign Trade and Energy Factor

Foreign trade is one of the transmission channels of the external shocks into the Russian economy under the economic and energy interdependence pattern. The Russian economy is built on the export of natural resources, primarily hydrocarbons: oil, gas, coal, and products of their primary processing. Russia's foreign trade turnover amounted to USD 667 billion in 2019 (exports – USD 423 billion, imports – USD 244 billion, surplus – USD 179 billion) (Federal Customs Service of Russia, 2021). Russia's total exports exceeded USD 490 billion in 2021, with an increase of 45% compared to 2020. The share of export in the Russian GDP varied from around 30% and the share of imports in the Russian GDP varied from around 20% from 2018 to 2019. Due to oil-gas resources, Russia had foreign trade surpluses after 1998, but the country had a chronic deficit in the service trade (Santander Trade, 2021). Russia's foreign merchandise trade has grown at an average annual rate of about 1%, which was much slower than world trade had (2%) per year growth on average from 2010 to 2019. The share of Russia's annual export in the total value of world exports was 2% in 2019, while the share of the Netherlands (400 times smaller than Russia for territories and 8 times smaller than Russia for population) was close to 3%.

The share of Russia's annual imports in the total value of world imports was 1.3% in 2019, while the share of the Netherlands's imports was close to 3% (WITS, 2021). The main commodities of Russia's exports were crude oil, refined oil products, gas, coal, and wheat exported mainly to China, the Netherlands, Germany, Belarus, and Turkey in 2019–2021. Some parts of ships and boats, weapons, and ammunition play a significant role in the Russian non-resource and non-energy exports (the total value exceeded USD 180 billion in 2021) (VED, 2021). The major importing commodities of Russia were vehicles and car parts, medicines, various equipment, airplanes, and space vehicles imported primarily from China, Germany, Belarus, the USA, and Italy (OEC, 2021). The main item of Russian imports remained machinery and equipment, with a share of 46% in the total volume in 2019. Russia ranked 22nd in world imports with a share of 1.2% in 2018.

The fuel and energy complex plays a decisive role in Russian export. Almost 40% of primary energy resources are exported, which reflects the orientation of the modern Russian economy towards exports of raw materials (FEC, 2019). Fuel and energy products continued to dominate in the structure of Russian exports, accounting for about 2/3 of their value in 2019. The raw material exports (crude oil and natural gas, wheat, steel, woods, platinum, diamonds, etc.) were around USD 200 billion or 47% of the total exports of goods. If we add oil products, the share of fuel and energy products could exceed 60% in the commodity structure of exports. Russia exported USD 260 billion worth of energy resources (crude oil, petroleum products, natural gas, LNG, coal, electricity) in 2021, accounting for 53% of its total exports (Federal Customs Service of Russia, 2021).

Russia ranked 1st in gas exports, 3rd in oil exports (after Saudi Arabia), and 3rd in coal exports (after Indonesia and Australia) in terms of physical export volumes in 2019. There has been a stable growth in Russian supplies of fuel and energy complex products (crude oil, petroleum products, natural gas, coal, electricity) to foreign markets in physical terms. The average annual growth rate of exports of the fuel and energy complex was 3% between 2010 and 2019. The export of fuel and energy complex products in value terms amounted to USD 263 billion in 2019, having decreased by 3% compared to 2010 (USD 270 billion). The persisting fuel and raw materials orientation of Russian merchandise exports, in the context of a decrease in world prices for hydrocarbons, determined the negative dynamics of both exports and the overall turnover of Russia at the end of 2019. *The foreign trade channel for the transmission of the economic crisis turned out to be the main factor in the decline in the indicators of the Russian economy.*

The EU remains Russia's largest trading partner, but its share has declined from 49% in 2010 to 42% in 2019 (WITS, 2021). In value terms, trade between Russia and the EU amounted to USD 278 billion, including Russian exports – USD 189 billion, and imports – USD 89 billion. The EU has a leading position in the geographic structure of Russia's foreign trade. The leading positions among the EU member states are occupied by Germany, the Netherlands, and Italy, which account for 46% of Russia's foreign trade turnover with the EU countries. The share of other largest EU partners of Russia amounted to 8% for Germany, 7% for the Netherlands, and 4% for Italy in 2019 (Figure 4.4).

In the geographical structure of Russian trade from 2010 to 2019, there was a significant increase in the role of the countries of the Asia-Pacific region. The share of APEC countries increased from 23% in 2010 to 32% in 2019 (VED, 2021). The countries of the APEC had the second position in terms of the foreign trade turnover of Russia. The most important foreign trade partners among the APEC countries are China, the USA, South Korea, and Japan, which accounted for 86% of foreign trade turnover with the APEC countries in 2019. China was Russia's largest foreign trade partner accounting for 17% of Russia's foreign trade turnover with USD 111 billion in 2019. China's share in Russian merchandise trade increased from 9.5% in 2010 to 17% in 2019 (because of the growth of Russian raw materials exports to China by 3 times, while imports from China increased by

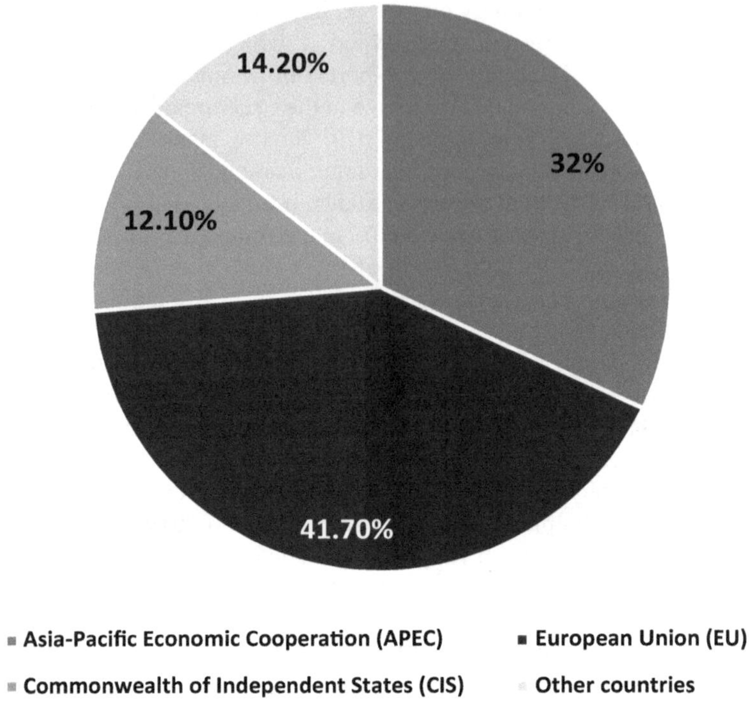

Figure 4.4 The geographic structure of Russia's foreign trade.
Source: VED (2021).

40%). Russia's exports to China alone (USD 68 billion) exceeded its total exports to all CIS countries (USD 65 billion) (Federal Customs Service of Russia, 2021). The role of the CIS countries in Russia's foreign trade has decreased over the past decade (the share decreased from 15% in 2010 to 12% in 2019), primarily because of a sharp decline in trade and economic cooperation with Ukraine. Russia's export to the CIS countries amounted to USD 53 billion and imports amounted to USD 27 billion. The share of the CIS countries was 12% and the share of the EAEU countries was 8.5% in Russia's foreign trade in 2019. Not only geopolitical reasons but also the fall in world prices for oil and gas led to a decrease in the value of Russian energy and non-energy exports to the countries of the EU and the CIS, especially from 2014 to 2016 (AC, 2020b, pp. 9–15).

Pylin (2012) argued that Russia's foreign trade relations with its East Asian neighbours developed more dynamically than with the EU and the CIS region (pp. 5–15). Russia's rapidly growing imports from the EU and East Asian countries largely compensated for the lower dynamics of imports from the CIS countries. The EU vector dominated Russia's foreign trade, which was largely supported by the high demand for Russian energy resources and the increase in imports of mechanical engineering products from the EU countries. Trade interaction between

Russia and the post-Soviet countries developed at a relatively slower pace against the background of a sharp decline in the share of the CIS region in Russian imports. Russia's foreign trade relations with rapidly growing East Asian neighbours developed at the highest rates, which largely led to a fourfold increase in the share of this region in Russian imports. China's total trade (import and export operations) with its major neighbours (Japan, Taiwan, Hong Kong, and South Korea) was USD 1.16 trillion in 2019. The USA's total trade volume with its neighbours (Canada and Mexico) was USD 1.12 trillion in 2019 (UNCTAD, 2021d).

Russia's foreign trade with the neighbouring CIS countries reached only USD 80 billion in 2019 (exports – USD 53 billion; imports – USD 27.0 billion) (VED, 2021). The share of non-CIS states in Russia's foreign trade turnover amounted to 88% in 2019 (in exports –87%, in imports –89%). These facts mean that Russia has less trade dependence on the neighbouring post-socialist countries that Russia declared as a "*sphere of influence*". Russia has asymmetric trade interdependence with particular CIS and non-CIS countries that could be the source of the country's manipulating energy power. Russia had higher trade interdependence with non-CIS countries such as the EU countries or the East Asian emerging markets. Additionally, Russia isn't a global and regional centre of attraction in terms of foreign trade turnover with the "near abroad" or geographically more distant countries.

Russia also has some untapped export potential in the petrochemical products that are by-products of oil-gas resources. China comes out as a major prospective market for the Russian untapped export potential for oil-gas and metals. Russia has the highest level of unrealized export potential with China, equal to USD 16 billion annually (almost 40% in oil-gas and metals) (ITC, 2021). Russian merchandise exports have slightly transformed over the past decade, maintaining a pronounced raw material orientation and a low level of diversification. Despite the increase in the number of competitive non-primary goods, the overall complexity of non-primary products exported by Russia has remained practically unchanged. Despite the increase (in value terms) of the share of non-primary goods in 2010–2019 from 47% to 53% (VED, 2021), Russian exports are still poorly diversified. Russia's raw materials exports, represented by energy products, rough timber, and metal ores, have a relatively higher *Revealed Comparative Advantage (RCA) Index* (UNCTAD, 2021e). Despite the chronic problems, competitive advantages of Russia's energy sector and energy system include rich natural resources, low production costs, proximity to the main sales markets (China and EU), a broader transport network and export routes, and qualified human resources. Export Potential Map developed by the International Trade Centre revealed that Russia has relatively higher export potential in commodities categorized as raw materials or lesser technology intensity.

4.1.6 Russia's Foreign Trade and Technological Backwardness

Russia mainly trades in less technologically intensive commodities that adjust the country's asymmetric interdependence affairs with the developed countries. In the Russian export basket, the share of products related to the use of advanced production technologies has halved in value terms – from 4.5% in 2002 to 2.2% in 2018. The share of the Russian high-technology exports in the total manufactured exports for 2007–2019 was 10% on average (World Bank, 2021d). Even though Russia trades aircraft, turbojet engines, ICT software, nuclear technologies and fuel, warfare technologies, medical products, and heat-generating fuel elements as an advanced commodities market, Russia isn't a leading actor in the trade of advanced high-tech products. The share of Russia in the world markets for products using advanced production technologies was 0.7% in 2018. Russia provides 17% of world exports in nuclear technology in 2018 as a leading country in the world in this sphere (Chebakova, Tkachev, & Skobelev, 2021). Russia has a high grade of specialization in reactors for nuclear power plants (NPP) based on the revealed comparative advantage (Table 4.2).

The share of Russia in the world export of machinery and equipment is less than 0.5%. But Russia is the world leader in the export of nuclear engineering products (38% of world exports in 2018). Supplies of nuclear engineering products are primarily represented by the export of fuel for nuclear power plants – fuel elements (TVEL). Russian TVEL exports amounted to USD 0.8 billion in 2019. The TVEL's main importing countries from Russia were Ukraine – USD 0.22 billion in 2019 (–35%), China – USD 0.15 billion (+18%), the Czech Republic – USD 0.13 billion (+13%), and Bulgaria – USD 0.12 billion (+70%) (Ministry of Economic Development of Russia, 2020a, pp. 3–43). In addition to nuclear technology and nuclear energy fuel, the main export items of advanced technologies from Russia are aerospace technology and weaponry systems where the country depends on the developed and some developing countries in terms of supply of crucial parts. Russia's share in the global markets of arms and aerospace was 1.2% in 2018 respectively. Aerospace technology and nuclear technology segments are characterized by the lowest growth rates among all markets for advanced manufacturing technologies in the world, and the defence industry accounts for only 0.2% of the total volume of advanced technologies markets (Tereshin, 2021). The USSR had a relatively developed biotechnology system, but independent Russia is one of the

Table 4.2 List of top-20 products with the highest RCA for Russia

No.	*Product (SITC Rev.3)*	*RCA*	*No.*	*Product (SITC Rev.3)*	*RCA*
1	Iron and steel ingots	10.7	11	Wood	4.6
2	Natural gas	9.3	12	Petroleum oils	4.4
3	Wheat and meslin	7.3	13	Silver and platinum	3.8
4	Fertilizers	6.6	14	Lignite and peat	3.7
5	Coal	6	15	Synthetic rubber	3.5
6	Crude fertilizers	5.3	16	Oilseeds	3
7	Crude oils	5.2	17	Sulphur	3
8	Nickel	5.2	18	Power generators	2.9
9	Barley	5.1	19	Iron/steel non-alloy	2.8
10	Pig and sponge iron	4.9	20	Aluminium	2.6

Source: UNCTAD (2021e).

lagging economies in life sciences and medicine. Russian exports in this field account for about 0.1% of GDP and the world export where Switzerland dominates with a 16.5% market share (ITC, 2020).

Technologies were imported to Russia from developed countries, and the country exported innovative products mainly to the post-Soviet region. Russia mainly imports ICT, electronics, and manufacturing products from Asian countries such as China and Japan; aircraft, medicines, biotechnology, machinery, and equipment from France, Germany, and Switzerland. Russia has a significant dependence on imports from these countries in this one-sided relationship. But the trade dependences change in the post-Soviet countries where Russia dominated in the trade flows with countries such as Ukraine, Belarus, Kazakhstan, Armenia, Azerbaijan, Uzbekistan, and Kyrgyzstan. Russia imports some critical technologies and products from post-Soviet countries such as Belarus (e.g., medicaments) or Ukraine (e.g., the aerospace industry). Russia increased advanced product exports (primarily ICT and weapons) to India and China and tech-related commodities' imports from France, the USA, Germany, and China from 2002 to 2018.

Russia's share in the global number of start-ups was 0.4% in 2018 and it was inferior not only to developed countries but also to the BRICS countries (except for South Africa) and some former socialist countries (Saltanova, 2021). The only industry where the share of Russian start-ups is higher than the global average is nuclear energy technology. Russia registered more than 23,000 trademarks in the Global Brand Database of the World Intellectual Property Organization (WIPO) in 2021, where one-third of all registered trademarks represented the advertising and business services sector, and the lesser portion was technology-related industries (around 20%) (WIPO, 2021a, 2021b). Patent applications by the Russian residents were almost 50 times less than the local Chinese patent applications in 2019 (23 thousand vs. 1.2 million) (World Bank, 2020b). Researchers in research and development per million people decreased 27% in Russia between 1996 and 2018, while the same indicator doubled in China for the same time interval (World Bank, 2020c). The share of research and development (R&D) expenditure in the Russian GDP was less than 1% in 2018, while the same indicator was higher in the majority of developed and developing countries (World Bank, 2019). Russia's R&D expenditure decreased by 23% from 2003 to 2018 (Table 4.3).

According to estimates of the Higher School of Economics in Moscow, Russia can be attributed to the group of countries that are significantly lagging behind not only in generating new ideas and patents for advanced products that require high technology but also in the export and import of advanced products. The export basket of Russia, heavily relying on oil-gas and other raw materials, isn't rich and diversified in terms of advanced products. Technological "catching up" strategies have failed so far, because of failures in investment in knowledge-intensive markets (Simachev, 2021, pp. 6–47). In March 2019, Deputy Prime Minister of Russia M. Akimov said that Russia must step up the technological development and digitalization of industrial processes including the energy industry to bridge the almost 100-year gap in labour productivity in comparison with the world's leading economies. The head of state-owned Rusnano company and former first deputy prime

Table 4.3 The share of R&D expenditure in the GDP (2018)

Country	*R&D expenditure/GDP*
Israel	5%
South Korea	4.5%
Japan	3.3%
Germany	3.1%
USA	2.8%
European Union (EU)	2.2%
Norway	2.1%
China	2.1%
Slovenia	2%
Czech Republic	1.9%
Brazil	1.2%
Poland	1.2%
Russia	1%

Source: World Bank (2020). R&D Data. https://bit.ly/3qsPYvp

minister of Russia, Anatoly Chubais, said that if the current economic growth rates are maintained, Russia will lag behind not only Europe but also neighbouring Kazakhstan (Vakhlachev, 2019). Russia has a strong scientific base and fundamental mathematical school that is the country's competitive advantage in high-tech sectors. Commercialization of innovative knowledge, efficient cooperation between industries and universities, highly effective R&D activities, and government's incentive towards high-tech development are very challenging areas. The raw material or resource-based economy of Russia is far from being one of the leading innovative economies in the world. Russia ranked 45th out of 130 economies in the 2021 Global Innovation Index (GII) staying behind many middle-income Asian countries such as Malaysia, Turkey, and Thailand (WIPO, 2021b, p. 4).

Technological dependence on foreign partners is relatively higher in the energy sector of Russia. The Russian fuel complex and energy sector need new and high technologies to reduce dependence on imports, increase production efficiency and develop green energy. In 2013, Russia imported about USD 2 billion worth of equipment for the oil and gas industry, but soon more than 50% of these purchases fell under Western sanctions. Difficulties arose in the oil-gas production related to the drilling tools, telemetry equipment, and IT solutions for the fuel and energy complex. In addition to replacing imports, oil-gas companies are constantly in need of new technologies. For example, tech solutions for the development of new fields and enhanced oil recovery (Makarova, 2021). European technological companies thoroughly ensured the technical modernization of Russian energy companies, especially Gazprom in the early 1990s. The need to develop and disseminate breakthrough technologies in the energy sector, including energy storage, is outlined in the Energy Security Doctrine (Energy Security Doctrine of the Russian Federation, 2019).

About 90% of the hydraulic fracturing market is accounted for by non-resident companies in Russia. Non-residents account for about 50% of the geophysics market. The horizontal drilling market is also highly dependent on foreign equipment, where the Russian companies' market share is approximately 25% (National Energy Security Fund, 2015). Thus, the more high-tech the service is, the higher the share of foreign companies. The main parts of oil-gas drilling rigs are imported, and parts and maintenance are also provided by Western companies. High-tech drilling services are 100% imported into Russia. The average age of 60% of all drilling equipment is estimated at more than 20 years (with a standard service life of 25 years; Deloitte, 2015).

Despite its severe technological dependence of Russia on Western energy technologies, it declared having an alternative to alter those technologies during political crises or technical emergencies. To create conditions for the widespread use of import substitution of oil-gas technologies: the dependence of oil workers on imports is critical: the share of imported equipment and technologies reaches 80%, and in some categories – equipment for offshore projects or software – can exceed 90%. The need to cooperate with foreign companies to receive high technology or financial resources limits Russia's "energy weapon" in the foreign energy policy. Russian fuel and energy complex needs integration into the world energy systems in terms of technologies and diversification of markets (Grigoriev, 2013). Mitrova (2021) argued that if market competition factors would determine Russia's energy strategies instead of a "geopolitical imperative" that promotes large pipeline projects or drilling very complex fields in the Arctic (the wider Arctic region provides 80% of gas and 20% of the oil output of Russia) to show power dominance, energy companies could make more rational decisions to introduce new technologies to explore new energy reserves (Mitrova, 2021).

4.2 Russia's Energy Resources and FEP

Almost all types of natural resources have been identified on the territory of Russia and its continental shelf. Russia is among the world leaders in the reserves, production, and export of hydrocarbons (crude oil, natural gas, coal), precious metals, and stones (iron ores, nickel, copper, aluminium, gold, palladium, platinoids, rough diamonds), and the non-metallic raw materials. With 6% of the global oil reserves, 20% of the recoverable gas reserves, 15% of total proved coal reserves, 13% of global iron reserves, 5% of global lead reserves, and 11% of global zinc reserves, Russia is one of the key players in the world energy and mineral markets (Accounts Chamber of Russia, 2020, pp. 3–26). In the structure of the mineral resource base of Russia, the main share (71%) is occupied by fuel and energy resources, represented by gas, coal, oil, 15% – of non-metallic raw materials, 13% – of ferrous and non-ferrous metals, and 1% falls on diamonds and precious metals (Larchenko, 2015, pp. 2–12; Table 4.4).

Russia was the second-largest producer of crude oil, gas condensate, and natural gas in the world after the USA in 2020. Russia is one of the largest coal producers in the world, with the largest coal reserves. The country is the number one exporter of natural gas and number three supplier of crude oil to the world energy market. Russia's energy exports target the European, Asian, and post-Soviet markets. The

Table 4.4 Selected world rankings of Russia's energy portfolio (2020)

	Reserves	*Production*	*Consumption*	*Exports*
Oil	6th	2nd	6th	3rd
Natural gas	1st	2nd	2nd	1st
Coal	2nd	6th	6th	3rd
Electric generation	NA	4th	4th	14th

Source: BP (2021).

Note: NA = not applicable.

Table 4.5 The market value of the Russian natural resources

Natural resources	*Value (trillion USD)*
Natural gas	9.2
Oil and condensate	4.5
Coal and shale	6.7
Ferrous metals	2
Non-ferrous and rare metals	1.8
Precious metals, uranium, diamonds	0.3
Other minerals	4.2

Source: Accounts Chamber of Russia (2020, pp. 3–26).

country also hosts strategic oil-gas transit pipelines connecting Central Asia and South Caucasus to the global market.

Currently, of the 283 types of minerals identified in the depths of Russia, 86 are mined, and the main production falls on 1/5 of these natural resources (oil, gas, coal, iron ores, copper, nickel, lead, zinc, tungsten, gold, silver, platinum, palladium, diamonds, phosphates, cement raw materials, and groundwater) (Accounts Chamber of Russia, 2020, pp. 3–26). The gross value of the explored and preliminarily estimated reserves of natural resources in the depths of Russia in world market prices is determined at *USD 28 trillion*. Three-quarters of this amount is accounted for by oil, gas, and coal (Table 4.5).

4.2.1 Russia's Oil Reserves

BP assessed Russia's total proved oil reserves as lesser than 15 billion tonnes or 108 billion barrels for 2020 that accounting for 6% of the world's total proved oil reserves. "*Reserves-to-production (R/P) ratio*" (the time span of current reserves' sufficiency if the current production level will be stable) for the Russian oil reserves is equal to 28 years. Russia's proven oil reserves decreased from 116 billion barrels in 1991 to 108 billion barrels in 2020 (7% drop in almost 30 years) (BP, 2021). Russia was the only country among the major oil-rich countries that the proved oil reserves declined from 1991 to 2020 (Table 4.6). For the Russian government's assessment, as of January 1, 2022, Russian recoverable oil reserves amount to 31 billion tons.

Various Russian state organizations have different evaluations for the sufficiency of oil-gas reserves. According to the Ministry of Natural Resources of

Table 4.6 The growth of proved oil-gas reserves for 1991–2020 (%)

Oil		*Gas*	
Country	*Change*	*Country*	*Change*
Venezuela	385%	China	732%
Canada	319%	Turkmenistan	674%
USA	114%	Qatar	271%
Libya	112%	USA	179%
Iran	70%	Iran	72%
Iraq	45%	Nigeria	69%
Saudi Arabia	14%	Venezuela	57%
Russia	–7%	Russia	10%

Source: BP (2021).

Russia, Russia's current oil reserves will be sufficient for almost 60 years, and natural gas for more than 100 years considering the current level of extraction (Vesti, 2021). According to the Federal Subsoil Resources Management Agency (Rosnedra), the exploitation of profitable oil resources will only last for 19 years. According to Rosgeologia estimates, Russia has sufficient oil reserves for 30 years (Orlov, Topalov, & Todorov, 2015) and gas reserves for 70 years. Gazprom stated that Russia has the largest accumulated oil-gas resources in the world and there will be no problems with raw materials for a century. For official information, the increase in crude oil reserves due to exploration and revaluation exceeded the production decline by 20% in 2019 (AC, 2020c).

An increase in the oil reserves of Russia was not due to the discovery of new fields, but due to additional exploration of the developed fields and the increase in the oil recovery factor. Ministry of Natural Resources and Environment of Russia officially declared crude oil and condensate reserves were around 20 billion tonnes for 2020. Russia's approximately 20 billion tons of proven oil reserves (8% of the world) would be sufficient for 30–35 years considering oil production volume that could be varied around 500–550 million tons per year (Badmayeva, 2021). Profitable oil reserves in Western Siberia would be sufficient for additional 21 years (Kommersant, 2021). These periods could be extended as technology diffuses and the volume of investments in geological exploration increases for hard-to-recover oil reserves in hard-to-reach places. Different and contradictory predictions on the energy reserves of Russia complicate the proper evaluation of energy power. The lack of clear insights and vision on energy reserves limits Russia's foreign energy policy and all studies related to the Russian FEP.

The share of high-quality oil reserves in Russia has been steadily declining. The quality of Russian oil is slightly inferior to the best foreign grades (Brent, Dubai Crude) in terms of density, sulphur content, and fractional composition. The main grade of Russian oil is the Urals, accounting for about 83% of Russian exports. It is distinguished by a high density, comparable to the Dubai Crude, and average sulphur content. The main Russian export-grade Urals is a mixture in the Transneft pipeline system of heavy, high-sulphur oil from the Urals and the Volga region.

Table 4.7 Main characteristics of oil grades of Russia and other countries

Grade	*Mining area*	*Density (kg/ cubic metre)*	*API density grade*	*Sulphur content (%)*
Foreign oil grades				
Brent	The fields in the North Sea, offshore Scotland, and Norway	825–828	39.4–40	0.37
West Texas Intermediate (WTI)	Texas (USA)	827	39.6	0.24
Dubai Crude	Dubai Emirate	870	31	2
Russian oil grades				
Urals	Bashkortostan, Tatarstan, Yugra	860–871	31–32	1.2–1.3
ESPO	Eastern Siberia	851–855	34.8	0.62
Sokol	Sakhalin-1	835–837	36.7	0.23
Siberian Light	Yugra (Khanty-Mansiysk)	845–850	36.5	0.57
Vityaz	Sakhalin-2	820–823	41	0.18
Arctic Oil (ARCO)	Prirazlomnoye	906	24	2.3

Source: CDU TEK (2021).

After the start of production on the Prirazlomnaya platform in Russia, a new grade of oil appeared – Arctic Oil (ARCO) (Gazprom Neft, 2021). The relatively low-sulphur and lighter ESPO (exported to the Asian market) accounts for about 12% of oil deliveries. Sokol, Siberian Light, and Vityaz grades of Russia are also in demand on the world oil market. Oil from fields in Eastern Siberia is one of the highest qualities in the country – it is light, low-sulphur, and has a low viscosity (Table 4.7).

About 2100 oil fields were exploited in Russia in 2019 that are concentrated in several oil and gas provinces. Commercial oil deposits were discovered in 37 regions of Russia including the offshore areas of the Okhotsk, Baltic, Caspian, Barents, Azov, Kara seas, and the Laptev Sea. Russia's resource base of liquid hydrocarbons is distinguished by the uneven distribution of its reserves. About 70% of total reserves are concentrated in 11 unique and 183 large multi-layer fields, located mainly in the West Siberia, which includes the subjects of the Ural Federal District (Khanty-Mansi Autonomous Region-Yugra, Yamalo-Nenets Autonomous Region, Tyumen Region), and the Siberian Federal District (Omsk, Tomsk, Novosibirsk Regions, and part of the Krasnoyarsk Territory) (Ministry of Natural Resources and Environment of Russia, 2020). The Ural Federal District provides 54% of the fossil fuel production in the country. About 10% of the total oil produced in the country was obtained from the fields of the Siberian Federal District in 2019.

The fate of the Western Siberia oil-gas region of Russia is uncertain for the rapid exploration of oil reserves. But Western Siberia which is relatively close to the European market will remain the main production region until 2035. More than 60% of Russian condensate reserves are concentrated in the northern part of the Yamal-Nenets Autonomous Region. Major oil and gas condensate fields with huge reserves in the Khanty-Mansi Autonomous Okrug-Yugra include Priobskoye, Prirazlomnoye, Samotlorskoye, and Krasnoleninskoye. These fields provide more than 30% of oil production in the Khanty-Mansi Autonomous Okrug-Yugra and 14% of oil production in the country. The share of oil production in the Khanty-Mansi Autonomous Region has been decreasing in recent years with an increase in the share of the Yamal-Nenets Autonomous Region and the Tyumen Region. Previously commissioned oil fields are reaching the production plateau. The most productive among the shelf zones are the shelves of the Okhotsk and Caspian Seas (Filanovsky oil field), providing more than 3% and 1% of oil production in Russia, respectively. Strategic importance is attached to the Russian coastal territories. About 5% of the country's oil reserves and 9% of the country's condensate reserves have been explored on the country's shelf.

Generally, the size of discoveries decreased in Russia. New discoveries decreased from large oil fields with 50 million tons of reserves to small deposits of 3 million tons reserves. Out of 18 billion tons of proven oil reserves, two-thirds (12 billion tons) are classified as hard-to-recover reserves (Shmal, 2016, pp. 256–260). If sustainable oil production with proven oil reserves of developed fields could be 35 years theoretically, it is less than 20 years when we exclude hard-to-recover oil reserves. It will be impossible to maintain the level of oil production without hard-to-recover reserves that require new technology and investments. The role of new oil fields would increase by 35%–45% after 2035, which means the need to involve new, hard-to-recover oil reserves in the exploration and attract huge foreign investments (State Duma Committee on Energy, 2021a). Also, the use of new technologies is required to increase the production of hard-to-recover oil reserves. Russia is not able to productively develop 50% of the resource-rich lands it already owns.

Alekperov (2011) argued that the possibilities of increasing the oil and gas production of onshore regions, or the land territory of Russia are limited (pp. 370–371). The development of the oil and gas provinces of Western Siberia, the Urals, and the Volga region is in the late stages of exploitation with declining production. The degree of depletion of proven reserves reaches 55%, and the degree of exploration of the initial total resources is 46% (Federal Agency for Subsoil Use, 2016). The number of out-of-work oil and gas wells in Russia is about 40% of the total number of production wells. About 55% of all oil wells could maximally produce 10 tons per day. At least 50% of Russia's oil reserves are economically unprofitable. Oil reserves of highly productive fields have been developed by over 50% (Alekperov, 2011, pp. 370–432). Most oil fields are characterized by high water cuts (the proportion of water in the produced fluid is 80%–95%) (Milov, 2020). Russia is still one of the global leaders on the level of associated gas flaring with an annual volume of 20 billion cubic metres. There is a lack of proper infrastructure to transport the associated gas in the remote areas of East Siberia of Russia (World Bank, 2021e). About 73% of Russian trunk oil-gas pipelines were built over 20 years ago requiring maintenance costs. From the early 1990s to the late 2010s, oil-gas fields have been explored 10 times less than in previous years when many more Soviet-era deposits are being depleted. Total 1150 oil and gas fields were discovered from 1992 to 2014 in Russia, but this was about one-third of the total number of known fields since the USSR period (Orlov, Topalov, & Todorov, 2015).

There is a lack of investments and strategic attention to geological exploration and upstream activities in Russia. The medium-scale geological mapping covered only 24% of Russia's territory in 2019 (in China, medium-scale mapping is done for 75% of the territory) (Prokopieva, 2020), and large-scale mapping, which was the basis for forecasting minerals in the 1990s, has been completely stopped due to the budget deficit. State investments in the reproduction of the mineral resource base currently account for 0.5% of the expenditure side of the federal budget. About 2%–5% of the state budget expenditure is spent for these purposes in most natural resource-rich states (Mordyushenko, 2021, p. 4). The government's programmes aimed at reproducing the mineral resource base at the expense of the federal budget are not fully implemented (RCC.ru, 2020). The oil price is another driver of oil production investments from domestic and foreign sources. The peak of activity on licensing and execution of oil extraction coincided with the oil price of USD 110–120 per barrel (Kutuzova, 2021, p. 4). The expected tightening of financial conditions for new fossil fuel production projects by EU's finance institutions will deteriorate Russia's oil-gas production perspective.

Russian government officials acknowledge that the country hasn't suitable conditions that would allow for a sufficient increase in the oil-gas and mineral reserves so that in the long term it remains always above production volumes. It is necessary to intensify the exploration of large new deposits and the development of the mineral resource base (hydrocarbons, coal, ferrous and non-ferrous metals) in Russia (TASS, 2021a). The significant challenges for oil production growth are as follows: (a) high depletion of large oil fields and the onset of a phase of declining oil production; (b) new fields are smaller in size and have more complex mining and geological conditions of development; (c) traditional oil reserves in large fields are being depleted and hard-to-recover reserves couldn't be developed effectively. The challenges related to the expansion of the resource base and actual oil-gas production are a fundamental constraint on Russia's foreign energy policy that aims to obtain geopolitical advantages and fiscal revenues through the export of fossil fuels. Also, hard-to-reach energy reserves and geographical distribution of the energy reserves increase the domestic fragility of the Russian FEP.

4.2.2 Russia's Oil Production

Oil production increased from 304 million tons per year in 1998 to 563 million tons per year in 2018 (Zapivalov, 2020, pp. 15–18). The production of liquid hydrocarbons in Russia between 2010 and 2019 increased by 11%, reaching approximately 561 million tons by 2019 (513 million tons in 2020, 525 million tons in 2021), including the volume of oil production exceeding 525 million tons, gas condensate – circa 35 million tons (Ministry of Natural Resources and Environment of Russia, 2020). The changes in Russia's oil production have a higher level of correlation

(0.7) with the variation of oil prices in the global market from 1999 to 2021. The volume of oil exports amounted to 240 million tons in 2020, which is 11% below the level of 2019 (Alifirova, 2021). Oil and gas condensate production was 524 million tons and gas production was 762 billion cubic metres in 2021 (Finmarket, 2022). Russia produced 10 million barrels per day of crude oil and gas condensate in March 2022 with a gradual decrease after the sanctions. "*Energy Strategy of Russia for the period up to 2035*" estimates ensure the annual crude oil and gas condensate output to be 555–560 million tonnes by 2024 (the war in Ukraine can negatively impact this scenario), then decrease to 490–555 million tonnes by 2035 (Ministry of Energy of Russia, 2020a). The exploitation of new oil fields to increase oil production is influenced by the conjuncture of the world oil market, macroeconomic factors, the balance of supply-demand, the geopolitical situation, access to advanced technology and finance, the rate of economic development, and sanctions (Figure 4.5).

Crude oil and condensate production in 2019 were carried out by approximately 300 oil and gas companies in Russia that include vertically integrated companies, independent or joint ventures operating based on a Production Sharing Agreement (PSA) regulating oil, gas, and mineral production in Russia by foreign companies. Major oil producers in Russia are Rosneft, Lukoil, Gazprom Neft, Surgutneftegaz, Tatneft, and Bashneft. The five largest Russian vertically integrated companies through the oil supply chain – Rosneft, Lukoil, Gazprom Neft, Surgutneftegaz, and Tatneft – produced 445 million tons of liquid hydrocarbons including oil and condensate in 2019 (80% of the Russian production). The leading position in the

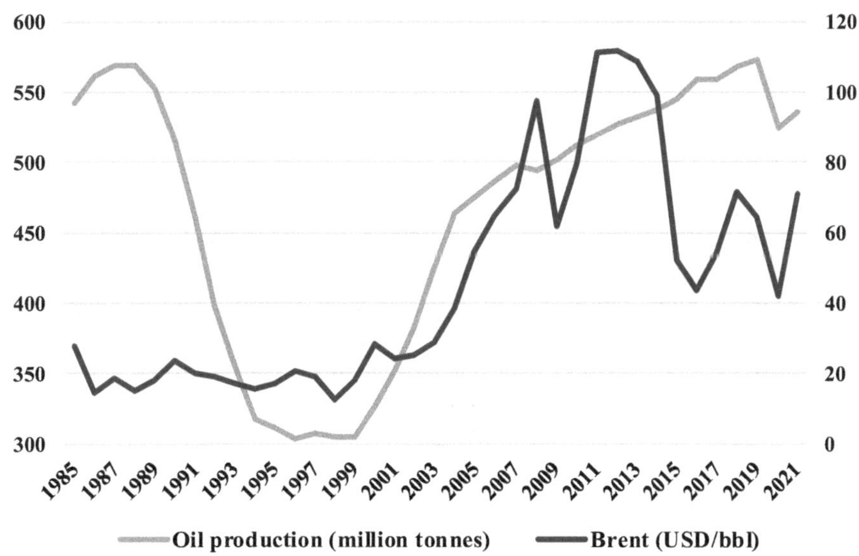

Figure 4.5 Russia's oil production and oil price.

Source: BP (2021).

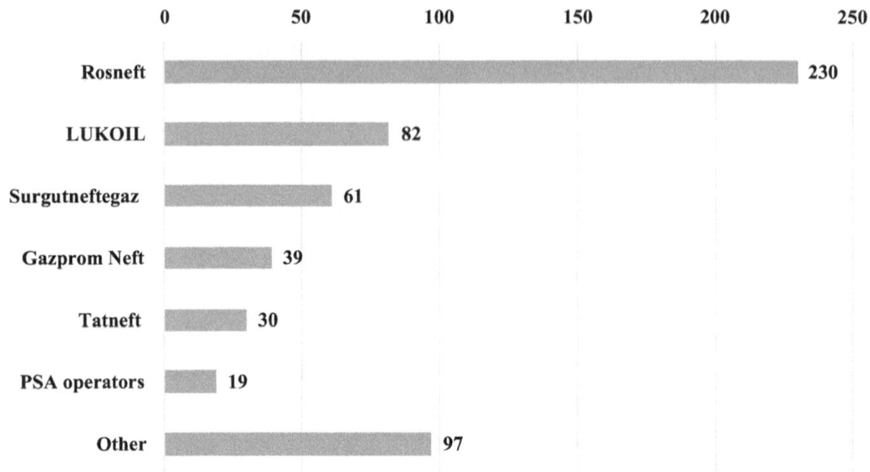

Figure 4.6 Oil and condensate production by the largest Russian companies and PSAs in 2019 (million tonnes).

Source: Ministry of Natural Resources and Environment of Russia (2020).

country in terms of the production of liquid hydrocarbons is held by the state-owned company Rosneft the largest subsoil user that provides more than 35% of the Russian total oil production. Lukoil is the second-largest oil company in Russia that operates oil fields in Western Siberia. Tatneft produces 5% of Russian oil in the Republic of Tatarstan (Neskuchnaya Ekonomika, 2021; Figure 4.6).

4.2.3 Russia's Crude Oil and Petroleum Products Export

In 2019, Russia ranked 2nd in the world in oil exports. The share of exported oil in 2019 amounted to 46% in the structure of Russian supplies of fuel and energy complex products (Ministry of Economic Development, 2020a, pp. 3–43). The volume of oil exports in 2019 amounted to 267 million tons which were equal to almost 50% of the total production (Interfax, 2020b). The export of Russian oil to non-CIS countries increased to 250 million tons, to the "near abroad" to 17 million tons in 2019 (TASS, 2020). The share of Asia-Pacific region countries in total Russian oil exports was 36% in 2019, while the share of neighbouring CIS countries was 8%. The leading country in terms of Russian oil imports was China (70 million tons) in 2019. The oil exports from Russia to China increased five times – from 13 million tons to 70 million tons the period 2009 to 2019 because of growing energy demand in China and the launching Eastern Siberia–Pacific Ocean (ESPO) oil pipeline (Figure 4.7). Russia exported 87 million tons of oil to the Asian market in 2021.

The share of European countries in the structure of oil supplies from Russia amounted to about 54% in 2019. The export of crude oil increased by 16% over the period 2010–2019, and the volume of oil product supplies decreased. EU countries

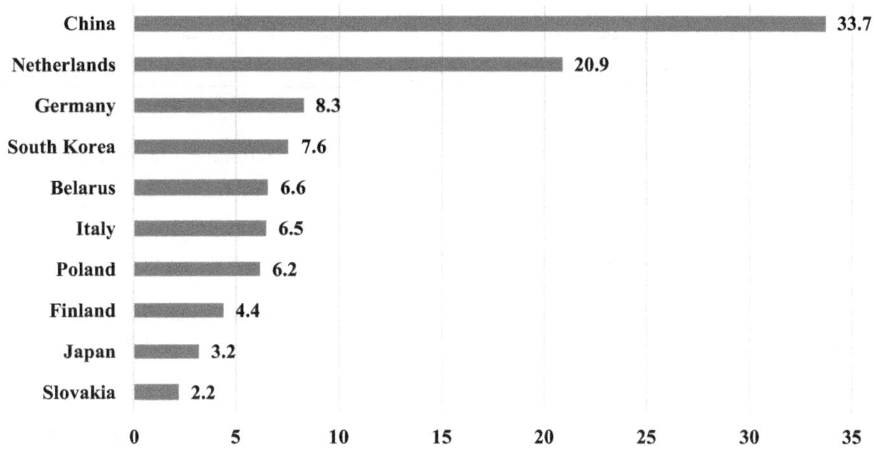

Figure 4.7 Value of Russia's crude oil export to major consumers (2019, billion USD).
Source: Federal Customs Service of Russia (2021).

remain the main destination for crude oil supplies, but their share has been decreasing. About 54% of exported crude oil was sent to the EU in 2019 which was 5% less than in 2018. The main consumers of Russian oil in the European region were the Netherlands (46 million tonnes in 2019), Germany (19 million tonnes), Italy (15 million tonnes), Poland (13 million tonnes), and Finland (10 million tons). In addition to the EU countries, Belarus is a major consumer of Russian oil in the western direction (18 million tons in 2019) (CDU TEK, 2021). The value of exports amounted to USD 120 billion in 2019 (Abay, 2020). Over ten years, oil supplies in physical terms increased by 7% (250 million tons in 2010), while in value terms it decreased by 10% (USD 135 billion in 2010). Russia's share in the EU's oil products import was 25% in the first half of 2021 (Eurostat, 2022) (Table 4.8).

The main oil refining capacities belong to major oil companies: Rosneft, Gazprom, Lukoil, and Surgutneftegaz. Rosneft as the largest state-owned oil company owns the largest refining capacities in Russia which accounts for one-third of the volume of raw materials processed in the country. The share of Russia in the world's oil refining capacity remains at 7% (BP, 2021). The oil refining capacity in Russian refineries is more than 5 million barrels per day (Oil & Gas Journal, 2021, pp. 12–13). More than half of the oil produced in the country is sent for refining by 38 oil refineries that were operating in Russia in 2019. The remaining portion of crude oil from domestic refining was exported from Russia together with oil products. 143 million tons of petroleum products (kerosene, diesel fuel, liquid fuel, etc.) were exported in 2019 (almost 50% of refined oil), of which 90% and 10% were accounted for by non-CIS countries and the CIS, respectively. The export of petroleum products from Russia decreased between 2012 and 2019 because of the conflict between Ukraine and the West. The main direction for the export of petroleum products remains the EU and the USA (Fadeeva & Tkachev, 2020), which

Table 4.8 Russia's major oil–gas export pipelines

Pipeline	*Throughput*	*Length*	*Route*
Natural gas			
Brotherhood, Soyuz, Progress	100 bcma	–	Russia-Ukraine-Europe (EU)
Yamal-Europe	33 bcma	2000 km	Russia-Belarus-Poland-Germany
Nord Stream	55 bcma	1224 km	Russia-Baltic Sea-Germany
Nord Stream-2	55 bcma	1200 km	Russia-Baltic Sea-Germany
Blue Stream	16 bcma	1213 km	Russia-Black Sea-Turkey
Turk Stream	31.5 bcma	930 km	Russia-Black Sea-Turkey
Power of Siberia	38 bcma	3000 km	Russia's Far East-China
Crude oil			
Druzhba	1.2–1.4 mmb/d	5500 km	1 Russia-Belarus-Poland-Germany 2 Russia-Ukraine-Slovakia (Hun.)
Eastern Siberia-Pacific Ocean (ESPO)	1–1.6 mmb/d	4800 km	Russia-China
Baltic Pipeline System ½	0.6–1.5 mmb/d	2170 km	Russia-Gulf of Finland
Caspian Pipeline Consortium (CPC)	0.7 mmb/d	1510 km	Kazakhstan-Russia- Black Sea
Baku-Novorossiysk	0.1 mmb/d	1330 km	Azerbaijan-Russia-Black Sea

Sources: Heinrich (2014, pp. 13–76), Soldatkin (2021) and IAOT (2021).

accounted for 75% of exports of petroleum products in 2019. Transportation of crude oil and petroleum products for domestic and foreign consumers is carried out through the main oil pipeline system of Transneft.

4.2.4 Russia's Gas Reserves and Gas Production

Russia is one of the key countries in the global gas industry, occupying leading positions in the scale of gas reserves, gas production, and gas exports to the world market. BP assessed Russia's total proved natural gas reserves as more than 37 trillion cubic metres for 2019 which accounted for 20% of the world's total proved gas reserves as the world leader in natural gas reserves. "*Reserves-to-production (R/P) ratio*" (the time span of current reserves' sufficiency if the current production level will be stable) for the Russian gas reserves is equal to 59 years. Russia's proven gas reserves slightly increased from 34 trillion cubic metres in 1991 to 37 trillion cubic metres in 2020 (a 10% rise in almost 30 years) (BP, 2021). Russia had the lowest growth rate of proved gas reserves between 1991 and 2020 in comparison with major natural gas countries. But Ministry of Natural Resources and Environment of Russia has claimed that the country possesses 25% of the world's gas reserves. For the Russian government, the country has the world's largest resource base of gas, and its total recoverable reserves amount to 73 trillion cubic metres (Ministry of Natural Resources and Environment of Russia and UNECE, 2016).

Russia has 49 trillion cubic metres of gas deposits that can be estimated with a high degree of confidence (classification of reserves: $A+B_1+C_1$), and 24 trillion cubic metres of natural gas deposits that can be estimated with a medium degree of confidence (classification of reserves: B_2+C_2) (Russian Federal Geological Fund, 2021). Russia had 10 fields with gas reserves of more than 1 trillion cubic metres and 21 fields with gas reserves of more than 500 billion cubic metres, which accounted for 70% of the total gas reserves in the country in 2019 (Ministry of Natural Resources and Environment of Russia, 2020). The Russian gas resource base is characterized by a high degree of unevenness in the territorial distribution of reserves – more than 80% of the reserves are concentrated in the Yamal-Nenets Autonomous Region, Yugra, and Khanty-Mansi Autonomous Region. Most of the largest fields in terms of gas reserves are in the West Siberian oil and gas province, mainly in the Yamal-Nenets Autonomous Region. Yamal-Nenets Region accounted for 84% of total domestic gas production in 2019 having a leading position in the country's gas production.

Russia is second only to the USA in terms of gas production while maintaining its leadership in gas supplies to the world market. Natural gas production in Russia has increased by 20% between 2010 and 2019, reaching 743 billion cubic metres in 2019 (Ministry of Natural Resources and Environment of Russia, 2020, pp. 41–54). It was a record figure for the entire period of Russian gas production. BP's global energy assessment reports indicated less gas production for Russia in 2019 (680 billion cubic metres) in comparison with the government information. But even for BP's assessment, the gas output result for 2021 was a record level for Russia. Russia's gas production trajectory partly overlaps with the changes in gas prices (the correlation ratio is 0.7 between natural gas production and gas price based on the NBP price benchmark; Figure 4.8).

The share of Russia in the global consumption of natural gas amounted to 12% in 2021. Gas production declined to 695 billion cubic metres in 2020 because of the global pandemic and recovered to 763 billion cubic metres in 2021 (ANGI, 2022). Russia's gas production in 2021 (763 billion cubic metres including around 100 cubic metres of associated gas) based on the "Zapolyarnoe" and "Bovanenkovo" gas fields was the peak or record production after 1991 (IEA, 2022c, pp. 6–18). The largest gas fields of Russia in the West Siberian oil-gas province of the Yamal Nenets Region (Yamburgskoye, Yuzhno-Russkoye, Bovanenkovskoye, Urengoyskoye, and Zapolyarnoye) accounted for about 40% of the gas production in 2018. New large gas fields discovered in Eastern Siberia, the Yamal Peninsula, and the Gydan Peninsula in the north are becoming a new gas production centre in Russia. Commercial gas production began at the Chayandinskoye gas field in the Far Eastern region in 2019 together with the launch of the Power of Siberia gas pipeline.

Almost 260 firms produce natural gas in Russia, but the leading producers are Gazprom, Novatek, and Rosneft. Gazprom's share in world gas reserves is 16%, and in Russian gas reserves – 70% (Gazprom, 2021b). Gazprom produced two-thirds of the Russian total gas production in 2019 (500 billion cubic metres) while the remaining energy companies account for only one-third of gas production. Even though Gazprom is the leader in the gas production sector in Russia, the volume

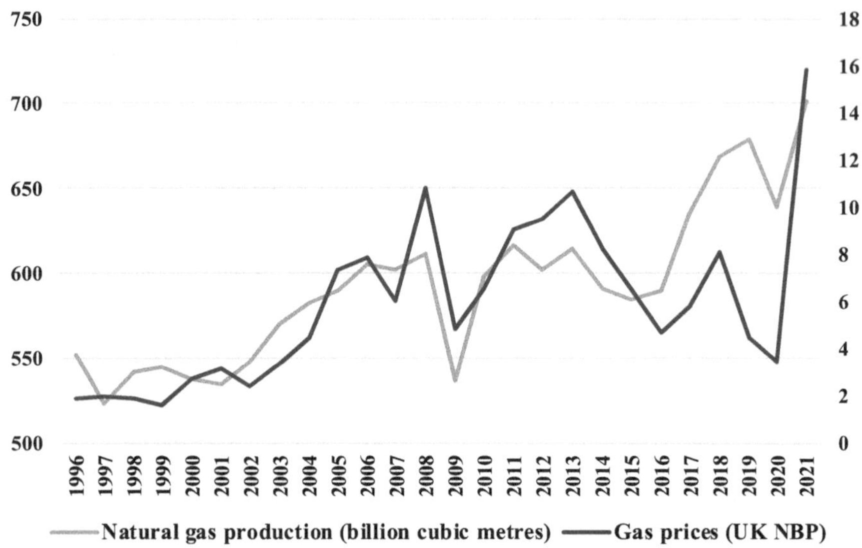

Figure 4.8 Russia's gas production and gas prices.

Source: BP (2021).

of gas production by the company decreased in recent years. Gazprom doesn't disclose segregated data about gas production by fields, but traditional large fields of Gazprom are in the stage of declining (replaced deposits of Yamal). Gazprom does not have many opportunities to increase gas production (Lyutova, 2021). The largest independent company and the second in terms of gas production in the country is Novatek exploring the South Tambeyskoye field (the Yamal Peninsula, Yamal LNG project). Most oil companies produce natural gas, the largest in terms of gas production are Rosneft, Lukoil, and Gazprom Neft (AC, 2020c). Foreign gas producers such as Exxon Neftegas and Sakhalin Energy were actively operating in Russia till February 2022 (Figure 4.9).

4.2.5 Russia's Gas Export

Russia is the world's largest gas exporter and provides nearly a third of the world's gas supplies. A third of the natural gas produced in the country is exported. Russia continues to maintain its leadership in the global export of gas, maintaining its share at about 20%. In 2019, gas exports from Russia reached 250 billion cubic metres: gas export via pipelines was 220 billion cubic metres and LNG export was 30 billion cubic metres. In 2021, gas exports from Russia reached 204 billion cubic metres: gas export to CIS countries was 35 billion cubic metres and gas export to non-CIS countries was 170 billion cubic metres (CBR, 2021). For the period 2010–2019, gas exports increased by 70%, including via gas pipelines – by 80%, and the LNG – by 25%. Russia received USD 50 billion in revenues from the gas export in 2019. From 2010 to 2019, the volume of gas supplies in physical terms increased

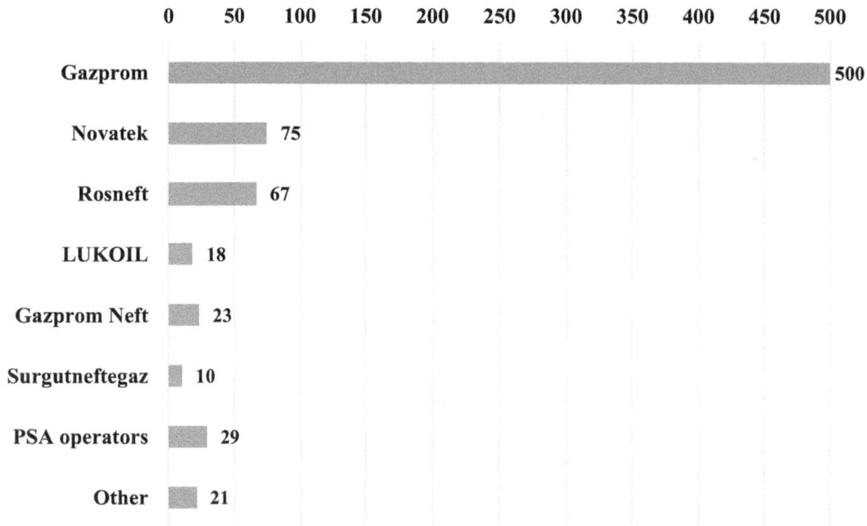

Figure 4.9 Gas production by Russian companies (2019, bcm).

Source: AC (2020c).

by 26% (175 billion cubic metres in 2010), and in value terms – decreased by 2.5% (53 billion US dollars in 2010). Russia's gas exports by pipeline decreased, but LNG supplies increased in 2019 (Figure 4.10).

Russia is the largest exporter of oil and gas to the EU market. Russia exported around 155 billion cubic metres of gas (140 billion cubic metres of pipeline gas and 15 billion cubic metres of LNG) to the European market in 2021 that equal to 45% of the EU's total gas imports and 40% of the EU's domestic gas consumption in 2021 (IEA, 2022d). The largest destinations of Russia's or Gazprom's gas export were Germany (55 billion cubic metres or 25% of total energy exports), Italy (22 billion cubic metres or 10%), Belarus (20 billion cubic metres or 9%), Austria (17 billion cubic metres or 8%), Turkey (15 billion cubic metres or 7%), and Italy (14 billion cubic metres or 6.5%) in 2019 (Gazprom Export, 2020). Russian government officials argue that the EU cannot completely replace Russian gas for at least 5 years after 2022, because of the lack of the necessary LNG and pipeline infrastructure for receiving gas supplies. But interconnected pipelines in the European states could partly solve the insufficient quantity of LNG infrastructure in the continent. Russian Deputy Prime Minister Alexander Novak (who coordinates the foreign energy policy in the government) believes that Russia pursues a rational foreign energy policy and that Russian energy resources could continue to play a crucial role in Europe's energy security (Novak, 2022).

The Russian gas exports to Ukraine decreased since 2014 for geopolitical confrontation and stopped after 2019 (Reuters Staff, 2021). Russia exported pipeline gas via the Yamal – Europe, Nord Stream, Power of Siberia, and Turkish Stream gas pipelines. The Nord Stream-2 gas pipeline (55 billion cubic metres capacity)

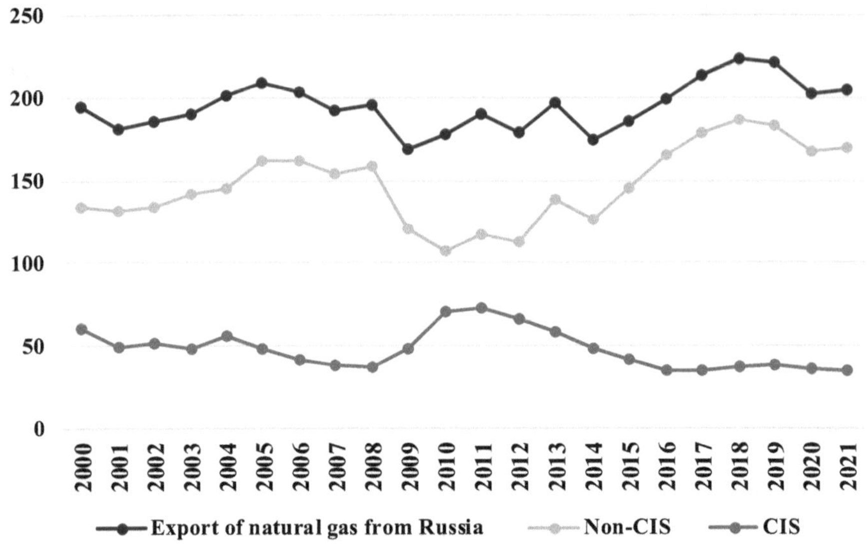

Figure 4.10 Russia's gas export via pipelines (bcm).

Source: CBR (2021).

and the Turk Stream gas pipeline (31.5 billion cubic metres capacity) appeared as a result of geopolitical and commercial disputes between the Kremlin, Ukraine as a transit country, and EU's gas-importing countries that were accompanied with the international sanctions. Russia imports a limited amount of natural gas from Kazakhstan and Uzbekistan annually. LNG production in Russia was 30 million tonnes in 2019–2020 and the country aims to be the top-2 country in the world for gas export by 2035 with 80–140 million tonnes of production. The production of LNG was ensured by an increase in production at the Yamal LNG plant and all the produced LNG in Russia was exported in 2020 (other LNG plants in Russia: Sakhalin-2 LNG, Cryogas-Vysotsk LNG, Arctic-2 LNG) (Kapitonov, 2020). Russia realized 51% of the LNG exports to Europe (France, the Netherlands, UK, Spain) from the Yamal LNG plant, 46% to Asia (China, Japan, South Korea, Taiwan) from the Sakhalin-2 LNG plant, and 3% to the Middle East and America (Figure 4.11).

Russia holds fourth position in the world among the largest LNG exporters after Australia, Qatar, and the USA in terms of export volumes (McKinsey & Company, 2021). The main superiority of LNG trade over pipeline gas is the lack of long-term contracts and long-run dependence on the exporting country. EU states approach LNG trade as a tool for energy import diversification.

4.2.6 Coal Reserves, Production, and Exports

Russia has the second-largest coal reserves in the world after the USA in 2019 (15% share in world reserves). Russia's share in world coal production increased to

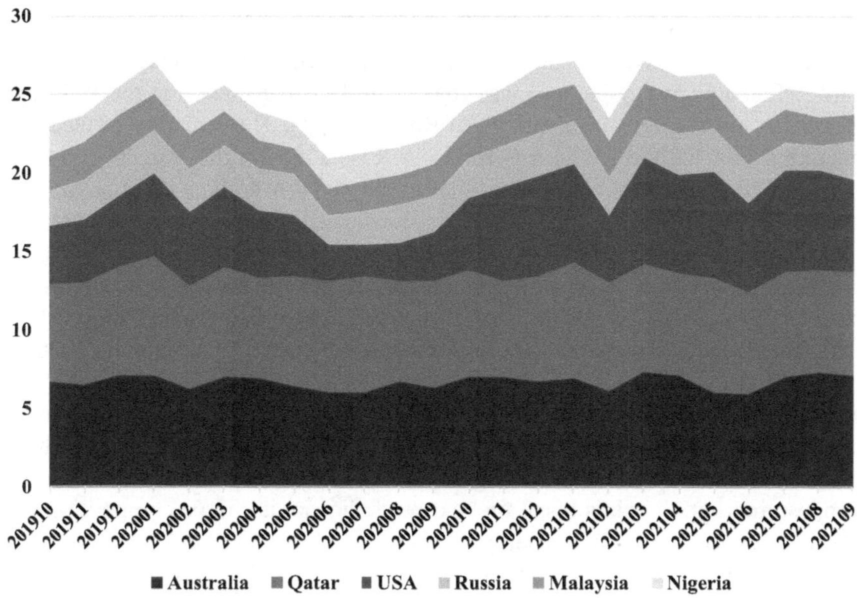

Figure 4.11 Volumes of LNG exports by country (million tons).
Source: McKinsey & Company (2021).

5% in 2019, making it the sixth-largest producer (BP, 2021). Russia was in fourth place in the world in terms of coal consumption (with a share of 3%) in 2018. The Institute for Natural Monopolies Research (IPEM)'s calculations revealed that the contribution of the coal industry to Russia's GDP reached 1% in 2018 (IPEM, 2019a). Russia is the third-largest global coal exporter with an 18% global market share in 2020. In 2021, Russia exported almost USD 18 billion worth of coal, of which almost USD 4 billion to the EU member states (Dzyadko et al., 2022). The volume of coal exports from Russia reached 218 million tons and China became the key destination for export supplies of coal in 2019. Russian exporters need permission from the government to export coal to Ukraine since 2019. There was an increase in export deliveries both to the Asia-Pacific countries and in the Atlantic direction. EU put into practice a ban on the import of coal and other solid fossil fuels from Russia in April 2022 (the cost of banned coal from Russia is around 4 billion Euro per year) (Dulneva, 2022). Zubarevich (2022) pointed out that applying restrictions on coal exports to Europe will cause severe consequences for the coal industry of the Russian regions. For example, the Kemerovo region accounted for 25% of all Russian coal exports before the sanctions. Zubarevich (2022) argued that "it is impossible to redirect such a volume of coal export from the Kemerovo region to the Asian market due to the capacity limitation of the Trans-Siberian Railway". This example is an indication of the challenges related to the shift in the energy export markets in the short term and the indirect costs of the vulnerability in the pattern of interdependence.

4.2.7 The Energy Balance and Renewables in Russia

The structure of Russia's fuel and energy balance is constantly changing. The main share in fuel and energy balance was coal in the 1970s, crude oil in the 1980s, and natural gas in the 1990s (Geography of Russia, 2021). The structure of electricity generation (1.1 trillion kWh) was stable in Russia during the last 20 years from 2000 to 2020. The average age of turbines in thermal power plants is about 35 years (IPEM, 2019b). Russia's energy balance consisted of 19% nuclear power, 17% hydropower, 16% coal, and 46% natural gas in 2020 (Figure 4.12).

Russia's share in the global renewable power generation and renewables consumption from wind, geothermal, solar, biomass, and waste sources were 0.1% in 2020. Russia accounted for 8% of the global nuclear energy generation in 2020 (4th position in the world after the USA, France, and China). Putin often expresses that Russia will continue to export nuclear technologies and contribute to the decarbonization of the global energy sector. The Russian government uses climate change and the EU's decarbonization strategy to justify its gas export tactics towards the European market. Russia's fossil fuel export is faced with fierce competition from the grown share of renewable energy sources in the EU energy balance. The energy transition creates serious challenges for the economy as the largest producer and exporter of hydrocarbons. The energy transition may lead to a reduction in Russian

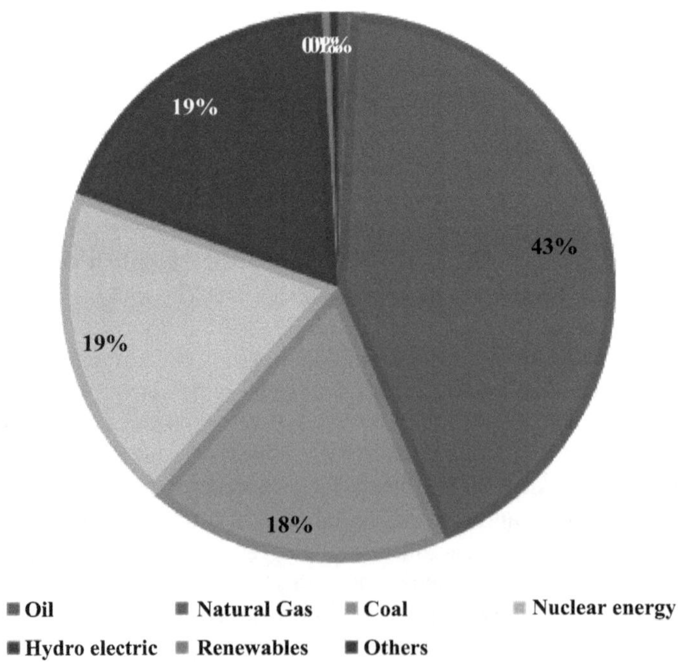

Figure 4.12 Russia's electricity generation by fuel (terawatt-hours, 2021).
Source: BP (2021).

energy exports by 16% by 2040 and a decrease in the average annual growth rate of the country's GDP by 1.1% per year (State Duma Committee on Energy, 2021b). Yergin (2020) argues that the energy transition from oil, natural gas, and coal to renewables will lead to deep shifts in the world economy and global power balance. Oil-exporting countries including Russia will be major losers in this process because of the lack of innovation. If Russia will not succeed to diversify and modernize its economy during the energy transition, the country's position in the global power system will be exposed to the risk the face of China as a world-scale growing power.

Averbukh (2021a) argued that Russia's natural resource export is under the devastating risk of green technologies: solar and wind power generation, the transition of the global car fleet to an electric and hybrid motor coupled with the refusal of an internal combustion engine that consumes gasoline and diesel. Russia attempted to move away from the export of raw materials to the export of higher added-value products massively supplying a high-tech final product to the world market. But Averbukh (2021b) argued that Russia cannot produce competitive products on the world market "surpassing the complexity of Kalashnikov assault rifle". Cordell (2021) argued that Russia has almost USD 4 trillion assets in the oil and gas sector that include oil-gas pipelines, drilling rigs, onshore and offshore platforms, and other related infrastructure. Almost 50% of the fossil fuel assets will be useless by 2036 because of the energy transition and net-zero targets of leading countries in the world. Bordoff and O'Sullivan (2022) argued that the demand for fossil fuels would rise before the permanent decline because of the energy transition. Therefore, petrostates such as Russia would continue to use an energy resource as leverage in the mid-term perspective until they reach the hard-to-reach and high-cost oil reserves (e.g., Arctic oil).

Russia has varying resources and capacities in renewable energy and metal bases that support alternative energy production. Russia owns almost 17% of the global proven *rare earth metals (REM)* reserves (for the government's assessment of 25% of the world's reserves), while its share in the annual production of REM was just 1% in 2020 (BP, 2021). The major responsible company for REM production is the state-owned nuclear energy company Rosatom, which was involved in producing REM, lithium, and cobalt in Russia, Argentina, Chile, and Congo. New energy geopolitics will increasingly be shaped by factors such as access to green technologies, REM, power lines, and energy storage. Lack of infrastructure and high technologies are major problems for Russia's competitive advantages in renewable energy.

If Russia will solve the serious challenges regarding access to finance and technology, the country will have strong global bargaining power and geopolitical advantage in renewable energy and its raw material base. Russia could compensate for its strategic losses in fossil fuel with the new domination efforts in the energy transition process as an alternative supplier of some rare earth metals, lithium, and cobalt to meet the growing demand from the EU. Even if the geopolitical advantage of Russia in fossil fuel will be decayed because of the global energy transition, the country could try to offset those losses with the geopolitical advantage and bargaining power in the renewables industry (if sanctions will be lifted by the developed Western states). The material foundation of the energy transition could potentially be a new dimension of the Russian foreign energy policy with new conflict and cooperation dynamics under the interdependence pattern with the EU and Asian emerging markets.

5 Major Actors of FEP

Energy Companies, Government, and Strategic Documents

5.1 Russian Energy Companies: Profiles and Global Networks

Continuous formal and informal interactions among governmental and nongovernmental representatives including representatives of state-owned and private energy companies, shape multiple channels of communications under the pattern of complex interdependence (example in the energy sector can be formal and informal communications in the framework of the World Economic Forum's (WEF) Annual Meeting in Davos, World Energy Council, World Petroleum Council, the UN structures, G-20 commissions, the Club of Rome, etc.). Also, the structure of the global energy market is very complex and multi-actor consisting of state-owned companies, private companies, government agencies, international/regional energy organizations (IEA, OPEC, and GECF), intergovernmental energy platforms, and individual and organizational energy traders (the largest crude oil traders such as Gunvor, Mercuria, Glencore, Trafigura, and Vitol).

Russian state-owned and private energy companies are leading actors in the country's energy sector and foreign energy policy. During 1991–1995, Russia's government formed powerful integrated energy companies such as Lukoil, Yukos, Surgutneftegas, SIDANCO, Slavneft, Komi-TEK, ONAKO, Rosneft, Tyumen Oil Company, Siberian Oil Company, Gazprom (the largest gas company in the world), Russian Coal Company, and RAO UES as the basis of the country's electric power industry. These energy companies operated in competitive energy markets and attracted foreign investments in the energy sector. Markov (1997) underlined that Russia's energy companies constantly increased their influence on the foreign policy of Russia from the early 1990s. There were mechanisms for the enormous Russian corporations to embody economic interests in foreign policy in the 1990s. The first mechanism was to pursue corporate interests through "direct diplomacy". The common expression was in the mid-1990s that "*Gazprom is Russia's Foreign Ministry of the 21st century*" (Markov, 1997). In 2003, Belarus's President Lukashenko noted that "*Gazprom is the second Foreign Ministry in Russia, but sometimes even more effective*" (Grib, 2003). Russia attempted to use its energy resources as an instrument through state energy companies to realize its strategic priorities in foreign policy. Mainly, Russia's four major energy companies (Gazprom, Rosneft, Transneft, and Rosatom) are actively used in foreign policy

DOI: 10.4324/9781003408482-5

as an instrument or "energy weapon" to achieve geopolitical and geoeconomically purposes. The purposes and missions of these four state-owned energy companies are different in terms of Russian foreign energy policy. The state affiliation of energy companies is one of the sources of Russia-EU gas conflicts. Umbach (2011) argued that Russia sought to increase the state's control over the energy sector through energy companies as a part of resource nationalism that was a primary driver of Russia's internal and external reinvigoration after 2000 (e.g., the seizure of the Yukos oil company in 2003) (pp. 23–38). Simultaneously, the EU accelerated energy (electricity and natural gas) market liberalization to decrease the dependence on the sole exporter. These opposite political economy trends in Russia and the EU set up deep political and economic contradictions. Russia's upstream and midstream companies in the gas sector are state-owned companies such as Gazprom, Rosneft, and Transneft, while the EU's gas distribution companies are primarily private operators.

Russian energy (oil, gas, nuclear, coal, electricity) production, transit, and transportation companies such as Rosneft, Gazprom, Lukoil, Rosatom, and Transnet sometimes had domestic and foreign political goals. Russia's oil-gas companies dominated domestic politics and the sphere of foreign policy in the 1990s and 2000s. These companies also fiercely compete in domestic and foreign markets over resource-rich territories and access to the energy export infrastructure. Gazprom and other public and private Russian oil-gas companies were regularly blamed to interfere in domestic politics actively (Germanovich, 1999). Poussenkova and Overland (2018) underlined that Russia's public and private oil-gas companies had a severe influence on the *parliament and the election cycle* in the 1990s. There were severe interconnections between the domestic political actors and the energy sector of Russia. During the press conference on 9 July 1996, Minister of Fuel and Energy of Russia Yuri Shafranik[1] openly expressed that "*it was the fuel and energy complex that ensured the victory of the President for election results in most regions*" (Boyko, 1996). Gazprom and Lukoil openly supported some regional candidates in local elections in 1999. Gazprom and RAO UES stopped gas supplies and electricity deliveries to Chechnya with the consent of Prime Minister Putin because of the military actions in the region (the official reason for that decision was large non-payments and debts of Chechnya (Klasson & Bushueva, 1999). Also, the Russian energy companies materially support the building of Russian "soft power" by sponsoring sports and cultural projects (Lomagin, 2019). The experience in the domestic political intervention created a behaviour pattern for Russia's energy companies to trace against foreign partners.

The behaviour of the Russian state-owned oil-gas companies to intervene in the political processes domestically in the 1990s accumulated experience and pattern for these companies to pursue and follow in the foreign energy interactions in the 2000s. These oil and gas companies were perceived as equivalent subjects of world affairs, reflecting asymmetric resources between the sizeable Russian energy companies and small post-Soviet countries. Russian state-owned and private oil and gas companies worked via government agencies that directly made decisions on critical issues taking into account the corporate interests of the companies. The most influential energy companies in terms of domestic and foreign policy were Gazprom, Lukoil, Rosneft, and Transneft. Examining energy companies' organizational systems and reactions to the external challenges, Overland and Poussenkova (2020, p. 2) suggested a hypothesis that "*Russian organizations, including oil companies, are not good at foreseeing and adapting to change*". Pusenkova (2010) asserted that Gazprom always had social and political functions and foreign energy policy functions. Gazprom symbolizes the power for domestic and foreign affairs of Russia. Gazprom mainly targeted "near abroad" and the Eastern European countries as an "energy weapon". It is claimed that methods such as restricting oil-gas supply to the receiving country, manipulating the carrying capacity of pipelines, and sudden increase in subsidized natural gas and electricity prices are employed. Domestic and foreign realms, including internal and external shocks, are profoundly intertwined in the company's actions. For example, Gazprom was hit by the non-payment crises in the domestic gas market in Russia and then in the CIS region during the mid-1990s. Gazprom had incredibly complex relations with Ukraine, a transit country for 95% of Russia's gas export in the 1990s, having chronic debt conflict. Gazprom's odious debts to Ukraine, Belarus, Moldova, and other CIS countries reached USD 10 billion in 1996. The debtors paid only 7% of Gazprom's receivables in cash, offering goods in return (agricultural, construction products, and metals) for the remaining 93% in 1996.

Strict measures of Gazprom (energy supply cuts, failed negotiations, legal mechanisms for the non-payments) against CIS states where the company had maintained Russia's geopolitical influence were partly driven by commercial considerations. Also, the global financial crises in 2008–2009, domestic and political consequences of the crises for Russia, and the geopolitics-based energy conflicts with Ukraine and the EU worsened Gazprom's capitalization, investment plans, production level, and market position. Belyi and Locatelli (2015) claim that the Russian oil industry led by Rosneft is much more centralized than the gas industry, where Gazprom experiences more global political and commercial pressure from the regional and global gas market players and actors (p. 3). But Rosneft's current management structures are much more international than Gazprom's. Gazprom is a unique case in the "state market" analytical framework because of the decision making process's de-facto "ministerial attribute".

5.1.1 Gazprom

The USSR Ministry of Gas Industry was reorganized into the State Gas Concern "Gazprom" in 1989. Gazprom was transformed from a state gas concern to a joint-stock company in 1992–1993 (Gazprom, 2021c). Currently, Gazprom is one of the largest oil and gas companies globally in terms of reserves, production volumes, and market capitalization. Specifically, Gazprom is the leading company globally for natural gas reserves and gas production. Gazprom's share in world gas reserves was close to 16%, in Russian gas reserves were 70% in 2020 (Gazprom, 2021d).

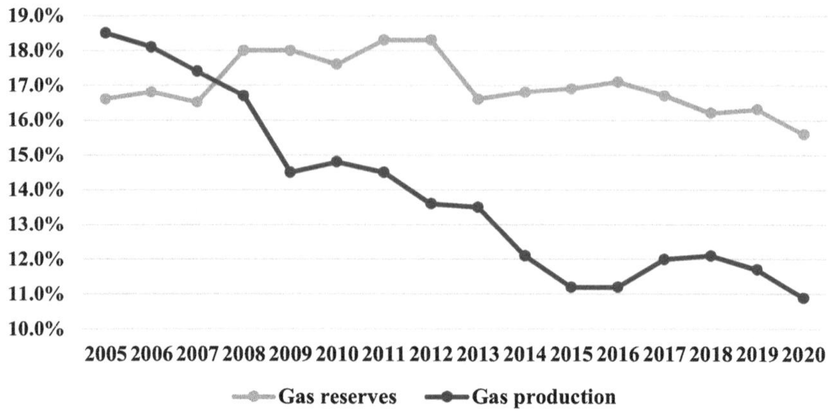

Figure 5.1 Share of Gazprom's gas reserves and production in global volumes (%).
Source: Gazprom (2021g).

Gazprom accounted for nearly 11% of world gas production and 66% of Russia's gas production in 2020 (Gazprom, 2021e). The share of Gazprom's gas reserves and production in the world declined permanently after 2012 (Figure 5.1).

The company owns the world's most extensive gas transmission system (177.000 km) in Russia's territory. Gazprom argues that if all the main gas pipelines of the company were pulled into a line, these pipes would encircle the Earth four times (Gazprom, 2021f). Gazprom has a diversified portfolio of assets and activities from the LNG business to oil and electricity/heat production. Gazprom's total installed capacity is 16% of the total installed capacity of the Russian energy system.

The company started to sign initial gas supply agreements with Gaz de France (France) and Neste (Finland) in 1993–1994 for 20 years. Currently, Gazprom operates in more than 20 countries around the world, and the number of markets to which the company's products are supplied exceeds 100. Gazprom has the first position globally in terms of gas sales and gas export. Gazprom supplies gas to more than 30 CIS and European markets. The share of gas supplies by Gazprom in gas consumption by European countries was 32% in 2020. The bulk of Gazprom gas sales fell on the Netherlands, Germany, Italy, Turkey, and France in 2020. Gazprom sells pipeline gas, LNG, CNG, crude oil, gas condensate, hydrocarbon processing products, petroleum products, electricity, and heat.

The geography of LNG supplies has expanded significantly in recent years, and the share of Gazprom supplies to the LNG market reached about 2% of the total global supply in 2020. India became the largest buyer of LNG from Gazprom in 2020 when more than 1.8 million tons of LNG (2.70 billion m^3) were supplied to this market (49% – in the Asia-Pacific countries, 37% – in the EU) (Burmistrova,

2021). Gazprom purchases gas from Central Asian states such as Turkmenistan, Kazakhstan, and Uzbekistan. Gazprom Neft is one of the leading Russian oil companies in producing and processing liquid hydrocarbons such as oil and gas condensate. Gazprom has first place in Russia for the installed capacity and electricity production in thermal generation. The share of Gazprom's personnel of the total number of employees in Russia was 0.7% in 2020 (478.000) (Gazprom, 2021h, p. 28).

Gazprom's net proceeds from sales of gas, oil, and gas processing products, crude oil and gas condensate, electricity and heat, and natural gas transportation services were around USD 88 billion in 2020. Gazprom's activities in Russia and foreign countries include search and exploration of hydrocarbons, extraction of gas and gas condensate, oil production, gas transportation, underground gas storage, gas distribution, gas processing, crude oil refining, production of petrochemical products, electricity, and heat production. Gazprom owns huge energy assets in Europe and post-Soviet geography, including underground gas storage facilities, oil refineries (Serbia, Italy, Kazakhstan), and other operating assets in gas and petrochemicals processing electricity facilities (Armenia, Serbia), and oil-gas export pipelines. Gazprom clinched Europe to Russia through a gas export pipelines network that possesses geopolitical and commercial noteworthiness. Gazprom owns the gas transmission system (GTS) of Russia having a monopolistic position in the Unified Gas Supply System (UGSS), with the length of its pipelines reaching 175 thousand kilometres (Heinrich, 2014, pp. 13–76). Gazprom has significantly expanded the geography of its activities. The company entered the market of the Asia-Pacific region (APR), began operations in Central Asia, Africa, and Latin America, and participates in the global LNG trade. In January 2020, gas supplies began via the Turkish Stream, a new export gas pipeline across the Black Sea. It is intended to supply Russian gas to Turkey and transit through Turkish territory to the countries of Southern and Southeastern Europe. In 2021, these countries were Bulgaria, Greece, North Macedonia, Romania, Serbia, and Bosnia and Herzegovina. Major projects of the Gazprom in the exploration and production of hydrocarbons abroad are

a *Search and exploration of hydrocarbons* in Bolivia (Acero block), the UK and the Netherlands (Winchelsea field), Iraq (Jackal block), Uzbekistan (Dzhel deposit), Algeria (El Assel area), Libya (areas No. 19 and No. 64), and Vietnam (blocks No. 112 and No. 129–132).
b *Gas production projects* in Bolivia (Ipati, Akio blocks), the UK and the Netherlands (Wingate deposits, Sillimanite), Uzbekistan (Shakhpakhty deposit), and Vietnam (Mok Tinh and Hai Thi fields).
c *Oil production projects* in Iraq (Badra field and Sarkala field in Garmian block).

Geological exploration of four investment blocks in the territory of Uzbekistan is being carried out by Gazprom and Uzbekneftegaz. Gazprom operates in gas distribution in Armenia (Gazprom Armenia) and Kyrgyzstan (Gazprom Kyrgyzstan). Gazprom has participation or shares in some European and CIS countries' underground gas storage (UGS) facilities: Austria, Serbia, Germany, the Netherlands, the Czech Republic, Belarus, and Armenia (Gazprom, 2021i, p. 59). Gazprom owns the 5th power unit of the Hrazdan TPP through its subsidiary Gazprom Armenia as the only foreign electricity asset of the company. Gazprom's strategic cooperation with foreign partners (e.g., Germany, the Netherlands, Japan, China, Korea, Uzbekistan) is carried out in the format of joint coordinating committees, whose work is focused on priority goals such as topical issues of development of partners companies in the modern gas, oil, and electricity markets. Gazprom is a shareholder in the German Wintershall's projects in Libya, the Netherlands, the UK, and Denmark through asset acquisition. Gazprom is a majority shareholder in the Serbian NIS oil-gas company that operates in Serbia Angola, Bosnia, and Romania (Table 5.1).

As a result, we can affirm that Gazprom's main activities in foreign countries are the exploration and development of oil-gas fields, the provision of oil-gas services, and the search and acquisition of new oil-gas assets in key strategic regions of the world. Investors from Europe and North America represent the bulk

Table 5.1 Foreign joint ventures of Gazprom for 2001

Country	*Joint venture*	*Gazprom share (%)*	*Foreign partner*
Germany	Wingas	35	Wintershall
	Wieh	50	Wintershall
	DH Gas	49	Siemens
	Gaz Import/Export	30	
	Kofag	13	
	FNG	5	
France	F.R.A. Gaz	50	Gaz de France
	Trading house Russia	3	
Italy	Promgaz	50	Snam
	Volta	49	Edisson
Austria	GVH	50	OMV
UK	Interconnector	10	BG Group
Finland	Gasum	25	Neste
Estonia	Eesti Gaas	30	
Turkmenistan	Turkmenrosgaz	45	Turkmengaz
Romania	Virom	25	Romgaz
Turkey	Gama-Gazprom	45.3	Botas
	Tur-Gas	50	
Greece	Prometheus Gas	50	Depa
Poland	EuroPolGaz	48	PGNiG
	Gas Trading	35	PGNiG
Hungary	Panrusgaz	50	MOL
Serbia	Progress Trading	50	
	Prometheus Gas Tr.	50	
Slovenia	Tagdem	85	Kovinotehna
Bulgaria	Overgas	50	Multigroup
	Topenergy	50	Bulgargaz

Source: Kommersant (2001).

of investments in shares of Gazprom on the Moscow Exchange (70% of total traded shares) in terms of the geography of institutional investors. Also, Gazprom has technological dependence on developed countries. To solve the problems of import substitution and determine Gazprom's need for import-substituting equipment and technologies, a set of measures has been implemented since 2015 when the crisis occurred in Ukraine. The intense instrumentalization of gas isn't only connected to the difference between oil and gas, but also a unique history of Gazprom that plays a vital role in this context. Gazprom was interlinked with Kremlin before Putin, but the functions were contrariwise. Gazprom had a vast network of joint ventures and affiliated companies around Europe and Central Asia even before Putin's rule.

President Yeltsin appointed Gazprom's Director Victor Chernomyrdin to the Prime Minister position in 1992 when the company's political influence started to heighten. During Yeltsin's rule, Gazprom instrumentalized the state institutions for its corporate interests, and Gazprom's CEO Rem Vyakhirev was considered as "*shadow minister of foreign affairs*". Putin appointed Alexey Miller as deputy minister of energy in 2000 and chairman of Gazprom in 2001. Miller worked with Putin in the External Economic Relations Division at the Saint Petersburg mayor's Office (Gazprom, 2021j). Viktor Zubkov, former deputy head of the foreign relations committee of the St. Petersburg mayor's office (where Putin also worked), was appointed chairman of the board of directors of Gazprom in 2008. Complete loyalty in political and financial matters was a guiding principle in the appointment of Miller and Zubkov. During Putin's order, the powers of state-owned and private energy companies were centralized under new and acted as a political tool of the Kremlin. But the position of Gazprom was always exceptional in the domestic and foreign policies of the Russian state.

5.1.2 Rosneft

The main assets of Rosneft were created during the Soviet Union period. The state oil company Rosneftegaz was established based on the nullified Ministry of the Oil and Gas Industry of the USSR in 1991. It was transformed into the state-owned enterprise Rosneft in 1993. Rosneft was reorganized as an open joint-stock company in 1995 (Rosneft, 2021a). Rosneft made two significant acquisitions in 2013 (TNK-BP) and 2016 (Bashneft), making it the largest publicly traded oil and gas company globally. Rosneft's principal shareholders are Rosneftegaz which is 100% owned by the state (40.4%), BP Russian Investments Limited (19.75% – this company decided to quit from Rosneft's portfolio in 2022), and the Qatar Investment Authority (18.46%) (Rosneft, 2021b). In 2012, Putin appointed Igor Sechin, another St. Petersburg-based colleague with solid international ties, as CEO of Rosneft. Gazprom's board included representatives of the oil business and politics in Europe, America, and the Gulf states till February 2022. Former Federal Chancellor of Germany Gerhard Schroeder held the position of Chairman of the Board of Directors and former minister of foreign affairs of Austria Karin Kneissl as Member of the Board of Directors of Rosneft (2021c).

Rosneft is one of the most significant oil production companies in the world, and its share in global oil production is 6% (4 million barrels per day in 2020). Its proven hydrocarbon reserves amounted to 39 billion barrels in 2020 (proven hydrocarbon reserves – 20 years sufficiency) (Rosneft, 2021d). It is the largest refiner in Russia, having 13 refineries, petrochemical, and gas processing enterprises. Rosneft is present in 23 foreign countries (Eurasia, the Middle East, Southeast Asia, Africa, Latin America) and 78 regions of Russia. It owns and operates 3,000 filling stations in Russia and foreign countries, including Belarus, Georgia (Abkhazia), Kyrgyzstan, and India (via Nayara Energy Limited, 49% owned by Rosneft). It performs refuelling services at 43 Russian and foreign airports. Rosneft is the largest oil exporter in Russia, exporting oil to Europe, the Asia-Pacific region, the CIS, and the international market. The export of crude oil in the Eastern or Asian direction reached 15 million tons in the second quarter of 2020, nearly 60% of the total oil sales volume to non-CIS countries (Rosneft, 2021e, p. 18). The share of oil and oil products supplies under long-term contracts (from one year and more) exceeded 90% of the export volume from Russia to the non-CIS countries.

Asian direction. Rosneft pursues the same "strategically balanced policy" between China and India as Kremlin. The Indian state oil company ONGC Videsh is one of the stakeholders in the Sakhalin-1 project having a 20% stake together with ExxonMobil (30%), a consortium of Japanese companies SODECO (30%), and Rosneft (20%). Nayara Energy (Rosneft's share -49%) owns and operates the largest Vadinar refinery in India, accounting for 8% of the Indian refining capacity (Rosneft, 2021b). Vadinar oil refinery is the second-largest refinery in India, with a total refining capacity of 20 million tons of oil per year. Rosneft acquired a stake in the Vadinar refinery and strategic infrastructure, including a deep-water port that can accept super-large tankers and an extensive network of filling stations. In 2021, Rosneft and Indian Oil Corporation Limited (IOCL) signed a contract to supply up to two million tons of oil to India through the port of Novorossiysk by the end of 2022 (Rosneft, 2021f).

Also, Rosneft continues to diversify its oil supply channels to China. The company is one of the leaders in supplying petroleum products (the supply of 35 million tons of petroleum products in 2009–2018) to China. In 2020, Rosneft signed the agreement with Beijing Gas on the acquisition by Chinese partners of a 20% stake in "Verkhnechonskneftegaz" to explore one of the largest producing fields in Eastern Siberia with a developed infrastructure and access to the ESPO pipeline. Rosneft was allowed to enter the domestic gas market of China through swap gas supplies, and both sides agreed to jointly develop a network of compressed natural gas (CNG) filling stations in Russia. These agreements allow Rosneft to expand sustainable and strategic partnerships with China. Rosneft is developing a project to construct an oil refinery and petrochemical complex in China. Also, the company designs a petrochemical production complex and oil refinery in Indonesia with a 45% stake.

European direction. Rosneft also strengthened international cooperation and a rising presence with the European companies in 2020. Rosneft entered the German refined products market in 2011 with the acquisition of a 50% stake in the Ruhr Oel GmbH (ROG) joint venture. Rosneft owns stakes (24%–54%) in three refineries in Germany through its subsidiary Rosneft Deutschland GmbH, controlling more than 12% of the country's refining capacity, and ranks third in this indicator in Germany with a refining capacity of 13 million tons. Despite the severe political confrontation of Russia with the EU over Ukraine, Rosneft signed new contracts with PKN Orlen SA in 2019 for the supply of oil to Poland and refineries in the Czech Republic (Rosneft, 2020a, p. 20). Rosneft signed a deal with Equinor company (Norway). The foreign company acquired 49% of KrasGeoNat Company, owning 12 exploration and production licences in areas with traditional reserves located in Eastern Siberia onshore. Trafigura (Swiss) acquired a 10% stake in the authorized capital of Vostok Oil Company to explore a hydrocarbon field in the north of the Krasnoyarsk Territory in 2020 (Rosneft, 2021g, p. 4). Rosneft has a stake in one of the largest gas distributors in the Baltic markets and is the operator of Latvian gas distribution networks. Rosneft indirectly owns 21% of shares in Mozyr Oil Refinery in Belarus (Table 5.2).

Global direction. Rosneft strives to expand its international presence in the most promising oil and gas regions of the world and increase its resource base. The company's target areas are South America, North/East Africa, the Middle East, and the Asia-Pacific region, where Rosneft operates already. Rosneft considers entering foreign gas markets and becoming a global player in the worldwide LNG market as one of its top priorities to form a balanced portfolio of assets in terms of risk profile. Rosneft has growing participation in the gas and condensate exploration and production projects in various countries as a shareholder and operator. Rosneft aims to be a global energy company with a diversified portfolio of international assets. But Rosneft acknowledged the risk of losing foreign assets because of political and economic risks. Also, Rosneft faced the risks of dependence on foreign products (e.g., catalysts for oil refining) and foreign technologies.

5.1.3 Lukoil

Lukoil was formed in 1991 as a result of the Decree of the Government of the RSFSR on the formation of the "LangepasUraiKogalymNeft" oil concern, which united three oil-producing enterprises from Kogalym, Langepas, and Uray, and

Table 5.2 Rosneft's oil-gas assets abroad

Country	*Assets*	*Share*
Egypt	Zohr gas field	30%
Iraq	Block 12 (oil)	100%
Myanmar	Block EP-4	90%
Vietnam	Block 06.1	35%
Vietnam	Block 05.3/11	100%
Vietnam	Nam Con Son gas pipeline	32.7%
Brazil	Solimoes Basin	100%
Mozambique	Blocks: A5-B, Z5-C, Z5-D	20%
Latvia	AS Latvijas Gaze	10.56%

Source: Rosneft (2021g, p. 97).

several oil refineries, including Perm and Volgograd (the name of the company is derived from the first letters of the Langepas, Urai, Kogalym oil-producing areas) (Lukoil, 2021a). Lukoil was the most active Russian company in terms of international projects from the early 1990s with the rapid expansion of the geography of oil-gas activities. Vagit Alekperov, the former first deputy minister of the oil and gas industry of the USSR from 1990 to 1991, was President and Chairman of the Management Board of Lukoil until April 2022 (Lukoil, 2021b). Alekperov had a powerful political and commercial network in the post-Soviet geography including Kazakhstan and Azerbaijan.

Lukoil prioritized the oil-gas resources in the post-socialist countries, Africa, and the Middle East regions. Lukoil's oil-gas and financial resources were comparable with the budgets of CIS states (e.g., Armenia and Moldova) in the mid-1990s. Lukoil's first international project was to obtain a 10% stake in the largest block of offshore oil fields, "Azeri-Chirag-Guneshli", in the Azerbaijani sector of the Caspian Sea in 1994. Lukoil actively participated in the exploration projects in Kazakhstan and Egypt in 1995. The company acquired a 15% stake in the project to develop the Karachaganak gas and gas condensate field and 5% in the Tengiz project in 1997. Lukoil is currently the most prominent Russian investor in Kazakhstan with USD 7 billion accumulated investments and providing 10% of the total hydrocarbons production. In 1997, Lukoil signed a contract with the Iraqi Oil Ministry to develop the world's largest oil field – West Qurna-2 (the project was frozen in 2002 because of the "9/11" terror attack). Acquisition of control over the Petrotel refinery in Romania was fulfilled in 1998, and the purchase of the refinery in Burgas (Bulgaria) happened in 1999 (Lukoil, 2021c).

After 2000, Lukoil expanded and acquired the downstream assets in Europe (a stake in a refinery in the Netherlands, filling stations in Benelux countries) and upstream projects in other parts of the world (Iran, Uzbekistan, Kazakhstan, Vietnam, Ghana, Sierra Leone, Saudi Arabia, Turkey, Italy, etc.) in alignment with Putin's global energy expansion strategy. The USA's ARCO energy company became a major shareholder and strategic partner of Lukoil in the 1990s. Lukoil expanded its presence in the USA after 2000 establishing oil-gas stations and signing strategic partnership deals (e.g., ConocoPhillips). Lukoil (20%) has steadily increased its stake in the Shah Deniz gas field's strategic exploration and production project, being the second-largest shareholder after BP (30%) in 2021 (Dmitrieva, 2021). Lukoil acquired lubricants business in Europe, invested in oil-gas processing complexes and renewable energy (solar power plant), and even put into operation the diamond deposit exploration with a diversified portfolio. Lukoil prepared a long-term forecast for the global liquid hydrocarbons market until 2035 in the context of the transformation of the world energy sector.

Currently, Lukoil is one of the largest private oil-gas companies globally, accounting for about 2% of world oil production and 1% of proven hydrocarbon reserves (Lukoil, 2021d). Lukoil involved energy projects covering geological exploration, crude oil and gas production, oil and gas processing and petrochemistry, energy sales and transport, and electricity sectors in 30 countries (Azerbaijan, Kazakhstan, Belarus, Belgium, Bulgaria, Serbia, Croatia, Ghana, Georgia, Egypt,

Iraq, Spain, Italy, the Netherlands, Luxembourg, Norway, Finland, Latvia, Romania, Montenegro, Cameroon, Congo, Macedonia, Mexico, Moldova, Nigeria, UAE, USA, Turkey, and Uzbekistan) (Lukoil, 2021e). Lukoil's oil and gas production in foreign countries accounts for almost 15% of the company's total production. Uzbekistan (13 gas fields from Kandym/Gissar clusters) accounted for 27% of the gas produced by Lukoil and it was 70% of its foreign gas production in 2020. The gas produced in Uzbekistan is exported mainly to China. Lukoil owned and operated more than 2500 oil-gas filling stations and other facilities of the sales network in Europe, the USA, and the "near abroad" countries in 2020 (Lukoil, 2021f).

5.1.4 Transneft

The government established Transneft in 1993 as the largest oil transportation company based on 16 oil pipeline enterprises of the former USSR (Transneft, 2021a). To bypass the transit states that used their bargaining power against Russia, Transneft developed an alternative pipeline towards European markets. For example, the Baltic Pipeline System (BPS) was created to bypass the Lithuanian Butinge oil terminal and Latvian Ventspils oil terminal that became a foreign asset for Russia after the collapse of the USSR. Transneft's oil pipelines directly connect the largest Russian oil fields with refineries and external markets or through seaports in Europe and Asia. The company's petroleum product pipelines connect refineries with the main consumption regions, seaports, and other domestic and export markets. Transneft developed oil pipeline transportation for the growing energy markets of the Asia-Pacific region. The Eastern Siberia–Pacific Ocean (ESPO) pipeline system with huge throughput capacity was the largest construction project in Russia.

Transneft is the global leader in oil transportation via pipelines and the natural monopoly operator of all trunk oil and oil product pipelines in Russia. It owns 51,000 km of crude oil pipelines and 16,000 km of oil product pipelines, more than 24 million m^3 of storage tanks, and more than 500 pumping stations. Transneft's oil and petroleum products turnover (billion tons/km) was 1,297 in 2019, which is higher than any other international oil transportation company (the second company was Canadian Enbridge with 178 billion tons/km) (Transneft, 2021b, pp. 38–55). The company realized 83% of crude oil and 30% of light oil product transportation in Russia in 2020 (Transneft, 2021c, p. 3). The labour productivity of Transneft lagged behind ExxonMobil (17.3 million tonnes km/person vs. 18.4 million tonnes km/person) in 2018. Transneft admits crude oil and oil products to its transportation system from Russia (95%), Kazakhstan (4%), Turkmenistan, and Azerbaijan.

Transneft delivered crude oil and petroleum products via its pipeline systems to Belarus, Uzbekistan, Kazakhstan, Germany, Poland, the Czech Republic, Slovakia, Hungary, and China. The share of China was 18% in the total oil delivery for 2019, while the share of European countries was 19% for the same period (Transneft, 2021b, pp. 38–55). In 2019–2020, Transneft was involved in resolving the consequences of the Druzhba pipeline incident. Transneft signed agreements on out-of-court settlement of the incident results with Lukoil, KazTransOil, Surgutneftegaz,

Gazprom Neft, and Rosneft concerning oil deliveries to Total Trading and Mozyr Oil Refinery. Transport also partly depends on imported equipment and technologies in the leading crude oil pipelines, petroleum product pipelines, and pumping stations. Therefore, Transneft categorized foreign trade restrictions, embargoes, blocking of accounts and settlements, US extraterritorial sanctions, and sanctions retaliation by Russia as significant external risks for its operations.

5.1.5 Inter RAO UES

Inter RAO was established in 1997 as a subsidiary of RAO UES of Russia, responsible for exporting and importing electricity. Inter RAO UES is an electricity company that manages assets in Russia, Europe, and the CIS. Its activities cover electricity and heat production, electricity sales, international energy trading, energy engineering, export of power equipment, and management of distribution power grids outside Russia. Inter RAO UES is the only Russian electricity operator that exports and imports electricity to/from Finland, Belarus, Lithuania, Ukraine, Georgia, Azerbaijan, Armenia, Turkey, Kazakhstan, China, and Mongolia (a totally of 14 countries) (Inter RAO Group, 2021a). Inter RAO UES operates in several segments of the electric power market outside of Russia that cover trading, generation, power grid facilities, sales activities, and engineering.

Inter RAO trades electricity on the Nord Pool Scandinavian market in the Baltic countries. Inter RAO realizes cross-border trading through RAO Nordic ("Nord Pool" platform in the Nordic area) (RAO Nordic, 2021) and Inter RAO Lietuva (Baltic States). Inter RAO's local energy trading companies in the Nordic and Baltic countries carry out trading operations to purchase and sell electricity on a single exchange platform Nord Pool and Nasdaq OMX Commodities, in Poland – on the national exchange "PolPx" (until 2022). These open trading platforms ensure transparency of the transactions and seriously prevent any misuse of electricity as an "energy weapon". Inter RAO operates foreign energy generating assets (Georgia, Moldova, Lithuania, Turkey) with a total installed capacity of 4,255 MW – including three thermal power plants (4,000 MW); two hydroelectric power plants (227 MW); one wind farm (30 MW). Inter RAO owns a distribution grid company that sells electricity to end consumers operating in Telasi (Georgia) with 5,820 km power transmission lines. The company possesses an electricity distribution company in Turkey – "Trakya Elektrik".

The main electricity export markets of Inter RAO UES are Lithuania, China, Finland, and Kazakhstan. The main direction of electricity import by Inter RAO is Kazakhstan. Finland and Baltic states accounted for 60% of Inter RAO's total commercial export of electricity for the nine months of 2021 (Inter RAO UES, 2021b). China accounted for 16% of Inter RAO UES's full commercial export of electricity for the nine months of 2021. Georgia and Kazakhstan accounted for 16% of Inter RAO's total commercial export of electricity for the nine months of 2021. Inter RAO supplied electricity to Turkey and Armenia in transit through Georgia in 2021. Kazakhstan accounted for 85% of Inter RAO's total commercial import of electricity for the nine months of 2021 (Inter RAO UES, 2021c). Inter RAO-Export

LLC is a specialized company of Inter RAO that exports power equipment and engineering services abroad. The main geographical area of Inter RAO-Export's presence is in South American countries such as Ecuador and Cuba (Inter RAO UES, 2021d). About 97% of all Inter RAO shares traded on stock exchanges belong to European and American investors (Inter RAO UES, 2021e, pp. 256–257).

Inter RAO UES has a development strategy for 2025–2030 that adopts the main principle of "promoting energy security and ensuring the strategic interests of Russia" as a strategic goal (Inter RAO Group, 2021f). Eurasian Economic Union countries (Russia, Armenia, Belarus, Kazakhstan, and Kyrgyzstan) signed a Protocol on the Formation of a Common Electricity Market in 2019. Its goal is to ensure free trade in electricity, its transit through the countries of the Union, and the distribution of the capacity of interstate power transmission lines. Inter RAO UES can play a central role in this regional integration. Inter RAO has strategic priority areas: (a) expansion of the geography: strengthening in the markets of Latin America, entering new markets in Africa, South, East, and Southeast Asia, the Middle East, and the CIS; (b) formation of stable long-term relationships with leading energy companies, government, and financial institutions in foreign countries; (c) cooperation with Ministry of Foreign Affairs and Ministry of Energy of Russia towards the export and access to technologies; (d) participation in international consortiums for the implementation of large energy projects in foreign markets; and (e) functioning in alignment with foreign economic policies and energy strategy of Russia.

Inter RAO faced regulatory and market-based challenges in foreign markets in 2020. After the launch of the Belarusian NPP unit built by Rosatom, the trading section of the "Nord Pool" Belarus-Lithuania market was closed, and a new trading section of the "Nord Pool" Russia-Latvia market was opened in 2020. Interstate relations between Ukraine and states that are not members of the Energy Community on electricity trade are restricted in 2020. A new Georgian wholesale electricity market model was launched in 2021 based on the Nord Pool market principles. These facts indicate that market-based and transparent regulatory frameworks in the target countries could restrict the zone of manoeuvres for the Russian energy companies.

5.1.6 Rosatom

Rosatom is one of the largest global nuclear energy companies owned by the Russian state. Rosatom pursues the state's unified atomic energy policy and strategy that includes developing geopolitically important Northern Sea Route in the Arctic and nuclear bomb-related projects, in addition to nuclear energy and nuclear materials. The state corporation united more than subsidiary enterprises and affiliated organizations in 2019, including the nuclear weapons complex' organizations and the world's only nuclear-powered icebreaker fleet (the company has initiatives on wind energy) (Rosatom, 2020a). Chairman of the Supervisory Board of Rosatom Sergey Kiriyenko was the Minister of Fuel and Energy, and the Prime Minister of Russia from 1997 to 1998 (Rosatom, 2020b). In addition to the Russian Orthodox Church affiliation, he is also the First Deputy Head of President's Administration, having

Table 5.3 Key performance indicators of Rosatom for 2021a, 2021b

Indicator	*Value*
Share of NPP generation in the total electricity generation in Russia	20.3%
The portfolio of NPP construction projects in the foreign countries	36 units
The portfolio of NPP construction projects in Russia	3 units
The share in the global nuclear fuel fabrication market	17%
Rank in the world on uranium mining	2nd
Rank in the world on the volume of the uranium mineral resource base	2nd
Rank in the global nuclear fuel market	3rd

Sources: Rosatom (2021a, 2021b).

ample ability to lobby Rosatom in the state. Rosatom's assets and competencies cover the entire supply chain of nuclear energy production (it is the only company in the world having this feature) that incorporate geological exploration and mining of uranium, conversion/enrichment of uranium, fabrication of nuclear fuel, engineering-design-construction of the nuclear power plants (NPP), operation of active NPPs abroad, management of spent nuclear fuel and radioactive waste (Table 5.3).

Rosatom is the number one nuclear energy company globally in terms of its portfolio of NPP construction projects abroad, which included 36 power units and uranium enrichment that generate more than 35% of the world market (2020) (Rosatom, 2021b, pp. 18–19). Rosatom is 2nd place in the world in terms of uranium reserves and 4th place globally in terms of its production. It has 2nd place in the world in terms of installed capacity among nuclear-generating companies and 17% of the nuclear fuel market. Rosatom has a long-term strategic goal to increase its share in international atomic energy markets, including its presence in more than 50 countries and its long-term portfolio of foreign orders to ensure leadership in the global nuclear energy market by 2030. In the annual report for 2020, Rosatom identified the ongoing foreign political pressure and the global trend towards increased protectionism as geopolitical risks that have the greatest impact on the company's international activities (Rosatom, 2021b, pp. 28–29). There are counterclaims that the nuclear energy agreement with Rosatom creates long-term nuclear dependence on Russia.

Experts argue that if gas supply contracts cover 10–20 years when Russia builds a nuclear energy reactor in the host country, it sets up the dependence for 100 years. The lifespan of nuclear energy blocks is around 100 years, meaning the 100 years of presence of the Russian state in the territory of other states via Rosatom (CACDS, 2020). Rosatom's annual report for 2020 acknowledges that the life cycle of a NPP is calculated for a period of about 100 years when the construction of NPP takes 5–7 years, operation of NPP takes approximately 60 years, decommissioning of NPP takes 20–45 years (Rosatom, 2021b, pp. 16–17). Rosatom has a few competitive advantages for foreign partners: a comprehensive offer for the entire "life

Table 5.4 Rosatom's NPP construction in foreign countries

Country	*NPP*	*Capacity (MW)*	*Power units*	*Reactor*
Turkey	Akkuyu	4800	4	VVER-1200
Egypt	El-Dabaa	4800	4	VVER-1200
Belarus	Belarusian	2400	2	VVER-1200
Hungary	Paks-2	2400	2	VVER-1200
Finland	Hanhikivi-1	1200	1	VVER-1200
India	Kudankulam	4000	4	VVER-1000
Bangladesh	Rooppur	2400	2	VVER-1200
China	Tianwan	4000	4	VVER-1000
China	Tianwan	2400	2	VVER-1200

Sources: Rosatom (2021c) and Rosenergoatom (2021).

cycle" of NPP (from fuel supply to construction) that guarantees a competitive cost per kilowatt-hour of produced electricity; assistance to find financing from the Russian government (the "*Build-Operate-Own*" scheme); training of human resources and preparation of local specialists in the Russian nuclear institutes. Under the portfolio of foreign NPP orders, Rosatom provides nuclear energy capacity for the first time in most client countries such as Turkey, Egypt, Belarus, and Bangladesh to obtain atomic energy and related strategic nuclear capabilities (Rosatom, 2021c) (Table 5.4).

Rosatom constructs almost 50% of all nuclear power plants under construction around the globe (the share of China is 20%, and the percentage of the USA is 2%) (Bordoff & O'Sullivan, 2022). This is a unique global advantage of Russia in terms of nuclear energy geopolitics that the Kremlin intends to use in the current decade (2021–2030) when the energy transition process will temporarily surge up the demand for nuclear energy. Ensuring an expansion into the world market, Rosatom constantly works in three key areas: modernization of existing technologies; creation of new technologies for energy markets; and modernization of existing and creation of new technologies for non-energy markets. The Committee on Energy of the State Duma of Russia presented recommendations on the "*Nuclear Energy Technologies of the New Generation: Legislative Aspect*" in 2017, where legislators acknowledged that the most critical state priorities and the strategic interests of the Russian Federation in the development of the nuclear energy include "preserving geopolitical positions of Russia and consolidation of the leading positions in the world market of nuclear technologies" (State Duma Committee on Energy of Russia, 2017). It means that Parliament officially recognized the geopolitical context and motivation of the Russian nuclear energy policy. The most important argument for developing nuclear energy is energy security and energy independence. Nuclear energy services and nuclear power plant construction by Rosatom in different European, Asian, and Middle East countries set up long-term technological (through Russian-made VVER reactors), financial (Russian state banks provide cheap loans to Rosatom's projects), human resource training, and fuel supply dependence of client countries on Russia.

President of the Center for Global Studies "Strategy 21" from Ukraine, Mikhail Gonchar argues that Rosatom and its powerful subsidiary – TVEL (producer and provider of nuclear fuel) cannot be exploited as Gazprom or Rosneft in the foreign energy policy (CACDS, 2020). If cutting or disrupting the gas supply by Gazprom has an immediate effect on the targeted country, Rosatom/TVEL couldn't follow the same method. Suppose Rosatom/TVEL decides to halt the nuclear fuel supply to any customer country to punish, intimidate, or motivate that country for political and economic purposes. From a technical point of view, the targeted country that operates NPP fills and discharges the nuclear fuel from and to the reactor on an annual or biannual basis.

Rosatom plays a crucial role in Russia's alternative energy and metal strategy. Russia's most significant player in the field of lithium production is Rosatom which has its lithium deposits in Eastern Siberia and Yakutia and also lithium resources abroad, especially in Latin America and Africa. Rosatom aims to secure 9%–10% of the world market of lithium production by 2030 (RBK, 2021). These new aspects stemming from the energy transition context increase the complexity of regional and global energy settings.

5.2 Concentration and Monopolization by the Russian Energy Companies

The Russian model of state capitalism determined the consolidation of economic power in the energy sector and emerging large energy corporations such as Gazprom, Rosneft, Lukoil, Transneft, and Rosatom after 2000. Putin declared strategic areas including the oil, gas, and minerals sectors and related strategic assets where participation of foreign companies had been gradually limited using administrative and legal mechanisms during Putin's rule. Despite Putin's specific energy market reforms between 2000 and 2004 (his first term in office), restrictions had already started to concentrate wealth and decision-making power related to the energy sector on the one hand (e.g., export pipelines were monopolized, and public ownership spread in the oil-gas industry). More state interventions in the energy sector and strengthening the role of state-owned energy companies (Rosneft, Gazprom) were widespread phenomena after 2004 (his second term in office). The turning point to construct the state capitalism initiated by Putin in Russia was the nationalization of Yukos energy company in 2003–2005. But state-owned energy companies (e.g., Gazprom, Rosneft) having enormous energy resources are managed by Putin's devoted "inner circle" with a security and business background while public companies are ruled based on private interests. This approach is an exaggeration of Putin's political personality but correctly underlines the private interest groups' function in the public energy companies.

There is growing *concentration and monopolization* in Russia's oil industry in terms of oil production by state-owned oil companies. The monopolization attitude in the Russian foreign energy policy over energy sources and transit pipelines through strong state-owned enterprises was an anachronism from the USSR period when the existing political and economic system denied any type of competition.

One of the features of Putin's era was a high level of total natural resources rents in the national economy between 2001 and 2011 which gave a chance to the regime to consolidate a domestic power through the accomplishment of total state control of the country's sovereign energy sector. The consolidation of power thanks to external rent revenues solidified Russia's foreign policy initiatives, as well. So, the main source of the economic power of Russia's state was oil-gas revenues that were dependent on foreign conditions including the global oil-gas market and the relations with consumer countries mostly in Europe. Russian governments (especially, during Putin's era) aimed to get the maximum concentration of power over the fuel/energy complex and the related financial inflows of the industry in the hands of the government as the decisive source of power in Russia.

After gaining total control over the state-owned energy companies, Putin decided to empower national energy companies and use their market power in foreign policy and domestic politics. In a later stage, empowered national oil-gas companies' profit-driven commercial interests (e.g., Gazprom controlled a very high number of media channels) were reflected in Russia's foreign energy policy reshaping official policy vis-à-vis energy importers via organizational and personal interactions. The level of concentration increased in the Russian oil industry after 2012 because of the rising role of state-owned companies in the industry, political concentration of power, and external circumstances (Kalyuzhnova et al., 2016, p. 120). The structure of oil production in Russia is characterized by a predominance of state-owned companies, with almost 40% of production accounted for by Rosneft by 2017. After the return of Bashneft to state ownership in 2017, the share of state-owned energy companies in Russian oil production reached 50% (compared to 33% in 2012) (Petlevoy & Toporkov, 2019). As described in the previous chapters, "resource nationalism" increased the state control over the oil-gas and minerals in Russia that can be used as political leverage in regional politics (UNEP & IRP, 2020).

The level of monopolization of the oil industry index has grown significantly as determined by the Herfindahl-Hirschman Index (Table 5.5).[2] The oil industry can be assessed as a highly monopolized industry in which the Herfindahl-Hirschman Index exceeds 1800 (Mitrova, Grushevenko, & Malov, 2018, pp. 24–25). The oil industry became highly monopolized after Rosneft's purchase of TNK-BP in 2013 and the acquisition of Bashneft in 2017. Monopolization in the oil-gas industries is

Table 5.5 The level of concentration of the oil industry in Russia

Years	*Herfindahl-Hirschman Index (HHI)*	*Major events*
2012	HHI=1416	
2013	**HHI=2097**	**Rosneft's purchase of TNK-BP**
2014	HHI=2044	
2015	HHI=2010	
2016	HHI=1997	
2017	**HHI=2252**	**Rosneft's purchase of Bashneft**

Source: Mitrova, Grushevenko, & Malov (2018, p. 25).

one of the crucial variables that determined the reinforcement of the state-owned oil-gas companies, and more reliance of the Kremlin on the state's energy companies in the offensive foreign energy policy. Mitrova, Grushevenko, and Malov (2018) argued that off-scale monopolization and nationalization in the energy sector revealed the growing inefficiency of state-owned companies that limit foreign energy policy and economic development. It can be argued that monopolization and nationalization in the oil-gas industries of Russia would potentially damage the energy interdependence with developed partner countries. But monopolization could increase the dependence of the Russian oil-gas companies on foreign energy technologies to stabilize productivity and prevent degradation in efficiency. Higher energy/metal prices and unequal distribution of natural resources trigger resource nationalism that deteriorates energy geopolitics and attitudes towards foreign energy companies. Despite all complexities, foreign companies operate in the country and produce hydrocarbon resources in Russia.

5.3 Foreign Energy Companies Operating in Russia

The presence of foreign companies in Russia, in parallel with the activities of Russian state companies abroad, can be considered within the framework of interdependence. Both directions generated energy conflicts in the last 30 years (1991–2021). In the early 1990s, the Russian state several consecutive steps to attract foreign energy companies with foreign investments: (a) partly privatization of Rosneft, Lukoil, Yukos, and Surgutneftegaz through the transfer of 15% of shares of these companies to foreign investors; (b) joint ventures (JVs) had the right to export all the produced oil; (c) favourable and stable tax regime in the production sharing agreements (PSA). In 2019, three PSA projects continued to operate: Sakhalin-1, Sakhalin-2, and Kharyaginskoye PSA. The largest PSA project being implemented in Russia is the Sakhalin-1 project (1995) which provides for the development of three oil fields. The shareholders of the Sakhalin-1 project are Exxon Neftegas Limited (30%, the operator of the project, (a subsidiary of ExxonMobil from the USA), the Japanese consortium SODECO (30%), as well as the Rosneft, and the Indian state oil and gas corporation ONGC Videsh Ltd (20% each) (Exxon Neftegas Limited, 2021). Sakhalin Energy, the operator of the Sakhalin-2 project (1994), is producing oil and gas condensate fields offshore Sakhalin Island (a strategic area close to Japan and the Asian market). The project shareholders are Gazprom (50%), Shell (27.5%), Mitsui & Co. Ltd (12.5%), and Mitsubishi (10%) (Sakhalin Energy, 2021). The operator of the Kharyaginskoye PSA is Russia's Zarubezhneft-Dobycha Kharyaga Company (20%), the other shareholders are Zarubezhneft (20%), Statoil Kharyaga (30%), Total (20%), Nenets Oil Company (10%). Gazprom Neft and Shell (Netherlands) are developing the Salym group of oil fields (Total Energies, 2021).

The negative change in Russian foreign policy was reflected in the state's approach to the foreign energy companies operating in Russia. Zaslavsky (2011) underlined that the state's attitudes towards foreign energy companies had undergone the boom-and-bust cycle under the influence of energy prices, domestic groups' preferences, and needs for investment and technology. As a result of the favourable investment climate, the government signed several with foreign energy companies. Firstly, local Russian energy oligarchs expressed concern and disagreement on the PSA condition favouring foreign energy companies in the late 1990s. From the early 2000s, the Russian state restored its self-confidence due to rising global energy prices and started revising the PSA contracts with foreign companies signed in the 1990s. Russian state-owned energy companies were not interested in attracting foreign companies based on production-sharing agreements to the energy sector under the higher oil prices condition in the 2000s. Russian state and Putin reflected the attitudes of state-owned energy companies and oligarchs towards foreign energy companies. The government tightened the tax regime and put pressure on foreign energy companies to transfer their shares and project operator status to the Russian state-owned oil-gas companies such as Gazprom and Rosneft.

Putin justified the government's PSA-related coercive actions using "resource nationalism" rhetoric expressing that "*the colonial method of using Russian resources will not work*" in the country anymore (Interfax, 2008). After the series of Russian government enforcements and claims on environmental violations, the largest shareholder of Sakhalin-2 PSA – Royal Dutch Shell agreed to sell 50% shares in the project's operating company (Sakhalin Energy) to Gazprom in 2007 (New York Times, 2007). The legal conflict between the shareholders of the Kharyaga field development project (Total and Statoil) resulted in the transfer of 20% of shares to the state-owned Zarubezhneft in 2009. Only the operator of "Sakhalin-1" PSA – ExxonMobil – could preserve its position in the project because of political and economic interconnections between Russia and the USA. But ExxonMobil encountered a problem selling the gas produced at Sakhalin-1 through pipelines controlled by Gazprom. After 2010, Russia again felt the need to cooperate with foreign energy companies that have the necessary technological and financial resources to develop the Arctic shelf's energy resources. After Gazprom's project's total failure to exploit the Prirazlomnoye field in the Arctic, the Russian state and public energy companies realized that these projects could be realized only with the engagement of foreign energy and technology companies.

Global energy companies such as BP, Shell, Exxon, and Equinor proclaimed to exit from the Russian energy sector's upstream, midstream, and downstream projects in March 2022, despite the huge cost of the withdrawal. Shell announced the USD 4–5 billion initial cost to stop energy projects in Russia in 2022 (New York Times, 2022). Also, the world's largest companies providing services in the oil sector and working to increase production in oil wells and oil fields (Schlumberger, Halliburton, Baker Hughes, Weatherford) announced the suspension of new investment projects and new technology transfer activities in Russia in March 2022 (because of Russia's military intervention to Ukraine). This step would have a negative impact on Russia's oil production level in the long run. Although the share of these companies in the total Russian oil services market is 15%, their share in the segments of the oil service market that require higher technologies (increasing production in old fields, software provision used to optimize production in the depleted fields) is between 50% and 60% (Bloomberg News, 2022).

The acute technological dependence of Russia on foreign energy companies partly compensates for foreign markets' needs for Russian fossil fuel resources. This pattern of interdependence has weakened the outcomes of Russia's military adventure in Ukraine in 2022 and Europe's real sanctions that targeted Russia's energy sector. Also, there are uncertainties and contradictions in the foreign energy companies' future activities in Russia after the international sanctions in March–April 2022. On one hand, several energy companies announced their withdrawal from the Russian market and the closure of production facilities in the country. But they are partly influenced by the political agenda that pushes them to withdraw from Russia's energy markets (the pattern of interdependence) and to relinquish income-generating assets in Russia. The Russian government created several obstacles to the withdrawal of foreign capital from the country, including oil and gas assets owned by foreign companies in March 2022 (Krugley, 2022). Also, there were clear signs of expropriation of the shares of foreign energy companies in the Russian oil-gas projects such as Sakhalin through newly-established state-owned giant energy company after the war in Ukraine in 2022 changing previous behavioural patterns towards external market players (Obayashi, Chow, & Bousso, 2022).

5.4 The Role of Government in the Russian FEP

Governments and complex interdependence patterns mutually affect each other through institutional paths in the foreign energy policy. The foreign energy policy of the Russian government should adjust to interdependence, but also their policies through government agencies such as the Ministry of Energy set up a modified interdependence pattern. In 1991, the Ministry of Energy of Russia was established as a federal institution responsible for the development and implementation of state policy and legal regulation in the field of the fuel and energy complex. The Ministry of Energy is a relatively powerful institution in Russia, and energy ministers were influential persons in the formulation and realization of energy policy. It has responsibilities ranging from energy security to reducing dependence on imported technologies and services in the energy sector. It defines the list of "backbone" energy enterprises (currently 126 companies) in Russia that are major energy producers and receive large financial support from the government during external shocks including sanctions (Alifirova, 2022). But also, political support always continued to function from the state apparatus to energy companies in the 1990s and 2000s. Yelstin, Putin, and Medvedev directly lobbied for the main interests of Russian oil companies in the CIS, EU, and the Middle East region.

Primakov (2009) underlined that despite the corporate interests of the oil-gas companies in the CIS and EU markets, the energy policy is shaped by the Russian government, not state-owned or private oil-gas companies. But when energy companies' corporate interest is particularly overpowered in the energy conflicts, the country's political leadership intervenes (pp. 23–141). After 1991, Russia's government intended to avert any alternative oil-gas producer from the post-Soviet region to enter the European market bypassing Russia. But the USA desired to support constructing an entire pipeline system to supply Central Europe with oil and gas from the Caspian basin and Central Asian region, bypassing Russia. As a compromise based on technological and financial dependence, Lukoil and Gazprom started to operate in Kazakhstan, Turkmenistan, and on the shelf of the Caspian Sea competing with major Western oil and gas companies. Russian energy and foreign affairs ministers directly supported the energy companies in the CIS and other markets.

In 1998, there was a shift in the Russian government and management system from the oil-gas and energy sector to the secret services and the military-industrial complex. The first and the second prime ministers of Russia were representatives of the oil-gas sector and energy complex. The first Prime Minister Victor Chernomyrdin was Deputy Minister of the USSR Gas Industry in 1982 and he was Minister of Gas Industry of the USSR between 1985-and 1989. Chernomyrdin was the Chairman of the Management Board of the "Gazprom" State Gas Concern between 1989-and 1992. He was appointed firstly Deputy Chairman of the Government for the energy sector and then Prime Minister of Russia in 1992. The second prime minister of Russia – Sergey Kiriyenko (1998) – worked as the President of the "NORSI-OIL" Oil Company from 1991 to 1997. Kiriyenko was the First Deputy Minister and Minister of Fuel and Energy of Russia from 1997 to 1998. Another influential figure of the Yeltsin period – Boris Nemtsov held the post of Minister of Fuel and Energy of Russia in 1997. Following two prime ministers, Yevgeny Primakov (1998–1999) and Vladimir Putin (1999–2000) were representatives of the secret services and the military-industrial complex. First Deputy Prime Minister of Russia Yuri Maslyukov (1998–1999) was the former chairman of the State Military-Industrial Commission of the Cabinet of Ministers of the USSR (Kolesnikov, Gevorgyan, & Timakova, 2000).

Militarization and securitization in the state's administration system and policy mechanisms influenced the roles of the state-owned energy companies and their exploitation in foreign energy policy. The Ministry of Energy of Russia and the Ministry of Foreign Affairs of Russia started to develop foreign policy concepts and energy strategies with energy security and energy diplomacy dimensions to assist the state-owned and private energy companies in accessing energy resources and foreign markets in the mid-1990s.

5.5 Russia's Strategic Documents on Foreign and Energy Policy

Changes and permanence in Russia's foreign policy and its energy policy dimension are better reflected in the foreign policy concepts and other strategic documents. Those documents that specified the country's foreign policy goals and priorities also emphasized the energy factor as a foreign policy mean directly and indirectly starting from the Soviet Union's last years and continuing in the era of the Russian Federation. The energy factor had been accentuated for the cooperation and integration of Russia with the post-Soviet countries and the West after 1991. The first sentence of the "Agreement on the Creation of the Commonwealth of Independent States (CIS)" (December 8, 1991) stipulated that "*the USSR as a*

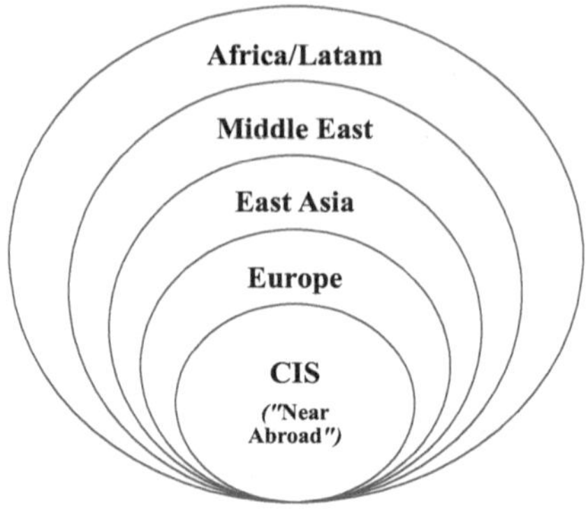

Figure 5.2 Regional priorities of Russia's foreign policy in the sequential concepts.
Source: Developed by the author based on foreign policy concepts of Russia.

subject of international law and geopolitical reality ceases to exist" (Consultant Plus, 2021). It also envisaged a "*refusal to use economic or any other methods of pressure*" that reflected the asymmetric power, including economic and energy resources among founding countries of CIS in favour of Russia (Figure 5.2).

Bobrov (2019) argued that Russian foreign policy concepts referred to CIS rather than "post-Soviet space", meaning geopolitical space and regional organization. CIS has historically been the most critical area of Russia's foreign policy. The CIS was mentioned as the regional priority in the foreign policy concepts (1993, 2000, 2008, 2013, 2016) (Bobrov, 2019). Russia's concepts and strategic documents identify two significant blocks of the aim of foreign policy: (a) security-based interests and (b) socio-economic development. The natural resources and energy industry is seen as a possible means and goal for the Russian state. In the context of the foreign policy concepts and other strategic documents, primary threats to Russian national interests and foreign policy are perceived as NATO's eastward enlargement towards Eastern Europe and the CIS region, and the disintegration of the relations with the CIS countries. Russia's foreign policy concepts and doctrines emphasize its aspirations multipolar/polycentric world order that should alter the US-led unipolarity. Emerging geographical interests of multidimensional Russian foreign policy are the Asia-Pacific area (as an alternative to the Transatlantic), BRICS, Latin America, Africa, and the Middle East. Güler and Teke (2021) argued that the Russian worldview about the end of the bipolar world order, the risks of the unipolar order for global stability, establishing a multipolar world order, regional integration, great power aspirations, and the power transition from the West to the East has constantly accompanied almost all foreign policy concepts of Russia from 1993 to 2016 (p. 27). Table 5.6 indicates the permanence of Russia's foreign policy goals.

Foreign policy concept of Russia (1993). President Yeltsin approved the "Concept of the Foreign Policy of Russia" in 1993. The main task of the concept was to establish Russia's (as a great power) stable positive relations with the countries

Table 5.6 Continuity in Russia's foreign policy aims

First Foreign Policy Concept (1993)	*Second Foreign Policy Concept (2000)*	*Third Foreign Policy Concept (2008)*	*Fourth Foreign Policy Concept (2013)*	*Fifth Foreign Policy Concept (2016)*
Sovereignty and territorial integrity	The great power status of Russia	Supremacy of international law	Polycentric international system	Polycentric international system
Independent role of Russia in the polycentric system	Multipolar structure of the international system	The great power status of Russia	Pragmatic foreign policy and "soft power"	Regional integration structures
		Multipolar structure of the international system	Interests of Russians abroad and relations with the CIS	

of the "near abroad" to overcome the destabilizing disintegration processes in the territory of the USSR (Russia Matters, 2021). The foreign policy concept of Russia (1993) openly stipulates that "*in the event of unilateral actions by other states of the 'near abroad', infringing on the interests of Russia, it will seek ways to protect its interests and the use of its response measures*" (Medvedev, 1993). These potential measures include energy power instruments, especially against the Baltic and Eastern European countries that the concept had already underlined. Russia aimed to retrieve relations with China and India. Business partnerships with Latin America had chances to take place in nuclear research, oil, and petrochemical industries. Russia's attitude to the Middle East region was determined primarily by its geostrategic and geopolitical significance, the role of the richest oil reserves available in the area for global energy, the presence of significant financial resources, territorial proximity to the borders of Russia with the CIS, which have the risks for the destabilization processes on the situation in the Caucasus and Central Asia. Russia had envisaged an energy partnership with the Gulf states to solve problems in the domestic energy sector.

President Yeltsin signed a decree "*On Approving the Strategic Course of Russia with the Member States of the Commonwealth of the Independent States*" in 1995. The document highlights that "the development of the CIS is in the vital interests of Russia, and relations with the CIS countries are an important factor in the inclusion of Russia into world political and economic structures" (Consultant Plus, 2005). The multidirectional interests of the CIS countries would be coordinated based on a balance of mutual compromises. "*Not harming the interests of Russia*" was confirmed as the principle of joint affairs. Mutually beneficial economic cooperation is a fundamental prerequisite for solving the entire range of relations with the CIS. The "*model of multi-speed integration*" has been proposed by Russia within the framework of the CIS as "*an important factor determining the scale of economic and military support from Russia*" (Kremlin, 1995). It means that Russia is not imposing its conditions on the CIS, but they should adopt Moscow's economic legislation and energy regulations.

Foreign policy concept of Russia (2000). The highest priority of the foreign policy of Russia due to the Foreign Policy Concept of Russia that was approved in 2000 by newly elected President Putin was to protect the interests of the state (Foreign Policy Concept of Russia, 2000). The foreign policy concept envisaged multipolar international order and visioned Russia as a great power and strategic balancer due to its geopolitical position as an immense Eurasian power. The geopolitical situation of Russia determines its multi-vectoral foreign (energy) policy towards Asia, Europe, and the Middle East. The top regional priority of Russia's foreign policy was the relations with the member states of the CIS that were linked to the country's national security objectives. The development of the relations with China and India was declared a foreign policy priority in Asia. The vital energy transit routes in the various regions were assessed as Russia's economic interests. Russia's foreign economic interests were described as resources for the foreign policy process. The concept describes foreign policy tools: political, diplomatic, military, economic (energy), and financial. Russia employs foreign economic policy instruments regarding the national interests and adequacy of the available means in terms of their actual contribution to reinforcing its global position and the complexity of foreign policy problems that target Russia's state sovereignty and economy. Russia will support and promote the interests of the state-owned and private energy and non-energy firms in foreign markets.

Foreign policy concept of Russia (2008). In 2008, President Dmitry Medvedev approved a new version of the "Foreign policy concept of Russia" (Foreign Policy Concept of Russia, 2008). The concept categorized Russia as "the largest Eurasian power" diagnosing that the West lost its globalization process monopoly. The development of relations with the CIS member states, China and India were priorities. In the 2008 foreign policy concept, priority was given to preserving the reputation of Russia as a responsible partner in the energy markets, ensuring the sustainable development of its economy at the expense of energy resources, and promoting the balance of world energy markets. The document also mentions for the first time "*energy security*" and notes that Russia uses all the economic levers and resources at its disposal to protect its national interests. The concept envisages ensuring equal positions for Russia and its companies in world economic relations. But also underlines that Russia achieves maximum benefits and minimizes risks with further integration into the world economy, considering the need to ensure the country's economic and energy security. Russia continues to build capacity and modernize the energy sector, confirming its reputation as a responsible partner in the energy markets and contributing to the balance of world energy markets. Russia strengthens strategic partnerships with leading energy producers and actively develops a dialogue with consumers and transit countries on energy security. Countermeasures must consistently support energy supplies to ensure demand stability and transit reliability.

Fundamentals of the state policy of Russia in the Arctic for the period up to 2020 were enacted by President in 2008. The leading national interests of Russia in the Arctic are (a) the use of the Arctic zone of Russia as a strategic resource base of the country, ensuring the solution of the tasks of socio-economic development of the country; (b) the use of the Northern Sea Route as the national unified transport route of Russia in the Arctic. Priorities were the development of the continental shelf and the oil-gas fields in the Arctic. The document strongly emphasizes the securitization of the region and militarization of energy policy: "*creating troops of the Armed Forces, military formations and border agencies in the Arctic zone of Russia, capable of ensuring military security in various conditions of the military-political situation*" (Council of Security, 2008). The foreign policy envisaged developing a beneficial energy partnership via the single energy system in Europe, achieving compliance with existing bilateral and multilateral contractual obligations in the energy sector (Kremlin, 2012).

Foreign policy concept of Russia (2013). The foreign policy concept of Russia that was adopted in 2013 (Foreign Policy Concept of Russia, 2013) anticipated strengthening the trade and economic positions of Russia in the system of world economic relations, diplomatic support for the interests of domestic economic actors (including energy companies) abroad, non-discrimination of Russian goods and investments, using the capabilities of international and regional economic and financial organizations for these purposes. The state aids energy companies in the development of new markets. Russia strengthens strategic partnerships with leading producers of energy resources, and actively develops a dialogue with consumer and transit countries since measures to guarantee energy supplies reliability should be supported by countermeasures to ensure the demand stability and reliability of transit. The use of innovative technologies (dependence) to extract hard-to-recover fossil reserves ensures transformations in the energy sector. Major hypotheses and prepositions of all foreign policy concepts of Russia didn't change since 1993. All concepts propose that using political and diplomatic, legal, military, economic, and financial instruments in solving foreign policy tasks should be proportionate to their real significance for ensuring Russia's foreign policy interests.

Foreign Policy Concept of Russia (2016) emphasized the formation of a polycentric global system (shift to the Asia-Pacific and declining Western powers), the complex international relations structure, and emerging new economic and political influence centres (Ministry of Foreign Affairs of Russia, 2016). The priorities of Russia's foreign policy in the energy-related fields were a diplomatic contribution to energy security, eliminating restrictions in world energy markets, the peaceful use of nuclear energy and strategic stability, access to advanced energy technologies, cooperation with leading producers of energy resources, energy consumer, and transit countries, ensuring the stable supply of energy resources. Russia aims to achieve geopolitical conditions for diversifying the energy resources in world markets by expanding the energy exports and the geography of foreign economic and investment ties, including the energy sector. Russia's foreign energy policy combines geopolitical, economic, military, and even demographic elements partly reflected in the country's foreign policy concepts (Table 5.7).

Russia's foreign energy policy and energy strategies. The Russian energy strategies define the main directions of energy policy, the goals, priorities, and mechanisms for the policy implementation. "*Energy Strategy of Russia for 2010*", as a fundamental and first energy concept, adopted in 1995 by the President, stipulated that the development of the energy sector would be built on two crucial elements:

Table 5.7 Russia's foreign policy concepts and energy factor

	1993	*2000*	*2008*	*2013*
Self-perception of Russia	Normal (European) power	Great power with strategic interests; Eurasian power	One of the influential centres in the modern world; the largest Eurasian power	One of the most influential and competitive poles of the modern world
Foreign policy direction	West	Multi-vector and specific path	Balanced and multi-vector	Eurasia
Relations with Asia	Formal approach	Russia's geographical proximity to the Asian region and the development of the Far East and Siberia regions.	Russia's geographical proximity to the Asian region and the development of the Far East and Siberia regions.	The global power shift towards Asia as a strategic and geopolitical zone; the development of the Far East, Siberia regions.
Role of the economic factor in foreign policy	Formal approach	Russia can utilize available economic resources for national interests	Economic interdependence is crucial to international stability and the use of all available economic tools and financial resources for foreign policy.	To determine the global agenda in energy security; diversify Russia's presence in global energy markets; to secure the transit status of Russia.
Energy as an economic power	Not mentioned	Energy export routes as an economic interest	Reliable partner in the energy market; contributing to the balanced world energy market; strategic cooperation with other energy producers; cooperation with transit and consuming countries based on energy security.	Shale revolution; increased and unfair competition; market diversification.

Sources: Lomagin (2015, pp. 16–18) and Kremlin.ru.

an increase in the export of natural gas and energy conservation (Podlipsky, 1995). "*The Energy Strategy of Russia until 2020*" (2000) fixed the following priorities of Russia's foreign energy policy: diversification of energy exports, optimization of export's commodity structure, the improvement of oil-gas infrastructure in the East Siberia, and increase in energy exports to the Asia-Pacific region countries.

Table 5.8 Changes in Russia's energy strategies

"Russia's energy strategy for the period up to 2020" (2003)	*"Russia's energy strategy for the period up to 2030" (2009)*	*"Russia's energy strategy for the period up to 2035" (2017)*	*"Doctrine of the Energy Security of Russia" (13/05/2019)*
"Russia has significant energy resources and a powerful fuel and energy complex, which is the basis of economic development, an instrument of domestic and foreign policy".	"The goal of Russia's energy policy is to maximize the efficient use of energy resources and the potential of the energy sector to sustain growth and strengthen foreign economic position".	"The fuel and energy complex of Russia makes a significant contribution to the national security and socio-economic development of the country".	"The significant contribution of the energy system to the national security with foreign economic and foreign policy threats to the Russian energy security".

Source: Ministry of Energy of Russia (2019, 2020a,b).

The same provisions were consistently reflected in the Energy Strategy until 2020 (2003), Energy Strategy until 2030 (2009), and Energy Strategy until 2035 (2020). If we compare the main definitions of the energy strategies and doctrine from 2003 to 2019, we can observe increasing "*securitization*" and constant emphasis on the foreign policy domain (Table 5.8).

"*Russia's energy strategy for the period up to 2020*" approved by the government of Russia in 2003, endorsed the goals and priorities of energy Russia's strategies for the period till 2020. The first sentence of the document links the Russian energy sector and energy infrastructure system with its foreign policy:

> *"Russia has significant reserves of energy resources and a powerful fuel and energy complex, which is the basis of economic development, an instrument of domestic and foreign policy. The country's role in world energy markets largely determines its geopolitical influence".*
>
> (Institute of Energy Security, 2003, p. 4)

The concept explains energy security as a set of measures against external factors such as geopolitical and macroeconomic (Ershov, 2004). It states that an essential component of the external conditions for the development of Russia is the solution to the problem of forming a unified energy and transportation infrastructure in the adjacent regions of Europe and Asia, the development of international energy transportation systems, and non-discriminatory energy transit (Institute of Energy Security, 2003, pp. 12–13). The updated energy strategy – "*Russia's energy strategy for the period up to 2030*" approved by the government of Russia in 2009, softens the link between energy and foreign policy underlying that

> *"the goal of Russia's energy policy is to maximize the efficient use of energy resources and the potential of the energy sector to sustain economic growth,*

> *improve the life quality of the population and help strengthen its foreign economic position".*
>
> (CenterPolit, 2020)

"*The energy security doctrine of Russia*" that was approved in 2019 by President Putin envisaged the challenges, threats, and risks of energy security in Russia under the context of the changes that have taken place in the international situation and domestic policy (Ministry of Energy of Russia, 2019). The doctrine defined "*energy security*" as the state of protection of the economy and the country's population from threats to national security in the energy sector. The energy industry contributes to the country's national security and socio-economic development. The energy sector of Russia includes oil, gas, and coal industries, electricity, and heat supply that play a crucial role in generating fiscal revenues. External economic challenges to energy security are relocating the centre of world economic growth to the Asia-Pacific region and increasing the share of renewable energy in the world energy balance. The technological independence in the energy industry, supporting the export of energy resources and the position of the interests of Russian companies. The doctrine considers "illegal seizure" (e.g., by Ukraine) of energy resources exported by Russia during their transportation through the territories of foreign states as foreign economic and foreign policy threats to energy security (Ministry of Energy of Russia, 2019).

"*Energy Strategy of Russia for the Period up to 2035*" (2020) proposed that

> *"the foreign policy of Russia in the field of energy is aimed at strengthening the country's position as one of the leaders in the world energy market, reducing risks and increasing the efficiency of foreign economic activity of Russian energy companies".*
>
> (Ministry of Energy of Russia, 2020b)

Russia aims to become a leading player in the Asia-Pacific markets via the spatial distribution of the energy infrastructure and oil-gas resources in East Siberia, the Far East, and the Arctic zone. The main priority of the state energy policy of Russia is a provision of energy security for the country and the constituent entities that locate in geostrategic territories.

Annual Messages of the President to the Federal Assembly of Russia. Russian President's annual messages to the Federal Assembly convey important communication and contain crucial details on the Russian foreign and energy policy. Messages underlined that military power is the guarantor of Russian statehood, but economic self-sufficiency based on the energy factor is also an essential factor. President Yeltsin sent the official "*Message of the President of Russia to the Federal Assembly*" as the first strategic document on the Russian state's leading domestic and foreign policy directions in 1994 (Message of the President, 1994). The message declared natural foreign policy allies of Russia without any mention of foreign energy policy. Russia's position in the world order is determined by preserving its status as a world nuclear power, but the state should maintain the modernization of strategic nuclear forces.

"*Message of the President of Russia to the Federal Assembly*" in 1995 pointed out that Russia's antitrust policy targeted government regulation of markets dominated by natural monopolies, including electricity and pipeline transport. Russia's disrupted energy and metal exports were described as an economic violation. The growing insolvency of the CIS states was concerning Russia, especially for energy supplies in 1995 (Message of the President, 1995). *The message of the President of Russia to the Federal Assembly in 1996* argued that Russia's position in the world has been determined by its power components: geographic scale and population, *natural resources (mainly oil and gas)*, and military strength (Message of the President, 1996). *The message of the President of Russia to the Federal Assembly in 1997* affirmed that control over natural monopolies, primarily in such sectors as the electric power and the gas industry, was a fundamental problem of state regulation of the economy. Russia's strategic partnership with China, India, and other ASEAN countries was prioritized in the multipolar world (Message of the President, 1997).

The message of the President of Russia to the Federal Assembly in 1998 argued that the Asian direction of foreign policy is an example of the practical implementation of the thesis about the unique role of Russia as a Eurasian power. The main task was to ensure favourable external conditions, including the global energy market environment for economic growth. Russia abandoned government procurement of crude oil and liquidated the system of special oil exporters. A unique role in overcoming energy debts or non-payments belongs to large production systems – "RAO UES" and Gazprom. The concept proposed that the Russian foreign policy should be "economized" for increasing the effectiveness of entire Russian diplomacy (the promotion of Russia's products on the world markets) (Message of the President, 1998).

The message of the President of Russia to the Federal Assembly in 1999 argued that Russia's foreign policy priority remained relations with the CIS that was based on long-term national interests. Russia has vital interests in the Transcaucasus in terms of *energy security*. Russia's strategic mission is to integrate not as a raw material or energy appendage into the world economy but as an advanced country with a high technological level. Russia's specialization in the production and export of raw materials, including oil-gas resources, intensified in the mid-1990s. This was causing the country significant losses due to the fall in global demand and prices for raw materials and energy resources. Criminal groups could influence the situation in entire regions and sectors of the economy, including the fuel and energy complex. Russian diplomacy should support business globally through participation in promising international projects, including energy projects (Message of the President, 1999). In his annual "*Message to the Federal Assembly of Russia*" in 2000, the newly elected President Putin stated that the basis of independent foreign policy is pragmatism, economic efficiency, and the priority of national objectives. The foreign policy concept of the Putin era (2000) recognized the importance of internal goals over external ones. The raw material orientation of the economy remained, and the budget revenues largely depended on the dynamics of energy prices (Message of the President, 2000).

Message to the Federal Assembly of Russia in 2001 argued that "*foreign policy is both an indicator and an essential factor in the state of domestic affairs*". Russia's economic system has changed very little and is based on oil, gas, metals, and other raw materials. The foreign policy should protect the economic interests of the Russian state and enterprises abroad (Message of the President, 2001). *Message to the Federal Assembly of Russia in 2002* argued that Russian foreign policy continued to be built purely pragmatically, matching capabilities and interests: military-strategic, economic, and political. Russia had many opportunities to implement large-scale joint infrastructure and energy projects in CIS countries. Russia was back to second place in the world in terms of oil production and first place in the world in energy trade in 2002 (Message of the President, 2002). *Message to the Federal Assembly of Russia in 2003* emphasized that the exports of crude oil, petroleum products, and gas increased in 2002–2003, and Russia was the largest exporter of fuel and energy resources globally (Message of the President, 2003). The unifying economic processes taking place in the CIS were associated with the integration of Russia into the world economy dynamically.

Message to the Federal Assembly of Russia in 2004 argued that the Russian Foreign Ministry and the government need to find more effective ways to increase Russian exports and reliably protect the interests of Russian companies abroad. Economic growth based on oil-gas sales affected the international position of Russia. Russia should use foreign policy instruments to implement the most critical national tasks for a more tangible practical return in the economy including the energy sector. The deterioration and low density of the oil pipelines, gas transportation system, and electric power infrastructure impose severe restrictions on the development of the entire Russian economy. Russia implemented a series of energy projects diversifying crude oil supplies via expanding the throughput of the Baltic pipeline system, putting into operation the Western Siberia–Barents Sea oil pipelines, determining routes from the fields in Eastern Siberia, bypassing the Bosporus and Dardanelles straits, and integrating the Druzhba and Adria oil pipelines. Russia developed the gas distribution network that would allow diversifying export flows by directly linking the networks of Russia and the Baltic states with the EU-oriented gas infrastructure (the construction of the North European Gas Pipeline) (Message of the President, 2004). *Message to the Federal Assembly of Russia in 2005* argued that Russia is interested in "synchronizing the pace and parameters of reform processes" in Russia and the CIS states. The energy infrastructures in the strategically important regions of Russia, such as the Far East, Kaliningrad, and border areas, become pivotal in Russia's cooperation with its neighbours (Message of the President, 2005).

Message to the Federal Assembly of Russia in 2006 contained parallel information on nuclear weapons and nuclear energy. Russian state strengthens its position in the world markets of nuclear engineering and the latest technologies such as reactors for atomic energy generation. The efficiency of energy use in Russia is lower than that of the country's direct competitors in world markets. Russia can play a positive role in shaping a common EU energy strategy and a stable position in the energy markets for the long term. Gazprom has come to third place in the world in terms of capitalization among the largest corporations in the world while maintaining low tariffs for Russian consumers (Message of the President, 2006). *Message to the Federal Assembly of Russia in 2007* argued that Russia ranked first in oil production globally, but Russia was significantly lagging in oil refining. Accumulated oil-gas revenues strengthened Russia's energy power. Russia couldn't form technological potential adequate to the modern challenges of world technological development. Significant changes are required in the structure of power generation – by increasing the share of atomic, coal, and hydroelectric power generation. Russia has enormous hydro resources and uses less than 20% of its potential, while other developed countries use 70%–80%. Putin proposed that it was necessary to start the construction of large hydroelectric power plants and nuclear energy blocks based on the most modern technologies. The economy is synonymous with state security, including protecting borders (Message of the President, 2007).

President's Message to the Federal Assembly of Russia in 2008 pointed out the importance to intensify actions in foreign economic policy to avert the self-isolation of Russia, and it promoted the process of integration into the global economy. The regional priorities were overlapping with foreign policy concepts such as Eurasian Economic Union, CIS, the EU, China, India, Japan, major Asian partners, Latin America, and even Africa (Message of the President, 2008). *President's Message to the Federal Assembly of Russia in 2009* underlined that Russia's crucial resources that formulate its great power, including oil-gas resources, nuclear weapons, and binding energy and transport infrastructure that remained from the Soviet time, become morally and physically obsolete. Chronic backwardness, dependence on raw materials exports, lack of innovations, and misconducts were featured as serious challenges. Russia couldn't innovate in traditional energy to increase the extraction of minerals and alternative energy, leading to inefficient energy resources. Russia's foreign policy must be highly pragmatic because of the economic backwardness strengthening multipolarity. Russia's foreign policy is developed due to the complex interaction of various social groups. President argued that foreign policy and active diplomacy should focus on economic interests, supporting the Russian companies abroad, attracting foreign investments and the high-techs to address the challenges of modernization and technological breakthrough in the energy sector (Message of the President, 2009).

President's Message to the Federal Assembly of Russia in 2010 linked Russia's foreign energy policy with militarism. A common economic area throughout Eurasia from the Arctic to the Asia-Pacific based on modern integration schemes and concepts of economic cooperation was proclaimed as Russia's strategy (Message of the President, 2010). *President's Message to the Federal Assembly of Russia in 2012* underlined that competition for resources (metals, oil, gas, and human resources) and geopolitical conflicts with economic and ethnic characters accelerated. Resource-rich Siberia and the Far East which have a geographical approximation to the Asian-Pacific market, are drivers of Russia's economic development (Message of the President, 2012). *President's Message to the Federal Assembly of Russia in 2013* underlined that Russia's pivot to the Asia-Pacific region that could drive the dynamic development of the Eastern territories would open new opportunities for the economy and provide additional tools for pursuing an active foreign energy policy. Putin reiterated that the Eurasian integration is based on real economic interests, and Russia will consistently advance in the process (Message of the President, 2013).

In the President's Message to the Federal Assembly in 2014, the import substitution, efforts on decreasing the critical dependence on foreign technologies and industrial products, and the increasing role of domestic raw material and energy companies were emphasized as a reaction to the sanctions and external restrictions. External circumstances defined Russia's self-isolation efforts after 2014, and it was believed that large projects on the development of oil-gas deposits in the Arctic shelf could boost demand for domestic manufacturer's products (Message of the President, 2014). *President's Message to the Federal Assembly of Russia in 2015* argued that external restrictions for Russia, such as low prices for raw materials, will last for a long time (Message of the President, 2015). The economic growth rate based on natural resources could fluctuate around zero. Russia and China reached an agreement on combining, synchronizing, and harmonizing the Eurasian integration in the example of the Eurasian Economic Union (EEU) with the Chinese initiative for the Silk Road or "Economic Belt" in 2015.

President's Message to the Federal Assembly of Russia in 2016 argued that Russia's idea is to form a multi-level integration model in Eurasia or an extensive Eurasian partnership. Large-scale energy projects are the strategic dimension of bilateral relations with India, China, and even Japan (Message of the President, 2016). *President's Message to the Federal Assembly of Russia in 2018* argued that the EEU will have a common market for electricity, crude oil, oil products, and gas by harmonizing and integrating markets to create a sizeable Eurasian partnership (Message of the President, 2018). Several large-scale industrial, transport, nuclear, energy, and military infrastructure projects were implemented in the Arctic as a strategically crucial region.

In the President's Message to the Federal Assembly of Russia in 2019, Putin emphasized economic cooperation as one of the priorities of foreign policy (Message of the President, 2019). Russia's mutually beneficial relations with China serve as an essential stabilizing factor in global affairs, ensuring security in Eurasia in terms of economic cooperation. European large and medium-sized companies are interested in economic and energy cooperation with Russia. The EU's politicians have divergent views on Russia and the USA deploys long-range missiles closer to the Russian border. *President's Message to the Federal Assembly of Russia in 2020* argued that Russia envisages that the five nuclear powers that are the UNSC permanent members bear a special responsibility for global ("hegemonic") stability and international political, economic, and military affairs ("*conservative vision for global order preservation ignoring changes and emerging powers*") (Message of the President, 2020). *President's Message to the Federal Assembly of Russia in 2021* argued that Russia needs to implement new initiatives in nuclear generation, hydrogen energy, and energy storage (Message of the President, 2021). Russia targeted to decrease the accumulated volume of net greenhouse gas emissions in the country less than in the EU. Russia's foreign policy priorities that are determined in the foreign policy concepts, energy strategies, and annual Presidential messages specify the dimensions and objectives of the country's foreign energy policy and patterns of the energy conflicts.

Notes

1 The prominent Putin-era Energy Minister Alexander Novak (2012–2020) has never dealt with the internal activities of energy companies but has dealt chiefly with global energy networks (e.g., "OPEC+").

2 $HHI = S_1^2 + S_2^2 + \ldots + S_n^2$; HHI is the Herfindahl-Hirschman Index; S_1 is the share of the largest enterprise; S_2 is the share of the next largest enterprise; S_n is the specific gravity of the smallest enterprise (the greater result of the index means higher monopolization and concentration).

6 Russia's Energy Conflicts and Supply Interruptions Dataset (RECSID)

6.1 Analysis of RECSID's Main Findings on Energy Conflicts in Russia

Studies indicated the instrumentalization of Russian energy resources for the foreign policy objectives. But "Russia's Energy Conflicts and Supply Interruptions Dataset" (RECSID) that will be presented in this chapter was developed as a complex dataset that contributes to understanding the clear link between Russia's energy conflicts (supply interruption cases), the interdependence pattern in the country's foreign energy policy and foreign policy goals. RECSID identified 813 energy conflicts and supply interruptions cases that Russia was directly involved from 1990 to 2021. These conflicts covered all types of energy including natural gas, crude oil, oil products, nuclear, electricity, and coal. RECSID disclosed that Russia used not only natural gas but also oil, nuclear energy, coal, and electricity for political purposes.

However, 64% of the total number of Russia's foreign energy conflicts and supply interruptions were solely related to natural gas (523 cases). About 21% of the total number of Russia's foreign energy conflicts and supply interruptions were related to crude oil and oil products (167 cases). About 6% of the total number of Russia's foreign energy conflicts and supply interruptions were related to nuclear energy (47 cases). About 5% of the total number of Russia's foreign energy conflicts and supply interruptions were compound conflicts with oil, gas, nuclear, and electricity components (40 cases). About 4% of the total number of Russia's foreign energy conflicts and supply interruptions were related to electricity (31 cases). Finally, 0.6% of the total number of Russia's foreign energy conflicts and supply interruptions were related to coal (five cases).

Natural gas that could cause a higher level of asymmetric interdependence is more prone to conflictual use by the Kremlin rather than other energy types such as oil or nuclear. RECSID findings conclude that natural gas is a geopolitical tool for Russia and crude oil is also "weaponized", but not on the same level as natural gas. One of the reasons is the perception in the Russian decision-makers that their crude oil has alternatives in the regional and global markets shaping more symmetrical interdependence, but in the case of natural gas, Russia has monopolistic dominance at least in the European and CIS markets.

DOI: 10.4324/9781003408482-6

Geographical distribution of Russia's energy conflicts. The study breaks up the geographical distribution of Russia's energy conflicts in alignment with foreign policy goals and trade interdependence. RECSID revealed that Russia had a higher number of energy conflicts with neighbouring post-Soviet countries and some large trade partners (despite the existing trade interdependence). One-third of Russia's foreign energy conflicts and supply interruptions (32%) were experienced with only four post-Soviet neighbouring countries – Ukraine (124 cases), Belarus (53 cases), Lithuania (43 cases), and Azerbaijan (39 cases). Russia had more energy conflicts with the former USSR countries that had deeper antagonistic political affairs such as Ukraine, Belarus, Lithuania, Azerbaijan, Georgia, Armenia, Moldova, Turkmenistan, Latvia, Kazakhstan, and Estonia. Russia had fewer (almost none) energy conflicts with the post-Soviet countries in the Central Asian region that hadn't a direct border with the country including Kyrgyzstan, Uzbekistan, and Tajikistan. There is a negative correlation between the distance from Russia to the target country and the number of the country's foreign energy conflicts and supply interruption cases (–0.13) (Table 6.1).

RECSID identified that Russia had 320 energy conflicts and supply interruption cases with the Commonwealth of Independent States (CIS) countries that accounted for 42% of total energy conflicts. Russia had 290 energy conflicts and supply interruption cases with the EU as a collective institution and its member countries that accounted for 38% of total energy conflicts. Russia had 60 energy conflicts and supply interruption cases with non-EU countries of the wider European region which accounted for 8% of total energy conflicts. Russia continued to renter to the continuous energy conflicts with the same post-Soviet and EU countries over and over in the 1990s and 2000s for various reasons and motivations using almost identical tools but with some evolution (Figure 6.1).

Russia had 57 energy conflicts and supply interruption cases with Asian, African, and MENA countries that accounted for 7% of total energy conflicts. *Asian energy partners have had fewer energy conflicts with Russia than European energy partners*. Russia had the same number of energy conflicts as China and the USA – 31 conflicts per country. Russia had 32 energy conflicts and supply interruption cases with the USA (31 cases) and Cuba (1 case) which accounted for 4% of total energy conflicts.

The remaining 1% of the total energy conflicts of Russia took place with international organizations such as OPEC and unrecognized "quasi-states". RECSID displayed that Russia had energy conflicts not only with legitimate nation-states but also with the unrecognized "quasi-states" or separatist units such as Transnistria (Moldova) and South Ossetia (Georgia). The separatist political regime (de-facto controlled by Russia) in the South Ossetia region of Georgia had an energy conflict with Gazprom in August 2009 (the first anniversary of Russia's recognition of the "independence of South Ossetia") over the construction of the gas pipeline from North Ossetia (Russia) and South Ossetia (Georgia). "Prime Minister" of the separatist South Ossetian political regime Vadim Brovtsev argued that "Gazprom is engaged not in the economic, but political project". Gazprom indirectly approved that the project on gas provision to South Ossetia could not be commercial in terms

Table 6.1 Russia's energy conflicts and supply interruptions by countries

Country	*Number*	*Country*	*Number*
Ukraine	124	CIS	4
Belarus	53	Transnistria (Moldova)	4
EU	53	Bosnia & Herzegovina	3
Lithuania	43	Croatia	3
USA	41	Kyrgyzstan	3
Azerbaijan	39	Netherlands	3
Poland	36	Norway	3
China	32	Sweden	3
Bulgaria	32	Uzbekistan	3
Turkey	28	Canada	2
Georgia	27	Slovenia	2
Armenia	22	South Korea	2
Moldova	21	Vietnam	2
Turkmenistan	20	Albania	1
Germany	19	Algeria	1
Hungary	17	Baltic states	1
Latvia	13	Central Europe	1
Kazakhstan	12	Cuba	1
Czech Republic	11	Denmark	1
Italy	11	Egypt	1
Slovakia	11	India	1
France	10	Israel	1
Estonia	9	Japan	1
Serbia	9	Jordan	1
Iran	8	Macedonia	1
Greece	7	Mongolia	1
Romania	7	Montenegro	1
UK	7	OPEC	1
Yugoslavia	7	Qatar	1
Austria	6	South Africa	1
Finland	6	South Ossetia (Georgia)	1
Iraq	5	Tajikistan	1

Source: RECSID.

of profitability (South Ossetia demanded Gazprom a lower gas price than for the gas exported to Georgia), but it was a political issue for Gazprom that led to the withholding (Allenova, 2009).

Russia had only one conflictual case with non-traditional countries with long distances from the country such as Albania, Algeria, Cuba, Denmark, Egypt, India, Israel, Japan, Jordan, Macedonia, Mongolia, Montenegro, Qatar, and South Africa. Russia had 52 energy conflicts towards not a single country, but regions demonstrating collective action such as the EU, CIS, Baltic region, and Central Europe. Russia also experienced an energy conflict with OPEC in 2002 when higher oil prices motivated Russia to raise oil export and Russia refused to cut oil production as an OPEC deal (Figure 6.2).

Timeframe of energy conflicts and power concentration in the energy sector. Unlike similar studies on the Russian energy conflicts that mostly concentrated

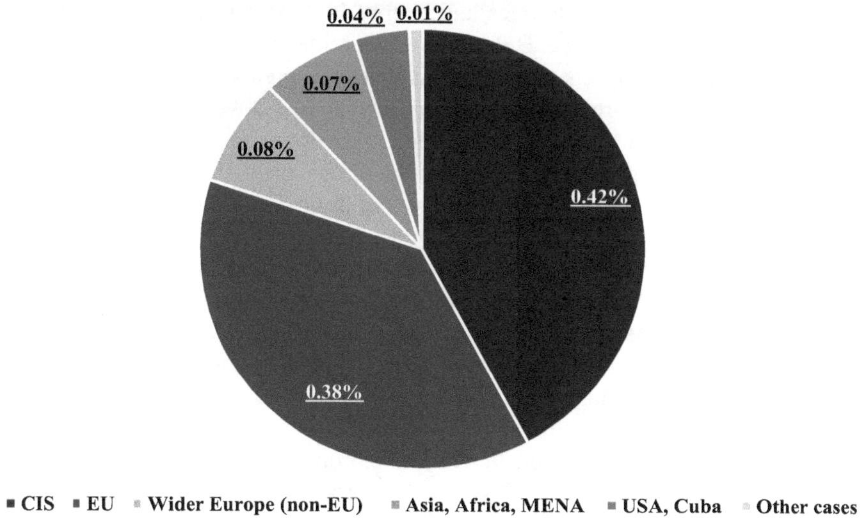

Figure 6.1 Geographical distribution of Russia's energy conflicts.
Source: RECSID.

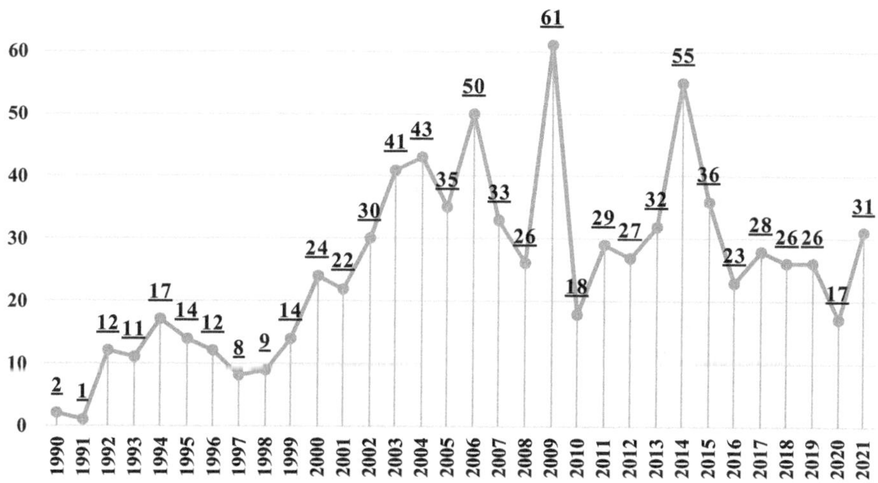

Figure 6.2 Number of Russia's energy conflicts and supply interruptions by years.
Source: RECSID.

on the ruling period of President Putin after 2000, RECSID covers the pre-Putin period between 1990 and 1999, as well. RECSID identified that 14% of all foreign energy conflicts and supply interruptions in Russia happened between 1990 and 1999. About 86% of all foreign energy conflicts and supply interruptions in Russia happened between 2000 and 2021 which could be named "Putin's ruling era".

Russia reinvented energy resources and energy infrastructure as a domestic and foreign policy tools after 2000. But RECSID identified the evidence of time overlaps between energy conflicts and geopolitical developments before 2000. RECSID identified that some gas-related energy conflicts in Russia were inherited from the USSR period. For example, the USSR-Greece gas supply agreement was signed in 1987. Greece could not realize the gas supply agreement with Russia in 1992, and it did not expand its infrastructure to receive natural gas.

RECSID includes the fact of the total stop of gas and oil supply to Lithuania in April 1990 as the first case of Russia's energy conflicts. Lithuania's independence movement caused the energy blockade by Moscow as economic and political pressure. As a result of the energy supply disruption, Lithuania's legislature decided to retreat from the independence act temporarily. Even though the conflict took place in 1990 when the independent Russian Federation didn't exist yet formally, it very well indicates the attitudes of the political elites of Moscow towards the political use of the energy factor. In 1991, Gazprom was not allowed to purchase Eastern German gas distributor VNG, and Gazprom's rival company Ruhrgas got control over the gas distributor company. Russia continued to use the oil-gas supply disruption for the destabilization of the Lithuanian economy and the Estonian economy in January 1992. As a result of the total stop of natural gas, crude oil, and oil product deliveries by Russia, Lithuania threatened Russia with the economic blockade of the Kaliningrad exclave, and Estonia had a negative perception of Russia. Also, Russia warned to stop the gas supply to Lithuania in 1992 to position Russian troops on the territory of Lithuania.

A gas pipeline explosion occurred in North Ossetia, as a result, the natural gas supply stopped to Armenia in 1992. Armenia demanded damage compensation from Russia for supply cessation. Russia halted the natural gas supply to Ukraine for the accumulated gas debt and payment currency (Ruble vs. USD) problems in 1992. Russia halted deliveries of natural gas to Estonia which was dependent on Russia for gas supply in June 1993; the main reason was the "discriminatory policies" allegedly towards ethnic Russians living in Estonia. The peak year of the Russian energy conflicts before Putin's ruling period was 1994 when Russia had natural gas, crude oil, and even nuclear energy conflicts with Ukraine, Azerbaijan, Moldova, Armenia, Belarus, Bulgaria, Kazakhstan, and Turkey. These facts represent the pattern that continued after the independence of the Russian Federation: (i) using oil-gas supply for political purposes and (ii) the deep apprehension in the foreign energy partner countries and companies on Russia's conflictual behaviour in the foreign energy policy.

The number of foreign energy conflicts and supply interruptions in Russia started to increase from the "bottom ground" in 1998–1999 reaching the first peak in 2000 with 24 energy conflicts and supply interruptions. The average number of energy conflicts and supply interruptions in the pre-Putin period (1990–1999) was 10, and the average number of energy conflicts and supply interruptions under Putin's rule (2000–2021) was 33. There are some evident examples of the energy conflicts of Putin's ruling period with political motives. Russia-Belarus negotiations on the Union State were in political deadlock in January 2007 when Belarus

President Lukashenko claimed Russia infringe sovereignty and independence of his country. Russia stopped the oil flows via the Druzhba pipeline, interrupting supplies to the EU states in January 2007. A sudden reduction of oil supply by 40% (from 0.5 million tons to 0.3 tons of crude oil) to the Czech Republic in July 2008 when Prague signed an agreement to station the USA's radar system against ballistic missiles on its territory was a very clear example on the "energy weapon" applied by Russia (Fabrichnaya, 2008). Socor (2008) argued that Putin gave an instruction to Russia's Ministry of Energy to restart crude oil supply to the Czech Republic in 2008, demonstrating the politicization of supply disruption.

The interruption of gas supplies to Yugoslavia by Gazprom with the political motivation of the Russian government at the end of September 2000, synchronous with the presidential election on 24 September 2000 in Yugoslavia resulted in the downfall of the long-run regime of Slobodan Milosevic and the new government of Vojislav Kostunica (Vedomosti, 2000). Gazprom stopped the natural gas supply to Serbia in 2014 for gas debt in parallel to the bilateral political negotiations. We can sum up that Putin's ruling era was more conflictual than Yeltsin's period in terms of energy conflicts and "energy weaponizing". But turning points started before Putin's ruling period in terms of energy conflicts, foreign policy, and even domestic politics. There are several prepositions about the turning points in pre-Putin and post-Putin periods such as 1993, 1998–1999, 2004, and 2007. But in both periods there were real cases and attempts to use energy resources as a political tool based on RECSID findings.

There is room to apply "weak signals" and "early warning systems" in the Russian energy conflicts based on the time dimension. We could attempt to use energy conflicts and supply disruption cases to predict future major ruptures through the concentration of data and early warning mechanisms. The theory of "*weak signals*" was firstly presented by Igor H. Ansoff (1975) envisaging the detecting of "early warning" signs on "surprises and discontinuities" of an uncertain domestic and foreign environment. He argued that "information noise" prevents governance systems to identify weak signals that come before "surprises and discontinuities" leading to the lack of effective strategic decision-making on trajectories of future events. As a result, improbable conditions and situations or "black swans" (Taleb, 2007) emerge suddenly. "Weak signals" of the "early warning systems" can also vary following the size, visibility, the level and likelihood of impact, and capacity of conjecturable aftereffects.

We can apply Ansoff's "weak signals" theory to the identification of the early warning impulses on Russia's energy conflicts with major partner countries, companies, and institutions based on RECSID. Also, "weak signals" could be the self-explanatory approach for the predictability of Russian foreign energy policy behaviour. Major components of "weak signals" in the Russian energy conflicts could be the content of the weak signal, size of the weak signal, objective and subjective visibility of the weak signal, the current impact of the weak signal, and future impact of the weak signal. Table 6.2 demonstrates examples of the major components of "weak signals" in Russia's energy conflicts and foreign energy policy.

Table 6.2 Components of "weak signals" in the Russian energy conflicts

Components of "weak signals"	*Examples from RECSID*
Content of the signal	Energy supply disruptions, failed energy negotiations, the change in energy price or volume of energy trade
Size of the signal	Duration of the energy conflict, quantities related to supply disruptions, threats of interruption, price rise, or volume drop
Visibility of the signal	Appearances and visibility in media, the reactions of officials and experts from target, resource-holder, and transit country
The current impact of the signal	Current consequences of energy supply disruptions or the change of pricing formula for the economies of target countries
Future impact of the signal	Future consequences of energy supply disruptions or the change of pricing formula for the economies of target countries

Sources: Ansoff (1975) and RECSID.

The major peak periods of foreign energy conflicts and supply interruptions of Russia were 2004, 2006, 2009, and 2014 which overlapped with the Russia-West geopolitical collision over the post-Soviet countries. There was an "earthquake effect" of the Russian energy conflicts meaning that major conflicts erupted in certain years (e.g., 2004, 2006, 2009, 2014), but those were followed by a series of "aftershocks" concerning energy partners. "Aftershocks" meant counter policy measures by partner countries' governments and companies to adjust their energy policies against Russia's energy supply. Also, before the "earthquake" year there were a series of "early warning (weak) signals" meaning pioneer energy conflicts (e.g., 2003 before 2004, and 2013 before 2014) that could be used to predict upcoming major energy-related collisions. But this kind of prediction requires additional case studies and qualitative analysis.

Scheme-6 shows the sequence of "weak signals" emerging in the Russian energy conflicts. The "weak signals" of energy conflicts depend on the environment of Russian foreign energy policy (political, economic, commercial, technological, social, and environmental). The interpretation of "weak signals" by decision-makers and experts enables the future trajectory of Russian foreign energy policy in terms of the size of impact, the scope of the conflict, timing of the subsequent events. We can indicate changing security configuration in Europe after Russia's military aggression in Georgia (2008) and Ukraine (2014) as an example of an environment where foreign energy policy operates and generate "weak signals". As another example of the "weak signals" theory, Russia's gas supply problems with Europe started in 2021 (well before the military conflict in Ukraine and major energy conflict with Europe in 2022) when Russia reduced the volume of pipeline gas to Europe triggering gas shortages and price hikes. The military aggressions undermined views and perceptions of Russia's reliability as an immediate energy supplier and created the groundwork for energy conflicts with serious repercussions at different time intervals. In addition to the military and security dimensions, the economic interdependence ("energy resources in return for technology and finance") also shape the environment of foreign energy policy that balances geopolitical and economic determinants of the energy conflicts. *The "timing factor" in the Russian energy conflicts is also a "motive identifier"*. It is not an easy task to reveal the political motivation of the energy supplier's disruption decision to the consumer or transit country (Figure 6.3).

Stegen (2011) proposed a model to examine the validity of energy's exploitation as a geopolitical or political instrument and that pattern incorporates the *timing* factor in the energy conflict. She points out that "to avoid international criticism, a supplier may attribute disruptions to weather, sabotage, technical problems, or other causes. What elicits suspicion in such cases is the timing of the disruption" (p. 6509). Martin Jirušek (2017) set forth four major factors to identify political motivation in Russia's energy policy actions including Kremlin's support for state-owned energy companies (especially, Gazprom) (p. 229):

1 *Timing of the energy policy action.*
2 *Context of the energy policy action.*
3 *Specific intervening variables for particular cases.*
4 *Operating circumstances of the energy policy action.*

Especially, the timing factor has very appropriate explanatory power for the political rationale behind Gazprom's behaviour towards partner countries and companies. He argued that the timing of the 2009 gas crisis among Russia, Ukraine, and the EU demonstrated the misapply of energy flows (e.g., gas) as an integral

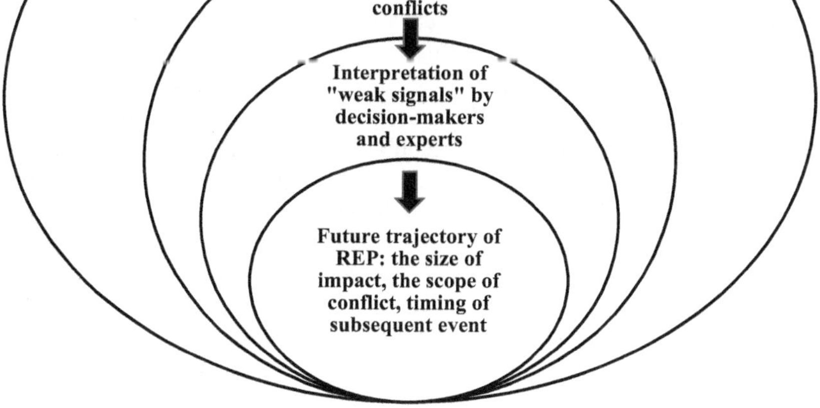

Figure 6.3 The sequence of "weak signals" emergence in the Russian energy conflicts.

component of "*Russia's foreign energy policy toolbox*". Dr Martin Jirušek from the Masaryk University of the Czech Republic in his interview with the author of this study underlined that identification of the non-economically motivated conduct of Russian energy companies is a challenging issue (Expert interview with Dr Martin Jirušek, 2019, Czech Republic). The only criteria to distinguish Russia's commercial energy moves from politically motivated acts are *timing and correlation* with other political and geopolitical events. In many cases, there was a clear connection between the energy and foreign policy of Russia. For example, when the government of Moldova signed the association agreement with the EU in 2014, Russia raised gas debts of that country including the Transnistria region. Moldova refused to recognize the gas debt of the secessionist Transnistria region. EU and Romania assisted Moldova set up an alternative gas supply to the monopolistic gas assets and infrastructure of Gazprom. Casinge (2014) links Gazprom's gas supply interruptions and trade sanctions by Russia with the Moldova-EU association agreement and political integration. The timing between Russia's energy conflict (gas price and supply cut) with Moldova and foreign policy interest to estrange the country from the EU coincided. Gas prices, energy supply manipulations, and threats of supply cuts by Russia sometimes overlap with worsening bilateral relations.

Before Russian Prime Minister Chernomyrdin's visit to the Czech Republic in April 1997, Russian ambassador Nikolay Ryabov threatened Prague with energy-related sanctions if the Czech Republic joined NATO. Ryabov said that the Czech Republic should think carefully before joining NATO because Russia could shut off the gas pipeline and Prague will simply freeze over in the coming winter. This was immediately connected with the prospects of gas supplies when the Czech Republic suffered from asymmetric gas interdependence with Russia. But as a result of the Ryabov's menaces, the Czech Republic did not agree to sign a new agreement with Gazprom on additional deliveries of 3 billion cubic metres of gas. The gas supply contract was concluded with Norway, despite the more favourable conditions proposed by Russia. During his negotiations in the Czech Republic, Chernomyrdin (who was associated with Gazprom all over Europe) had to repeatedly emphasize that the basis of Russian gas supplies was a pure market, and not political at all. But the reason for the turn of Prague from Moscow to Oslo is obviously political and the loss of the Russian side was around USD 5–5.5 billion. Chernomyrdin demonstrated a different tactic and tool of "gas pressure" on Prague saying that the issue of paying off Russian debts would be linked to the dynamics of Russian gas supplies to the Czech Republic. Many local political forces argued that dependence on an eastern neighbour threatened the Czech national security.

When we research Russia's energy conflicts, it is important to count not only real already completed facts but also energy threats that Russian officials openly stated. Because those officials' statements about the "energy weaponizing" by Russia create fear and a negative conception of the reliability of Russia's oil-gas supply. RECSID offers a shred of rich evidence on the timing factor in the Russian foreign energy conflicts. Table 6.3 demonstrates the time overlap between the political events and Russia's energy conflicts.

Table 6.3 Timing factor in Russia's foreign energy policy conflicts and "spurts"

Year	*Russia's energy conflict*	*Time overlaps with political events*
06/1993	Russia halted deliveries of natural gas to Estonia which was dependent on Russia for gas supply.	The main reason was the "discriminatory policies" allegedly towards ethnic Russians living in Estonia.
09/2000	Gazprom interrupted the natural gas supplies to Yugoslavia at the end of September 2000.	The presidential election took place in Yugoslavia in September 2000 resulting in the downfall of the long-run Slobodan Milosevic's regime.
01/2003	Russia halted oil deliveries to Latvia's Ventspils terminal referring to a limited pipeline capacity.	Latvia's "potential" mistreatment of the ethnic Russian minority in the country disturbed the Russian government.
01/2004	Russia restricted gas supply to Georgia formally due to disagreements between Gazprom and Itera.	The timing of the gas supply interruption synchronized with the election of the new pro-Western President of Georgia – M. Saakashvili.
01/2005	Gazprom shut down gas supplies to Ukraine after it rejected a swift price hike. The "gas war" led to short supply interruption to European consumers.	V. Yushchenko came to power jeopardizing the relations with Moscow in the cause of deeper integration with the EU and NATO.
01/2006	Explosions occurred on gas pipelines connecting Russia to Georgia and Armenia leading to supply disruption in both countries.	Georgia's ultra pro-Western political power led by President Saakashvili had a strong political will for the deeper integration with NATO and the EU.
07/2006	Russia halted crude oil supplies to Lithuania referring of the pipeline outflow.	The measure coincided with the transfer of a Mazeikiu refinery in Lithuania to Poland (PKN Orlan) ignoring the Russian energy interests.
01/2007	Russia blamed Belarus for withdrawing oil from the export pipe. Russia stopped the oil flows via the Druzhba pipeline, interrupting supplies to the EU states.	Russia-Belarus negotiations on the Union State were in political deadlock in January 2007 when President Lukashenko claimed Russia infringe sovereignty and independence of his country.
05/2007	Russia stopped the oil product supplies to the Estonian market and coal transit via Estonia.	A decision fall in with mass protests in Moscow about Estonia's removal of a Soviet Union's war memorial from the city centre in Tallinn.
11/2019	Russia agreed to provide a substantial gas discount to Moldova (26%) starting from January 2020.	In June 2019, the pro-Russian Socialist Party and the pro-Western bloc ACUM formed a coalition in Moldova supported by Russia and the West.

Source: Bergin (2008).

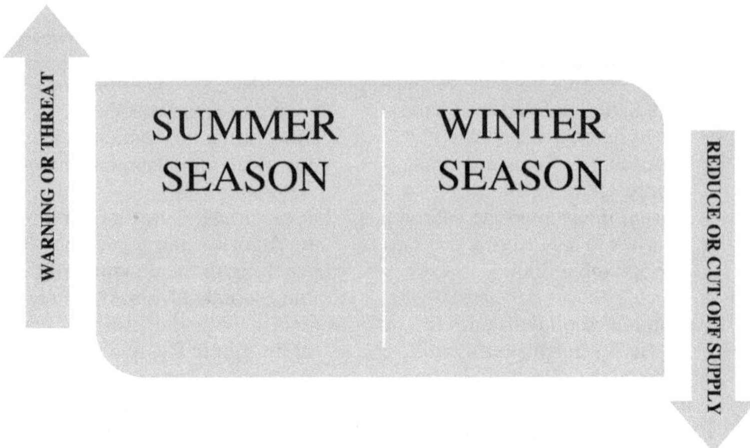

Figure 6.4 Seasonal behaviour in the Russian supply-based energy conflicts.

In terms of timing, RECSID uncovered that Russia usually made political pressure on CIS and EU countries in the winter seasons using oil-gas supply. In February 2012, Russia officially used the argument that the weather was extremely cold in Russia and reduced the gas supply to several European countries including Austria, Bulgaria, Germany, Greece, Hungary, Italy, Poland, and Slovakia. Natural gas supply disruption has deteriorated the energy relations with Europe. RECSID identified that Russia mostly warned about the supply disruption in the summer seasons and had realized "these promises" on oil-gas supply cut in the winter season (Figure 6.4).

Russia's energy policy moved on contemporaneous with the foreign policy goals in an ideologically "blind" way without differentiating "friends from enemies" (this reality is against the *constructivist* assumption of diverse perceptions of counterpart countries) and repercussions for Russia. RECSID discloses numerous cases of energy conflicts and supply disruptions coinciding with political disagreements between Russia and target countries.

6.2 Russia's Energy Conflicts and Energy Types Based on RECSID

Russia's natural gas conflicts: RECSID findings. RECSID identified 562 natural gas-related conflicts between 1990 and 2021. Thirty-two out of 562 natural gas-related conflicts were combined oil-gas conflicts; 6 conflicts had oil, gas, nuclear, and electricity dimensions. Russia had multidimensional energy conflicts mostly with the USA and EU. Russia had more intense natural gas conflicts with Ukraine (92), the EU (38), Belarus (30), Lithuania (25), Poland (23), Turkey (23), Azerbaijan (21), Turkmenistan (20), Moldova (19), and China (18). Russia engaged the gas conflicts with unrecognized "quasi-states" such as Transnistria (Moldova) and South Ossetia (Georgia; Figure 6.5).

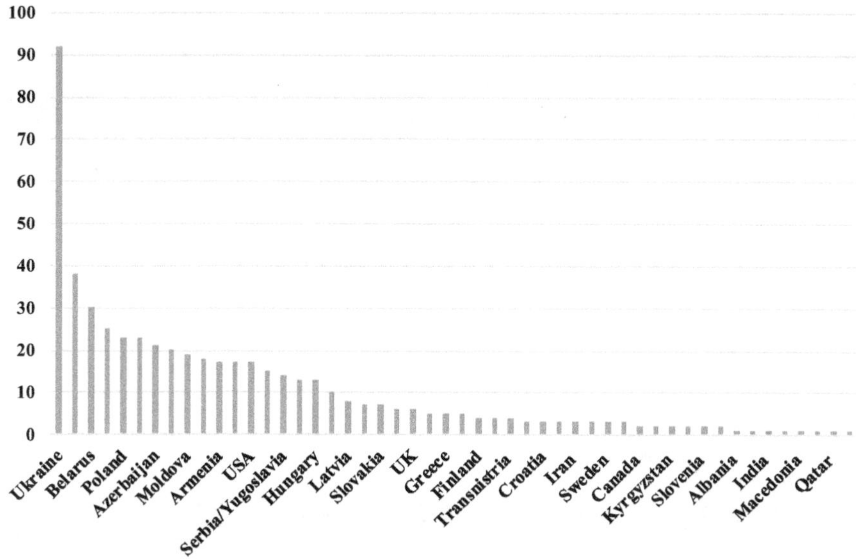

Figure 6.5 Number of Russia's gas conflicts and supply interruptions by country.

Source: RECSID.

Russia mostly had natural gas conflicts in 2006, 2009, and 2014 when its political and economic relations worsened with the CIS and the EU countries. In the 2006 gas crisis, Russia had natural gas conflicts with almost all the CIS partners including even politically loyal allies such as Belarus (5) and Armenia (3). More "problematic" post-Soviet countries such as Azerbaijan (2), Georgia (2), Lithuania (2), Turkmenistan (2), Ukraine (2), and Moldova (1) had fewer gas conflicts with Russia in 2006. In 2009, Russia conflicted mainly with the EU as an institution (e.g., European Commission's energy regulations triggered conflicts), EU member countries (e.g., Hungary, Italy, Bulgaria, Poland), and primarily with Ukraine (5) and other post-Soviet countries such as Turkmenistan (3). One-third of the total gas conflicts were driven by Ukraine in 2014 (13 out of 39). EU member countries, the USA, and politically loyal countries such as Serbia and China also dominated Russia's foreign energy conflicts in 2014 (Figure 6.6).

The *intensity* and the *peak* intervals of Russia's natural gas conflicts overlap with the geopolitical rift periods with the West over the "near abroad" regions. Russia's natural gas conflicts could be classified into the following large categories in terms of the types:

1 *Reducing the natural gas supply*
2 *Warning to stop gas deliveries*
3 *Total stop of the natural gas supply*
4 *Raising the natural gas prices*
5 *Consumer demands gas price discount*

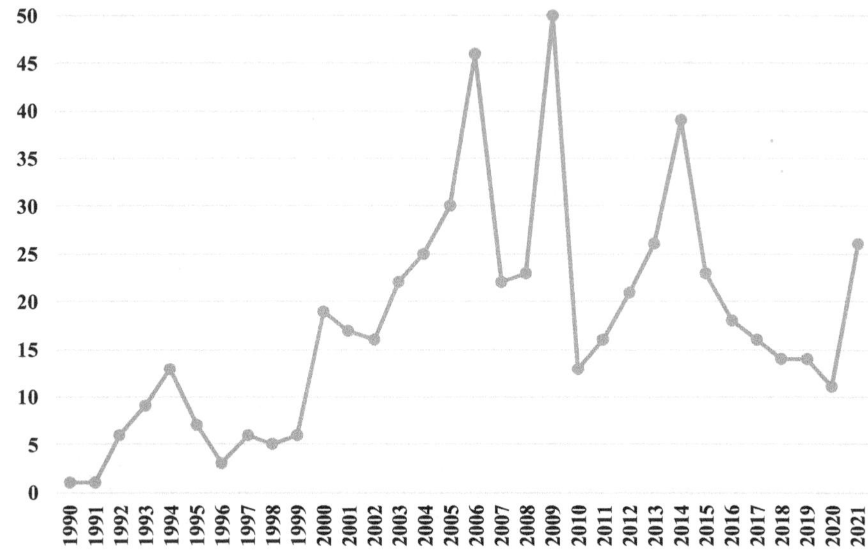

Figure 6.6 Number of Russia's gas conflicts and supply interruptions by years.
Source: RECSID.

6 *Failed gas supply negotiations*
7 *Filing a lawsuit against energy partner*
8 *Termination and refusal of the gas contract*
9 *The dispute on the gas transit tariff*
10 *The dispute on the access to pipeline*
11 *Conflict in the asset transactions*
12 *Threatening with international arbitration*
13 *Raising gas debt or demanding debt payment*
14 *Antitrust investigations against the companies*
15 *Gas export routes and sources diversification*
16 *Explosions in the natural gas pipelines*

Large categories of Russia's natural gas conflicts overlap with the *instruments* of the country's foreign energy policy. *Reducing the gas supply* to the consumer country was the most widely used instrument of the Russian foreign energy policy. RECSID identified 74 cases of the reduction of natural gas deliveries which was equal to 14% of the total energy conflicts in Russia from 1990 to 2021. Russian companies had decreased the gas supply to Ukraine (11 cases) and Belarus (8 cases) more frequently. Other EU and post-Soviet countries that often suffered from the reduction of the Russian gas were Bulgaria (4 cases), Hungary (4 cases), Lithuania (4 cases), Poland (4 cases), Georgia (4 cases), Moldova (4 cases), Austria (3 cases), Slovakia (3 cases), Romania (3 cases), and Turkey (3 cases). The main actors from Russia were state-owned Gazprom and the private Itera gas companies. In 2021,

Gazprom caused a price hike in the European market booking less gas via the Yamal-Europe gas pipeline. Belyi (2022) argued that reducing gas supply towards a multi-actor and more competitive Western and Northern European gas market with diversified gas networks isn't feasible for Russia. But reducing the gas supply could be effective in Eastern Europe where a gas supply is more "unidirectional", demonstrating Gazprom's dominant position.

RECSID identified 55 cases of the *warnings or threatening to stop or reduce the gas supply* to the counterpart countries by Gazprom's leadership, Putin, or other Russian officials. These were more than 10% of the total energy conflicts from 1990 to 2021 and Russia mostly used these warnings against the former USSR countries including Ukraine (15 cases), Belarus (6 cases), Moldova (4 cases), Georgia (4 cases), Armenia (3 cases), Azerbaijan (3 cases), and Kyrgyzstan (1 case). But it also warned the EU (6 cases) at large, EU's member countries (Latvia, 2 cases; Lithuania, 2 cases; Bulgaria, 2 cases; the Czech Republic, 1 case; Estonia, 1 case), and Balkan countries (Serbia (Yugoslavia), 2 cases; Bosnia and Herzegovina, 1 case) to halt or decrease the gas supply. These facts demonstrate the conflict dimension of Russia's foreign energy policy where Russia exploited "energy threat" not only against post-Soviet countries but also against EU countries, perhaps, with less intensity. Russia warned the EU countries about the supply cut but it implemented less gas supply disruption against the EU.

RECSID has identified 52 cases of the *total stop or full disruption of gas supply* mostly by Gazprom, but in a few cases by Itera against the consumer countries between 1990 and 2021. Russia halted the gas supply mostly to Ukraine (nine cases), Azerbaijan (five cases), Serbia/Yugoslavia (four cases), Georgia (three cases), and Lithuania (three cases). Other post-Soviet (Armenia, Belarus, and Moldova), EU countries (Austria, Bulgaria, the Czech Republic, Estonia, Germany, Greece, Hungary, Italy, Poland, Romania, Slovakia, Slovenia, and Croatia), and non-EU Balkan countries (Albania, Bosnia and Herzegovina, Macedonia, and Montenegro) also faced the total gas supply disruption by Russia, but with less intensity. Politically loyal post-Soviet countries such as Armenia and Belarus, and Russia's large trade partners from the EU region (e.g., Germany) encountered fewer cases of full gas supply interruption.

RECSID has identified 55 cases of *price-related gas conflicts* between 1991 and 2021. Under this category, Gazprom raised the gas price or threatened to hike the price, consumer countries protested the high gas prices or resisted not paying a higher price, Gazprom and the partner country/consumer failed to deal with the price issue, and the buyer country demanded from Gazprom to lower price, the consumer country/company filed a lawsuit against Gazprom in the international arbitration to change gas price, the gas exporter country (e.g., Turkmenistan or Uzbekistan) raised the gas price to Russia, Gazprom cancelled gas price discount. Belarus (nine cases), Ukraine (seven cases), Moldova (five cases), Lithuania (five cases), and Armenia (four cases) had more intense price-related gas conflicts with Russia. Post-Soviet countries and other partner countries often criticized the way of price-setting for natural gas and ceilings of energy prices that were misused by Russia. For example, Lithuania suggested to Gazprom (i) to link the price of gas to the price of fuel oil; (ii) to establish a maximum limit on gas prices to insure against changes in the price situation on world markets. Traditional and largest gas importers of Russia that have fewer energy conflicts such as Germany (three cases) and China (three cases) have entered frequent gas price conflicts with Russia.

Also, Russia had a higher number of *failed gas supply negotiations* with China (4 cases) rather than any other partner country. Gazprom *filed a lawsuit* or had undergone a similar counterclaim through an international arbitration mostly with Naftogaz (Ukraine), BOTAS (Turkey), PGNiG (Poland), and a Lithuanian energy company. RECSID revealed that energy debts have triggered Russia's energy conflicts. Some partner countries offered the Russian company Gazprom to accept the payment of debt for the supply of natural gas as a share of some local companies due to the lack of cash (e.g., Serbia offered Gazprom a share in the capital of the chemical plant, manufacturer of fertilizers and other enterprises in 2002). Gazprom's gas conflict with some partner countries including the Baltic states was sometimes related to the transactions (to buy or to sell) on the gas grids, interconnector pipelines, or the stakes in the companies of the host country. Russia had sanction-related gas conflicts mostly with the USA and EU after 2014.

Generally, Russia had 35 *pipeline-related gas conflicts* with consumer, host, and transit countries for RECSID. Poland and Ukraine were more problematic gas transit countries, and Turkmenistan was a more challenging gas source country for Russia in terms of the relevant conflict intensity. Russia had a few cases of pipeline-related conflict with China regarding the route and capacity of the export pipelines. Also, there were a series of explosions and attempts to blow up the infrastructure in the gas pipelines that connected Russia to South Caucasus countries (Armenia, Georgia, and Azerbaijan), Ukraine, and Turkmenistan. These explosions occurred in critical periods (e.g., 1992, 2006, 2009, and 2014) when Russia had geopolitical and geo-economic clashes with the target countries. For example, the Urengoy-Uzhgorod gas pipeline exploded as a result of the terrorist attack on the gas pipeline in Poltava in June 2014 when Russia entered the de-facto war in Eastern Ukraine. Therefore, Gazprom was accused of being behind these explosions in the gas pipelines (Figure 6.7).

Russia's oil conflicts: RECSID findings. RECSID identified 206 oil-related conflicts between 1990 and 2021. One hundred and sixty-seven out of 206 oil-related conflicts were pure oil conflicts, and 39 cases were combined oil-gas and more complex energy or multidimensional conflicts. Russia had more intense oil conflicts with Azerbaijan (23), Belarus (19), Ukraine (15), China (14), Lithuania (14), the USA (14), the EU (8), Hungary (7), Bulgaria (6), Kazakhstan (6), Latvia (6), Poland (6).

Azerbaijan's "leadership" in this ranking, as an oil-gas producer country, is a new phenomenon in the context of existing literature and "conventional wisdom" on Russia's energy conflicts and foreign energy policy. This finding can be considered as one of the contributions of RECSID to the existing literature on the Russian FEP. Russia engaged in the oil conflict with OPEC, CIS, and the Central European region, as well. Top-3 CIS countries (Azerbaijan, Ukraine, Belarus) that had more oil conflicts with Russia accounted for almost 30% of the total oil

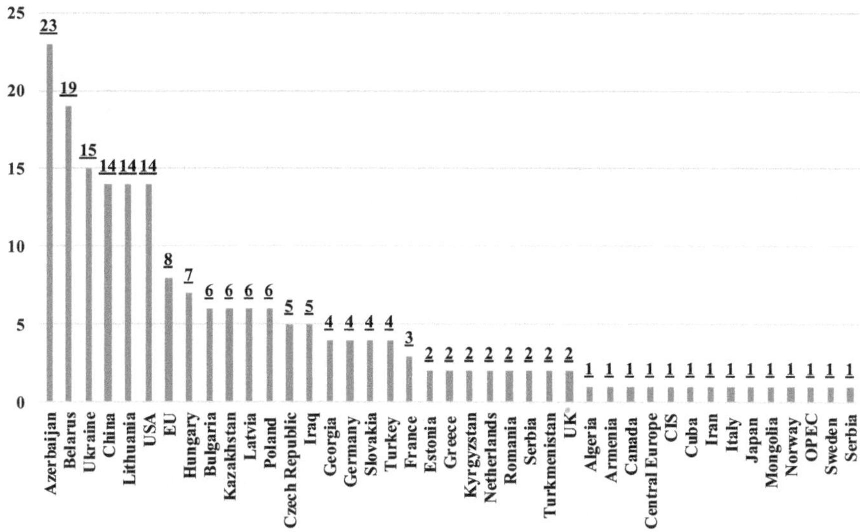

Figure 6.7 Number of Russia's oil conflicts and supply interruptions by country.
Source: RECSID.

conflicts with Russia. Even though Russia had more gas conflicts (18 cases) with China rather than oil conflicts (14 cases), the share of the Russia-China oil conflicts in the total oil-related conflicts doubled the share of the gas conflicts in the total gas-related conflicts (7% vs. 3.5%). Generally, the entire oil-gas affairs between Russia and China are prone to be tense and conflictual. Also, CIS countries and EU countries where Russia had a high number of energy conflicts were almost identical (e.g., Ukraine, Belarus, Azerbaijan, Lithuania, Poland, Hungary, and Bulgaria; Figure 6.8).

Almost 25% of Russia's oil-related conflicts with consumer and transit countries occurred between 1990and 1999 ("pre-Putin era"), while only 10% of gas conflicts took place at the same time interval. It means that Russia's oil-related conflicts prevailed over gas-related conflicts in the 1990s in comparison with the 2000s (market factor), not in absolute numbers but in proportion. In the early 1990s, Russia's oil production and export sectors were heavily regulated by the state and the Russian government strictly controlled the volume and price of produced and exported crude oil by considering inter-state agreements, but non-considering open market principles. Therefore, in that period, Russia easily manipulated oil export, as well, towards "problematic partners" such as the Baltic states and Ukraine.

The peak of the Russian oil conflicts was in 2003 when the country had 16 oil-related conflicts with a wide range of consumer and transit countries that included Azerbaijan, Belarus, China, Georgia, Greece, Hungary, Iraq, Japan, Latvia, Lithuania, Ukraine, and the USA. That peak year did not coincide with the peak period of the gas-related conflicts. Subsequent peak periods of the oil-related conflicts overlap with the peak years of the gas-related conflicts in 2009 and 2014. After 2014,

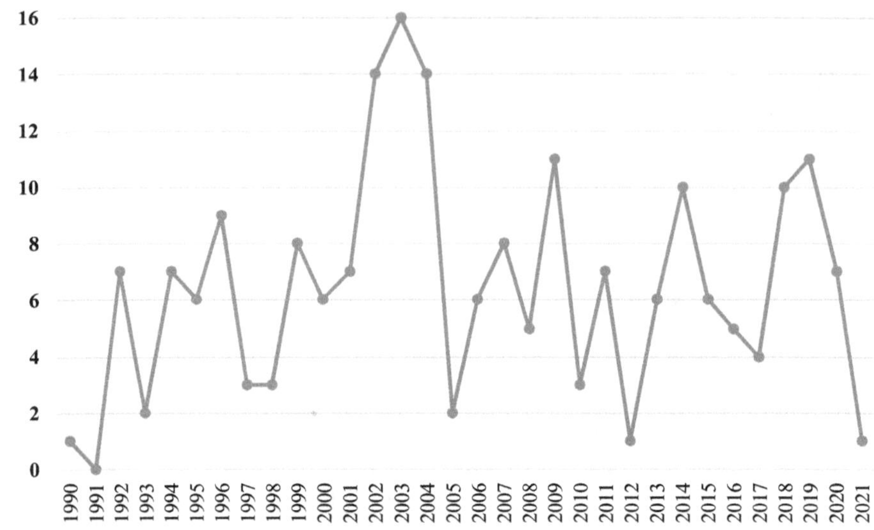

Figure 6.8 Number of Russia's oil conflicts and supply cuts by years.

Source: RECSID.

the gas-related conflicts decreased continuously, but oil-related conflicts started to increase after 2017 reaching the next peak in 2019.

The fluctuations of the oil-related and gas-related conflicts do not coincide and cohere with each other reflecting different dynamics of the energy conflicts because of the type of energy. Russia's oil-related conflicts could be classified into the following large categories in terms of the types and tools of the conflicts:

1 *Doubling or increasing the price of the supplied Russian oil*
2 *Investigation or auditing against the Russian oil companies*
3 *Foreign oil companies had a problem in Russia and left the country*
4 *Refusing to extend oil transit or oil supply deal*
5 *Conflicts over oil export or oil transit pipelines*
6 *The competition between Russian oil-gas companies*
7 *Sabotage and explosions against oil infrastructure*
8 *Reducing oil supplies to consumer countries by Russia*
9 *Total stop of the delivery of crude oil and oil products*
10 *Filing a lawsuit against the Russian oil companies*
11 *Seizing the assets of the Russian oil companies abroad*
12 *Oil supply disruption is used as an economic sanction*
13 *Oil payment debt is used as a political instrument*
14 *Russia used terrorism or revolts to get an oil deal*
15 *The conflict over the oil transit tariff and oil price*
16 *Russian oil companies' foreign transactions failed*
17 *Russia exports the contaminated oil to the foreign buyers*

RECSID identified only 14 cases of *the reduction of crude oil and oil product deliveries*, against 74 cases of the reduction of natural gas deliveries. Russia used reduction of the crude oil and oil products supplies mostly to post-Soviet and post-socialist countries such as Ukraine, Belarus, Lithuania, Estonia, Latvia, Azerbaijan, and the Czech Republic frequently in the early and mid-1990s. RECSID identified 34 cases of *the total stop of crude oil and oil products delivery*, against 52 cases of the total stop of gas supply. Russia frequently used oil supply disruption "tool" against EU member countries (80% of the Russian oil supply stoppages were against the Czech Republic, Germany, Hungary, Estonia, Latvia, Lithuania, Poland, and Slovakia) rather than CIS countries, in contrast to the gas supply interruption (40% of the total stop of gas supply was against EU countries). It means symmetric economic interdependence wasn't a "risk mitigator" in the oil conflicts on contrary to the gas conflicts. Russia usually used *warnings to reduce or stop the crude oil and oil products' deliveries* against Belarus (4 cases) and the EU (2 cases). Russia had the same number of oil supply crises as China (2 cases) and Ukraine (2 cases) when Russia did not give state guarantees for oil supplies, the consumer country insisted on a new scheme for the oil supply or Russia continued the oil blockade of the target. When Russia really reduces oil and gas production to apply an "energy weapon", it negatively influences the productivity of the wells in the future and creates additional costs for the production recovery. It also means that energy's "weaponization" can be feasible and applicable only for a short-term period.

Intergovernmental *oil negotiations failed* mostly with post-Soviet countries such as Belarus, Azerbaijan, Kyrgyzstan, Lithuania, Poland, and Turkmenistan on oil supply, oil transit, oil price, and contract conditions. Contrary to the gas transit where Russia had the main problem with Ukraine, in the oil transit issue, the country had more problems with Azerbaijan when Russia acted as a transit country. Azerbaijan several times refused to extend oil transit deals or to sign a new oil supply contract via the Baku-Novorossiysk pipeline. Also, oil transit countries such as Ukraine increased the tariff for the Russian oil transit. Russia had a less price-related conflict in the oil sector in comparison with the gas sector. Russian oil companies did not agree on oil prices mostly with China. Russia used the oil price increase and oil related debts as political leverage against CIS countries such as Ukraine. Turkey as a transit country restricted the pass of the Russian oil tankers in the Bosporus strait with economic, environmental, political, and energy motives.

Foreign oil companies mainly from the USA, Canada, France, the Netherlands, Italy, and the UK operating in Russia had serious problems in the country. Foreign oil companies withdrew from some oil production and exploration projects in Russia, filed a series of claims against the Russian government and companies, foreign oil-gas companies left Russia, suspended joint oil ventures with the Russian public and private oil companies, and faced administrative barriers in the country. Foreign companies were not satisfied with the conditions in the "problematic" PSA contracts such as the Sakhalin-2 project. Russian oil companies *filed claims and lawsuits* against foreign oil companies (e.g., Chinese, and Ukrainian oil companies) in international arbitration and courts. Also, foreign oil and gas companies from the

USA and the EU member countries filed claims and lawsuits against the Russian oil companies in arbitration and courts. Oil-gas companies such as BP, ExxonMobil, Shell, Total Energies, and Equinor suspended new investments in Russian oil-gas projects in March 2022 due to the Russia-Ukraine war. Foreign energy companies working in the framework of oil-gas projects on Sakhalin hesitated to withdraw from the lucrative projects. If Shell, ExxonMobil, or other foreign energy companies plan to sell assets (which have fallen in price due to sanctions) of the oil and gas sector of Russia, then a potential buyer of such shares must obtain approval from the Central Bank of Russia and the Ministry of Finance of Russia. These assets must be sold either to Russian energy companies or to foreign energy companies (e.g., Chinese, or Indian oil companies), which will be allowed by the Ministry of Finance and the Central Bank of Russia. The pattern of interdependence was bound and fastened by the energy regulation framework of Russia.

Sanction-related oil conflicts between Russia frequently occurred in the USA after the 2014 crisis in Ukraine. The US sanctioned Russian oil, gas, and electricity companies; US sanctions targeted the Arctic shelf oil reserves of Russia. Rosneft warned the USA and EU of retaliation against their sanctions in 2014 and finally, Russia adopted countersanctions against the USA and EU. The USA and the EU were ready to impose sanctions if Russia again used energy as a "weapon". About 60% of the total transaction-related oil conflicts of Russia occurred with EU countries where the asset acquisition efforts of the Russian oil companies were hampered by various methods. The EU member countries refused or cancelled to transfer or sell oil-related infrastructure to the Russian companies. Also, some Chinese companies such as CNPC refused several times to purchase a stake in the Russian oil companies for political motivation.

Russian oil companies were expelled from the management and ownership of oil fields and sometimes their contracts were terminated mostly in Iraq and Kazakhstan. The Russian companies had similar problems in small and medium-sized oil-producing countries such as Algeria, Azerbaijan, and Cuba. Also, Russian oil companies were removed from oil-related foreign assets in post-Soviet countries such as Belarus, Lithuania, and Ukraine (Russian foreign energy assets were partly confiscated in the EU countries in 2022). *Investigations* against Russian oil companies (first, Lukoil) were carried out mainly in Bulgaria (four cases). Also, investigations and asset seizures based on tax, customs, and against the Russian oil companies happened in Azerbaijan, Romania, Belarus, Lithuania, Serbia, and the USA. Russia's oil sector encountered competition from the oil companies from different Asian countries such as China, India, and Japan. The competition or rivalry between the Russian oil companies has impacted the targeted consumer countries.

Russia had serious disagreements on *oil export pipeline* routes and pipeline-related oil conflicts (blocking Russia's pipeline projects, the delay in pipeline projects) mostly with China and some transit countries such as Belarus, Bulgaria, Poland, and Mongolia. Diversification of oil export routes by oil-rich post-Soviet countries (e.g., Azerbaijan and Kazakhstan) and diversification of the sources of oil imports by consumer countries (e.g., EU member countries) led to the oil-related conflicts with Russia and respective countries. EU aimed to reduce oil dependence on Russia through diversification of oil imports. Russia has manipulated the energy dependence of the target country to get economic benefits or to achieve a political aim (e.g., Hungary).

Russia was involved in a series of politically motivated *explosions and sabotage* against oil pipelines connecting the country to Georgia and Azerbaijan (e.g., in 2003–2004), as in the gas pipelines. Russian oil-gas companies (Lukoil, Rosneft, Gazprom) had a conflict with the local authorities in host countries where these companies had a stake in the oil and gas fields. Russia had oil conflicts with political and security motivations mostly with Azerbaijan (5 cases), Georgia (3 cases), and Ukraine (2 cases). Russia used the Karabakh "card" and the opposition to organize the revolt in Azerbaijan for oil-related purposes. Russia used the PKK terror organization against Turkey and Azerbaijan to block oil export pipeline projects. Russia has intimidated Georgia politically to eliminate oil transit via this country. Russia used "energy leverage" for recognition of South Ossetia and Abkhazia after 2008. Russia militarily intervened in the Tuzla Island of Ukraine to block promising oil-gas fields in the Azov Sea in December 2003. In these political and security-motivated oil conflicts, the Ministry of Foreign Affairs and counterpart countries were actively involved in the process. The *contamination of exported oil* can be a new energy tool for Russia to damage the quality of products in the oil refineries of counterpart countries (mostly, neighbours and European countries). As a result, the loss of Belarus from the supply of poor-quality Russian oil via the Druzhba pipeline was estimated at hundreds of millions of dollars in 2019. The export of the contaminated oil damaged Russia's reputation as an oil exporter in the European and CIS markets.

Russia's nuclear energy conflicts: RECSID findings. RECSID identified 52 nuclear energy-related conflicts between 1994 and 2021. Five out of 52 nuclear conflicts were deeply complex dissension with the USA, the EU, Turkey, and Hungary having nuclear dimensions. Russia had more intense nuclear energy conflicts with the USA (8), Ukraine (7), Bulgaria (7), Iran (4), the EU (3), and the Czech Republic (3). In addition to the European countries, Russia had nuclear energy-related discordances with new energy partners from the Middle East (Turkey, Egypt, and Jordan), Asia (Vietnam), and Africa (South Africa). Russia mostly had nuclear energy conflicts in 2014–2015 when its political and economic relations worsened with major Western partners. Russia's nuclear energy conflicts could be classified into the following large categories:

- *Disagreements and negotiation failure on the construction plan of the nuclear power plant* by Rosatom in terms of the cost and time of the project ("Belene" NPP in Bulgaria, "Bushehr" NPP in Iran, "Belarus" NPP);
- *Counterpart countries abandoned the plan to build a nuclear power plant* with political, commercial, and ecological considerations (Bulgaria, Vietnam, Jordan, and South Africa);
- Rosatom failed to win *the nuclear power plant construction bid* or Russian-made NPP was closed with political occasions (Finland, the Czech Republic, and Lithuania);

- Rosatom warned to raise *nuclear fuel prices and disrupting nuclear energy supply*, some delays in the fuel supply process, and non-payment in the nuclear energy supply through which Russia used counterpart's nuclear energy (nuclear fuel or nuclear technology) dependence (Ukraine, the USA, and Hungary);
- The *sanctions towards Russia or countersanctions by Russia* affected nuclear energy affairs, general disruption of political and economic affairs influenced the nuclear energy, Russia warned the partner countries with retaliation (the EU, the USA, and Turkey);
- The traditional partner country of Rosatom in the nuclear energy field preferred to cooperate with *the rival company from the USA, France, and Japan* with political considerations (Ukraine and Kazakhstan);
- Rosatom's active foreign nuclear policy aggravated *political fear in the target country* and major companies abandoned the creation of the joint venture together with Rosatom with political and commercial considerations (the UK, the Czech Republic, Germany, and France);
- *Third parties concerned about Rosatom's NPP project* with the partner country (the USA opposed Russia-Iran nuclear energy cooperation, the EU started an investigation against Rosatom, Austria had opposed the "Paks-2 NPP" in Hungary, Lithuania protested the Belarus NPP; Figure 6.9).

Western countries had negative prejudice against Rosatom claiming its coordinated efforts with Kremlin to fortify Russia's geopolitical position in critical regions and countries. European countries considered nuclear power plants as an instrument of Russia's geopolitical plans. Rosatom faced strong opposition in the

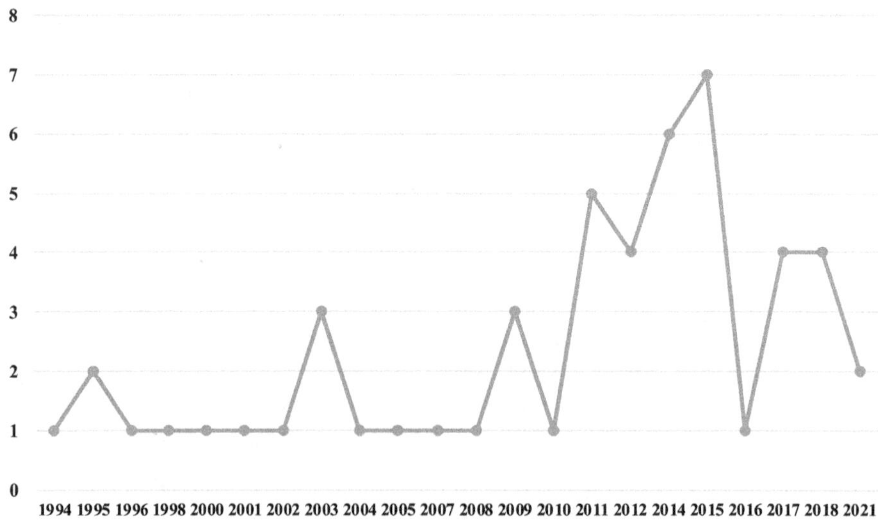

Figure 6.9 Number of Russia's nuclear energy conflicts by years.

Source: RECSID.

EU countries with political and environmental motivations. Generally, the European states and societies were against nuclear energy, also, target countries aimed to reduce their nuclear energy dependence on Russia. But the European Commission presented green sustainable energy source status to the nuclear and gas in 2022 to accelerate the domestic energy capacity and decrease the energy dependence on Russia. Cesnakas and Juozaitis (2017) argued that the geopolitical motivation of Rosatom (TVEL) prevails over commercial incentives in the Hanhikivi NPP (Finland), where there is a considerable discrepancy between Russia's project financing and confirmed electricity price. A similar geopolitical motive may dominate in Astravets NPP built by Rosatom's construction branch on the Belarus-Lithuania border.

In some European countries, higher political and military elites protested Rosatom's projects. In 2010, the National Security Council of the Czech Republic postponed the construction of the new units of the Temelin NPP when Rosatom was the main pretender to construct the units and supply nuclear fuels. The Czech Republic's CEZ company cancelled the Temelin NPP building project in April 2014 when Rosatom and Westinghouse had a fierce competition over the project. As a result of the political crises with the Western power in 2014–2015, Rosatom partly lost the European nuclear energy market. Political and security-related disagreements with the target consumer countries led to the nuclear energy-related conflict with Russia. Putin and Medvedev directly lobbied for the interests of Rosatom in the CIS, EU, and the Middle East region.

As a result of the nuclear-related conflicts, Rosatom was partly pulled out from the nuclear energy market of some European, post-Soviet, Asian, and Middle East countries. Rosatom's reputational risks, stemming from the risk of nuclear fuel supply disruption, were especially high in the USA and the EU market complicating its access to the advanced Western technology and financial resources. To compensate for the losses after the sanctions, Russia was forced to issue a state loan for the foreign NPP project that was very attractive for the target country. Anti-Russian sanctions of the USA on restrictions of imports of low-enriched uranium (LEU) affected Rosatom in 2018 while the company received huge revenues from LEU. Rosatom often competes with developed countries' nuclear energy companies (e.g., Westinghouse from the USA, Toshiba from Japan, and Areva from France) over post-Soviet markets such as Ukraine and Bulgaria. Russia often delayed the NPP's construction in various partner countries. Mutual banning of nuclear fuel supply and nuclear fuel transit occurred between Russia and Ukraine in 2014–2015 for political reasons. The years 2014 and 2015 were the peak of the Russian nuclear energy conflicts with 13 cases targeting mostly Ukraine, the EU, and Turkey. Nuclear energy has the potential to shape long-term structural dependence (longer than oil and gas) on Russia in terms of nuclear reactor maintenance and nuclear fuel supply (e.g., in Akkuyu NPP of Turkey).

Bowen and Dabbar (2022) pointed out that Russia is the largest exporter of nuclear reactors. Also, Rosatom is a key service supplier to developing and developed countries (including the USA) related to mining, conversion, enrichment, fabrication, and utilization of nuclear fuel. Russia is the largest player in the global market of nuclear fuel conversion and enrichment with approximately 40%–50% market share. Rosatom provided one-quarter of the USA's annual fuel enrichment needs in 2021, but the USA plans to decrease this dependence ratio to 15% in 2030 (Bowen & Dabbar, 2022). Interdependence exists not only in fuel conversion and enrichment segments of nuclear energy but also in the supply of necessary services and some technologies to the Russian-made VVER nuclear reactors. Despite the global rejection of all types of Russian energy after the military intervention in Ukraine in 2022 and diversification plans, it is time-consuming for reactor-holders to relinquish Russia's presence in the nuclear energy market. Also, Rosatom is unwilling to lose its dominant position in the global nuclear energy market because of Kremlin's geopolitical manoeuvres.

Russia's electricity and coal conflicts: RECSID findings. RECSID identified 33 electricity-related and five coal-related conflicts between 1990 and 2021. Russia had more intense electricity conflicts with two South Caucasus countries – Georgia (seven cases) and Armenia (four cases). In addition, Bulgaria (three cases), Ukraine (three cases), Belarus (two cases), Lithuania (two cases), the USA (two cases), and Moldova (two cases) encountered electricity-related conflict with Russia more than once. The geographical proximity of the electricity importer countries connecting to the Russian electricity grid network determined the neighbouring countries that had an electricity-related conflict with Russia. Russia has misused Georgia's complex energy dependence on Russia with political and security motivations. Chechnya war, border security problems, Russian-backed separatism in South Ossetia and Abkhazia, Georgia's pro-Western domestic political settings, and Georgia's transit opportunities for the oil-gas resources of Azerbaijan determined the political-security and pure energy dimensions of the electricity conflicts with Russia.

Russia terminated the electricity export deal with Georgia, Inter RAO UES warned to file a lawsuit against Georgia, Russia used the electricity factor to achieve international recognition of the separatist regions of Georgia (South Ossetia and Abkhazia), and Russia's behaviour caused the chain of shutdowns in the electricity network and domestic political scandal in Georgia. Inter RAO UES had a competition with the US company that owned a power network in Tbilisi and with Iran which desired to control Tajikistan's electricity sector. Also, Georgian authorities and oppositional forces blamed Gazprom for the explosion and the sabotage of the power transmission system connecting Russia and Georgia in 2006. Also, during the 2003 electricity crisis, Putin ordered to restart the electricity export to Georgia (Figure 6.10).

Russia used the increase in electricity tariff as a political tool against CIS countries and especially, Georgia. RAO UES had planned to increase the tariff in the mid-2000s arguing that the export tariff was adjusted to the market rate. Russia used electricity debts as leverage against another CIS country – Kazakhstan – and finally, electricity debts were written off in return for energy assets in 2000. Political and economic factors also created serious problems in Russia-Armenia electricity affairs. Inter RAO UES left Armenia due to low tariffs and RusHydro decided to sell the energy assets in the country in 2017–2019. The US and EU sanctions

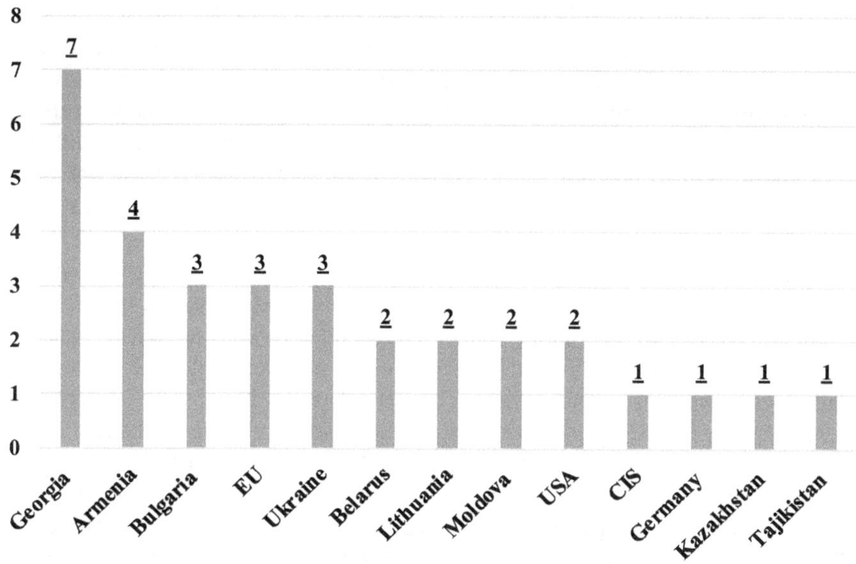

Figure 6.10 Number of Russia's electricity conflicts by country.

Source: RECSID.

targeted Russia's electricity sector after the 2014 Ukrainian crisis and the military intervention in this country in February 2022. EU expanded sanctions against Russia that ban the supply of energy equipment to the country after the Crimea crisis. As a response, Moscow made a political decision to stop the supply of electricity to Ukraine in 2014. The total stop of the electricity supply by Russia forced Ukraine to work with the separatist "Donetsk and Luhansk" regions (Dzhumaylo et al., 2014).

The first wave of the Russian electricity conflicts occurred in 2003–2005 when Russia had serious energy crises and geopolitical clashes with the Western powers over the post-Soviet region, especially Georgia and Ukraine. The second wave took place between 2014 and 2017 when a new round of tension appeared in the West-Russia affairs mainly over Ukraine, Georgia, and Armenia. For RECSID results, Russia's state-owned Inter RAO UES applied a *total cut-off of the electricity flows* towards Georgia (three cases), Moldova (one case), and Ukraine (one case) in the early 2000s. Inter RAO UES reduced the electricity export to Belarus in 2011 and Belarus abandoned the electricity import to Russia. Russia never used electricity supply interruption against the Baltic countries that were partly dependent on the Russian power grid. Inter RAO UES is a major energy exporter of Russia that supplies electricity to Azerbaijan, Belarus, China, Finland, Georgia, Kazakhstan, Lithuania, and Mongolia (Inter RAO Group, 2021a).

RECSID identified ten cases when partly state-owned efforts of RAO UES and Gazprom *to privatize power grids* in the Eastern Europe and CIS region failed as an evolving energy conflicts tactic or tool. As a result, Gazprom decided to exit the electricity sector of Lithuania with mutual lawsuits. RAO UES failed to privatize the power grids of Moldova and the USA indirectly intervened in the privatization process in 2004. RAO UES encountered very serious problems in the privatization of energy distribution companies in Bulgaria. Bulgaria's accession to the EU influenced the deal with RAO UES in 2005 and finally, Bulgaria rejected RAO UES's application to take part in the privatization and postponed the agreement with the Russian electricity company that used the electricity market liberalization in Europe.

RECSID identified four cases of *the coal-related energy conflicts* of Russia with Ukraine (two cases), Estonia (one case), and Kazakhstan (one case). In 2007, Russia halted deliveries of steam coal transit to Estonia reviving the "energy weapon" fears. The motivation for the coal-related conflict was political as Estonia moved a statue of a Red Army soldier in Tallinn. Boykov (2020, pp. 389–406) argued that Putin's power starting in 2000 marked the beginning of the next stage in Russia's policy towards the Baltic states. Moscow's new foreign policy line could be described as "*energy diplomacy*" aimed at overcoming dependence on the ports of the Baltic countries for the export of energy resources, primarily oil. The events of "Bronze Night" in 2007 influenced both the political atmosphere of Russian-Estonian relations and its economic component. As a result of measures taken by Russia, the volume of cargo transportation in 2007 decreased by 35%, the volume of transportation of crude oil fell by 34%, gasoline by 50%, and coal by 60% compared to the same period in 2006 (Boykov, 2020, pp. 389–406).

In 2014, Moscow made a political decision to stop the supply of coal to Ukraine forcing the country to work with separatist "Donetsk and Luhansk" regions. In 2015, Kyiv blocked electricity supplies to Crimea and as a response, Russia stopped coal supply to Ukraine again. Ukraine was forced to resume the electricity supplies to Crimea in 2015. Russia's coal-related conflict with Kazakhstan also was related to Ukraine. Because Russia aimed to restrict the coal supply to Ukraine limiting a coal transit from Kazakhstan in 2019. Hurska (2019) argued that Russia used coal exports as a "weapon" against Ukraine obstructing Kazakhstan's exports to this country. Russia pursues three main aims in that policy: (a) Moscow assures its control over Ukraine's occupied eastern part (Donbas), where coal smuggling is a tool for managing and financing local armed pro-Russian groups; (b) Through controlling East Ukraine's coal resources and not allowing Kazakhstan and other countries to export coal to Ukraine with full capacity, Moscow is able to make additional pressure to Kyiv, especially in the wintertime; (c) The coal trade sustained an important source of illegal income for the Russian business elite that were close to the political regime. Russia's radical decision to limit the coal transit from Kazakhstan to Ukraine led to the intervention by the Eurasian Economic Commission to prevent the energy conflict. In this context, the behaviour of the European Union and the Eurasian Economic Commission overlapped with Russia's foreign energy policy. *Regional institutions limited the manoeuvre capacity of Russia in the foreign energy policy*. Coal also was used as a political pressure instrument by Russia against the CIS and the EU. Coal can be further researched as Russia's "energy weapon" separately based on RECSID findings.

6.3 The Energy Conflicts, Oil Prices, and Domestic Politics Based on RECSID

Energy conflicts, oil prices, freedom, and democracy. The transmission channels between the domestic and foreign realms of Russia are not clear to theorize in terms of foreign energy policy. But as one of the variables, oil price fluctuations can (i) alter the vulnerability of energy-rich countries under the interdependence pattern of bilateral and multilateral foreign affairs; and (ii) affect the power consolidation of domestic politics. The correlation ratio between the number of Russia's foreign energy conflicts and supply interruptions and oil prices (Brent benchmark) is equal to 0.53 from 1990 to 2019 and 0.8 from 1990 to 2006 (high correlation ratio breaks down after 2006 when fluctuations in the oil price went up). The current year's oil and gas prices are reflected in the subsequent year's state budget of Russia as oil-gas revenues. Therefore, if we correlate the current year's conflict intensity with the previous year's oil price then the correlation ratio reaches 0.61 for 1990–2019 (0.73 from 1990 to 2006, and a high correlation ratio breaks down after 2006). Based on statistical analysis and RECSID's findings, we observed that not the trend of the crude oil prices in the world market, but the difference between the price's static "snap" level and fiscal breakeven level (or the critical threshold that was USD 40 per barrel) makes more sense for Russia's domestic political repressions and foreign aggression. Also, we must take into account that oil price fluctuations could influence foreign energy policy as a transmission channel in interdependent energy affairs.

IR's liberal school proposes that autocratic political leaders and authoritarian states that are less accountable to the citizens promote and trigger interstate conflicts. Doyle (1983) argued that peaceful conflict resolution mechanisms, collective moral values, and economic cooperation among democratic states found "democratic peace" in the global system. Domestic democratic reforms can be considered an effective way to avoid interstate conflicts, even wars from a liberal perspective. The authoritarian systems can more easily decide to start various interstate conflicts including energy conflicts in the case of Russia. The democratization trend worsened in parallel to the growing energy conflicts and "energy weaponization" (e.g., "gas wars") starting between 1991 and 2019. The correlation between the total "democracy index"[1] and the number of Russia's foreign energy conflicts and supply interruption cases was (−)0.6 from 1991 to 2019. Russia had relatively more energy conflicts and supply disruption cases when the country had a relatively lower democracy score and higher domestic political repression (Figure 6.11).

The sensitivity to the oil price changes was different in the Kremlin's domestic and foreign policy. Despite the medium-level correlation between the number of Russia's foreign energy conflicts and supply interruptions and oil prices based on RECSID findings, the oil price had an influence and repercussions on Russian domestic and foreign policy (Figure 6.12). Friedman (2009) argues that the price of crude oil and the status of freedom always move in opposite directions in oil-rich states that are simultaneously dependent on oil production for the exports and GDP while having weak state institutions or outright authoritarian governments ("*the first law of petropolitics*") (Friedman, 2009).

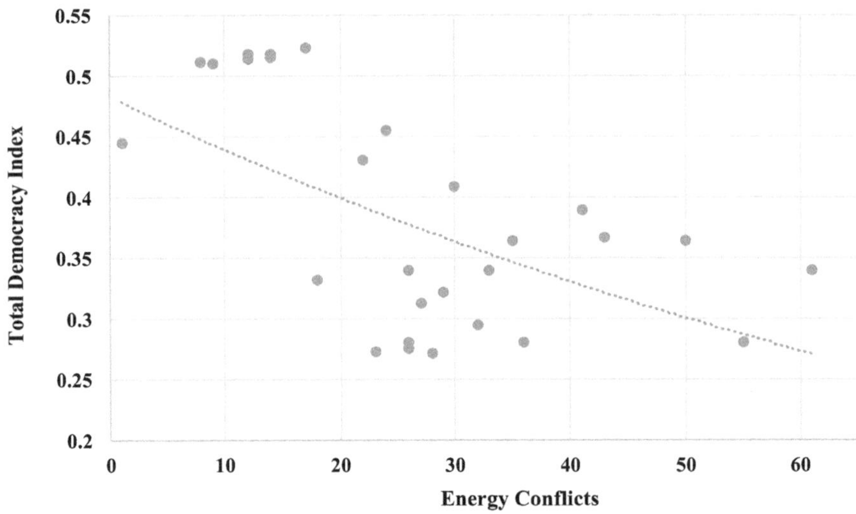

Figure 6.11 Democracy and energy conflicts in Russia.
Sources: RECSID and Democracy Matrix (2021).

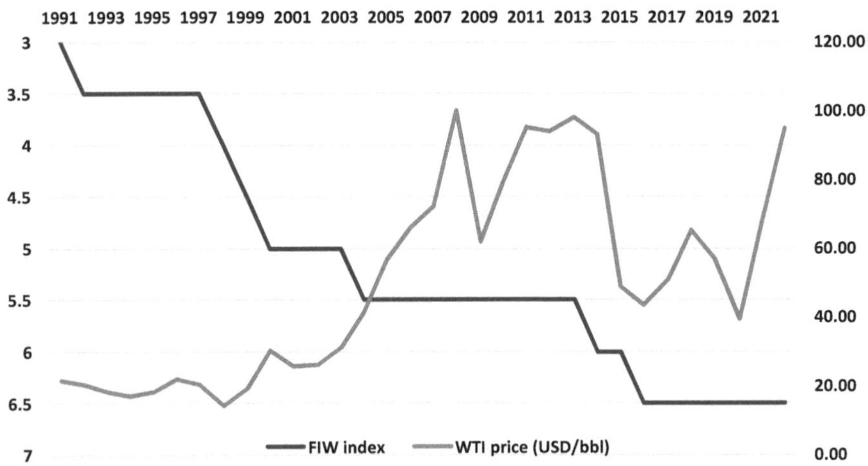

Figure 6.12 Oil price and freedom in Russia.
Sources: Freedom House (2020); BP (2021); and author's calculations.

The lower crude oil prices force political leaders to act sensitively against outside forces considering alternative options to attract foreign investments.[2] But the higher the average global crude oil price, the domestic environment for freedom and independent political and state institutions are worsening. Figure 6.12 compares the upward trend of WTI brand oil price (approximate to the price of Russia's exported "Urals" brand oil) and "Freedom in the World" (FIW) survey ratings for political rights and civil liberties (indexes moving from 1 to 7 with worsening trends). There are double aims here to reveal the opposite correlation that was equal to (−)0.7 and to identify the turning points.

In the domestic policy, there was a steady unvarying phase between 2004 and 2013 even though the oil price had risen between 2004–2008 and 2010–2013. But at the same time, Kremlin pursued very aggressive foreign policy and foreign energy policy between 2004 and 2013 (the well-known speech at the Munich Security Conference in 2007, the military invasion of Georgia in 2008, "gas war" with Ukraine in 2009). There was a rapid decrease in the oil price between 2014 and 2016, but Kremlin continued foreign policy and energy policy confrontation with the West and "near abroad" countries. Russia's domestic political developments were more sensitive to the oil price changes than its foreign policy including foreign energy policy that relies on more stable principles and vital interests.

In addition to the domestic political settings of Russia, also, the domestic system of the "target" countries can affect the energy conflicts. Ethnic Russians can be seen as a potential determinant of energy conflicts. One of the motives for Russia's aggressive foreign energy policy could be to exploit energy leverage to making pressure on the "near abroad" countries to protect ethnic Russians. There is a significant ethnic Russian population in 17 post-Soviet and Eastern European countries. There is no significant statistical correlation between the share of ethnic Russians in the total population of the target countries and the number of Russia's foreign energy conflicts and supply interruptions cases with the same countries (0.2). If we exclude Ukraine, then the correlation ratio between the share of ethnic Russians in the total population of the target countries and the number of Russia's foreign energy conflicts and supply interruptions scales down to a negative relationship (−0.1; Table 6.4).

Table 6.4 Ethnic Russians abroad and energy conflicts

	Share of ethnic Russians in the total population	*Number of Russia's foreign energy conflicts and supply interruptions*
Armenia	0.50%	22
Azerbaijan	1.30%	39
Belarus	8.30%	51
Estonia	24.80%	10
Georgia	1.50%	27
Kazakhstan	19%	12
Kyrgyzstan	5.50%	3
Latvia	25.20%	14
Lithuania	5.80%	43
Moldova	4.10%	21
Bulgaria	0.40%	31
Finland	0.50%	6
Slovakia	0.30%	11
Tajikistan	1.10%	1
Turkmenistan	4%	20
Ukraine	17.30%	117
Uzbekistan	2.30%	3

Sources: RECSID and CIA (2021).

The share of ethnic Russians in the total population is higher in Latvia (25%), Estonia (25%), and Kazakhstan (19%) where Russia had an insufficient number of energy conflicts and supply interruptions (respectively 14, 10, and 12). Despite the low level of energy conflict intensity, Russia had decided to halt natural gas supply to energy-dependent Estonia in June 1993 arguing discriminatory policy towards ethnic Russians in the target country. Almost ten years later in February 2003, Russia had decided to stop the oil delivery to Latvia claiming that the country mistreated the ethnic Russian minority. Russia had a higher number of energy conflicts and supply interruptions cases with the post-Soviet states that accommodate relatively fewer ethnic Russians (e.g., Azerbaijan, Bulgaria, and Georgia). But also, Russia used the ethnic Russians as a pretext against some post-socialist countries (e.g., Estonia and Latvia) in the foreign and energy policy.

6.4 Energy Conflicts and Economic Interdependence Based on RECSID

Economic interdependence has several channels of transmission including foreign trade and investment in terms of foreign energy policy. Also, several economic indicators shape domestic economic settings and related fragilities. The correlation between energy conflicts and economic indicators is crucial to revealing the pattern of interdependence through a set of vulnerabilities and sensitivities. RECSID revealed that the correlation ratio between the total natural resources' rents (% of GDP) and the number of Russia's foreign energy conflicts and supply interruptions was equal to 0.55 from 1990 to 2019.

The correlation ratio between the oil rents (% of GDP) and the number of Russia's foreign energy conflicts and supply interruptions was equal to 0.54. The correlation ratio between the GDP per capita (current USD) and the number of Russia's foreign energy conflicts and supply interruptions were approximately equal to 0.5. The correlation ratio between the net FDI inflows into the Russian economy as a percentage of GDP and the number of the country's foreign energy conflicts and supply interruptions was equal to 0.5 from 1990 to 2019. There is a negative correlation (−0.2) between Russia's net foreign assets and the number of energy conflicts and supply cuts from 2001 to 2019. The correlation between Russia's energy conflicts and international (foreign exchange reserves and gold) reserves was 0.5 from 1992 to 2019.

RECSID revealed that one-sixth of Russia's energy conflicts and supply interruptions (16%) were experienced with the largest trade partners such as the EU, China, the Netherlands, Germany, and Turkey. The correlation between Russia's export to the target country and the number of the country's foreign energy conflicts and supply interruptions is equal to 0.2. This weak correlation strengthens limitedly if we exclude Ukraine – the leader country in the list of Russia's foreign energy conflicts. The correlation between Russia's export to the target country and the number of the country's foreign energy conflicts and supply interruptions is equal to 0.32 without Ukraine which is an outlier case in the statistical analysis. The correlation between Russia's imports from the target country and the number of the country's foreign energy conflicts and supply interruptions is equal to 0.25. It means that mutual trade interdependence and the volume of the trade turnover didn't prevent the energy conflicts between Russia and the major trade partners. But RECSID identified that Russia did not implement the most radical means of "energy weapon", such as a direct cut-off of energy (gas) supplies, against its biggest trading partners such as China and Germany. RECSID revealed that even though the fact of *interdependence* isn't a major restrictive factor for the Russian foreign energy policy, it mitigates Russia's implementing tools against major energy trade partners. The energy disputes and sensitive prejudices between Russia and neighbouring countries were not antagonistic, and economic and trade interdependence adducted two sides to find a common ground for cooperation. The pattern between Russia's energy conflicts and trade-based interdependence is verified when we segregate the country's total export into electricity natural gas and crude oil.

Russia's electricity export and energy conflicts. Russia's largest electricity export markets were Finland, Lithuania, China, and Kazakhstan in 2019. Russia had not experienced any electricity-related conflicts except in Lithuania. Finland and Lithuania have accounted for almost 70% of Russia's total electricity export in 2019. Russia has only two electricity-related conflicts with Lithuania that were mainly the negative repercussions or "side effects" of Gazprom's failure in the country's gas market, rather than any thoroughgoing measures by Russia to "weaponize" the electricity against the Baltic country (Table 6.5).

Russia had no electricity-related conflicts with Finland, China, and Kazakhstan which make up 60% of the total Russian electricity export. Russia had the highest number of electricity-related conflicts with Georgia that accounting for only 3% of the country's total electricity export in 2019. The composition of Russia's electricity export by countries for 2019 hasn't undergone a drastic change to a large extent over at least the last 15 years (2004–2019). It means that the Baltic countries, Nordic countries, Kazakhstan, and China led the list, and the other post-Soviet countries such as Ukraine and Georgia relatively lagged. Generally, there is a slight

Table 6.5 Russia's electricity export and conflicts by countries (2019)

Country	*Million kWh*	*Electricity conflicts*
Finland	7,607	0
Lithuania	6,285	2
China	3,099	0
Kazakhstan	1,472	1
Georgia[a]	670	7
Mongolia	372	0
Ukraine	329	3
Norway	93	0
Azerbaijan	91	0
Belarus	31	2

Source: Federal Customs Service (2020a).

[a]Includes South Ossetia.

negative correlation between Russia's electricity-related conflicts and the electricity export to certain countries (−0.3). It purports that electricity trade volume as a component and contributor of the energy interdependence played an "alleviating" function in Russia's foreign energy policy and energy conflicts.

Russia's natural gas export and energy conflicts. Russia's largest natural gas export markets were Germany, Turkey, Austria, Italy, France, Belarus, the Netherlands, the UK, and Poland in 2019. The main gas export destination was Germany which has gas-related conflicts with Russia. Also, Russia has a higher number of gas conflicts with Turkey and Belarus which possess a significant share in the country's gas export. But at the same time, Russia had a multitude of gas conflicts with Ukraine and Lithuania that both countries occupy a minor portion of the total country's gas export. But both countries have a "transit power" in terms of Russia's energy exports (Table 6.6).

RECSID has identified that Russia implemented "the total stop or full disruption of gas supply" (directly targeting specific country) tool mostly against post-Soviet or post-socialist countries such as Ukraine, Azerbaijan, Serbia/Yugoslavia, Georgia, and Lithuania that had a lower share in the Russian total gas export. Russia didn't prefer to employ this type of radical energy conflict tool against major gas export destinations such as Germany. European countries have faced total gas supply disruption or reducing gas inflow cases mostly as an aftereffect of Russia-Ukraine gas transit conflicts. Even though Gazprom has warned and threatened the EU as a collective entity on supply cut plenty of times, Kremlin was cautious in selecting an "energy weapon" toolkit against large European gas-consuming states. But this cautiousness didn't prohibit Gazprom from raising the gas prices for Germany by around 40% in January 2006 to adjust the gas prices to the market level and political reasons. So, there is no clear positive and negative correlation between Russia's gas-related conflicts and the gas export volume by country (+0.03).

Table 6.6 Russia's gas export and conflicts by countries (2019)

Country	*Value of gas export (billion USD)*	*Gas conflicts*
Germany	10.6	13
Turkey	4.5	23
Austria	3.2	5
Italy	3.1	10
France	3.1	6
Belarus	2.7	30
Netherlands	2.4	2
UK	2.3	6
Poland	2	23
Norway	1.6	3
Czech Republic	1.6	3
Hungary	1.5	13
Slovakia	1.3	7

Source: Federal Customs Service of Russia (2020a).

Russia's crude oil trade and energy conflicts. The relationship between Russia's crude oil export and oil-related conflicts is analogous to natural gas, lacking any clear and modest correlative pattern. But in comparison with gas conflicts, Russia had relatively more oil-related conflicts with the largest oil trade partners (correlation ratio: +0.3), especially with China (Asia). Russia had 14 oil-related disputes with China as the largest oil-importing partner. Still, it had only two oil-related conflicts with the second-largest buyer of Russian oil – the Netherlands (the country is also the largest importer of Russian petroleum products) as the EU member state. Russia had the highest number of oil-related conflicts with oil-rich Azerbaijan, which plays an insignificant role in the Russian crude oil and oil products exports. Also, it had intense oil-related conflicts with Belarus that deeply integrated with the Russian oil products processing and mutual trade (Table 6.7).

Even though Russia often used the "instrument" of disrupting oil supplies against EU member states, it ruled out the Netherlands as the largest importer of Russian crude oil and petroleum products. In addition, Russia has never stopped supplying crude oil and petroleum products to China as the largest buyer from the Asian continent. Energy interdependence through energy trade isn't a "*valid preventer*" but a "*confined mitigator*", under certain conditions, in Russia's aggressive foreign energy policy and energy conflicts. The major exception is an electricity export that is accompanied by the low intensity of the conflicts. *But we cannot compare Russia's limited electricity export with its crude oil and natural gas export's considerable volume and value.*

Table 6.7 Russia's crude oil export and conflicts by countries (2019)

Country	*The volume of crude oil export (million tonnes)*	*Gas conflicts*
China	70.63	14
Netherlands	46.2	2
Germany	18.9	4
Belarus	18.1	19
South Korea	15.3	0
Italy	14.6	1
Poland	14.1	6
Finland	9.9	0
Turkey	8.2	4
Japan	6.4	1
Slovakia	5.1	4
USA	4.7	14
Hungary	4.3	7
Czech	3.8	5
Bulgaria	3.5	6
Romania	3.2	2
Lithuania	3.1	14
India	2.5	0
UK	2.4	2
Greece	2.3	2

Source: Federal Customs Service of Russia (2020a).

Russia's energy conflicts and trade openness. The intense conflicts in the Russian foreign energy policy and trade openness had a slight negative correlation. The correlation ratio between the number of Russia's foreign energy conflicts (plus supply interruptions) and the primary trade openness indicator ((import (+) export) (/) GDP) was (−)0.3 from 1992 to 2019. The trade openness index of Russia for 2019 was around 20% (UNCTAD, 2021f). This level was the worst indicator compared to other post-Soviet states because the resource-rich national economy of Russia is based on the non-diversified export of oil-gas and mineral resources. Russia's trade openness and energy conflicts increased parallelly between 1997 and 2000. After 2000, the trade openness gradually decreased while energy conflicts followed zigzagging trends with rapid soars occasionally (e.g., 2006, 2009, 2014). Trade openness is a multidimensional variable that depends not only on structural factors but also on pure market-based or even seasonal factors. But Russia's growing energy conflicts between 2004 and 2014 partly coincided with the period when the country's trade openness level shrank (Figure 6.13).

Energy conflicts and complex influence. Russia's energy conflicts could be examined concerning the country's complex influence on the target countries using various indices. Foreign Bilateral Influence Capacity (FBIC) Index (developed by Josef Korbel School of International Studies at the University of Denver) measures the influence capacity of major global and regional powers including Russia in terms of economy, politics, and security (The University of Denver, 2020). RECSID and FBIC Index 2019 results have disclosed that there is a negative correlation (−0.2) between Russia's economic, political, and security influence in the target (mostly neighbouring and post-socialist countries) countries and the number of

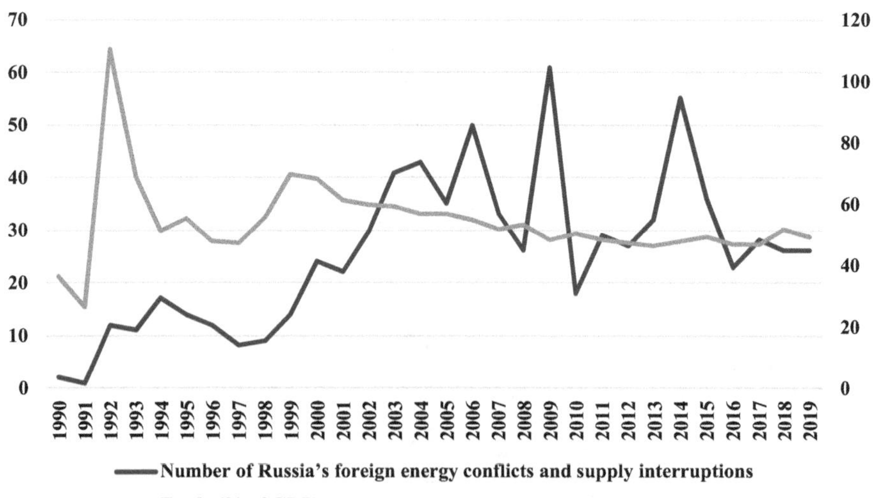

Figure 6.13 Russia's energy conflicts and trade openness.

Sources: RECSID; World Bank Data; and UNCTAD.

foreign energy conflicts and supply interruptions. Economic, political, and security interactions could increase Russia's influence on the "receiver" country and also, scale up the target country's dependence on Russia. But this complex influence and complex dependence could contrarily relate to energy affairs.

Russia could have more energy conflicts with the target country that it has less economic, political, and security influence (based on FBIC results). For FBIC Index 2019, Russia had relatively moderate and low levels of economic, political, and security influence on Azerbaijan, Ukraine, and Lithuania where it had a higher number of foreign energy conflicts and supply interruptions. The only exception is the case of Belarus. For FBIC Index 2019 results, Russia had the highest level of economic, political, and security influence on Belarus which is the number two country in terms of energy conflicts with Russia. Also, Russia had relatively higher levels of economic, political, and security influence on the post-Soviet countries in Central Asia including Kyrgyzstan, Kazakhstan, and Tajikistan which had a lower number of foreign energy conflicts (Table 6.8).

Energy conflicts and energy dependence. The share of Russian natural gas in the total gas consumption of the selected European and post-Soviet countries varied from 10% to more than 100% (RIA Novosti, 2018). But the level of gas import dependence of the consumer countries on Russia isn't a determinant and single trigger of the Russian foreign energy conflicts and energy supply interruptions. Russia could have fewer energy conflicts with countries that had higher energy dependence on Russia. For example, the share of Finland's gas import from Russia in the country's total gas consumption was 125% in 2018, but the country has only 6 minor energy conflicts with Russia from 1990 to 2019. Lithuania's gas dependence on Russia was 45%, but the country had 42 energy conflicts with Russia. But Latvia's gas dependence on Russia was 77%, but it had 13 energy conflicts with Russia

Table 6.8 Russia's influence and energy conflicts

	FBIC Index (2019)	*Number of energy conflicts*
Belarus	0.996	51
Kyrgyzstan	0.802	3
Kazakhstan	0.744	12
Armenia	0.628	22
Georgia	0.62	27
Tajikistan	0.524	1
Azerbaijan	0.386	39
Mongolia	0.273	1
Ukraine	0.21	117
Turkmenistan	0.174	20
Uzbekistan	0.135	3
Moldova	0.08	21
Lithuania	0.09	43
Latvia	0.09	14
Estonia	0.08	10

Sources: RECSID and The University of Denver (2020).

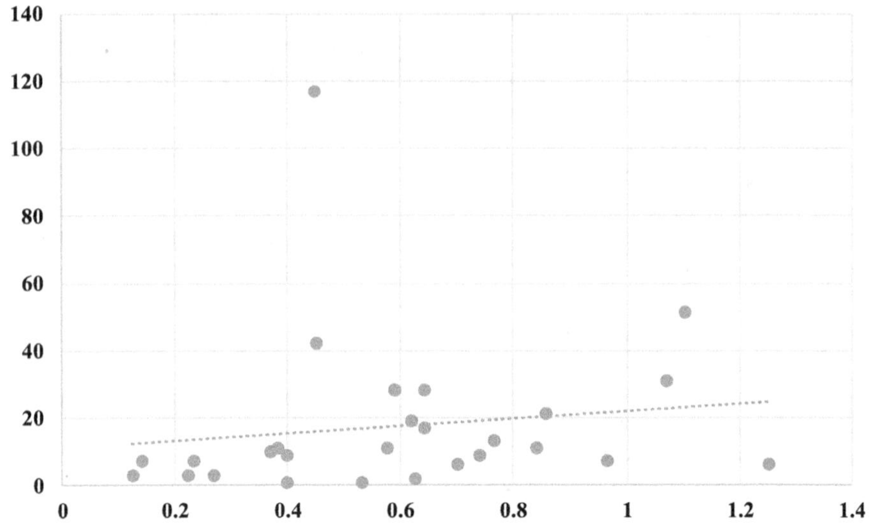

Figure 6.14 Russia's energy conflicts and the EU's dependence (%) on gas import.

Sources: RIA Novosti (2018) and RECSID.

(Figure 6.14). The correlation ratio between the energy dependence of European countries on Russian gas and the number of Russia's foreign energy conflicts and supply interruptions is very weak (0.13).

When we examine not only natural gas but all energy types, the energy imports dependency of the EU-27 was higher than 60% in 2019 (the portion of imports in total energy consumption) (Eurostat, 2021a). Small EU countries such as Malta, Luxembourg, and Cyprus had an energy import dependency ratio between 90% and 100%. Italy's energy imports dependence was 77.5%, in Hungary – 70%, Germany – 67.6%, France – 47.6%, the UK – 35%, and Sweden – 30%. The major exporter country that those European countries depend on is Russia. The share of Russia in the EU's total natural gas import was 41%, crude oil was 27% (two-thirds of the non-EU's crude oil imports), and coal was 47% in 2019 (Eurostat, 2020).

Europe was the largest buyer of Russian oil before the war in Ukraine (also, the share of Russia in the EU's annual oil imports was 36% in early 2022) and more than 40% of Russia's oil exports fell to Europe in 2021. EU's crude oil import from Russia decreased to 4% of total crude imports in December 2022 (Russia supplied 10% of EU's imported oil products for the same period) after the import prohibition on Russia's seaborne crude oil (the 6th package of EU's energy-related sanctions) (Eurostat, 2023). One-third of Russia's budget revenues come from oil revenues (gas exports provide 7% of budget income) and the federal budget's dependence on fossil fuels (oil and gas) increased after the sanctions in 2022. Kudiyarov (2022) defined the gas affairs between Europe and Russia as an "*umbilical cord*" that isn't easy to cut suddenly. In 2021, the EU imported 155 billion cubic metres of natural gas from Russia, which is about 45% of the total imports of EU countries (40%

of the EU's total gas demand) and about 30% of total consumption. Also, the EU accounts for three-quarters of Russia's pipeline gas exports, which is equivalent to almost a third of Gazprom's total annual production. It means that Russia also couldn't repudiate Europe as a major buyer of natural gas. For Kudiyarov (2022), the specific operations and export-import transactions in the gas market are carried out by pragmatic and rational commercial companies, not by emotional politicians. From this position, it is not Germany that buys gas from Russia, but the German RWE company from the Russian Gazprom company. The affairs amid coeval companies are "a tangle of complex interactions" (The Economist, 2022) that on one hand offer alternatives for the supply of goods (and increase the adjustability to the realities) but also accelerate the contagion effect of the energy supply interruptions.

Russia and Europe have an interdependence pattern related to the energy trade. But the EU primarily depends on Russia as the number one country for oil, gas, and coal imports. This dependence creates a certain level of vulnerability and sensitivity in the European countries in the face of Russia. Russia's exploitation of this dependence as political leverage could be modified according to the "dependent" countries' (geo)political loyalty and Russia's key national interests. When interdependence theory exhausts itself in explaining the foreign energy policy of Russia, we refer to the country's security (e.g., NATO expansion) and geopolitical considerations or motivations.[3]

Notes

1 "Total Value Index" of the Democracy Matrix (three dimensions: freedom, equality, control; five institutions: elections, civil society, free media, judiciary, effective/accountable power) developed by the University of Würzburg (https://www.democracymatrix.com/conception/democracy-matrix#c525).

2 There is a strong negative correlation (−0.8) between the two sets of values [Russia's energy disputes/cases in International Arbitration (Stockholm Chamber of Commerce) and crude oil prices] indicating that Russia had more energy-related cases in international arbitration when crude oil prices were lower in global markets.

3 For example, Finland's political and security neutrality or the number of ethnic Russians in Latvia could be the determinants in the Russian foreign energy policy towards the countries.

7 Motivations, Determinants, and Constraints of Russia's FEP and Energy Conflicts

7.1 Russia's Energy Conflicts with Major Energy Partners

Russian foreign energy policy cannot be understood as a "united" phenomenon. There is a need to fragmentize the energy conflicts into country-based cases (with countries where Russia had more intense energy conflicts) to reveal real motives.

Russia-Ukraine energy conflicts: RECSID findings. RECSID identified 124 energy conflicts with *Ukraine* in 1991–2021 that were mostly related to natural gas (approximately 80%). Russia had a few energy conflicts with Belarus on crude oil, oil products, nuclear energy, coal, and electricity (approximately 20%). Only 15% of the energy conflicts between Russia and Ukraine occurred before 2000, and 85% of the energy conflicts took place after 2000. Based on historical evidence, analysis of energy conflicts in Russia, and strategic documents of the country, we should reasonably conclude that Russia's energy policy towards Ukraine has a unique historical, political, and economic background. The energy conflicts with Ukraine cannot be used to interpret patterns of Russia's foreign energy policy and energy conflicts with other actors.

Russia and Ukraine had all types of energy conflicts with various applied tools: Gazprom and Naftogaz filed overmuch lawsuits against each other; Gazprom reduced the gas supply to Ukraine; Rosneft or Transneft reduced the oil deliveries to Ukraine; Russia warned to stop or reduce the oil-gas supply to Ukraine; Russia totally stopped the oil-gas supply to Ukraine; Gazprom raised gas prices and used gas debt as a political pressure tool; Rosatom delayed the delivery of nuclear fuel for the NPP; Russia stopped coal supply to Ukraine; Russia organized the terrorist attack to gas pipeline in Ukraine; both sides warned each other to terminate gas transit contracts. Chronic non-payment problem and gas debts to Gazprom, Ukraine's unique historical relations with Russia and domestic politics, Ukraine's relations with EU and NATO, Russia-Ukraine disputes on the Black Sea Fleet, Russia's expansionist energy policy towards "near abroad", gas supply disputes between Gazprom-Naftogaz-Itera, and Ukraine's decision to increase the tariff for oil-gas transit triggered oil-gas crises between two countries. As a result of the Rosatom-Westinghouse competition over the Ukrainian nuclear energy market, Rosatom warned to raise nuclear fuel prices and delayed the delivery of nuclear fuel for the nuclear power plants of Ukraine. Ukraine signed a fuel supply deal

DOI: 10.4324/9781003408482-7

with Westinghouse in 2008 and Kyiv aimed to increase fuel purchases from the USA after the 2014 crisis when Ukraine extended the contract with Westinghouse (2014) and terminated the contract with Rosatom (2015). Russia stopped coal and electricity supplies to Ukraine in 2014, and it supplied power to the unrecognized "Lugansk" separatist region with political motivation. Russia-Ukraine energy conflicts combined the complex conjunction of geopolitical and commercial motivations based on the unique history of bilateral affairs.

Russia-Belarus energy conflicts: RECSID findings. RECSID identified 53 energy conflicts with *Belarus* in 1991–2021 that were mostly related to natural gas (59%) and oil (37%). Russia had a few energy conflicts with Belarus on nuclear energy and electricity issues. Only 10% of the energy conflicts between Russia and Belarus occurred before 2000, and 90% of the energy conflicts took place after 2000. Gazprom warned to cut off the gas and oil supplies to Belarus with economic and political incentives. But also, RECSID has identified the real facts when Gazprom halted the gas supply and oil deliveries to Belarus and oil-gas transit via Belarus. Gazprom has warned Belarus about gas price hikes and even threatened to double gas prices for economic and political reasons. Belarus protested Gazprom for a higher price and a large-scale "trade war" had started between the two countries. Russia used oil-gas debts as political leverage and Belarus refused to pay the oil-gas debt. Even the Ministry of Foreign Affairs of Russia sent a note to Minsk on gas prices for the chronic gas debts to Gazprom in 2010. In Moscow-Minsk conflicts regarding the oil-gas supplies and higher oil-gas prices, the MFA of Russia acted as the energy sector's powerful actor.

Belarus demanded a unique position in terms of oil-gas debts and oil-gas prices that could be adjusted to the Russian local price level. Adjustment of the Russian oil-gas price to the market level was painful for Belarus and Lukashenko threatens Russia with retaliation. Russia failed in intergovernmental oil-gas negotiations with Belarus in 1996 when Russia made political pressure on Belarus after the referendum. Russia had a challenge in the oil-gas transit via Belarus when the transit country used its bargaining power. Oil-gas debt and price issues were often discussed at the highest political level between the two countries, but Putin and Lukashenko often failed to be agreed on the energy conflicts.

Moscow demands from Minsk to recognize South Ossetia and Abkhazia in return for energy concessions, but Minsk refused to recognize the separatist units of Georgia. Belarus has delayed the transactions of the Russian oil-gas companies to control the country's oil-gas assets and infrastructure. The privatization of Beltransgaz and Mozyr Oil Refinery led to political disputes between the two countries. Belarus and Russia had unique energy conflicts, especially in the oil sector on duty-free supplies of oil deliveries and importing contaminated oil with a high concentration of chlorides. Belarus has abandoned the oil, gas, and electricity import from Russia to protest its foreign energy policy. Belarus decided to annul the Russian ownership of the oil pipeline and claimed that the energy price hikes and energy supply disruptions were a "political order". Russia was seeking alternative routes for oil-gas exports and Transneft decided to reroute crude oil and refined products for alternative buyers as a part of its export diversification strategy. Even though actual commercial motivations prevailed in the Russia-Belarus energy conflicts, political factors also played an important role in containing the difficulties of the integration projects.

Russia-Lithuania energy conflicts: RECSID findings. RECSID identified 43 energy conflicts with *Lithuania* in 1990–2021 that were mostly related to natural gas (57%) and oil (33%). Russia had energy conflicts with Lithuania on nuclear energy and electricity issues, as well. Gazprom was a major actor in the energy conflicts between these two countries. Gazprom filed a series of lawsuits against Lithuania and encountered counterclaims by the target country. Gazprom raised the gas prices against Lithuania with economic and political motives. Lithuania warned to raise the tariff for gas transit when Gazprom warned to stop gas supply for geopolitical reasons. Gazprom reduced and fully halted the gas supply to Lithuania. Also, Lukoil reduced and halted the oil deliveries to Lithuania. Baltic states including Lithuania were punished for political disloyalty through adjustment of the oil price to the market, as a result, Vilnius refused to buy Lukoil's oil products in 2005.

Lithuania has excluded Gazprom and Lukoil from tenders with political concerns to purchase the local energy assets in the country such as Mazeikiai Oil Refinery. Lithuania insisted on revising the gas price and gas volume by Gazprom using its transit power. Lithuania protested the construction of the Belarus Nuclear Power Plant by the Russian state-owned Rosatom corporation very close to the Belarus-Lithuania border that Vilnius considered a part of Russia's geopolitical plan. The dispute over the Belarus NPP had repercussions on the oil-gas affairs between Lithuania and Russia. US's entry into the global gas market with LNG and expansion towards the Baltic countries including Lithuania created a harsh rivalry with Russia. RECSID findings disclosed that Russia-USA competition over the Lithuanian market was one of the main determinants in the energy conflicts between Russia and Lithuania (political and commercial rivalry). Also, Russia-Poland energy and geopolitical competition had a negative repercussion on the Russian oil-gas affairs with Lithuania ("*third-party effect*").

Russia-Azerbaijan energy conflicts: RECSID findings. RECSID identified 39 energy conflicts with *Azerbaijan* that were distributed equally between the oil and gas sectors between 1992 and 2016. Russia and Azerbaijan had all tools of energy conflicts: explosions and sabotage in the oil-gas pipelines and oil fields' drilling platforms (*Map*); failure to sign or extend oil-gas deal; failed oil-gas negotiations; gas price disputes; gas volume disputes; oil transit disputes; energy debts and non-payment issues; some delays in the oil-gas exploration projects; complex energy conflicts that directly related to the security and politics; investigations against the Russian oil-gas companies; reducing the gas supply; warning to stop the gas supply; total stop of gas supply; challenges in the transactions and foreign assets acquisitions of the Russian oil-gas companies in Azerbaijan.

Russia's geopolitical confrontation with global and regional powers over the South Caucasus, the war in Chechnya and the tension in the North Caucasus, the legal status of the Caspian Sea, the transit routes of Azerbaijan's oil-gas reserves bypassing Russia, domestic political events, and integration attempts towards Western alliance very much determined political components of the bilateral energy affairs between Azerbaijan and Russia. The war in Chechnya and Karabakh conflict has influenced Azerbaijan's decision on the early oil export routes. Lukoil, Gazprom, and Transneft were actively involved in the energy conflicts with Azerbaijan and state-owned SOCAR. Despite all political tensions and energy conflicts, intense negotiations on bilateral oil-gas cooperation continued and Russia participated in oil-gas projects with Azerbaijan. Azerbaijan succeed to diversify oil and gas export routes bypassing Russia, but also resumed crude oil export via Novorossiysk port. Azerbaijan-Turkey energy rapprochement made tense in the energy affairs and oil-gas conflicts with Russia ("*third-party effect*"). Political and geopolitical motivations prevailed in the Russia-Azerbaijan energy conflicts in comparison with a commercial determinant.

Russia-Bulgaria energy conflicts: RECSID findings. RECSID identified 32 energy conflicts with *Bulgaria* in 1991–2021 that were mostly related to natural gas (48%), nuclear energy (23%), and oil (19%). Russia had a few energy conflicts with Bulgaria on electricity issues. Only 13% of the energy conflicts between Russia and Bulgaria occurred before 2000, and 87% of the energy conflicts took place after 2000. Russia and Bulgaria had direct natural gas-related conflicts on the South Stream gas pipeline project when the EU's political position affected Bulgaria's decisions. Russia-Ukraine energy conflicts and the supply disruptions in the winter seasons created second-tier gas conflicts between Russia and Bulgaria as a repercussion. Gazprom warned to stop gas supply, reduced the volume of gas supply, halted the gas supply totally, and raised the gas prices from 1994 to 2014.

Almost all nuclear energy bilateral conflicts were related to the Belene Nuclear Power Plant (NPP) project in 2011–2012 when Bulgaria refused to finance the project, suspended official negotiations with Rosatom, abandoned the building of the NPP, and finally, refused to pay Rosatom's penalties after the mutual litigations. Oil-related conflicts have emerged mainly in 2011–2016 when Bulgaria investigated Lukoil for antimonopoly policies and the company was suspected of abuse of market rules. The electricity-related bilateral conflicts were pertinent to the Russian RAO UES's company and its foreign asset transactions in Bulgaria. Domestic political changes and political opposition against the Russian energy companies (e.g. Lukoil, Gazprom, RAO UES, and Rosatom) deeply impacted on Russia-Bulgaria energy conflicts. Also, we have to take into account that Russia's energy conflicts with the target country often had negative consequences for third countries ("*third-party effect*"). For example, Russia-Ukraine energy conflicts affected the EU, and Russia-EU energy conflicts negatively affected Bulgaria (e.g., the refusal of the Belene NPP project). Political and commercial motivations coexisted in the energy conflict between Russia and Bulgaria.

Russia-China energy conflicts: RECSID findings. RECSID identified 32 energy conflicts with *China* in 1991–2021 that were mostly related to gas (55%), and oil (45%). All energy conflicts between Russia and China took place after 2000. Generally, we could differentiate between conditions-based energy conflicts (related to the contract conditions such as prices, volumes, and export routes) and punishment-based energy conflicts (supply cuts, manipulations with oil-gas exports, sabotages, etc.). Bilateral gas conflicts related to the conditions (price, volume, route) of the gas supply from Russia to China. CNPC and Gazprom had a series of failed gas supply negotiations. CNPC and Gazprom seriously disputed gas prices and gas export routes, as a result, Gazprom postponed the gas supply to China through the pipeline. Gazprom aimed to supply natural gas to China at the EU price level. China presented a tough position on the gas price and Gazprom resisted changing its pricing policy. The base gas price and formula for its indexation led to the gas conflicts. The long-awaited gas contract failed for the gas price in the early 2010s and led to political and economic bargains among countries. Putin and Xi Jinping directly intervened in the price disputes to solve the conflict in 2014. Putin instructed Gazprom on the new supply route to China.

CNPC insisted on revising the gas pricing formula by the Russian side and Gazprom claimed advance payment from China. China did not guarantee the volume of the gas purchase in Russia. China did not need the Russian gas urgently, but it demanded the Russian gas for energy security and diversification. The inauguration of the Turkmen-China gas pipeline also triggered a dispute between Russia and China ("*third-party effect*"). China gradually pulled out of Russia from the Central Asian region starting with energy and continuing to politics. Russia lost bargaining power not only with China but with the EU, as well, when China could easily agree with Turkmenistan on gas price and gas export volume. China refused to invest in the Russian energy infrastructure including the Yamal LNG project several times when Chinese funds tried to avoid US sanctions. So, the US sanctions on Russia's energy sector influenced China's position.

Regarding the bilateral oil-related conflicts, Rosneft and Sinopec did not agree on oil price, Rosneft had a conflict with CNPC on oil price, there was a disagreement on oil export pipelines routes, Rosneft rejected to renew oil supply deal to China, China didn't pay for oil supply to Transneft, China warned about the delay and changes in oil pipeline projects, Russia did not give state guarantees for oil supplies, Yukos stopped shipping oil to CNPC, Lukoil started a lawsuit against Sinopec on oil disputes, China insisted on a new scheme for the oil supply. The rerouting of the oil export pipeline by Russia was viewed as a political step on the Chinese side. Russia and China had oil transaction-related conflicts, as well when Chinese oil-gas company CEFC decided to freeze a purchase of Rosneft's 14% stake in 2018 and CNPC refused to buy Slavneft in the auction in the early 2000s. Russia's internal group interests led to delays in the oil-gas projects with China. RECSID disclosed that China-Russia energy conflicts were mostly determined by commercial disputes.

Russia-USA energy conflicts: RECSID findings. RECSID identified 41 energy conflicts with the *USA* in 1991–2021 that were combined pure gas conflicts (32% of the total), pure oil conflicts (23%), nuclear energy conflicts (19%), and composite energy conflicts (oil, gas, nuclear, electricity –26%). Only 13% of the energy conflicts between Russia and the USA occurred before 2000, 87% of the energy conflicts took place after 2000 when Putin started to rule the country. In Putin's ruling period, the Russian economy was more integrated into the world economy, but energy conflicts increased. Russia-USA energy conflicts included competition over the European market, nuclear energy competition between Rosatom and Westinghouse, the

US sanctions imposed on the Russian oil and gas companies, lawsuits against the Russian energy companies, and problems of the US oil-gas companies in the Russian energy market (especially, ExxonMobil), failed negotiations on nuclear fuel supply, and the US opposition against Russia's energy transactions towards assets acquisitions. More than 50% of the total energy conflicts between Russia and the USA were related to unilateral sanctions against Russian energy companies after 2014.

In 2001, the US investigated Lukoil's assets outside of Russia and the US had a sceptical view of Lukoil's expansion when Lukoil bought the network of gas stations in the US. In March 2003, the US invasion of Iraq didn't regard Russian energy interests. As a result, Russian oil companies suffered losses, and bilateral relations "cooled" temporarily. In January 2004, Russia changed its attitudes towards foreign oil-gas companies. ExxonMobil and Chevron lost the right in Sakhalin-3 and foreign oil companies hesitated about Russia. In January 2008, the sale of 51% of Serbia's NIS to Gazprom resulted in the US opposition to Russia's energy assets in Serbia. Rosatom-Westinghouse competition on Bulgaria's nuclear energy market deferred the nuclear deal of Russia with Bulgaria in 1995. But Rosatom continued to enter that Eastern European market after 2000. Russia built nuclear power plants in Iran and China. As a result, the US refused to import Russia's nuclear fuel in 2001. Also, the USA was against Russia-Georgia natural gas cooperation in 2003. Russia confronted the USA in the Georgian market and it had supported the Baku-Tbilisi-Erzurum gas pipeline project. The US had made continuous political pressure on Germany regarding Russian gas imports.

US sanctions reduced the number of Western partners of Rosatom and Gazprom. After 2014, ExxonMobil stopped cooperation with Rosneft, while EU and US sanctions did not impact the Sakhalin oil projects. Gazprom and Rosneft warned the USA of retaliation in 2014 when access to technology and finance was an issue for the Russian companies. In 2015, ExxonMobil changed its rhetoric against Russia, and it warned to file a claim against the country. In 2018, the US's energy and finance sanctions triggered Russia to adopt counter-sanctions against the USA complicating bilateral energy ties. In 2019, ExxonMobil faced administrative barriers and restrictions in the Sakhalin-1 project when the company could not use vessels under a foreign flag. In January 2019, the US envoy in Germany directly intervened in Nord Stream-2 pipeline project, and the US aimed to replace Russian gas with its LNG resources in the European market. Germany decided to freeze the Nord Stream-2 gas pipeline project because of serious political pressure from the USA related to the Ukrainian war in February 2022. RECSID revealed that USA-Russia energy conflicts were caused by geopolitical competition over critical regions and the "third-party effect" of Ukraine as a "vibrant detonator".

Russia-EU energy conflicts: RECSID findings. RECSID identified 53 energy conflicts with the EU as a political entity by 2021 that were mostly related to natural gas (approximately 83%). Russia had a few energy conflicts with the EU on oil, nuclear, and electricity (approximately 17%). Russia's oil-gas export to the EU had a long history (gas cooperation started in 1968, and oil affairs even have a more extended history). All energy conflicts between Russia and the EU as a political entity occurred after 2000 during the ruling period of Putin. Russia-EU energy conflicts included market abuse by the Russian energy companies, warning by the Russian side to reduce or stop gas supply, reducing the oil-gas supply to the EU zone, investigations, and lawsuits against the Russian energy companies, inefficacious energy transactions of the Russian energy companies that were blocked by the EU, price-related and energy transit conflicts, pipeline route, and oil-gas diversification efforts by EU.

RECSID identified that Russia had problems with the EU on gas affairs from the mid-2000s. Russia's refusal to sign the Energy Charter with the EU intensified energy isolationism in 2006. In 2006, the EU coordinated countermeasures for Gazprom when the gas monopolist squeezed the foreign investors out of the Sakhalin-2 oil-gas field. The EU changed its position on Russia's energy sector after the military aggression of Russia against Georgia in 2008. EU blamed Russia for using oil and gas as a political weapon. The EU aimed and officially expressed to reduce energy dependence on Russia by realizing a supply diversification strategy. EU proposed a series of alternatives against Russia in the gas supply including "Caspian-Black Sea-Baltic Energy Transit Space".

In 2006, Russia menaced the EU with gas supply to China and the EU harshly criticized Gazprom for "natural gas blackmailing". Gazprom reduced its gas exports by 21% to the EU in 2008 for commercial, technical, and political reasons. Ten years later in 2018, Russia reduced the crude oil (with increasing sulphur content) exported via Transneft pipelines to the EU while high-quality oils were exported to China. In October 2008, a short after Russia-Georgia-West political-military crisis, Gazprom applied record high prices for the EU (USD 500 per 1,000 cubic metres of gas), but it couldn't keep high gas prices for the EU because of existing alternative suppliers. The natural gas price hike was a response to the EU's efforts to diversify gas imports. In 2009, Putin called on the EU to support the South Stream gas export project threatening the EU with expensive LNG.

In 2009, Russia did not guarantee Europe for gas supply interruptions while Russia-EU energy politics tension over the Ukrainian transit lasted. In 2009, President Putin stated that the EU ignores Russia's interests and directly warned of new gas supply disruptions in the EU. Russia warned to stop the gas supply to the EU to force the Union to refuse alternative gas sources in 2009 while the EU decreased gas imports from Russia. In the winter 2009, Putin directly warned the EU about the new gas crisis for political reasons and the gas debt payment issue with Ukraine. In 2009, Rosneft's CEO Sechin warned Europe of a new oil-gas crisis when Russia was against the Odessa-Brody oil pipeline. Gazprom raised the gas prices for the EU as a political enforcement mechanism when the EU denied providing special status to Gazprom in 2011.

EU countries had attempted to show a consolidated position against Russia after 2008 and strongly backed the Southern Gas Transport Corridor and Nabucco project. EU approved the third energy package in 2009 as a part of the gas market liberalization plan, but Gazprom couldn't reach end consumers in the EU after the package. In 2007, the EU proposed very tough energy market reforms and as a result, Gazprom was refused to get electricity grids in the EU. Not only Gazprom but also RAO UES suffered from the EU laws on the energy market. Gazprom was accused to violate consumers' rights in the EU market and the EU charged Gazprom with market abuse in 2015. Gazprom committed to complying with EU rule in 2018 offering a natural gas discount to the EU. In 2019, amendments to the EU gas directive were debated and Gazprom considered the rule that Nord Stream-2 gas pipeline should not be operated by the company, as discriminatory.

RECSID specified that Russia and the EU had a series of conflicts regarding the gas supply pipelines. In 2013, the EU openly threatened the South Stream project that could connect Russia with the South-Eastern European gas market. EU openly struggled with the natural gas supply project of Russia. In 2014, EU-Russia gas negotiations on the South Stream pipeline failed and the EU didn't exempt South Stream from the gas market regulation rules. In 2014, the EU blocked the South Stream pipeline project after the annexation of Crimea, and Russia abandoned the gas pipeline project. From 2013 to 2019, Russia and the EU couldn't agree on the capacity of the OPAL ("Ostsee-Pipeline-Anbindungsleitung") gas pipeline throughout Germany, and Gazprom's expanded access to 90% of the capacity of the OPAL pipeline was cancelled by the EU's Third Energy Package. In 2017, Gazprom refused to raise gas transit via Ukraine as a reaction to a lawsuit from Poland against Gazprom's access to the OPAL gas pipeline. In 2018, Russia halted natural gas supply in the Yamal-Europe and Nord Stream gas pipelines. An official reason was preventive maintenance, but some technical closures were related to politics. In 2019, EU countries' refineries refused to pay for contaminated oil flowing via the Druzhba pipeline. As a result, Surgutneftegaz and Rosneft faced material loss in the EU.

EU countries were divided on Gazprom's position when the EU's energy security plans were against Russia. EU launched a series of antitrust investigations and inspections against Gazprom suspecting the company's monopolistic position in the gas market of the EU and separate member countries such as Italy. EU member countries such as Bulgaria, Poland, Estonia, and Lithuania supported the EU's antitrust investigation on Gazprom's gas sales, gas prices, and the Nord Stream-2 pipeline project. In 2011, Gazprom aimed to control a gas storage facility in the EU. But the EU successfully blocked Gazprom's deal on Austria Gas Hub and the company was expelled from the spot gas trade in the EU. In 2014, the EU threatened Russia with a lawsuit in WTO because of export duty exemptions and privileges to China for oil fields in Siberia that gave China an advantage over the EU.

In 2014, EU-Ukraine-Russia gas negotiations failed while Gazprom warned to reduce gas supply and the EU released a stress test on gas supply stoppage. In 2015, Gazprom CEO Miller directly warned and threatened EU states and consumers with gas supply cuts as a reaction to a new concept of the EU Energy Union. RECSID identified that the EU's investigations against the Russian energy companies weren't limited only to the natural gas and oil sectors, but included nuclear energy, as well. The EU started an investigation against Rosatom's deal with Hungary on Paks NPP in 2015 claiming that both sides signed a contract without a tender procedure. EU succeeded to block the Russia-Hungary nuclear deal in 2015 that envisaged Rosatom as the only fuel supplier to the Paks NPP. The EU's energy conflicts with Russia adversely impacted the energy policy and security of some member countries in the gas, oil, nuclear, and even coal (especially, after the energy embargo related to the war in Ukraine in 2022). The unloading of Russian oil into the EU ports was prohibited from 5 December 2022. The intense energy conflicts between Russia and the EU were a complex combination of commercial and geopolitical determinants.

7.2 Motivations of Russia's Energy Conflicts

Country-based analysis of energy conflicts based on RECSID findings has revealed that Russia's energy conflicts had geopolitical and commercial motives. RECSID contains a series of energy conflicts between Russia and counterpart countries with geopolitical and commercial motivations. Although there is an interconnection between these two types of disputes, it is difficult analytically to determine a solid cause-and-effect relationship between commercially motivated and geopolitically motivated energy conflicts. RECSID's findings revealed the cases of the energy conflicts with energy geopolitics dimension and commercial motives. The geopolitical importance of the energy export routes and geopolitical narratives in the concrete energy projects were shown up in the Russian foreign energy policy. Also, energy assets' privatization, energy investments, the costs of the energy projects, and conditions of energy transit could trigger energy conflicts as a commercial motivation (Table 7.1).

Energy conflicts of Russia with geopolitical motives. Geopolitical motives prevailed in the energy conflicts between Azerbaijan and Russia over explosions and sabotage in the Baku-Novorossiysk pipeline in 1999 when the Chechnya-Russia war and the Baku-Supsa pipeline project triggered energy geopolitics. Also, there were geopolitical motives behind the total stop of oil export in the Baku-Novorossiysk pipeline by SOCAR in 1999 when the state of Azerbaijan openly stated that it preferred the Baku-Tbilisi-Ceyhan export pipeline. In the early 2000s, Lukoil decided to drop the bid for the privatization of Polish Rafineria Gdanska of Poland when Lukoil was perceived as a Russian geopolitical tool in the former socialist bloc countries. In 2002, Lukoil sold its stake in Azerbaijan's Azeri-Chirag-Guneshli project to the Inpex company of Japan, but at the same time, Lukoil had wanted to strengthen its position in Iraq's oil sector as a part of the USA-Russia geopolitical deal. In 2004, oil tankers passing via the Bosphorus strait restricted by Turkey and Russian oil companies suffered heavy losses, as a result of geopolitical disputes over the Chechnya war and the Kurd issue.

In 2014, the Crimean referendum raised geopolitical risks and as a result, Gazprom and Rosneft were sanctioned by the EU and the USA. EU blocked energy supply to Crimea in 2014, but Russia had to cooperate with Ukraine on Crimea. In 2017, the EU expanded sanctions against Russia, and electricity sector officials were sanctioned by the EU after the supply of Siemens turbines to Crimea. EU sanctions reduced the number of the Western partners of the Russian energy companies and access to technology and finance was a serious issue. The geopolitical rift between Ukraine and Russia has caused a warning to the address of the EU and

Table 7.1 Energy conflicts with geopolitical and commercial motivations

Energy conflicts with geopolitical motivation	*Energy conflicts with a commercial motivation*
In October 1997, Russia warned to stop natural gas deliveries to Bulgaria. It was claimed that gas disruptions had a political motivation to provoke public discontent in Bulgaria.	In November 1994, there was sabotage in the Russia-Armenia gas pipeline that led to the interim cessation of gas supplies to Armenia. The motive was the privatization of Armenian energy assets.
In February 1999, sabotage occurred on the Baku-Novorossiysk oil pipeline, which halted the export of Azeri crude oil. The reason was the geopolitical conflict between Azerbaijan and Russia over the war in Chechnya.	Gazprom stopped the gas supply to Georgia in January 2001. The motivation was the competition with the US energy company and the suspension of RAO UES from the electricity tender.
In January 2000, Russia demanded the payments of USD 4 billion energy debts of CIS countries to Russia. Russia used debts as political leverage demanding political loyalty from CIS states.	Russia-China negotiations on oil export pipeline routes failed in March 2003. Rerouting of the pipeline was viewed not only as a political step by China but also raised the project's costs.
In February 2004, tankers pass via Bosphorus restricted and Russian oil companies suffered losses. The motive was a geopolitical dispute between Russia and Turkey on Russian support to the PKK terrorists.	Russia intended to pull out of Iran from the electricity market of Tajikistan in October 2004. Iran and Russia had competed in the energy resources and market of Tajikistan increasing energy investment.
In March 2011, Gazprom had a problem with Moldova regarding the gas debt payment. The motive was the Kremlin's geopolitical interests in the Transnistria separatist region of Moldova.	Gazprom filed claims against Lithuania ("Kauno Energija") in March 2010 and warned to exit from the heat and power plant deal. Lithuania accused Gazprom of non-compliance with the contract.
Putin personally warned to limit gas supplies to Ukraine in April 2014. The motive was political discord and a geopolitical clash between Ukraine and the EU.	In May 2015, Gazprom filed a new lawsuit against Naftogaz (Ukraine). The motive was mutual gas debt and gas price claims that strained bilateral gas relations.
In December 2014, Russia decided to abandon the South Stream gas pipeline when the EU blocked the project after the annexation of Crimea. The geopolitical confrontation of Russia prevailed over the economic role of the project.	In May 2018, Jordan's negotiations with Rosatom on nuclear power plant (NPP) construction failed. Jordan claimed about the extremely high cost of the NPP by Rosatom.
In February 2018, Rosneft had a problem with the Iraqi authorities. Baghdad rejected Erbil's (KRG) separate deal with Rosneft and its contracts with the Kurdish government for oil supply.	In February 2018, Russia and Belarus had harsh competition for oil transit from Belarus. Belarus preferred to use Baltic ports for oil export and Russia had to offer low transit tariffs for oil.
The USA imposed sanctions on Nord Stream-2 and Turkish Stream gas pipelines in December 2019. The USA had opposed Russian gas supply projects towards the EU with geopolitical motives.	In December 2019, Russia and Belarus could not agree on conditions for the supply of Russian oil to refineries. Belarus has aimed to diversify its oil supply from other sources for commercial motives.

Source: RECSID.

Ukraine to limit natural gas supplies directly by Putin. In 2014, Russia abandoned the South Stream gas pipeline when the EU blocked the project for the annexation of Crimea and geopolitical significance exceeded the economic role. In the early 2010s, Gazprom had a gas debt payment problem with Moldova when Transnistria had a different view on the gas debt issue and Gazprom suffered from Kremlin's geopolitics. Moscow had special geopolitical interests in Transnistria related to Ukraine and Romania. In 2017, Lithuania protested the Belarus NPP project of Rosatom banning electricity import from Belarus and Russia, because Vilnius considered the nuclear power plant (NPP) project as Russia's geopolitical ambition that was situated in the critical border region between Lithuania and Belarus.

RECSID disclosed that Russia's policy towards states in its periphery has become a source of recurrent tension and rivalry between Russia and the West. The geopolitical competition is increasingly intertwined with other issues, including foreign energy policy and energy conflicts with Russia. Russia used energy exports including not only oil and gas but also nuclear fuel, coal, and electricity export as a "political weapon", intervening in the post-Soviet countries' internal politics, putting pressure on their foreign policy decisions, and reducing supplies to the larger European trade partners. But interdependence patterns could avert severe foreign energy policy tools such as a total disruption of energy supply by Russia against the EU states.

Restoring state control over the Russian energy sector in the era of Putin's rule magnified the risk of re-using "energy weapon". Russian energy policy turned from an economic asset into a potential instrument of political pressure before and after 2000. Russia's decision-makers and policymakers deeply believe that country's dominant position in global energy markets should enable it to achieve its political goals in the "near abroad" and gain a sphere of influence in the post-USSR countries. Moscow traditionally used "energy weapon" tools against disloyal neighbours: in 1990, they were used against Lithuania, in 1992 against all the Baltic states in response to their demands for the withdrawal of Russian troops remaining on their territory, in 1993–1994 against Ukraine, in February 2004 against Belarus. Yukos case in 2003–2005 and the "gas war" with Ukraine in January 2006, 2009, and 2014 fully undermined the reputation of Russia as a reliable supplier. The reputational risk made Russia's "energy weapon" less effective in the long run and Russia realized the limitations of the FEP under the energy interdependence. But it didn't relinquish to use of energy export for geopolitical aims.

Russia's conflictual foreign energy policy towards Belarus, Ukraine, and other CIS countries could be interpreted only through the complex and very specific social, economic, legal, and political interrelations of Russia with these countries in the post-Soviet period that subsume the deep legacy of Soviet era. But the energy market conditions and the nature of the energy sector are also crucial factors. Since the early 1990s, NATO expressed interest in integrating the Baltic states, Ukraine, and Georgia into the European security mechanisms of the bloc. At the same time, these are countries that Russia has more aggressively approached in matters of foreign energy policy and energy conflicts related to oil, gas, and transit. These overlaps mean that the relations of the partner country with NATO are a very important determining factor in the energy policy of Russia and its conflictual attitude to this respective country. This attitude was supported by the expert interviews and content analysis of the official documents.

Russia's misemployment of oil-gas resources against Ukraine and other CIS and European countries has a security-oriented geopolitical context and background together with commercial interests (in the case of Ukraine, there was a long history of energy disputes over non-payment of the debts and oil-gas prices starting from 1992 to 1993). "Energy counterattack" as a reaction to NATO's enlargement is one of those factors. But economic interdependence that was asymmetric for the benefit of the West constrained Russia to openly threaten the counterpart countries' energy interests. But starting from 2003 to 2004, asymmetric interdependence became more symmetric, and the threat perception imposed by the West on Russia sharpened. These factors triggered Russia to use "energy weapon" more actively and even openly against the CIS and the EU countries.

Generally, geopolitics, security concerns, and grand strategy objectives cannot fully explain Russia's foreign energy policy and cannot determine the outcomes of FEP. But also, the map of the Russian energy conflicts intensity overlaps with the country's overarching strategic aims for geopolitical expansion based on the grand strategy: Ukraine and Belarus as a Slavic dimension of the grand strategy, Azerbaijan and Georgia as Caucasus dimension of the grand strategy, other post-Soviet countries as a "near abroad" region of the vital strategic interests of Russia, the EU countries reflecting a western expansionism dimension of the grand strategy, Turkey reflecting the Mediterranean and the Black Sea dimension of the grand strategy, and China reflecting an eastern expansionism dimension of the grand strategy. Russia occupying *Eurasian* heartland had two geopolitical extremities that are the EU in the western direction and China in the eastern direction where it had serious energy conflicts and strategic energy interests. The energy conflicts blanket all border perimeters of Russia including most of the neighbour countries of this "insecure" land power (except, Mongolia). Especially the western and southern bordering countries had a higher level of conflictual nature in the energy affairs in alignment with the goal of the grand strategy of Russia on domination in the "Greater Eurasia".

Figure 7.1 demonstrates that Russia had more intense energy conflicts (especially, gas-related conflicts) with the post-Soviet countries that Russia aims to dominate geopolitically (proof of the hypothesis on the geography of energy conflicts). Therefore, it can be argued that the use of energy for foreign policy purposes could not be fully motivated by economic and commercial reasons. But we cannot fully ignore the multiple actor structure of the energy market, energy interdependence pattern, and the existence of commercially motivated energy conflicts.

We can introduce some brief examples of *Russia's energy conflicts with commercial motives*. Russia and China had a series of oil-gas conflicts on pipeline routes based on the project costs and oil-gas prices. Jordan failed negotiations with Rosatom on nuclear power plant (NPP) construction in 2018 because of the extremely high cost of the NPP. Russia and Belarus had a series of oil conflicts in 2018–2019 on the level of transit tariffs and oil supplies to refineries. As a

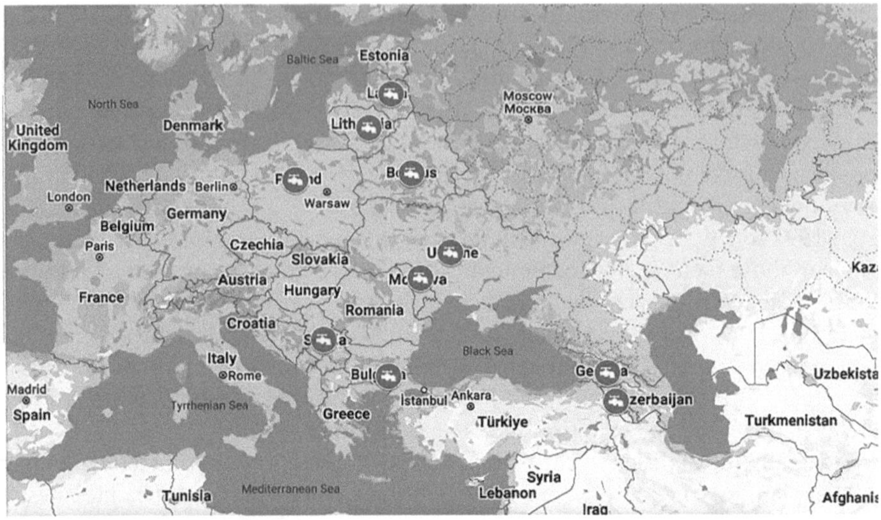

Figure 7.1 The countries that Russia had more intense energy conflicts.

Source: Author's compilation in the "create my map" function of the Google Map. https://bit.ly/3qoIB4z.

result, Belarus planned to diversify its oil supply from alternative sources for commercial motives. RECSID revealed that the majority of Russia's energy conflicts have commercial motivation. Acute energy conflicts that could last a long time with more stiff tools such as a total stop of the energy supply could have geopolitical motivation. The risks of politically motivated supply interruptions and even commercially motivated persistent energy conflicts may contribute to fundamental changes in the behaviour of energy consumer countries from "near abroad" and the EU market towards *diversification* strategies in terms of alternative energy sources and supplying countries (diminishing return of "energy weapon").

7.3 Rebalancing of the Interdependence: Energy Diversification and Sanctions

Diversification strategies of energy-importing countries determine the outcomes of the Russian "energy weapon". Diversification of energy types, diversification of energy-exporting countries, creating of strategic energy storage, availability of alternative energy supply infrastructure, and elastic energy systems enabling to use of alternative energy sources could be considered as ways to ensure energy security by the CIS and EU countries against Russia's energy power. Russia is a major oil-gas supplier to Europe and European states are major foreign investors in the Russian economy. But EU's energy diversification intends to reduce drastically Russia's economic and energy presence in Europe after the "gas wars". Russia is the major exporter of gas, oil, and coal to the EU market. Russia provides 40% of the EU's annual gas imports on average.

After the collapse of the USSR, the EU raised the diversifying energy supplies. Russia was considered an overly dominant country, and the post-Soviet countries were already perceived as potential alternatives. The main question was about the natural gas supply because crude oil was a global commodity, and there were enough options for obtaining it from other countries (Simonov, 2020). Latynina (2014) argued that the Russian state's "energy superpower" concept triggered an "energy weapon" that led to the decline of Gazprom's deliveries to Europe and its share in the EU gas market (Latynina, 2014). Germany began to develop renewable energy, Lithuania acquired an LNG terminal, and the shale gas boom started to squeeze Gazprom from the European market. Russia's foreign energy policy towards the CIS and the EU that used an energy resource as a coercive measure to obtain political and economic concessions strengthened these countries' energy security plans and relevant initiatives towards the diversification of energy import routes (emerging LNG import routes with related regasification infrastructure), energy suppliers (from Russia to LNG exporters or other energy producers such as Norway, Qatar or Azerbaijan), and energy resources (from fossil fuels to renewables). For example, even though South-eastern European countries (Greece, Balkan states, Bulgaria) historically had positive relations with Russia, these countries implemented energy import diversification strategies to limit energy import dependence on Russia.

In addition to the Turk Stream pipeline that brings Russian gas to this region, bypassing Ukraine, the region also imports gas from Trans Adriatic Pipeline (TAP) which brings the gas from the Caspian Sea and new LNG terminals (e.g., Krk LNG terminal in Croatia) that deliver the liquefied natural gas from the USA and the Gulf countries (Gurkov, 2021). Even though the annual throughput capacities of the LNG terminal in Croatia and the TAP pipeline are less than Turk Stream's second line that exports natural gas to Europe, the presence of the alternative infrastructures circumscribes Gazprom's monopolistic power in the region. The EU and the CIS states intended to continue energy cooperation with Russia, but without violating its principles of diversification of reliable energy supplies to fortify the resilience against Russia's energy dominance.

The time-consuming nature of energy import diversification strategies has increased the political leverage of Russia. Manipulation with energy supply volume and oil-gas-electricity-coal prices could be considered as Russia's power exercising techniques and forms in terms of "energy power". Destabilization of the Western world and building a "sphere of influence" over "near abroad" could be a strategic objective of Russia's energy power. But when we look at the control over outcomes throughout exercising Russia's "energy power" based on RECSID findings, we could observe that it was "negative power", rather than "positive power" for Russia. The energy power and conflictual foreign energy policy can be assessed through power resources and means, but it can be evaluated via outcomes, as well. Oil-gas producers that follow aggressive foreign energy policy may face a decrease in revenues from the energy sale, the diminishing reputational risk, and growing diversification efforts by the energy importers. The regional and global geopolitical and geoeconomics risks and vulnerabilities will endanger energy security and effective diversification strategies.

The energy power used by Russia against target countries couldn't potentially produce the desired long-run outcome for Russia by directing energy importing countries to renewable sources and alternative regions. Renewable power generation increased more than 40 times in the EU market from the early 1990s to 2019 (Eurostat, 2021b). But despite the huge growth, still, the share of renewables in the EU's final annual consumption was only 22% in 2020, and the energy import dependence ratio increased from 56% to 60% between 2000 and 2019 (Eurostat, 2021a). Especially, some Eastern European and Baltic states that import Russia's energy resources more widely increased their energy import dependence rate (e.g., Lithuania increased energy import dependence from 58% in 2000 to 75% in 2019). In addition to the efficiency and climate change, one of the major motivations of European countries for energy transition was to decrease the "toxic" energy dependence on Russia's energy resources. The correlation between Russia's total energy conflicts (RECSID) and Europe's energy transition towards renewable energy sources was 0.93 from 1990 to 2004 and negative 0.31 from 2005 to 2019. The share of renewables in the EU's energy balance increased in parallel to the growing number of energy conflicts with Russia between 1990 and 2004. The role of energy from renewable sources continued to grow in Europe after 2005, while Russia's energy conflicts had demonstrated more fluctuations.

With the energy import diversification strategies of the energy-importing countries and energy transition, long-term predictions about the declining fossil fuel demand may decay Russia's "energy weapon" in the long run. Rühl and Erker (2021) argued that oil efficiency based on new technologies leads to the "*2.2 million barrels of oil less to sustain the same level of global GDP*" (Rühl & Erker, 2021) and this factor also can decrease the demand for the Russian energy resources. The report by the Global Commission on the Geopolitics of Energy Transformation (2019) argued that the Russian economy is relatively sizeable and more diversified than the economies of the oil exporters from the Middle East. These actors may mitigate the economic repercussion of the global energy transition for the Russian economy. But generally, it will encounter an onerous adaptation process, because of high fiscal reliance on oil-gas incomes (40%) and technological backwardness in renewables.

IGU's Global Gas Report (2022) argued that gas import diversification is a time-consuming and capital-intensive process requiring long-term vision and deliberate actions. But the war in Ukraine accelerated the energy diversification plans in the EU that included new LNG terminals in new coastal areas and new investments in floating storage and regasification units (FSRU) to diminish the gas dependence on Russia by approximately 66% in 2022 with the vision about zero-level dependence on Russian oil, gas, and coal by 2030 (IGU, 2022, pp. 20–41). The speed of EU and post-Soviet states' energy diversification process is high, but it varies across countries descending the overall effect of diversified energy portfolio on Russia's foreign energy policy based on realities of the energy market.

The results of energy diversification strategies of the EU and post-Soviet countries don't ensure to claim a tectonic change in the energy dependence on Russia in the short and medium-term. Small European countries such as Malta, Luxemburg, and Cyprus had a higher level of energy imports dependence on Russia between 2000 and 2019. IEA calculates and publishes the fuel reliance for the separate fuel types and total fossil fuel reliance on Russia by the various European and other developed countries. When calculating the fuel reliance for the separate fuel types, the formula divides fossil fuel (separately oil, gas, and coal) imports from Russia by the target country's total energy supply (TES). When calculating total fossil fuel reliance, the formula divides the sum of all fossil fuels (totally oil, gas, and coal) imports from Russia by the target country's total energy supply.

$$Reliance_{fuel} = \frac{Fuel\ imports\ from\ Russia}{TES_{fuel}}$$

$$Reliance_{Fossil\_Total} = \frac{Coal\ imports_{from\ Russia} + Oil\ imports_{from\ Russia} + Nat\ gas\ imports_{from\ Russia}}{TES_{Total}}$$

Source: IEA (2022b). Reliance on Russian Fossil Fuels Data Explorer.

Baltic states and Central and Eastern European countries have a higher reliance on the Russian oil, gas, and coal resources. The ratio of Lithuania's oil imports from Russia to the country's total energy supply was 279% in 2019. Hungary, Slovakia, the Czech Republic, Estonia, and Latvia had the highest gas reliance on imports from Russia. Lithuania, Finland, Slovakia, the Netherlands, and Bulgaria had the highest oil reliance on imports from Russia. Denmark and Cyprus had the highest coal reliance on imports from Russia. The EU imports almost 70% of coal from Russia, which has the highest quality in terms of heat transfer coefficient (Table 7.2).

When we analyse the total fossil fuel reliance on Russia, the leading countries are Lithuania, Hungary, Slovakia, the Netherlands, Finland, Bulgaria, Greece, Poland, Latvia, Germany, Italy, the Czech Republic, Turkey, Estonia, and Romania

Table 7.2 Fuel reliance on Russia (2019)

Country	*Energy*	*Reliance*
Lithuania	Oil	279%
Hungary	Gas	175%
Finland	Oil	175%
Denmark	Coal	150%
Slovakia	Oil	141%
Slovakia	Gas	137%
Netherlands	Oil	127%
Cyprus	Coal	118%
Bulgaria	Oil	113%
Czech	Gas	109%
Estonia	Gas	104%
Latvia	Gas	100%

Source: IEA (2022a).

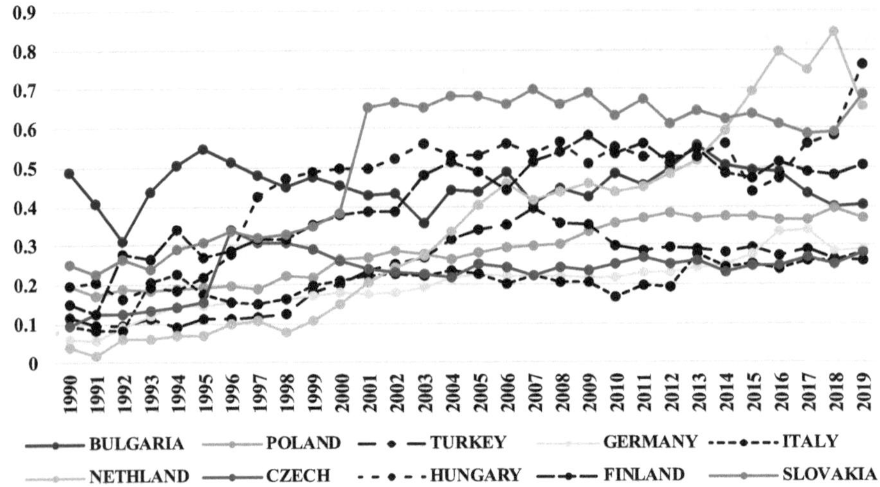

Figure 7.2 European countries' total fuel reliance on Russia (%).
Source: IEA (2022a).

(IEA, 2022a). Some of these countries (e.g., Lithuania and Bulgaria) have a relatively higher level of energy conflicts and supply interruption disputes with Russia. The correlation between the number of energy conflicts and supply interruptions with Russia and the total fossil fuel reliance on Russia was around 0.4. It means that Russia could initiate energy conflicts with both less and more dependent countries (Figure 7.2).

European countries followed different paths in terms of energy reliance on Russia. If we look at the largest energy importers in terms of volume of fossil fuels (Germany, Italy, Turkey, and the Netherlands) or the countries having a higher level of energy dependence on Russia (Lithuania, Hungary, and Slovakia), we could observe that European countries didn't have serious progress so far in the significant decrease of the energy reliance on Russia. Energy expert Ilham Shaban (2018) argued that Europe's goal is not to reduce energy imports from Russia, a geographically close largest resource country, because the EU needs the energy for economic growth. Europe's policy is based on the minimization of Russia's use of energy as a political tool; renewing the energy infrastructure that existed during the Soviet period in Europe, mainly at the expense of Russia; constantly placing Russia in a position to make long-term and stable, but also cheaper energy imports. EU has rational energy affairs with Russia-based chiefly on commercial and technological motives rather than political ones. Europe has begun to reduce its crude oil imports from Russia. Still, the imported high-quality oil products increased because that crude oil refining hurts the environment. Nuclear energy can be a significant contributor to ending Europe's energy dependence on Russia, but NPPs are shutting down rapidly in Europe for ecological motives (this trend reversed after the energy crises in 2021–2022) (Expert interview with Ilham Shaban, 2018, Baku).

Bordoff (2022) and Popkostova (2022) affirmed that Russia accomplishes its gas supply commitments to Europe based on long-term contracts and it continued even in the war period in Ukraine throughout February–April 2022. Despite the sanctions, the transit of Gazprom's gas through Ukraine continued during the war remaining at a high level in compliance with the committed volumes of the long-term contracts (more than 100 million cubic metres daily) (Interfax, 2022b). In February 2022, Putin stated that Russia remains a part of the world economy and it is not going to damage the world economic system as far as Russia itself remains the part (TASS, 2022). It means Putin recognized the pattern of interdependence offering stable gas supplies in return for avoiding harsh sanctions that could disconnect from the international energy market and financial system. Gazprom supplied gas through the territory of Ukraine in the regular transit mode, in accordance with the requests of European consumers in February–April 2022 (Neft i Kapital, 2022). This important fact again demonstrated the limitations of the Russian energy power and foreign energy policy under an interdependence pattern. But Liuhto (2010, pp. 51–52) argues that the interdependence in Russia-EU energy relations contains multi-level asymmetries: (a) time-based asymmetry meaning that Russia's dependence on oil-gas revenues from the EU is more time-consuming than the EU's needs for Russian energy resources in terms of the impact of external shocks; (b) company-level asymmetry meaning the different level of "negotiation-power" in oil (more competitive private business) and gas (less competitive state business) sectors. He believes that energy interdependence will not cause deeper integration of Russia into the EU system and the EU will need to readjust in this unsafe asymmetry via a united external energy policy.

In addition to revenue generation and political motivation, Russian gas transit to Europe via Ukraine wasn't deeply affected by the Russian military intervention from February 2022 to May 2022, also because Ukraine preserved its key role in the gas transit (despite alternative transit pipelines) with around 40 billion cubic metres annually (one-fifth of Russia's annual gas export to the EU in 2021). Russia's gas transit to Europe through Ukraine exploits two routes: Sokhranovka and Sudzha. Gas transit continued to use the Sudzha route despite the war in 2022, but Ukraine decided to stop gas flows via the Sokhranovka route in May 2022 which accounted for 8% of gas flows to Europe (IGU, 2022, pp. 20–41). Before the war, Ukraine was a transit for almost 25% of the total volume of Russian gas in the European market which was equal to 155 billion cubic metres (IEA, 2022c, 6–18). Still, Russia refused to supply more gas in 2021–2022 based on spot market rules intentionally or enforcedly because of internal gas output challenges and political reasons.

In addition to Russia's gas supply problems as an external factor, the EU's energy policies towards a shift from oil price-indexed long-term gas contracts to spot markets, lowering fossil fuel investments in the energy transition period, deactivating active gas fields in Europe such as Groningen field in the Netherlands, lack of commitment-based regulations on strategic reserves of the Union and gas storages owned by Gazprom have led to the energy crises. Gas production was reduced by 50%, oil, and coal production by about 35% in the EU from 2009 to 2019. The EU cut its domestic hydrocarbon (oil, gas, and coal) production in a short period under diversification and net-zero strategy, without considering the temporary and additional medium-term demand for hydrocarbons stemming from energy transition and environmental and political force majeure. Overland (2017) had characterized the EU's strategy to exploit an energy regulation for bolstering political and security plans as a "liberal mercantilist" tool in answer to Gazprom's dominant position (pp. 115–130). The EU's energy import diversification policies collide with the Russian energy companies' market diversification strategies.

In the expert interview, Martin Jirusek (Czech Republic) argued that Russia had very intense energy conflicts and energy supply disruption cases with the Central and Eastern European (CEE) region where Gazprom had a monopolistic position. CEE region has realized the very swift diversification policy from Russian energy. CEE countries have better regulation, less misconduct, and more effective governance that limits Russia's political goals through energy policy. Russia economically falls behind the CEE countries in terms of national income per capita (see Figure 7.3). The economic and institutional backwardness of Russia in comparison with the post-socialist CEE countries (such as Slovenia, Estonia, the Czech Republic, Poland, Lithuania, Slovakia, Latvia, Hungary, and Romania) trigger the energy conflicts and disputes between Russia and CEE countries because of "retribution attitudes" (Figure 7.3).

CEE countries' demeanour to diversify oil-gas and even nuclear fuel imports, may give rise to Russia's more aggressive foreign energy policy towards the region. Gonchar (2022) argued that Russia "systematically and consistently" worked

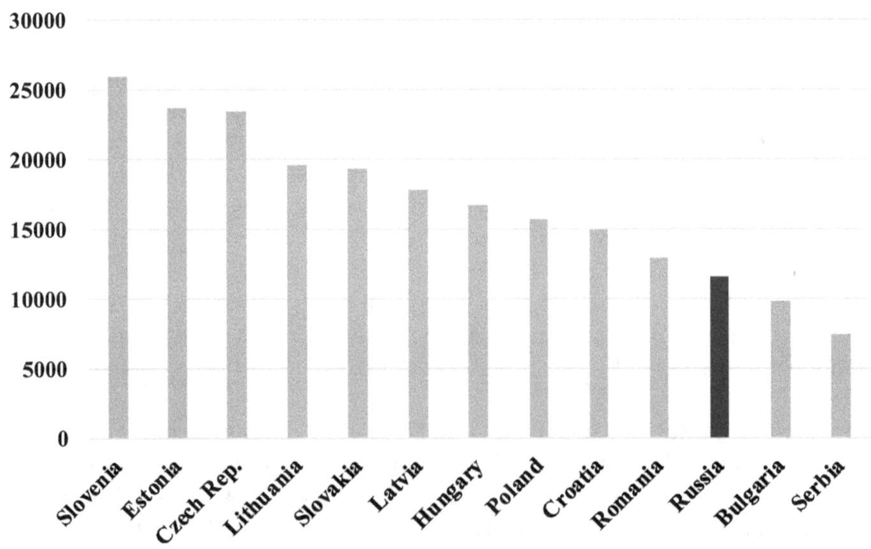

Figure 7.3 Russia versus CEE: GDP per capita (current USD, 2019).

Source: World Bank (2021).

towards the EU energy market gradually capturing at least 40% of the market. But the EU states have an alternative source in this interdependent setting meaning that Russia's foreign energy policy gained tactical gain the Europe, not "strategic victory". Also, Russian foreign energy policy and Europe's energy diversification strategies depend on domestic political systems and the ruling coalitions in the EU states, especially Germany (Gonchar, 2022). Not only domestic factors in the energy importing countries or Russia's geopolitical strain with the CEE countries but also the power of transit countries such as Ukraine, Poland, and Belarus to manipulate Russia's oil-gas export to Europe caused frequent energy conflicts and supply disruptions. Russia stopped the oil flow via the Druzhba pipeline (Belarus, Ukraine) and gas supply via the Brotherhood pipeline system (Ukraine) to the Central European region several times accusing not final consumers but mostly transit countries of siphoning off oil and gas in pipelines. As a result, Russia's oil and gas supply reliability was damaged in the CEE region.

As a "*vicious circle*", the diminishing credibility of Russia as an energy supplier stimulated a new wave of energy import diversification strategies by geopolitically crucial countries. This "vicious circle" unsharpened Russia's "energy weapon". Russia's aggressive foreign energy policy eroded the credibility of Russia as a reliable energy supplier navigating target countries (such as the EU members or Ukraine) to diversification strategies. But the energy diversification strategies of the target countries again make Russia's foreign energy policy towards these states even more aggressive (the second "vicious circle"). The EU decision-makers made a sharp turn towards the energy independence, energy security, and energy diversification of the member states after the Russian military aggression against Ukraine.

Like the EU states, Ukraine also realizes an energy diversification strategy to reduce "toxic" dependence on Russia. Ukraine's electricity system was swiftly disconnected from the Russian grid in March 2022 and synchronized to the European grid further weakening Russia's "energy weapon" (Blaustein, 2022). Also, the portion of renewable energy supply in Ukraine increased from 1.7% to 4.9% between 2007 and 2019 (187%). Despite the high growth in the share of renewables in energy consumption, the share of coal, oil, gas, and nuclear energy in the primary energy balance was around 95% in 2019 (State Statistics Service of Ukraine, 2021). There is a negative correlation between the share of renewable energy supply in Ukraine and the number of Russia's foreign energy conflicts and supply interruptions from 2007 to 2019 (–0.23).

Ukraine has a higher dependence on Russia for oil, natural gas, and partly nuclear fuel. Nuclear dependence is an integral part of Ukraine's energy dependence on Russia. In March 2014, when pro-Russian separatist forces started to destabilize Eastern Ukraine and Russia started to annex Crimea, the government of Russia stated that the transit of nuclear materials through Ukraine and the direct supply of the nuclear fuel to the country became risky for the military situation. The Eastern European countries perceived the fact of "blackmailing" as utilization of Rosatom's market position for the foreign policy and economic expansion by the state of Russia. Rosatom intends to keep post-Soviet countries that have nuclear power plants to be dependent on Russian technologies and services by preventing their efforts to produce high technologies and finding alternative countries to cooperate in the nuclear industry.

The host country could break fuel dependence through (i) diversification of nuclear fuel imports from different suppliers and (ii) strong domestic political resistance against nuclear energy. Ukraine realized a diversification plan in three directions: nuclear fuel supply diversification, the storage of wasted nuclear fuel, and the construction of new nuclear power plants. Ukraine could achieve 50% diversification of nuclear fuel import by signing an agreement with Westinghouse (USA) during 2014–2015. The energy diversification strategy of Ukraine cannot be considered fully successful in terms of real outputs and outcomes except for the nuclear sector. The structural energy dependence complicated the scramble against Russia's energy power or "energy weapon". But Ukraine didn't give up on the reform agenda and the integration efforts towards the EU/NATO meaning that Russia's "energy weapon" couldn't generate vivid and real outcomes in the long run.

Referring to Ukraine's potential membership in NATO, President Putin officially recognized the separatist regions of Ukraine (DNR/LNR) as "independent states" on 21 February 2022 (RBK, 2022), and Russia started direct military intervention in Ukraine on 24 February 2022. Western countries have imposed numerous economic sanctions on Russia in response to the military intervention in Ukraine. The harsh international sanctions against Russia's finance and the energy sector were imposed by the USA, the UK, and Germany including stopping Nord Stream-2 pipeline project. On February 23, 2022 (one day before the Russian military intervention in Ukraine), Deputy Chairman of the Security Council of Russia Dmitry Medvedev warned Europe of 2,000 euros per 1,000 cubic metres of natural gas after the discontinuation of the certification of the Nord Stream-2 gas pipeline by Germany (Antonov, 2022).

The EU has banned the supply of goods and technologies for the Russian oil industry. The EU imposed sanctions on the supply of equipment for oil refining (e.g., technologies for aromatic hydrocarbon production, naphtha isomerization, hydrocracking reactors, catalytic cracking, hydrogen production technology, polymerization, and technology for sulphur recovery) and liquefaction of natural gas (e.g., technologies for gas cooling, the separation, and fractionation of hydrocarbons, the liquefaction of gas, cold rooms for LNG, cryogenic heat exchangers (100% imported by Russia in 2019), and cryogenic pumps (95% imported by Russia in 2019)) (Energy Intelligence Group, 2022) to Russia in April 2022. Prohibiting LNG technologies will adversely impact the Arctic LNG-2 and Baltic LNG plants that are constructed by NOVATEK, Gazprom, and Sibur (Interfax, 2022c). Also, it was officially acknowledged that Russia needs foreign technologies for modelling the oil-gas fields, well logging and drilling, oil refining technologies, and power equipment. Russia imports 60% of the gas turbines that are used in electricity production and almost 50% of transformers that are used in the electricity transmission that was sanctioned (Novak, 2022).

After the introduction of sanctions against Russia to freeze foreign currency accounts, President Putin instructed to transfer payments for gas supplies to "unfriendly countries" into rubles to gradually move away from the dollar and the euro on March 23, 2022. On March 30, 2022, Medvedev again warned that measures and sanctions towards Russia including the freezing of the Nord Stream-2 pipeline project, blocking the assets of the Central Bank of Russia, the refusal of payment for Russian gas in rubles based on the currency rate in the gas contracts, conducting investigations in the offices of Gazprom in Germany will "leave Europe without gas" (Radio Sputnik, 2022).

In April 2022, Putin recognized that the Russian oil and gas sector faced problems in terms of the logistics of energy exports and delays in the transfer of payments by banks from "unfriendly countries" for exported energy resources (Kremlin.ru, 2022). Gazprom halted gas supply to Poland and Bulgaria (both countries had around 40% energy reliance on Russia's energy resources) in April 2022 demanding to follow a "double-account mechanism" through opening ruble and foreign currency accounts in Gazprombank to make payment for the imported gas. Unlike Bulgaria, Poland has alternatives in the gas supply. But Gazprom didn't take a similar measure against Germany where the level of interdependence and the political-economic cost of the "exit" was relatively higher. Also, dozens of gas-importing countries from Europe (including firms from Germany, Austria, Hungary, and Slovakia) agreed to open "double accounts" in Gazprombank (that hasn't been excluded from SWIFT), even though practically nothing changed for gas importer companies in the payment procedure. But the officials from Russia and the EU intentionally politicized the payment procedure issue: Putin demanded from "unfriendly countries" pay the gas payment exclusively in rubles, while EC President Leyen cautioned EU's gas-importing firms to reject opening ruble/euro/dollar accounts in the Russian bank (Elliott, 2022).

In May 2022, EU members concurred on an embargo on the import of seaborne oil from Russia (under the sixth sanctions package) that could adversely impact 75%–90% of the oil import from Russia. This move considered the huge dependence of Central European countries such as Hungary (60% dependence on Russian oil), Slovakia (approximately 66% dependence on Russian oil), and the Czech Republic that would continue to import Russian oil through the Druzhba oil pipeline (this pipeline accounts for only 10% of Russia's total oil export to Europe). The EU's constraining actions towards Russia's oil trade took cognizance of varying dependency ratios of member countries on Russian crude oil and oil products. For example, the dependency rate varies from 25% in Southern Europe to 70% in Northwest Europe for diesel imports in 2022 (Perkins, Kumagai, & Wang, 2022). The pattern of interdependence in the oil trade between Russia and the EU was taken into account by both sides in the tool selection of foreign energy policy, even though the attempts to change the pattern will bear costs for the EU (the cost of refineries to switch from Russian oil to alternatives, price fluctuations in the global oil markets, etc.) and Russia (finding new markets in the Asian region, offering price discounts to potential buyers, additional transfer costs, etc.) (Hickin, Coleman, & Perkins, 2022). Fishman and Miller (2022) argued that sanctions against Russia's oil export should be redesigned to cut back the country's oil revenues (a quarter of the federal budget) without limiting oil volumes entering the global market (e.g., fixing the maximum price for Russian oil through cartel mechanism of oil-importing countries). Otherwise, the decreasing volumes of Russian oil in the global market will increase the inflationary risk for developed countries as the vulnerability cost of energy interdependence.

Sanctions revealed the scope of the economic interdependence between Russia and the Western countries. Also, sanctions carry the risk to push Russia out of the interdependent setting of multilateral and bilateral affairs, isolating the country from international interactions, and making it more aggressive in its foreign energy policy. Major Western energy partners of Russia including Germany acknowledge that economic sanctions are a "double-edged sword". It negatively impacts the economy of the target country, but also rising prices for coal, oil, and gas have the opposite effects on those countries that impose these sanctions. But the level of interdependence determines the outcome of the sanctions in terms of the long-run policy changes of the conflict sides that are hurt deeply by sanctions. Germany had long-term plans to become independent from the import of Russian energy carriers, but the war in Ukraine accelerated this process by supporting the decision on the embargo on coal imports from Russia and the gradual replacement of the Russian oil. Germany planned to significantly reduce its dependence on Russian gas (through building new pipelines and interconnectors from alternative gas-rich countries such as Norway and LNG terminals), coal, and oil during 2022–2024 (RIA Novosti, 2022). Norway surpassed Russia as Germany's largest gas supplier, providing 33% of Germany's natural gas imports in 2022 (Humpert, 2023). Marin (2022) argued that Russia accounted for 55% of gas imports, 34% of oil imports, and 26% of coal imports in Germany. To halt gas imports from Russia could lead to a 0.5%–2.2% contraction of GDP in Germany, while the pandemic contracted GDP by 4.6% in 2020. Bachmann (2022) and his research team predict that maximum output losses (electricity production + industrial production) would be 3% of GDP for the refusal of Russian fossil fuel by Germany. The cost of an energy embargo against Russia would be around 1%–1.5% of the total GDP of the entire EU economy annually. It means the vulnerability cost of the German economy and the EU under economic and energy interdependence with Russia is serious in the short term (high energy prices, energy deficit, etc.), but not very disastrous in the long run. The costs of energy diversification reshape the fractional degree of vulnerability for the EU states where relatively cheaper energy alternatives should be available. The cost of import substitution strategies after international sanctions targeting high technologies can be a cost of vulnerability interdependence of Russia.

The material and political costs of exit from an energy-based interdependence pattern are mutual for energy importing and exporting countries (İpek, 2019). For an energy importing country (Germany), the cost is switching to an alternative energy type or alternative energy supplier, and temporary shutdowns in the production facilities; for an energy exporter country (Russia), the cost is switching to the alternative energy markets (e.g., to find alternative markets for at least 55 billion cubic metres of gas that Gazprom exported to Germany in 2020 or searching new and more distant markets (such as India) for oil export) that can require new energy infrastructure (pipeline, etc.), access to energy technology and finance under sanctions, temporary discounts (around 20%–30%) in the energy sales, and accumulation of free reserves in the onshore/offshore storages without "sales perspective".

Currently, post-Soviet countries and major EU states have energy import diversification strategies that target Russia directly, despite the collective action problem in the EU. It makes Russia more aggressive in its foreign and energy policy towards these regions to maintain its dominance in energy markets and avoid the higher cost of the exit from interdependence. But handicap of Russia's aggressive foreign and energy policies and the "energy weapon" is the reality that when Russia increases the global energy security apprehensions using military tools against Ukraine or energy blackmailing, it doesn't only promote energy diversification strategies of the energy importing countries and sanctions. Russia also pushes the energy prices up when higher oil and gas prices create favourable conditions for the private oil-gas producers and oil service companies around the globe. Oil-gas producer companies could benefit from higher oil (for the oil industry it could be USD 100 per barrel) and gas prices to mount up exploration and production (E&P or upstream) investments. As a result, more oil-gas production based on switching "short-cycle" E&P projects to "long-cycle" E&P projects will increase the energy supply filling the withdrawn volumes of Russian energy resources from energy markets after sanctions (Spencer, 2022). Energy diversification efforts of both energy exporting and energy importing countries, and mutual sanctions related to the energy sector can be seen as "strategic adjusters" of the energy-based interdependence setting between Russia and energy importing countries. "Strategic adjusters" were devised to redistribute the costs of the exit from interdependence and rebalance the complex political and economic affairs that exist between conflicting parties.

7.4 Assumptions of Expert Interviews on Russia's FEP and Energy Conflicts

The actual intention of Russia towards the use of energy power and the real outcomes of the "energy weapon" can be qualitatively examined by interviewing energy experts on the Russian foreign energy policy. In this book, experts touched upon various aspects of Russian foreign energy policy from the point of view of Russia and the target countries. The components and constraints of the foreign energy policy were described by the experts (Table 7.3).

Explanation and narratives of the expert interviews. The expert interviews revealed a similar pattern of Russia's foreign energy policy behaviour based on corresponding assumptions including the country's security considerations such as *NATO's eastward expansion.* Ukrainian energy security expert Andrii Chubyk noted that the main driving incentive for the Russian "energy weapon" is a defence against NATO and the EU's expansion. Linking Russia's foreign energy policy with the country's security concerns is popular among some Ukrainians and even Russian analysts. Another Ukrainian analyst Khylko (2021) argued that Russia employs natural gas as an "energy weapon" against the EU, deliberately restraining natural gas supplies. The lack of clear vision of the EU, Germany, and the USA on the gas import from Russia and the Nord Stream-2 gas pipeline launch significantly

Table 7.3 Assumptions from the expert interviews on Russia's FEP

Interviewee	*Assumptions and keywords*
Giorgi Mukhigulishvili (Georgia)	Russia has the ability even to use *terror attacks* against oil-gas pipelines and electricity transmission lines (Georgia, 2006).
	Despite all contradictions, Georgia and Russia continued energy *cooperation* (transit of gas to Armenia and Abkhazia).
	Russia planned to use the electricity tariffs and natural gas tariffs as a political tool to influence the *domestic political process.*
	Russia's political and economic influence on the neighbouring countries using energy factors or resources depends on *the level of dependence* on Russia's energy sector.
Andrii Chubyk (Ukraine)	The main driving incentive for the Russian "energy weapon" is a defence against *NATO and the EU's expansion.*
	The gas crisis in 2009 was Russia's attempt to *provoke social tension* in the industrial east and south of Ukraine.
	The interdependence (energy in return for revenues) pattern with the EU is a serious limitation for Putin's foreign energy policy.
Prof. Dr Eckart Stratenschulte (Germany)	Russia-EU *mutual energy dependence* ("supply/receipts") can force two sides to cooperate rather than conflict.
	There is a difference in Russia's *behavioural pattern in foreign energy policy towards* "near abroad" and European countries.
	German decision-makers believe that *Russia isn't a reliable energy partner* and increases gas storage capacity against potential gas supply disruptions by Russia.
Dr Stanislav Pritchin (Russia)	Russia has political purposes in foreign energy policy, but Gazprom mostly wishes to focus on *commercial aspects* of FEP.
	Russia has *asymmetric interdependence* with its main counterpart countries (the Western states and China) in energy technologies.
	Rosatom's plans to build *nuclear power plants* abroad create a *long-term dependence* of the host state on Russia.
Dr Alexey Belogoryev (Russia)	Oil is less politicized in Russia, but natural gas is a "*political commodity*" since the early 1990s.
	Russia mostly uses energy factors as a political instrument against CIS states and it intends to keep a *reliable reputation* as an energy supplier for EU members.
	The main purposes of the Russian FEP are *diversification* of energy export markets towards Asia and *cooperation* with global actors to attract FDI to the energy sector.
	The *energy strategy* of Russia is an inert and formal document that defines the general aims of energy policy.
Dr Marcel Salikhov (Russia)	Russia subsidizes the Rosatom from the state budget to be more active abroad on *nuclear energy with political motivation.*
	The level of *technological dependence* on foreign countries is more severe in oil (45%–50%), rather than natural gas.
	Russia is motivated to be very active in the international energy market and to pursue an *active foreign energy policy when the oil price is low.*

(*Continued*)

Table 7.3 (Continued)

Interviewee	*Assumptions and keywords*
Dr Olga Bogdanova (Latvia)	Baltic states (e.g., Latvia) never had serious *politically motivated natural gas and electricity disruption* by Russia. There weren't any *serious politically motivated accidents* in the Belarus-Russia-Baltics electricity grid. Russia knows *the non-readiness of Baltic states* for disconnection from the Russian grid.
Dr Andras Deak (Hungary)	The *domestic settings* of recipient countries are an important factor in Russia's foreign energy policy. Russia has a *dependence on Europe* to receive revenue in return for energy export. Russia wants political loyalty and *long-term cooperation* from "friendly countries" in return for cheap energy. Russia combined "soft" and "hard" energy policy tools based on strategic ambitions *without a clear strategic vision* and foreign energy strategy.
Dr Martin Jirusek (Czech Republic)	Not only state-owned but also Russian private oil-gas companies follow Kremlin's line with *political loyalty* and do not criticize the government as a baseline. Pre-conditions of the energy market against Russia's aggressive energy policy are *free and fair competition, and better regulations* in the domestic energy market. The only criteria to distinguish Russia's commercial energy moves from politically motivated acts are *timing and correlation* with other events.
Dr James Henderson (UK) and Vaclav Bartushka (Czech Republic)	The *realist* view on EU-Russia energy relations is valid and rapid *energy transition* can create chaos. Oil is simultaneously a revenue generator and political tool for Russia; it was used by Russia to cement a *geostrategic alliance with China* against the USA. *Technological dependence* is Russia's motivation to continue cooperation with Western energy companies. *China's strategy to diversify oil imports* from the Middle East overlaps with Russia's strategy to diversify the oil export market. Antidote against Russia's "energy weapon" contains these components: *diversification* in the energy mix, more effective *regulations*, and *alternative routes*

decreased the West's deterrence power against Russia. Reducing dependence on gas transit through Ukraine seriously radicalized Russia to deepen the military conflict with Ukraine and demand security guarantees from NATO and the USA about the stop of NATO's expansion to the east (especially towards Ukraine or the borders of Russia) (TASS, 2021b).

There were contradictory views on Russian *energy companies' position* on the foreign energy policy. Stanislav Pritchin (Russia) has defended the argument that Russia has shown political purposes in foreign energy policy, but state-owned energy companies such as Gazprom mostly wish to focus on commercial aspects of

FEP. Martin Jirusek (Czech Republic) defended another extreme assumption that not only state-owned but also Russian private oil-gas companies follow Kremlin's political directives. The Kremlin supports its public and private oil, gas, coal, electricity, and nuclear companies comprehensively (financial, diplomatic, technical, and political support). Marcel Salikhov (Russia) argued that Russia subsidizes the Rosatom from the state budget to be more active abroad on nuclear energy with political motivation. Rosneft generates revenues from oil sales, but also it is a geopolitical tool for Russia to cement a geostrategic alliance with China against the USA.

Technological dependence was notified as Russia's motivation to continue cooperation with Western energy companies. The level of technological dependence on foreign countries is more severe in oil (45%–50%), rather than natural gas. Russia has asymmetric interdependence with its main counterpart countries (the Western states and China) in energy technologies. In addition to technological dependence, the *interdependence* ("energy supplies in return of fiscal revenues from sales") pattern with the EU was underlined by the experts (e.g., Eckart Stratenschulte from Germany) as a serious limitation of Russia's foreign energy policy. Therefore, there is a difference in Russia's behavioural pattern in foreign energy policy towards "near abroad" and European countries.

Alexey Belogoryev (Russia) noted during the interview that technological dependence is more severe in the oil, rather than gas industry. The level of foreign technological dependence is around 50% in the oil sector, and it partly limits Russia's independent foreign energy policy. Belogoryev, who actively participated in the preparation of Russia's long-term energy strategies, underlined that Russia mostly uses energy factors as a political instrument against CIS states and it intends to keep a reliable reputation as an energy supplier for EU members. Olga Bogdanova (Latvia) argued that there weren't any serious politically motivated accidents in the Belarus-Russia-Baltics electricity grid for the EU member Baltic countries, despite the reality of asymmetric interdependence.

About the nature of Russia's use of energy as political leverage and *energy cooperation*, Andras Deak (Hungary) argued that Russia combined "soft" and "hard" energy policy tools based on strategic ambitions without a clear strategic vision and foreign energy strategy. Crude oil is less politicized in Russia, but natural gas is a "political commodity" since the early 1990s. This very important assumption also overlaps with RECSID's findings and conclusions. Also, he added that domestic political crises, domestic political debates, or domestic political changes in the consumer countries (Hungary, Ukraine, Bulgaria, or the UK) could trigger the energy (mostly, gas) crisis with Russia derailing energy cooperation. Marcel Salikhov (Russia) argued that Russia is motivated to be very active in the international energy market and to pursue an active foreign energy policy when the oil price is low. But James Henderson (UK) expressed that economics is fundamental and geopolitics is a response to the realities in Russia's foreign energy policy.[1] Higher oil prices make Russia more aggressive in its foreign energy policy, but energy price volatility forces Russia to concentrate on optimal trade. Energy price volatility is alleviating Russia's "energy weapon". Russia wants political loyalty and long-term cooperation from "friendly countries" in return for cheap energy resources. Despite all contradictions, Russia continued energy *cooperation* with energy-importing countries from the "near abroad" and the EU to maintain the interdependence pattern to various degrees. Also, Russia's reliability as an energy supplier possesses a long-term risk to lose critical consumer markets.

Russia's foreign energy policy wasn't correctly analysed in the West, where most assessments relied on geopolitical games. Another common argument underlined by experts was about the *domestic domain* of the energy importing countries. On one hand, the domestic settings of recipient countries are an important factor in Russia's foreign energy policy. Experts underlined that the foreign energy policy is a partial reflection of the domestic preferences of influential energy-related groups. Western public opinion often ignores the commercial interdependence dimension of the energy markets demanding cooperation, a higher level of misconduct in Russia's bureaucracy (a factor that creates reverse dependence on the Western circles), and the interests of domestic political, and economic groups.

Pre-conditions of the energy market against Russia's aggressive energy policy are free and fair competition and better regulations in the domestic energy market. James Henderson (UK) and Vaclav Bartushka (Czech Republic) underlined when they answered the author's question on the Russian FEP that the antidote against Russia's "energy weapon" contains diversification in the energy mix, more effective regulations, and alternative routes. On another hand, Russia uses energy factors, mostly electricity and natural gas, as a political tool to influence the domestic political process, especially during the electoral cycle. Also, Russia may use the energy crisis to provoke social tension in the target country's sensitive regions. Giorgi Mukhigulishvili (Georgia) accused Russia to use terror attacks against oil-gas pipelines and electricity transmission lines. This claim overlaps with REC-SID's findings of the critical explosions in the energy infrastructure (pipelines and pump stations) of Georgia, Ukraine, Turkmenistan, and Azerbaijan for various critical periods.

Mukhigulishvili also claimed that Russia used the electricity tariffs and natural gas tariffs as a political instrument to influence society and the process of elections not only in Georgia but also in Armenia. He argued:

> *Russia's political and economic influence on the neighboring countries using energy factors or resources depends on the level of dependence on Russia's energy sector. If the level of dependence is high, then Russia can potentially start using the energy factor as a foreign policy tool. But if the level of dependence is low or moderate, and there are regulatory sound market conditions then Russia's capability to influence negatively will be getting limited. Georgia became a member of the EU-affiliated Energy Community to harmonize and transpose EU energy directives and regulations into the national legislation. If the government and private actors will support the energy efficiency and renewable development measures, in the future Georgia can achieve strong energy security and energy independence. Georgian decision-makers and policymakers in the field of energy perceive Russia as*

> *a non-reliable energy partner. But Georgian private energy companies that have business relations with Russia's energy companies don't have such perception.*
>
> (Expert interview with G. Mukhigulishvili, 2018, Tbilisi)

The different actors (e.g., energy companies and government) can demonstrate different behavioural patterns in different settings of the energy policy and energy markets.

Case study of Russia-Georgia energy conflict based on expert interview (Expert interview with G. Mukhigulishvili, 2018, Tbilisi). In 2006, when the energy conflict had broken out with Russia, Georgia had energy connections and *gas* transmission lines from Russia. The country had complete –100% – dependence on Russian natural gas. Also, Georgia received electricity through two different transmission lines from Russia. In the winter of 2006, when there was a shallow temperature in Tbilisi and entire Georgia, the Russian side provoked by blowing up the gas transmission line that Georgia received gas in the winter season. There was a total disruption in gas supply for a week. Still, the Baku-Tbilisi-Erzurum gas pipeline started to operate, carrying gas from Azerbaijan's "Shah Deniz" offshore field. The pipeline has been operational since late 2006, transporting natural gas firstly to Georgia and starting from 2007 to Turkey from the colossal "Shah Deniz" field. The Georgian government asked the government of Azerbaijan to supply additional gas volumes to Georgia. Initially, the Russian side announced that the explosions were just terrorist attacks. But when the Georgian government asked the Russian side to use the gas pipeline infrastructure of Azerbaijan to supply additional gas to Georgia to compensate unexpected cutoff, Russia refused to accomplish the demand. Finally, Georgia was supplied natural gas by Azerbaijan and Iran in the winter of 2006.

At that time, Azerbaijan had insufficient gas to increase its supply to Georgia. Therefore, the Iranian side sold additional gas to Georgia via Azerbaijan. Azerbaijan already had a gas transmission line with Iran, but that pipeline was lousy, causing severe losses during the gas transfer. In 2008, Georgia's natural gas and electricity system switched to Azerbaijan during the short Russia-Georgia war. Azerbaijan exported gas to Georgia using its new South Caucasus Pipeline (SCP) or Baku-Tbilisi-Erzurum gas pipeline from the "ShahDeniz" field. Georgia had enough gas to switch to Azerbaijan and diversify the gas supply sources to avoid suffering from Russia's cutoffs. Russia's fighter jets bombed the close areas of the Baku-Tbilisi-Ceyhan oil pipeline and Baku-Tbilisi-Erzurum gas pipeline in the 2008 military conflict. Russia just demonstrated to the EU and USA that it has the capacity to control/affect these pipelines and will not allow the increase of the volumes transferring from those strategic routes – the Southern Energy Corridor to the EU via Georgia. Also, the Trans-Caspian Pipeline was a prevalent issue in 2006. Russia's energy aggression was a clear message for investors and international financial institutions. It meant that if they intended to build the Trans-Caspian Pipeline from Turkmenistan to Europe via Georgia and Azerbaijan, they had to be aware and inoculated about the security risks of the project.

After the energy crisis with Russia during the 2006–2008 period, Georgia limited the import of Russian gas to 10% of total natural gas consumption. Azerbaijan supplied 90% of the natural gas consumption of Georgia. Russian natural gas giant Gazprom competed with Azerbaijan state oil-gas company SOCAR to retake the Georgian gas market control. Then Georgia entirely relied on Azerbaijan, having 100% natural gas dependence. Azerbaijan's state oil-gas company SOCAR and the international consortium for developing the "Shah Deniz" gas condensate field were the leading gas suppliers to Georgia. Georgia would completely switch to gas supply from Azerbaijan and wouldn't purchase gas from Russia after 2016.

In 2016, Georgia started to negotiate a new energy agreement with Russia. Russia refused to pay Georgia an in-kind transit fee of 10% of all the natural gas that passed from Russia to Armenia via Georgia. It intended to renew that condition in the new energy deal switching from "*the commodity scheme to cash payments*". The extension of the old contract was delayed until April 2016 since Gazprom insisted on monetary payment for transit. But this kind of change was not profitable for Georgia, as cash payments were vulnerable to natural gas price fluctuations and currency devaluations. But Russia achieved to sign a new deal with the Georgian government to switch the payment method for transit gas in 2017. Then Georgian side received cash for Russian transit gas to Armenia via Georgia three times lower than the previous in-kind transit fee.

In terms of *electricity*, Russia blew up one of the electricity transmission lines in Georgia in 2006. But currently, Georgia has relatively favourable conditions for electricity where it has local hydro-power plants to generate electricity that covers 80% of total annual consumption by households. Imported natural gases are used in thermal power plants to produce electricity. But Georgia has imported a severe quantity of electricity from Azerbaijan and Russia because of a temporary deficiency. Russia occupied almost 20% of the territory of Georgia including the Abkhazia region. The government of Georgia made the decision to supply electricity to the Abkhazia region *free of charge*. Georgia had a shortage of electricity in the 2017–2018 period because of the rehabilitation of the largest hydropower plant in the Gori region. Georgia purchased electricity from Russia to supply to Abkhazia for no charge in 2017–2018. Russia has military bases in Abkhazia, but they use the free electricity provided by Georgia. Because of free and very cheap electricity from Georgia, some Russian service and manufacturing companies started to produce their products in Abkhazia. *This short case study reveals the tools (explosions and disruptions) and limits (availability of alternative suppliers) of the Russian foreign energy policy in the example of the energy affairs with Georgia under the asymmetric interdependence setting as a source of energy power. Russia's instrument selection reached very radical tools from an "energy power toolset" against a small-size target country with a high level of sensitivity and vulnerability in energy interdependence.*

7.5 Basic Content Analysis of the Official Texts on the Russian FEP

The Russian foreign energy policy parameters and key trends were examined through the content analysis of official foreign policy concepts and annual presidential messages in this research. These documents and annual speeches can be indicative in terms of the operational environment of the foreign energy policy. Content analysis of the texts of the Russian President's annual messages to Parliament and foreign policy concepts included 13 keywords as a "*smallest recording unit*" (Frankfort-Nachmias, Nachmias, & DeWaard, 2015, pp. 276–278): *NATO, Eurasia, Ukraine, China, India, the West, Europe, threat and aggression, cooperation, energy, oil, gas, and nuclear*. These words appertain to uncodified categories on the geographical priorities of the foreign policy (West vs. Eurasia), the nature of the foreign policy in terms of worldview (threat and aggression vs. cooperation), strategic balance in the foreign policy (China vs. India), the energy dimension (general and oil, gas, nuclear) of the foreign policy.

Basic operationalized categories in the text-based analysis are (a) geographical priorities and strategic balance; (b) actor's world outlook; and (c) energy dimension. This relational content analysis tests to reveal the interlinked changes and evolution of Russian foreign policy's geographical priorities, worldview, and energy dimension. The text-based analysis, referring to the primary source documents of the government, partly incorporates discourse analysis, meaning that the study counts the number of keywords and analyses the discourse in that these keywords were used. For example, "West" was used for positive agenda based on mutually beneficial cooperation from 1993 to 2000, but the discourse had shifted to a more negative connotation after 2000 (Table 7.4).

The word "strengthening" ("*ukrepleniya*") of the state, national interests, and foreign policy was used 23 times in 1999. If the foreign policy concept of 1993 mentioned the keyword "*West*" 30 times and mainly in the context of cooperation, the foreign policy concepts of 2000 and 2008 referred to the same word only two times each in the context of containment, power decline, rivalry, interventionist, and other negative connotation in addition to bilateral partnership. The "*NATO*" was always mentioned in the context of the risky enlargement towards the East and possible cooperation mechanisms. There is a growing use of the "*Eurasia*" concept in the foreign policy documents in terms of great regional integration and new emerging pole of new multipolar world order (Figure 7.4).

From the early 1990s, *India* was mentioned in equal numbers as *China* in the Russian strategic documents (correlation ratio: 0.9). Even Russian strategists sometimes used the concept of "*Indochina*" combining these two regional powers in one great geopolitical space in terms of economic power and market size. But later China had the edge over India in the Russian strategic foreign policy documents reflecting the real power advantage of China in its relationship with Russia vis-à-vis India till 2000. After 2000, Russian foreign policy concepts again had used "China" and "India" in nearly equal proportion. China-India tandem was used as an internal (against each other) and external (Primakov's "triangle" against the collective West) strategic balancer. Even though Russia had a higher level of energy conflicts and supply disruption cases with *Ukraine*, this country was mentioned less and less in the annual messages and the concepts (excepting 2014).

The frequency and intensity of keywords and their relationship to the context of the selected categories reveal several clear trends and features in the official texts. The word "*energy*" had started to be integrated into the foreign policy documents

Table 7.4 Content analysis of the texts of the Russian president's annual messages to parliament and foreign policy concepts

	Basic categories in the text-based analysis												
	Geographical priorities and strategic balance							*World outlook*		*Energy dimension*			
	Keywords in the text-based analysis												
	NATO	*Eurasia*	*Ukraine*	*China*	*India*	*West*	*Europe*	*Threat*	*Cooperation*	*Energy*	*Oil*	*Gas*	*Nuclear*
	Frequency of "keywords" in the texts												
1993	**5**	**1**	**4**	**7**	**6**	**30**	**50**	**9**	**79**	**6**	**3**	**0**	**14**
1994	0	0	0	1	1	4	5	8	2	1	2	0	4
1995	6	0	6	3	2	3	24	12	27	3	0	0	10
1996	1	0	3	1	0	2	5	12	3	6	4	1	4
1997	2	0	2	3	1	0	8	7	7	1	0	1	4
1998	5	1	2	2	1	2	11	4	10	1	2	3	0
1999	4	0	2	2	2	3	21	19	18	5	1	0	6
2000	0	0	0	0	0	0	1	6	0	3	0	0	0
2000	**6**	**1**	**0**	**3**	**3**	**2**	**16**	**9**	**23**	**1**	**0**	**0**	**11**
2001	2	1	0	0	0	0	5	3	2	3	1	2	0
2002	1	0	0	0	0	0	2	3	0	3	2	0	0
2003	0	1	0	0	0	0	8	16	5	1	2	1	2
2004	0	1	0	2	1	0	5	5	2	1	5	5	1
2005	1	1	0	0	0	1	6	3	2	2	0	0	0
2006	0	1	0	1	1	0	3	13	2	10	1	2	15
2007	5	2	0	0	0	0	11	2	4	11	9	7	7
2008	2	2	0	1	1	0	8	7	4	1	1	1	0
2008	**6**	**6**	**1**	**6**	**6**	**2**	**28**	**22**	**41**	**14**	**0**	**0**	**14**
2009	2	0	0	1	0	0	3	1	0	18	2	3	10
2010	1	3	1	3	2	0	5	2	7	5	2	0	2
2011	0	4	0	0	0	0	5	0	2	3	1	0	3

(Continued)

Table 7.4 (Continued)

	Basic categories in the text-based analysis												
	Geographical priorities and strategic balance						*World outlook*			*Energy dimension*			
	Keywords in the text-based analysis												
	NATO	*Eurasia*	*Ukraine*	*China*	*India*	*West*	*Europe*	*Threat*	*Cooperation*	*Energy*	*Oil*	*Gas*	*Nuclear*
	Frequency of "keywords" in the texts												
2012	0	1	0	0	0	0	1	3	0	2	2	2	1
2013	0	3	3	0	0	0	2	2	0	1	1	1	12
2013	**6**	**7**	**1**	**6**	**5**	**3**	**31**	**24**	**62**	**8**	**0**	**0**	**15**
2014	0	2	17	0	0	2	5	4	3	2	1	1	1
2015	0	3	0	1	0	1	1	5	2	3	3	1	0
2016	0	3	0	2	2	0	3	4	5	2	0	0	0
2016	**4**	**6**	**2**	**4**	**3**	**3**	**23**	**26**	**64**	**11**	**0**	**0**	**16**
2018	3	4	0	2	1	0	4	11	3	15	2	1	27
2019	0	4	0	2	1	0	5	9	5	2	0	2	4
2020	0	0	0	0	0	0	2	5	1	1	0	0	2
2021	0	2	2	0	0	2	2	4	2	9	0	10	4
SUM	62	60	46	53	39	60	309	260	387	155	47	44	189
AVE	2	2	1	2	1	2	10	8	12	5	1	1	6

Notes: "threat" means foreign and domestic threats or aggressions towards Russia's statehood; "cooperation" means positive collaboration between Russian federal regions, and between Russia and foreign partners. "AVE" means a simple average of indicators.

in the foreign policy concept of 2008 mostly in the context of national security and supply/demand security. The "energy" concept was primarily utilized as a major component of Russia's comprehensive *cooperation* with external actors and an element of national *power*. The "Energy" phrase has been increasingly used in the context of domestic economic efficiency and global climate change. The "*nuclear*" was used in the context of energy, weapon, war, global stability, and security. *Nuclear energy was used in parallel to a nuclear weapon*. This context validates that the expansion of nuclear energy by Rosatom around Eurasia and the Middle East has strong geopolitical stimulus and nudge from the Kremlin (Akulov, 2021). Nuclear energy and nuclear weapon have serious interlinks; therefore, Russia's nuclear defence project gave the country nuclear energy (Table 7.5).

The weight of the energy dimension has grown in parallel with the increasing emphasis on "threat" (correlation ratio: 0.8). Russian foreign policymakers and Putin accentuated the "energy" factor as a power accumulation and cooperation instrument against rising external threats and risks. The foreign policy concepts

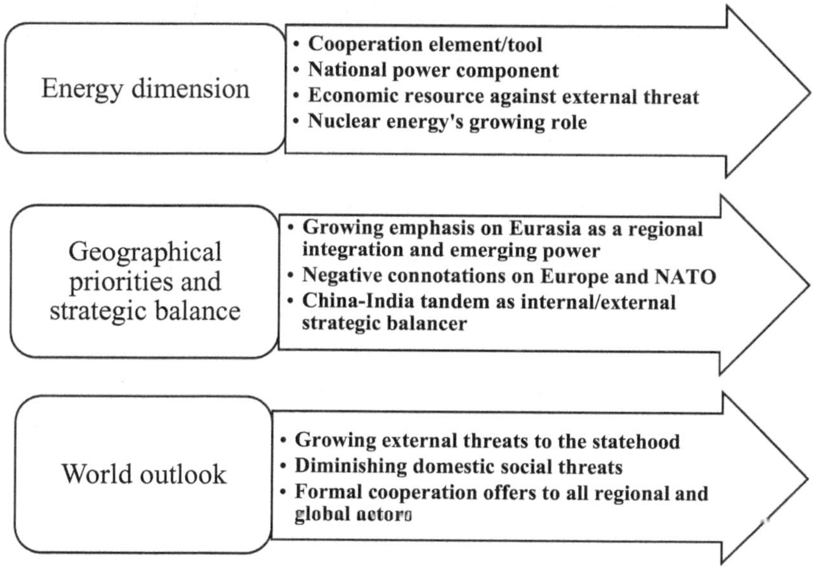

Figure 7.4 Result of relational content analysis: relations with categories and context.

Table 7.5 Correlation matrix for keywords

	Nuclear	*Threat*	*India*
Energy	0.73	0.8	
Threat	0.8		
Cooperation	0.74	0.9	
China			0.9

assessed growing foreign "*threats*" to Russia's national security from 2000 to 2016 (more emphasis on internal threats from 1993 to the early 2000s). Russian foreign policy documents consider the growing foreign "threats" and deep challenge to the nation-state as a globalized and transboundary phenomenon under the "conditions of rising interdependence of all states" (Ministry of Foreign Affairs of Russia, 2016). The frequency and intensity of "cooperation" firstly decreased, but then rapidly increased after 2010. Russia has not refused to offer opportunities for co-operation, at least at the level of official discourse, especially to EU partners, which are becoming increasingly interdependent with Russia.

The analysis of official foreign policy concepts and annual presidential messages reveals that "*economic interdependence* doesn't totally eradicate the 'energy weapon' of Russia but limits and mitigates its real adaptation and active implementation in terms of instruments, methods, timeframe, and desired ends/targets". The EU officially indicated that in the event of an armed confrontation between Russia and Ukraine after 2015, the commissioning of the Nord Stream-2 gas pipeline will be terminated. This factor limited Russia's use of gas pipelines as a geopolitical pressure instrument and military intervention in the "near abroad" that generates direct and indirect "threats" for Russia (Akhtyrko, 2021). The "threat" context and rhetoric were related to securing Russia from various forms of military and political pressure and potential external aggression after the mid-2000s.

NATO plays important role in Russia's foreign threat perception that affected foreign energy policy. Zevelev (2011) affirmed that NATO's eastward enlargement isn't only perceived as an essential threat to Russia's security, but also was the external factor that mobilized the Russian political and military elites. USA's holistic support to the Caspian Basin's oil-gas countries (Azerbaijan and Kazakhstan) to bypass Russia in the oil export was a factor that negatively impacted Russia-NATO (West) relations (Zevelev, 2011). Hashim (2010) underlined the role of the Russia-NATO struggle over Europe and the post-Soviet region as a crucial determinant of the energy dimension of the Russian foreign policy during Putin's rule (263–274). Vital security threats such as NATO's military manoeuvres could stir up Russia to apply "energy weapon" against the EU states. "*Military Doctrine of Russia*" which was enacted by the President in 2014, elaborated that despite the reduction in the probability of a macroscale war unleashing against Russia, the military danger for Russia is intensifying in several areas. The main external military threat for Russia is the military infrastructure of NATO members close to the borders of Russia. The doctrine envisaged "*build a new security model in the Asia-Pacific region based on collective non-bloc principles*" in cooperation with CSTO, SCO, CIS, and BRICS (Rossiyskoy Gazety, 2014). The use of the military infrastructure with Belarus (military space overlaps with key energy transit infrastructure) against NATO and the joint military doctrine with Belarus was one of the main priorities of the regional military alliance-building strategy (Ministry of Foreign Affairs of Belarus, 2019).[2]

The role of NATO's expansion on Russia's foreign energy policy and its tools should be analysed quantitatively. Final declarations of the series of NATO summits between 2002 and 2009 (Prague in 2002, Istanbul in 2004, Riga in 2006,

Table 7.6 Number of mentions of energy security and Russia in NATO's declarations

NATO's summit	*Energy security*	*Connotations*	*Russia*	*Connotations*
Prague Summit (2002)	0	–	6	Cooperation
Istanbul Summit (2004)	0	–	5	Cooperation and slight disagreement
Riga Summit (2006)	4	Risks for energy infrastructure	10	
Bucharest in 2008	6	Institutionalized role of NATO on energy security	22	Early signals on security concerns
Strasbourg/Kehl Summit (2009)	11	Elaborating the energy security	31	Condemnation of Georgia, concerns

Source: NATO (2021).

Bucharest in 2008, Strasbourg/Kehl in 2009) that was a period of the primary wave of Russia-NATO confrontation, were examined in terms of growing emphasis on energy security in parallel to the negative connotations on the relations with Russia. The mentions of energy security were increased in parallel to the increase in references to Russia (correlation ratio: 0.97) (Table 7.6).

The declaration of NATO's Prague Summit in 2002 alluded to Russia-NATO Council in terms of cooperation without any reference to energy security (NATO, 2002). The declaration of NATO's Istanbul Summit in 2004 mentioned Russia in the context of collaboration and some restrained discord on Russia's military presence in Moldova and Georgia (NATO, 2004). This declaration did not mention energy security and energy factor. The statement of NATO's Riga Summit in 2006 referred to energy security in the context of "risks and security of energy infrastructure" (NATO, 2006). Riga Summit's declaration mentioned Russia in higher quantities with the combining context covering collaboration and slight confrontation on the post-Soviet countries. The declaration of NATO's Bucharest Summit in April 2008 was one of the negative turning points in Russia-NATO relations because of the potential membership perspective of Georgia and Ukraine. After three months of NATO's Bucharest Summit, Russia militarily intervened in Georgia in August 2008. In the winter season of 2008–2009, Russia launched a new wave of energy conflict with all post-Soviet (Ukraine and Georgia) and EU members. That declaration has mentioned security concerns regarding Russia's practical steps and "artsy" policies that threatened NATO's regional security arrangements. Bucharest declaration introduced energy security and defence of crucial oil, gas, and electricity infrastructure as an institutional responsibility of NATO (NATO, 2008). The declaration of NATO's Strasbourg/Kehl Summit in 2009 has elaborated more details on energy security (e.g., diversification and uninterrupted energy flows) as a critical area of NATO's responsibilities (NATO, 2009). The same document emphasized serious security concerns on Russia's military intervention in Georgia as a fracture point in NATO-Russia complex affairs. NATO developed energy security agenda as a reaction to Russia's energy conflicts with the EU and post-socialist countries. Also, US's National Security Strategy claims that Russia expands its influence in different parts of Europe and Central Asia via control over key energy resources juxtaposing the regional position of Russia with the energy and security context (Martsinkevich, 2018).

On the Russian side, the securitization of energy also reached to peak after 2014. In the "*National Security Strategy of Russia*" enacted by the President in 2015, the national security concept of Russia covers the defence of the country and all types of security including economic and energy security. Strategy stipulates that national economic security depends on energy security through durable energy demand, application of high technologies, building strategic energy reserves, strengthening energy companies, rising energy efficiency, prevention of energy shortages, and stable energy supply. The strategy underlines the facts about preventing discrimination against Russian energy suppliers in foreign energy markets during the development of hydrocarbon fields outside the country. For Russia, there are attempts of several countries to regulate energy markets based on political rather than economic feasibility. The Strategy affirms the reduction of critical dependence on foreign *technologies* and reinforcement of the leading position in nuclear energy as one of the measures fulfilled by state authorities to counter threats to the economic security of Russia ("clause No. 60–62 in the Strategy") (The Council of Security, 2015). Securitization of energy affairs in terms of discourse, narratives, official statements, and rhetoric doesn't decrease the importance of the interdependence theory that determines the outcomes of the energy power.

7.6 Determinants and Constraints of Russia's Foreign Energy Policy

The expert interviews, RECSID, content analysis, and review of existing literature revealed various determinants of the Russian foreign energy policy. These driving factors include economic interdependence and corporate interests towards profit maximization; energy prices, energy revenues, and technologies; external threat perception, securitization, and militarization of the discourse; aspirations towards hegemonic expansion based on grand strategy objectives; and the personality of rulers in the power and domestic political setting. These determinants have different degrees of influence on foreign energy policy. The evaluation of intensity or severity of the driving factors can be categorized as "low", "moderate" and "severe" based on the expert interviews, RECSID, and exploration of open-source information. The personality of rulers or leaders in power is an influencing factor even though RECSID evidenced that the pre-Putin period was also conflictual in terms of energy interactions of Russia with counterparts.

From the quantitative perspective, the Russian energy conflicts and supply disruption cases don't strongly correlate with crude oil and gas prices and revenues ("low" level of influence). But the increasing energy revenues contributed to the domestic and foreign power consolidation in Russia that led to the more aggressive foreign energy policy. External threat perceptions by the state, attitudes towards securitization, and militarization of external and internal affairs, hegemonic power expansion trends had a high influence on Russia's foreign energy policy's "foreign policy dimension". Russian state-owned energy companies have corporate interests and profit maximization stances that also determine Russia's foreign energy policy and critical energy decisions. Economic and energy interdependence (through trade, investment, technologies, and energy needs), the structure of the energy market, and the complexities of the energy sector had "severe" or high influence on Russia's foreign energy policy's "energy policy dimension".

In addition to the tentative evaluation of the influence of various determinants of FEP, the current research developed Russia's Energy Interdependence Model (REIM) based on Grigas's (2017) accurate contributions. Energy researchers who shifted to the energy discipline from IR and political science are prone to explain energy affairs with geopolitical narratives. Still, energy scholars with technical, engineering, and economics backgrounds are inclined to underpin classic and complex interdependence arguments ("epistemological and ontological divergence in the scholars based on professional background"). Having an economics background and experience in the gas sector, Grigas (2017) proposed a detailed framework for interconnections between gas-exporting, gas-importing, and gas-transit countries (pp. 19–20). Firstly, she argues that *flawless interdependence is the infrequent case between gas producers and gas consumers*, while some analysts argue that there is no perfect dependence between two parties.

Therefore, while some scholars argue that lack of pure dependence excepts full politicization of gas affairs, Grigas (2017) points out that lack of pure interdependence always paves the way for a certain degree of politicization of foreign energy affairs (maybe not only in gas but also in oil and coal). As importing states depend on reliable energy supply for industrial production and social welfare, exporting states depend on the stable revenues from the energy sales markets. So, despite the power and geopolitics dimension of foreign energy policy, real-life energy affairs are *complex and interdependent*. Grigas (2017) believes that an accurate and full pattern of interdependence can ensure steady energy flow from the producers to consumers. But we look at the degree and proportionality of interdependence through the size of the importers' market, the extent of available alternative energy resources, and the ready-made energy infrastructure. The dynamic processes in regional and global energy markets (supply-demand equilibrium, developments in energy reserves and energy extraction technologies, growth trends, etc.) constantly change the interdependence pattern (Table 7.7).

Russia's Energy Interdependence Model (REIM) indicates that the sizes of Russia's domestic energy market and export markets, available alternatives for Russia and importing countries, and available energy infrastructure for Russia and importing countries could partly ensure a classic interdependence pattern[3] in the country's foreign energy policy. Suppose there is a one-sided dependence pattern between energy exporters and importers in favour of the first group. In that case, gas producers can misuse this pattern (toolset: price manipulation, export volume manipulation, etc.) to realize national political and security interests using the energy factor ("supply weapon"). Suppose an inverse pattern exists in energy relations

Table 7.7 Russia's Energy Interdependence Model (REIM)

Conditions of energy interdependence					
Market size		*Degree of alternativeness*		*Energy infrastructure*	
The size of the importer's market	The size of the exporter's market	The alternative import sources and routes	The alternative export sources and routes	Energy import infrastructure	Energy export infrastructure
Example: Ukraine, Belarus, Georgia, China, EU	Example: Russia's oil–gas market and dominant size	Example: LNG opportunities (Qatar, the USA, etc.), Turkmen gas, Iran gas	Example: LNG routes, China, Middle East (NPP)	Example: LNG and pipelines, nuclear power plants	Example: LNG and pipelines, nuclear techs

Source: Modified from Grigas (2017).

when energy importing countries benefit from the asymmetrical interdependence. In that case, consumers use energy leverage against producers via manipulating import volumes, demanding more price discounts, diversification of energy sources and destination countries, and applying additional and complicated energy market regulations ("demand weapon").

Grigas (2017) assumed that Russia could use an energy "supply weapon" (or "the politics of supply" as the author has described) against Latvia which has higher energy dependence on Russia with a smaller energy market and lack of alternatives (pp. 19–20). But she believes that Russia cannot use the same leverage against China which has more deterrence power against Russia with its large market size and available energy import alternatives. Varol (2013) underlined that Russia pursues an interest-based foreign energy policy that included direct supply disruptions for the former-soviet republics. Russia didn't often use harsh tools of foreign energy policy such as gas supply cuts against the major EU economies such as Germany because of existing "commodity-revenue" interdependence (pp. 20–397). Contrary to Grigas's and Varol's argument, RECSID revealed that Russia had interstate energy conflicts with energy importers having a large market size and alternative energy sources such as China and Germany. But RECSID uncovered that Russia used less severe tools of energy power against the countries that have circa symmetric interdependence with the country. Russia should be convinced of the symmetric interdependence of energy relations. Otherwise, it can potentially misuse seasonal conditions or energy shortages momentums to "punish" the target country under the framework of aggressive foreign energy policy.

Russia has a vast informal economy and informal networks that feed its real geopolitical power and foreign energy policy. But Formun Üstü also, energy-rich countries including Russia encounter complex challenges that limit their foreign energy policy. Also, RECSID findings, the expert interviews, and literature review revealed the following constraints that could potentially limit Russia's foreign energy policy: the level of energy-based economic interdependence, the initial costs of vulnerabilities and sensitivities based on the pattern of economic interdependence, domestic political economy settings, diminishing oil-gas revenues, lack of competencies and capabilities in the energy sector, shift to renewable energy, energy supply diversification strategies by the target countries, decreasing oil-gas reserves and production, exploration of hard-to-reach oil and gas reserves, technological backwardness, outdating the tools such as subsidies, global trade regulations towards trade openness, new "non-friend" political regimes, lack of trust and reliability by consumers, the maximum capacity of energy infrastructure, and finite and depleted oil-gas resources under the "peak oil" concept.

Some analysts argue that Russia's foreign energy policy based mostly on oil and gas resources has similar patterns to other countries that race for the dominant position. Russia invests heavily in other energy-rich countries (Libya, Iraq, Venezuela, Indonesia) to keep control of oil-gas production and export on a global scale (Kalantzakos, 2019, p. 7). Because the "peak oil" argument forces other key oil-gas countries to have a global strategy to control more resource basins. The "*peak oil*" approach means that oil (or gas) production will peak and then decline after spending some period on the plateau. It isn't an uncomplicated issue to predict a precise time of "peak oil", but we can consider it one of the factors affecting the outcomes of Russia's foreign energy policy and energy power as a constraint (Smil, 2020). Geological and technological challenges for Russia to enlarge its natural resource base and energy production are one of the fundamental limitations of Russia's foreign energy policy to gain geopolitical advantages using fossil fuels exports.

International sanctions (imposed in 2022) will further worsen the resource base for oil and gas exports through technological challenges that will prevent the recovery of declining production in Russia's traditional oil-producing regions.[4] A sharp reduction in the export of petroleum products due to sanctions and embargoes will lead to full capacity filling of existing storage facilities and a partial shutdown of production at the Russian refineries. Sanctions targeted the Russian energy sector and their long-term results function as an impediment to the foreign energy policy by restraining energy production and export. Decreasing energy production and export in Russia can potentially contribute to the reduction of the higher level of energy dependence on Russian fossil fuels in the key energy-importing countries. Less reliance on Russian energy resources and more diversifications could fundamentally shift the symmetricity of the existing interdependent setting. However, this scenario depends on how quickly the major Russian energy importers implement their diversification plans.

Notes

1 *James Henderson* (UK) and *Vaclav Bartushka* (Czech Republic) expressed their opinions to the author during the question and answer (Q&A) session of the Energy Summer School in the Czech Republic in August 2019.

2 Signed by the heads of states in 1999, the Agreement on Establishment of the Union States of Belarus and Russia sets up a legal basis for integration between the two countries.

3 Economic interdependence has some limitations to prevent interstate conflicts, because "traders" and "soldiers" think and act differently in interstate affairs. Generally, the mindset of the strategic decision-makers is a "black box" for outsiders that prevent economic actors to evaluate the rationality of the key decisions.
4 Russia relies on China to offset the technological gap in the energy sector. But China also depends on foreign technologies in the critical areas (e.g., South Korea and Japan supply key LNG technologies).

8 Conclusion and Policy Implications

The book examined Russia's foreign energy policy, energy resources, and energy conflicts in the context of interdependence patterns and strategic goals of foreign policy. The research examined tools, constraints, patterns, and determinants of the Russian foreign energy policy. The RECSID findings, semi-structured expert interviews, basic content analysis, and literature review revealed the determinants of the Russian FEP. The factors determining Russia's conflictual foreign energy policy actions and policy pattern against partner countries are the target country's military and political relations with NATO and EU institutions; Russia's foreign policy goals based on grand strategy; the level of the target country's energy (oil, gas, coal, nuclear, and electricity) dependence on Russia; the volume of mutual trade turnover and FDI flows shaping interdependence; energy companies' corporate interests and income generation functions; Russian energy companies access to local energy infrastructure; competition with rival states and energy companies; geopolitical interests in the territory of the partner country; the geographical proximity of the target country domestic political and economic setting; energy reserve and oil-gas production capacities; oil-gas prices in global energy markets; energy transition and diversification plans; and behaviour of oil-gas transit countries.

Russian foreign energy policy combines market-based interdependence patterns (ensuring energy supply to receive revenues from competitive energy markets) and security-based foreign policy attitudes (e.g., prevention of NATO's enlargement). When we match the foreign policy goals based on the grand strategy with the foreign energy policy of Russia, it could be observed that major components of the grand strategy have corresponding goals and actions in the foreign energy policy. Foreign energy policy is an outcome of national, regional, and global situations where interactions between global great powers', nation-states, non-state actors, and market players install an environment for the functional operation. The valid narrative about the Russian foreign energy policy backed by evidence was that it used its geography, natural resources, and energy infrastructure as an "energy power" to increase geopolitical influence. Even though the current research widely uses the concept of "energy weapon", it distinguishes it from "energy power" where the former is used mainly with political context while the latter can be operationalized from a theoretical standpoint.

DOI: 10.4324/9781003408482-8

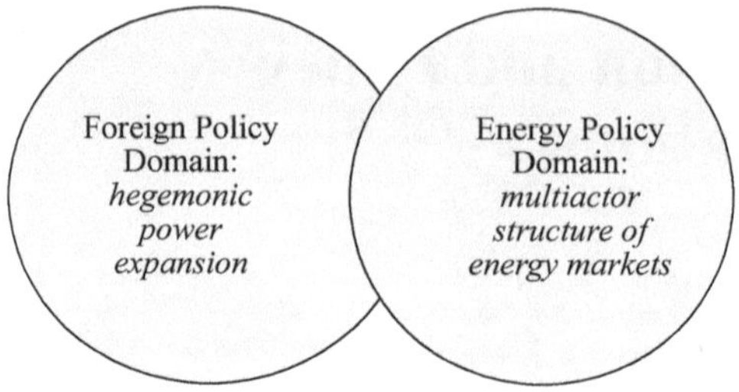

Figure 8.1 "Double domains" of the Russian FEP.

Different components of Russia's foreign energy policy, such as major propositions of foreign policy, energy strategies, energy conflicts, and energy diplomacy can be explained by different theoretical frameworks. We presume that foreign energy policy is situated in the "junction" of Russia's foreign policy and energy policy ("*double domains*"). Russian foreign policy could be explained mainly through neorealist theories (mostly, offensive neorealism) with a materialist ontology and hegemonic expansionism (Figure 8.1).

The foreign policy domain of the Russian FEP is influenced by the deep insecurity perception that is not only generated from the anarchic international system as the realist school argues but also from unique history and domestic discourses in alignment with social constructivist and liberal essentialist discourses. In contrast, the energy policy domain externalizes some reverberations of complex and classic interdependence based on liberal institutionalist ontology and the multi-actor structure of energy markets (market principles and previous behavioural pattern of actors may totally deform, especially in period of war). Also, it partly overlaps with the "state-market" interaction proposition. Russia's "energy weapon" could be occasionally exaggerated, ignoring the interdependence that oil-gas pipelines, energy trade, energy-related investments, energy technologies, and energy-related institutions shape.

The main argument of the book is that the interdependence pattern through energy trade, energy investments, energy technologies, and complex interactions isn't a "valid preventer" but a "confined mitigator", under certain "tranquil" conditions (partly depending on energy types), in Russia's foreign energy policy and energy conflicts in terms of the tool selection. Patterns of interdependence with counterparts can be asymmetric in terms of the costs of the exit from this pattern, providing additional "bargaining power" to Russia in conflictual interstate affairs to accomplish (geo)political and economic goals. The energy diversification efforts and sanctions against Russia by the Western countries could be seen as the efforts to rebalance the energy-based interdependence framework in terms of adjustments to the material costs and political consequences of vulnerability and sensitivity. RECSID's findings, semi-structured expert interviews, case studies, and basic content analysis allow the formulation of more precise conclusions on Russia's foreign energy policy and energy conflicts in alignment with the initial hypothesis (H) of the book based on the main argument of the research.

H-1: *Russia cannot "weaponize" all types of energy including gas, oil, electricity, uranium, and coal for grand strategy and foreign policy goals considering the fact that the energy type is globally traded shaping interdependence pattern.*

RECSID's didn't fully verify this hypothesis demonstrating that Russia's energy conflicts embrace all energy types including gas, oil, electricity, nuclear, and coal, but to a different degree. Some studies (Baldwin, 2016; Bogaturov, 2017; Pirani, 2010; Dannreuther & Ostrowski 2013) argue that oil and gas have a different level of conflictual nature in the Russian FEP. It is true that the number of gas-related conflicts outpaced oil-related and other energy conflicts (the presence of market in particular energy types played a role as a factor). Russia's energy conflicts with other energy types including crude oil, oil products, nuclear, electricity, and coal could have regional and global repercussions. The fluctuations of the oil-related and gas-related conflicts do not coincide and cohere with each other reflecting different dynamics of the energy conflicts because of the type of energy. Even though gas revenues are less than the oil incomes of oil-gas exporting countries; therefore, we can argue that natural gas is less prone to conflicts. But in the case of Russia's gas-related disputes, we could see that the energy security of the EU rapidly increased the strategic importance and conflictual attribute of the gas resources. We could examine the characteristics of various energy types in terms of RECSID's findings.

- *Natural gas* (that doesn't have a well-functioning global market like oil) is more prone to conflictual use by the Kremlin as a foreign policy tool rather than other energy types such as oil or nuclear. Crude oil and petroleum products are also "weaponized", but not on the same level as gas. One of the reasons is the perception in the Russian decision-makers that their crude oil has alternatives in the *regional and global markets*, but in the case of natural gas, Russia has monopolistic dominance at least in the European and CIS markets.
- Russia had more intense *oil* conflicts with Azerbaijan, and this is a new phenomenon in the context of existing literature and "conventional wisdom" on Russia's foreign energy policy. Russia's oil-related conflicts prevailed in gas-related conflicts in the 1990s in comparison with the 2000s, not in absolute numbers but in proportion. Russia frequently used oil supply disruption "tool" against EU members rather than CIS states (that import lesser oil from Russia), in contrast to the gas supply stoppage.
- Russia had more intense *nuclear* energy conflicts with the USA, Ukraine, Bulgaria, Iran, the EU, and the Czech Republic. In addition to the European countries, Russia also had nuclear energy-related discordances with new energy partners from the Middle East, Asia, and Africa. Russia mostly had nuclear energy conflicts in 2014–2015 when its political and economic relations worsened with major Western partners. European countries had negative prejudice against Rosatom claiming its coordinated efforts with Kremlin to fortify Russia's geopolitical position in the critical regions and countries.
- Russia had more intense *electricity* conflicts with two South Caucasus countries – Georgia and Armenia. Russia misused Georgia's energy dependence on Russia

with political-security motivations. Russia used the increase in electricity tariff as a political tool against CIS countries especially, Georgia. The *geographical proximity* of the electricity importer country that is connecting to the Russian electricity grid network determined an electricity-related conflict with Russia. But Russia never used electricity supply interruption against the Baltic countries (e.g., Lithuania) that were partly dependent on the grid.

- RECSID identified some cases of Russia's coal-related energy conflicts with Ukraine and Estonia. Russia has halted deliveries of *coal* transit to Estonia and Ukraine reviving the "energy weapon" fears. The motivation for the coal-related conflicts was political with Ukraine and Estonia. Moscow made a political decision to stop the supply of coal to Ukraine forcing the country to work with separatist regions. Russia's decision-makers believe that country's dominant position in global energy markets including coal should enable it to achieve its political goals in the "*near abroad*" (asymmetric dependence).

H-2: *Complex interdependence in energy trade and economic parameters (energy domain of the FEP) can partly limit Russia's aggressive FEP and diminish the "returns" of energy conflicts and FEP's applied and evolved tools.*

RECSID's findings, semi-structured expert interviews, case studies, and basic content analysis proved this hypothesis in terms of limitation and availability of various tools rather than direct determinant. Firstly, we should recognize that the operationalization of complex interdependence theory for data analysis is challenging. The book used energy and trade interdependence (that shape multiple channels and multiple agendas in energy affairs) in data analysis. One-sixth of Russia's foreign energy conflicts and supply interruptions were experienced with the largest trade partners such as the EU, China, Germany, the Netherlands, and Turkey. It means that trade interdependence and the volume of the trade turnover didn't fully prevent the energy conflicts between Russia and the trade partners. But RECSID identified that Russia did not implement frequently the most radical and costly means of energy power, such as a direct cut-off of energy supplies, against its biggest trading partners such as China and Germany.

Sometimes the energy clashes were purely driven by the commercial interests of Russian energy companies to maintain a dominant market position and multiple actor structures of energy markets and systems facilitated the solutions to the conflicts (however, the previous hypothesis demonstrated that Russia could use globally traded energy types in the energy conflicts, but in less intensity). The "multiple actor" approach overlaps with Strange's (1988) global power diffusion and state-market interactions theory, and Keohane/Nye's complex interdependence theory. Energy firms' solid corporate interests and profit maximization stances partly determine Russia's FEP and conflictual energy decisions. Also, Russia's state-owned and private energy companies' behaviour abroad reflects their behaviour in the domestic energy domain and the discourse of political economy.

Expert interviews and literature review indicated that pre-conditions of the energy market against Russia's aggressive energy policy are free and fair competition and better regulations in the domestic energy market. Russia resorted to the use of energy as a tool for achieving foreign policy goals considering the energy-intensive and gas-consuming nature of the economies of the target countries, and the level of energy production and energy prices. The energy sector sometimes acted as a platform that drove the energy dialogue and diplomacy between Russia and global actors. Also, Russia has an energy interdependence tie with the consumer countries through oil-gas revenues. Russia as an energy exporter relies on the revenues from the energy sales in the energy-scarce countries' markets, but energy importers also depend on the uninterrupted oil, gas, electricity, and nuclear fuel supply from Russia. Energy interdependence relationship with main partners could be asymmetric that provide additional power to Russia in interstate interactions. RECSID partly proved the assumption that Russia is pursuing a more aggressive foreign energy policy towards countries with deeper vulnerabilities in terms of dependence on the Russian energy resources, or the potential to exploit energy transit capacity as leverage against Russia.

H-3: *Under the pattern of interdependence, Russia's relatively aggressive foreign energy policy and energy conflicts don't depend on the political personality of President Putin and had a similar behavioural pattern in the pre-Putin period, as well.*

RECSID partly supported this hypothesis meaning that Russia had politically motivated energy conflicts in the ruling period of Yeltsin (1992–1999), but Putin's ruling era after 2000 was more conflictual than in terms of energy conflicts and "energy weaponizing" (but expert interviews asserted the importance of rulers personality). Metrics of foreign energy policy and constraints revealed that the personality of rulers or leaders in power is an influencing factor even though the pre-Putin period was also very conflictual (domestic and foreign dimensions) in terms of energy interactions of Russia with counterparts. Russia's assertive foreign policy with a robust foreign energy dimension under Putin's rule was based on Primakov's statist stance in the foreign policy seeking great power status for Russia in a preferable multipolar system. The majority of the Russian energy conflicts and supply interruptions occurred between 2000 and 2021 which could be characterized as "Putin's ruling era". The major peaks of foreign energy conflicts and supply interruptions of Russia were 2004, 2006, 2009, and 2014 which overlapped with the Russia-West geopolitical confrontation over the post-Soviet states. Russia mostly had gas conflicts in 2006, 2009, and 2014 when its political and economic relations worsened with the CIS and the EU countries.

Thorun (2009) asserted that Russian foreign policy was relatively cooperative towards the external world (especially in energy and security relationship with the West) between 2000 and 2004, while RECSID revealed that the cooperation mood in that period (first term of Putin's presidency) limitedly influenced Russia's energy conflicts and supply disruptions (60 conflicts and interruptions were identified on that period). The then US President Obama's "reset" initiative towards Russia in 2009 aimed to integrate the country into the regional and global affairs more profoundly with recognition environment limitedly affected Russia's foreign policy and foreign energy policy. RECSID reveals that the number of Russia's foreign energy conflicts and supply cuts decreased from 61 in 2009 to 18 in 2010

(Medvedev's presidency). But the country's foreign energy policy didn't totally become conflict-free, partly invalidating the constructivist arguments that recognition by the West as a great power can make Russian foreign policy and foreign energy policy less assertive. This means that energy conflicts were not entirely due to the confrontation between Russia and the West. But this is partly due to the dynamics of the energy sector and energy markets and the domestic consolidation of power (political and economic) in Russia.

The intensity and the peak intervals of Russia's natural gas conflicts overlap with the geopolitical rift periods with the West over the "near abroad" regions. Also, there was a shift in the Russian government from the oil-gas and energy sector to the secret services and the military-industrial complex. After gaining total control over the state-owned energy companies in the early 2000s, Kremlin under Putin's rule decided to empower national energy companies and use their market power in foreign policy and domestic politics. State-owned energy companies (e.g., Gazprom, Rosneft, Rosatom, Transneft, Inter RAO) dominate Russia's energy sector securing its domestic and foreign energy policy. Partly, the monopolization attitude in the Russian foreign energy policy over energy sources and transit pipelines through strong state-owned enterprises was an anachronism from the USSR period when the existing political and economic system denied any type of competition. Therefore, Putin's period has similarities with Yeltsin's period and even the USSR period in terms of the state's behaviour towards the energy policy. The foreign energy policy of Russia directly links to the domestic political, economic, and institutional systems. Under Putin's ruling, the security apparatus of the Russian state ("siloviki") intends to position Russia's foreign energy policy in the juxtaposition of new military doctrine and more aggressive foreign policy under the grand strategy. But in fact, Russia's foreign energy policy is partly developed by the complex interaction of various social groups.

H-4: *Foreign policy domain of the FEP determines the growing external threat perceptions and "securitization of energy" that increase the geographical coverage of the energy conflicts of Russia in alignment with foreign policy goals.*

Basic content analysis of the official texts revealed that Russian foreign policymakers and Putin accentuated the "energy" factor as a power accumulation and sometimes dialogue instrument against rising external threats and domestic risks based on insecurity perceptions. Therefore, Russia applied coercive "energy power" measures (cutting off energy supplies in the winter seasons, increasing energy prices, and gas price discrimination depending on the political loyalty of the energy-importing countries) against energy-consuming post-Soviet such as Ukraine openly unlocking their desires to integrate into the NATO and the EU. Russia's energy policy moved on contemporaneous with the foreign policy goals in an ideologically "blind" way without differentiating "friends from enemies" (e.g., intense energy conflicts with Slavic nations such as Ukraine and Serbia). Russia's conflictual foreign energy policy towards Belarus, Ukraine, Georgia, and other CIS states could be interpreted only through the complex and very specific social, economic, legal, and political interrelations (asymmetric interdependence) of Russia with these countries in the post-Soviet period that subsume the deep legacy of

USSR. Since the early 1990s, NATO expressed interest in integrating the Baltics, Ukraine, and Georgia into the pan-European security mechanisms of the bloc. At the same time, these are countries that Russia has more aggressively approached in matters of foreign energy policy and energy conflicts related to oil, gas, and transit. These overlaps mean that the relations of the partner country with NATO are a very important determining factor in the energy policy of Russia and its conflictual attitude to this country.

Transit countries' behaviour also was perceived as an energy security risk for Russia. Therefore, one-third of Russia's foreign energy conflicts and supply interruptions were experienced with only four post-Soviet neighbouring countries – Ukraine, Belarus, Lithuania, and Azerbaijan – where three out of four countries are simultaneously energy transit countries for Russia. Russia has had more energy conflicts with transit countries than with end-user countries. Russia had fewer energy conflicts with the post-Soviet countries that hadn't a direct border with the country. Russia always attempted to control the oil-gas transportation systems of Ukraine, Belarus, Moldova, Central Asia, and Caucasus countries through Gazprom, Rosneft, or joint energy transit companies. Russia aimed to create a network of subsidiaries owned by Gazprom, Rosneft, or Transneft in the "near abroad" region and Central and Eastern Europe to control oil-gas flows. Russia could have more energy conflicts with the target country from the post-Soviet region that it has less economic, political, and security influence (e.g., Azerbaijan, Ukraine, Lithuania). Russia had a higher number of energy conflicts and supply interruptions cases with the post-Soviet countries that accommodate relatively fewer ethnic Russians (e.g., Lithuania and Azerbaijan).

The geography of the Russian foreign energy policy and energy conflicts are widespread. The energy dimension plays a critical role in the Russian foreign policy towards the West and the East. Russia mobilized crude oil, natural gas, nuclear energy, coal, and electricity resources, energy export opportunities, and energy transit capabilities to achieve the strategic goals not only in Europe and CIS but also in Asian and the Middle East regions. Russia used "energy power" not only against post-Soviet countries but also against EU states, perhaps, with less intensity. Asian energy partners have had fewer energy conflicts with Russia than European energy partners (the geographic location of energy reserves and energy markets matters). Russia had energy conflicts not only with legitimate nation-states but also with the illegal and unrecognized "quasi-states" or separatist units such as Transnistria (Moldova) and South Ossetia (Georgia).

RECSID revealed that Russia's energy conflicts with the "target" country often had negative consequences for third countries, also Russia's geopolitical confrontation with regional and global powers triggered ("*third-party effect*"). The high intensity of Russia's energy conflicts and supply disruption cases with neighbouring post-Soviet countries coincide with the ultimate aim of the Russian grand strategy to be the dominant power in the post-Soviet region without any serious competitor. Russia's energy conflicts with EU countries and global powers such as the USA and China serve the strategic goal of being recognized as a "great power" globally. Especially the western and southern bordering countries had a higher level of conflictual nature in the energy affairs in alignment with the goal of the grand strategy of Russia on domination in the "Greater Eurasia" region. This overlaps between energy conflicts and grand strategy goals represent the foreign policy dimension of the Russian FEP, and it isn't a sufficient condition to evaluate the outcomes of the FEP and energy power that are partly determined by the realities of the energy sectors and energy markets based on interdependence and complex affairs.

Policy implications. From the perspective of policymaking, it is a challenging task to evaluate the effects of foreign energy policy and the energy power of Russia, because there is uncertainty about energy resources, energy production, and supply-demand equilibrium. Policymakers should take into account the contradictory info and statistics about the energy systems of Russia that are also open for manipulations diverting predictions. Identification of political or geopolitical motivation for energy supply disruption is a crucial element of the understanding of the Russian foreign policy that has several components for verification:

a Timing and correlation with coincided political and economic events
b Behavioural patterns and traditions in the previous (energy) conflicts
c Domestic political structure and decision-making process in the state
d The level of energy and economic interdependence with target states

But the major criteria to distinguish Russia's commercial energy moves from politically motivated acts are *timing and correlation* with other political and geopolitical events. In many cases, there was a clear connection between the energy and the foreign policy of Russia. RECSID offers a shred of rich evidence on the timing factor in the Russian foreign energy conflicts that exploit a broad toolset. Ansoff's "weak signals" theory has the potential for the identification of the "early warning signals" and "aftershocks" of Russia's energy conflicts with major partners and target countries, companies, and institutions. But there is a need for further operationalization of that theory and to add detailed case studies on the domestic settings of the target countries in the future researches.

RECSID and expert interviews showed that Russia's foreign energy policy *tools* evolved over time and the applied tools of the Russian aggressive foreign energy policy differed from the 1990s to the 2000s. Also, reducing the natural gas supply to the consumer country was the most widely used instrument of the foreign energy policy. But in terms of policy implications and filling the gap in the existing literature, the book also concentrated on the *nuclear* dimension. Russia halted not only the oil-gas supply but also the deliveries of nuclear fuel, electricity, and coal for political reasons. Russia's intense nuclear energy conflicts with partner countries would have policy implications for relatively newly emerging nuclear energy countries, which built long-term cooperation with Rosatom. The cooperation with Rosatom in the nuclear energy field has an advantage for the host country, such as technology transfer, commercial conditions, financing mechanism based on Russian state loans, and human resource preparation. At the same time, nuclear energy creates a longer-term dependence on the supplier than on oil, gas, and coal. Evidence-based findings of the book identify strategic, geopolitical, domestic stability, and also commercial considerations of the foreign energy policy and its applied tools including expansionary nuclear energy policy. There is a "vicious circle" in the foreign energy policy meaning that as a part of strategies to ensure energy security, various energy consumer states realize energy import diversification policies to reduce energy dependence on Russia.

The success rate of these diversification policies will determine the outcomes of the Russian "energy power". The energy transition is a "double-edged sword" for Russia because the "energy transition" could have serious geopolitical implications for the country's foreign energy policy weakening the influence of fossil fuel resources. But Russia has huge renewable energy potential and the energy transition also would boost energy cooperation among self-sufficient countries. The outcome and intensity of Russia's conflictual foreign energy policy can vary depending on the political and economic policies of the energy-importing or transit "near abroad" and the EU countries. Market-based and regulatory energy frameworks in the target countries could restrict the zone of manoeuvres for the Russian energy companies. Russian IR scholars acknowledged that the lack of economic resources and ideological foundation prevent Russia from pursuing long-term conflict with the West which plays a crucial role in the Russian economy in terms of the sales market of hydrocarbon and sources of investment and high technology. It means the level of foreign technological dependence in the energy sector partly limits Russia's foreign energy policy. The lack of a clear correlation between Russia's energy conflicts and oil prices demonstrates that instead of a one-sided influence on the Russian foreign energy policy, oil prices rather acted as a "double-edged sword" for the country (Figure 8.2).

Based on a broad literature review and empirical research, we could formulate the "*Input-Output Approach*" as a new factorial pattern on the Russian foreign energy policy including long-run outcomes. The inputs of Russian foreign

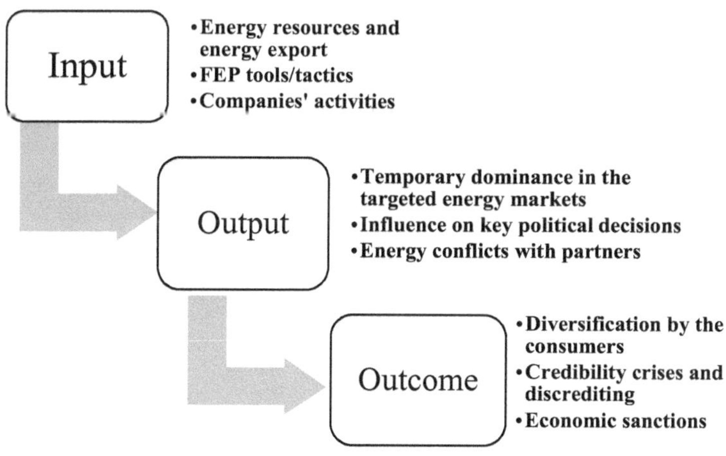

Figure 8.2 Input-output approach in the Russian foreign energy policy.

energy policy include energy resources and energy export, FEP tools and tactics, and energy companies' activities. The outputs of the Russian foreign energy policy comprise temporary dominance in the targeted energy markets, widespread influence on key political decisions, and energy conflicts with partners. The desired outcome of the Russian FEP would be (a) to deter "near abroad" countries from full integration into the EU and NATO; (b) to dominate the energy markets and energy assets of the EU and "near abroad"; and (c) to increase oil and gas revenues for the fiscal system and achieve economic development. But the real long-term outcomes of the Russian FEP are reputational and credibility crises, international sanctions including new sanctions applied in 2022, energy diversification strategies by the energy consumers, and the withdrawal of the Russian energy companies from the energy projects and energy assets of the European and post-Soviet countries. In the pattern of interdependence, political control over material inputs doesn't automatically ensure "command" over the final outcomes of the foreign energy policy. The asymmetrical energy interdependence of Russia couldn't be "per se" transformed into desired political and economic outcomes because of the political bargaining conducts and the quality of foreign energy policy and institutionalized interactions with domestic and foreign actors.

APPENDICES

Appendix 1

Correlation Ratios of Energy Conflicts and Various Indicators

Indicators	*Number of Russia's energy conflicts and supply interruptions*	*Period*
The distance from Russia to the target	(−)0.13	2019
Oil prices (Brent)	0.53	1990–2019
Oil prices (Brent)	0.8	1990–2006
Prior year's oil price	0.61	1990–2019
Prior year's oil price	0.73	1990–2006
Total democracy index	(−)0.6	1991–2019
FBIC Index	(−)0.2	2019
Russia's export to the target country[a]	0.32	1991–2019
Russia's imports from the target country	0.25	1991–2019
Electricity export to the target country[b]	(−)0.3	2004–2019
Trade openness	(−)0.3	1992–2019
Gas import dependence of EU states on Russia	0.13	2018–2019
Total natural resources rents (% of GDP)	0.55	1990–2019
Oil rents (% of GDP)	0.54	1990–2019
GDP per capita (current USD)	0.5	1990–2019
The net FDI inflows	0.5	1990–2019
Russia's net foreign assets	(−)0.2	2001–2019
Share of ethnic Russians with Ukraine	0.2	Various years
Share of ethnic Russians (without Ukraine)	(−)0.1	Various years
International reserves	0.5	1992–2019
Renewable power generation in Europe	0.93	1990–2004
Renewable power generation in Europe	(−)0.31	2005–2019

Source: Author's calculations based on RECSID findings.

[a]Excluding Ukraine as an outlier case in the statistical analysis.

[b]Only Russia's electricity-related conflicts.

Appendix 2

Indicators of the Energy Strategy of Russia for 2035

Indicator	*Indicator values*		
	2018 (baseline)	*2024*	*2035*
Oil industry			
Oil and gas condensate production (million tons)	556	555–560	490–555
Gas industry			
Gas production (billion m^3)	669	795–820	860–1000
A place in the world gas export market	1st place	1st or 2nd place	1st or 2nd place
The throughput capacity of export gas pipelines (billion m^3) *including:*	240	363	405
Westbound	240	325	325
Asia-Pacific region	–	38	80
LNG production (million tons)	18.9	46–65	80–140
International energy market			
The share of the Asia-Pacific countries in the total exports of the Russian energy resources	27	40	50

Source: Ministry of Energy of Russia (2020a).

Appendix 3

Ten Major Indicators for National (Economic and Military) Power (2019)

	EU	*USA*	*China*	*Russia*	*World*
GDP (trillion USD)	15.6	21.4	14.3	1.7	87.8
Exports of goods and services (billion USD)	7711	2515	2641	481	24890
Manufactures exports (% of merchandise exports)	79	59	93	20	68
High-tech exports (% of manufactured exports)	16	19	31	13	24
R&D expenditure (% of GDP)	2.18	2.84	2.19	0.98	2.27
Industry (value-added per worker USD)	74,321	107,025	24,773	28,880	25,129
Number of universities in the top 500	140	160	39	4	500
Population (million)	448	328	1398	144	7674
Military expenditure (billion USD)	220	732	261	65	1868
Armed forces personnel (000)	1920	1,380	2,695	1454	27,642

Sources: World Bank (2021a) and Webometrics (2022).

Appendix 4

Examples from RECSID (Energy Conflict Tracker for Russia)

The cause of energy conflict and supply interruption	*Energy type*	*Country*	*Date*	*Type of energy conflict or supply interruption*	*Result*
Russia intended to destabilize the Lithuanian economy	Oil products	Lithuania	January 1992	Total stop of oil products delivery	Lithuania threatened the blockade of Kaliningrad
Russia's political demands from Ukraine	Oil	Ukraine	January 1993	Reducing oil supply to 20 million tonnes	Yeltsin recognized the effects of "supply cut"
Discriminatory policy of Estonia towards ethnic Russians	Natural gas	Estonia	June 1993	Total stop of gas supply	Estonia was deeply dependent on Russia for gas supply
Political and security-related disagreements	Nuclear energy	Ukraine	March 1994	Delays in the delivery of fuel for the NPP	Ukraine was seeking political support from the USA on fuel supply
The contract for the Caspian shelf oil-gas fields by Azerbaijan	Oil-gas	Azerbaijan	September 1994	Russia organized the "futile" revolt in Azerbaijan	Russia participated in Azerbaijan's oil-gas projects
The privatization of the Armenian energy assets	Natural gas	Armenia	November 1994	The sabotage in the gas pipeline	Complete cessation of gas supplies to Armenia
Russia-Iran contract for the Bushehr NPP	Nuclear energy	USA	April 1995	Disruption of political and economic affairs	Russia-Iran nuclear energy cooperation continued to exist
Rosatom-Westinghouse competition on Bulgaria	Nuclear energy	USA	May 1995	Deferring the nuclear deal with Bulgaria	Rosatom continued to enter the Bulgarian energy market
The political position of Russia in the Bosnian conflict	Natural gas	Bosnia & Herzegovina	August 1995	Total stop of gas supply	Bosnia refused to pay the natural gas debt
Russia was not allowed to get Ventspils Nafta	Oil	Latvia	September 1996	Russia cancelled oil transit exemptions	Economic and political pressure on Latvia continued
Political pressure on Belarus after referendum	Natural gas	Belarus	December 1996	Reducing the supply of gas by Gazprom (50%)	Two countries carried out gas cooperation

Czech Republic intended to join NATO	Natural gas	Czech Republic	April 1997	Warning to cut off gas supplies	Prague signed a gas contract with Norway
To provoke public discontent in Bulgaria	Natural gas	Bulgaria	October 1997	Warning to stop gas deliveries	Bulgaria's intelligence claimed that gas disruptions had social & political motivation
Response to the actions of Gazprom in Ukraine	Natural gas	Turkmenistan	March 1998	Gazprom has stripped the gas pipeline	The conflict has affected grand politics
Discrimination against local Russians	Oil	Latvia	April 1998	Reducing the crude oil and oil products supply	A government crisis erupted in Riga
Political motives including the disputes in the Chechnya	Crude oil	Azerbaijan	February 1999	The sabotage in the Baku-Novorossiysk pipeline	The Baku-Supsa oil pipeline project's realization was accelerated
Lithuania's decision to sell the Mazeikiu refinery to the US	Crude oil	Lithuania	April 1999	Total stop of oil delivery	Vilnius managed to resume the oil supply
Destabilizing Serbia via social protests	Natural gas	Serbia	March 2000	Reducing the gas supply 3 times	Gazprom agreed to resume the gas supply
Chronic non-payment for the gas purchase	Natural gas	Belarus	April 2000	Reducing the gas supply by 30% by Gazprom	Rescheduling for paying off debts
The competition with the US energy company	Natural gas	Georgia	January 2001	Total stop of the gas supply	RAO UES was suspended from the electricity tender
Corruption scandal in the Blue Stream gas pipeline project	Natural gas	Turkey	January 2001	Turkey-Russia energy corruption scandal	Gazprom was blamed to expand corruption
Russia wanted to own a gas pipeline from Iran to Armenia	Natural gas	Armenia	July 2001	Armenia's gas debt paid off in lieu of a pipeline	Armenia tried to diversify gas import using Iran
Norex Petroleum and Calgary Overseas were expelled	Oil-gas	Canada	November 2001	Canadian oil-gas companies left Russia	High oil prices changed attitudes toward foreign companies
Commercial and political disputes with partners	Oil	Poland	July 2002	Lukoil drops bid for Polish Rafineria Gdanska	Lukoil was perceived as a Russian political influence tool
Economic & political pressure on Belarus	Natural gas	Belarus	November 2002	Warning to stop gas deliveries	The large-scale "trade war" had started
Duma called not to admit the CNPC to the auction	Oil-gas	China	December 2002	CNPC refused to buy Slavneft in the auction	Russia-China energy affairs continued

(Continued)

The cause of energy conflict and supply interruption	*Energy type*	*Country*	*Date*	*Type of energy conflict or supply interruption*	*Result*
Russia delayed the NPP's construction in Bushehr	Nuclear energy	Iran	December 2002	Iran and Russia couldn't agree on the NPP schedule	The USA made pressure on Russia on Iran's NPP
Complex problem: Chechnya, BTC, politics, debts	Electricity	Georgia	January 2003	Russia-Georgia deal on electricity terminated	Putin ordered the start of electricity export to Georgia
Russia-Georgia border issue on Chechnya and BTC	Natural gas	Georgia	January 2003	The Mozdok-Tbilisi gas pipeline was disabled and the accident on the Transcaucasus pipeline	Russia restored the gas pipeline to Georgia
Russia discussed rerouting an oil-gas pipelines	Crude oil	China	March 2003	Failed negotiation on oil export pipelines routes	Rerouting of pipeline viewed as a political step by China
Iraq made that decision with the US political pressure	Oil	Iraq	April 2003	Lukoil's West Qurna-2 contract was terminated	Lukoil's affairs with the US have been tense
The USA was against Russia - Georgia gas cooperation	Natural gas	USA	May 2003	Russia confronted with USA in the Georgian market	The USA supported the Baku-Tbilisi-Erzurum gas pipeline
Technical connection problem and political motivation	Electricity	Georgia	August 2003	Total stop of electricity supply and the chain of shutdowns in the electricity network	Russia supplied electricity to Georgia via Abkhazia
Russia's internal group interests (Transneft-Yukos tension) led to delay	Oil	China	September 2003	China warned about the delay and change in the pipeline project	Russia owed to realize the agreed oil pipeline
The secessionist "regime" demanded to write off the natural gas debt	Natural gas	Transnistria (Moldova)	November 2003	Transnistria blocked Russia's gas export to Moldova	Transnistria lifted the blockade after the debt write-off
Gazprom's problems with the acquisition of SPP	Natural gas	Slovakia	January 2004	The corruption scandal related to Gazprom	Gazprom's image in the European gas market was tarnished
Russia changed its attitudes toward foreign oil companies	Oil-gas	USA	January 2004	Exxon & Chevron lost the right in Sakhalin-3	Foreign oil companies hesitated about Russia
Total gas blockade of Belarus by Russia	Natural gas	Germany	February 2004	Total stop of gas supply to Eastern Germany	For Germany, the gas flow stop was the rare case

Energy & political conflict with CIS/EU	Natural gas	Poland	February 2004	Total stop of gas supply	Poland demanded fair compensation
Chechnya and the Kurdish issue and geopolitical disputes	Oil	Turkey	February 2004	Oil tankers pass via Bosphorus restricted	Russian oil companies suffered heavy losses
A terrorist attack with political motivation	Oil-gas	Azerbaijan	May-June 2004	Explosions in the Kazimagomed -Mozdok and the Baku-Tikhoretsk oil-gas pipelines	Oil-gas flows were restored very swiftly
Russia-Georgia political tension on South Ossetia	Natural gas	Georgia	July 2004	Warning to cut off the gas supply	Economic pressure to achieve political results
Russia intended to pull out Iran from the market	Electricity	Tajikistan	October 2004	Iran and Russia signed competing energy deals	Russia raised energy investment in Tajikistan
Transnistria forms an energy company and elections factor	Natural gas	Transnistria (Moldova)	March 2005	Gazprom threatened to raise gas prices	Moldova-Transnistria-Russia gas talks failed
Ukraine raised the price of uranium supplied to TVEL	Nuclear energy	Ukraine	December 2005	Rosatom warned of raising nuclear fuel price	Russia offered to unify the nuclear energy complex
Gas debt and new gas prices for Ukraine	Natural gas	Austria	January 2006	Reducing the gas supply	EU had concerns about supply security
Adjustment of the price to the market and politics	Natural gas	Germany	January 2006	Gazprom raised gas prices by 40%	Germany searched for an alternative gas source
Gas debt, adjusting new prices, and political issues	Natural gas	Ukraine	January 2006	Total stop of gas supply	Ukraine decided to go Stockholm Arbitration
For Russia, the Energy Charter was economically unfit	Oil-gas	EU	September 2006	Russia refused to sign the Energy Charter	Russia's energy isolationism started
Russia accused Belarus of siphoning off oil in the pipeline	Oil	Belarus	January 2007	Total stop of the oil flow via the Druzhba pipeline	Russia's oil supply reliability was damaged
Estonia moved a statue of a Red Army soldier in Tallinn	Coal	Estonia	May 2007	Russia halted deliveries of steam coal transit	The cut-off revived "energy weapon" fears
Lukoil aimed to acquire refineries in Europe	Oil	Germany	August 2007	Total stop of oil export via Druzhba pipeline by Lukoil	This supply cut fact was economic blackmailing

(*Continued*)

The cause of energy conflict and supply interruption	*Energy type*	*Country*	*Date*	*Type of energy conflict or supply interruption*	*Result*
The victory of the "orange" coalition in Ukraine	Natural gas	Ukraine	October 2007	Warning to stop the gas supply	EU focused on the energy supply security
Prague signed a deal with the US on the missile system	Oil	Czech Republic	July 2008	Total stop of oil delivery	Russia continued supply halt with a political drive
Russia created problems for foreign workers at BP	Oil-gas	UK	July 2008	BP withdrew from Russia all its employees	Russia changed its attitude toward BP.
South Ossetia and Abkhazia were recognized by Nicaragua.	Oil and electricity	Georgia	September 2008	Russia used an "energy card" for recognition of South Ossetia and Abkhazia	Russia promised energy projects to Nicaragua.
Response to EU efforts to diversify gas import	Natural gas	EU	October 2008	Gazprom applied 500$ record-high prices for the EU	Gazprom couldn't keep high gas prices for the EU
The gas debt and higher gas prices were demanded	Natural gas	Ukraine	January 2009	Total stop of gas supply	Russia-Ukraine-EU trilateral negotiations
Gazprom aimed to buy all gas from the Shah Deniz field	Natural gas	Azerbaijan	April 2009	Gazprom and SOCAR disputed on gas volume	Suspect terrorist attack in State Oil Academy of Azerbaijan
Explosion in the Central Asia-Center gas pipeline	Natural gas	Turkmenistan	April 2009	Total stop of gas import from Turkmenistan	Gazprom did sabotage to block Nabucco
Hungarian politicians were against the deal	Oil-gas	Hungary	May 2009	Surgutneftegaz failed to get a 21% stake in MOL	Gazprom aimed to block Nabucco pipe via MOL
Disagreement on the cost of the project and credit	Nuclear energy	Belarus	August 2009	Russia-Belarus a conflict on the building of NPP	Russia and Belarus continued the nuclear deal
South Ossetia demanded from Gazprom low prices	Natural gas	South Ossetia (Georgia)	August 2009	Gazprom and "South Ossetia" had a gas conflict	Gazprom was engaged in a political "project"
Accusing Belarus of siphoning 79000 tons of oil	Oil	Belarus	October 2009	Total stop of pumping oil via the Druzhba pipeline by Russia	Europe's trust in Russia's reliable energy supply had been shaken

Lithuania accused Gazprom of contract non-compliance	Electricity	Lithuania	March 2010	Gazprom filed claims against Lithuania ("Kauno Energija" case)	Gazprom warned to exit from the heat and power plant deal
EU took radical measures to replace Russian gas	Natural gas	Croatia	December 2010	Croatia abandoned the gas supply contract with Gazprom	ENI became the only gas importer to Croatia
CNPC claimed that Rosneft demanded higher oil price	Oil	China	March 2011	Rosneft had a conflict with CNPC on oil price	Rosneft/Gazprom-CNPC oil-gas price conflicts were regular
Political discords on energy supply and the NPP project (the EU factor)	Nuclear energy	Bulgaria	July 2011	Mutual litigations on the Belene NPP project	Rosatom (ASE) lost the Bulgarian nuclear energy market
Iran dissatisfied with the passivity of the company	Oil	Iran	August 2011	Iran terminated the deal with Gazprom Neft	Gazprom Neft and Lukoil lost a few oil fields in Iran
The official reason was the cold weather in Russia	Natural gas	Greece	February 2012	Reducing the gas supply by 10%	Deterioration in the relations with Europe
High cost of the NPP and political disagreements	Nuclear energy	Bulgaria	March 2012	Bulgaria abandoned the Belene NPP building	Russia intended to raise the compensation issue
Economic pressure to increase the price	Oil	Czech Republic	April 2012	Reducing the oil supply	EU states continued to revise the terms
Yamal LNG would be costly in the EU market	Natural gas	Qatar	March 2013	Qatar withdrew from the Yamal LNG project	Novatek started to look for new investment partners
SOCAR pumped less oil via the Baku-Novorossiysk pipe	Oil	Azerbaijan	May 2013	Russia ended oil transit deal with Azerbaijan	Azerbaijan succeeded to diversify oil export
Gazprom resisted changing its pricing policy	Natural gas	China	June 2013	CNPC insisted on revising the gas pricing formula	CNPC and Gazprom couldn't agree on the price
The base gas price and formula for its indexation	Natural gas	China	October 2013	CNPC-Gazprom failed gas supply negotiations	Russian President Medvedev intervened to end the price dispute
Armenia had pro-EU aspirations of signing the DCFTA	Natural gas	Armenia	December 2013	Russia canceled the 35% duty on oil products to Armenia	Armenia refused to sign DCFTA and decided to join to EEU

(*Continued*)

The cause of energy conflict and supply interruption	*Energy type*	*Country*	*Date*	*Type of energy conflict or supply interruption*	*Result*
Mutual banning of fuel supply and fuel transit	Nuclear energy	Ukraine	March 2014	Nuclear energy cooperation halted	Risk of energy supply disruption in Eastern Europe
The overthrow of Yanukovych and the Crimea issue	Natural gas	Ukraine	April 2014	The gas discount was canceled and gas price doubled	EU mediated the gas price negotiations
The Urengoy-Uzhgorod gas pipeline exploded	Natural gas	Ukraine	June 2014	The terrorist attack on the gas pipeline in Poltava	Gazprom transferred an advance payment
224 million USD gas debts of Serbia to Gazprom	Natural gas	Serbia	November 2014	Russia cut gas supplies to Serbia by 28%	Serbia had an intensive negotiation on debt
The politically-motivated debate on Turkish Stream	Natural gas	Turkey	March 2015	Gazprom-Botas conflict on gas price discount	Turkey was delaying the permits for Turkish Stream
Sanctions with Russian energy companies	Oil	France	June 2015	Total withdrew from some projects in Russia	Total continued to exist in Russian gas projects
Gas price disputes between Gazprom and Botas	Natural gas	Turkey	August 2015	Reducing the gas supply	Turkey refused to pay high gas prices
Turkish Air Force shot down a Russian Su-24 jet	Nuclear energy	Turkey	November 2015	Russia suspended talks on Akkuyu NPP	Bilateral energy affairs had temporary tension
Kyiv totally blocked electricity supplies to Crimea	Coal	Ukraine	November 2015	Total stop of the coal supply by Russia	Kyiv had resumed electricity supplies to Crimea
Price issues with private partners and political disputes	Natural gas	Turkey	February 2016	Reducing gas supplies by 40% by Gazprom	Turkey reduced its gas dependence on Russia
Disputes on supply route, gas prices, and volumes	Natural gas	China	June 2016	Russia-China gas supply negotiation failed	Western gas supply route was necessary for Gazprom
Russian companies were accused of unfair pricing	Oil products	Bulgaria	October 2016	Investigations against Lukoil and Gazprom Neft	Restrictive measures were applied to the Russian companies
The high cost and debt burden of NPP building	Nuclear energy	Vietnam	November 2016	Vietnam refused the nuclear power plant project	Rosatom offered a state loan to build NPP
Reaction to the lawsuit of Poland against OPAL	Natural gas	EU	February 2017	Gazprom refused to raise gas transit via Ukraine	Gazprom lost access to the OPAL gas pipeline

Baumgarten distribution station had an explosion	Natural gas	Austria	December 2017	Total stop of gas supply	Gazprom could not use alternative supply routes
Disputes on electricity tariffs with the government	Electricity	Armenia	April 2017	Rus Hydro warned to sell energy assets in Armenia	Russia energy holdings lost the local assets
Rosneft's contracts with the Regional Government in Iraq for oil supply bypassing Baghdad	Crude oil	Iraq	February 2018	Regulatory procedures against Rosneft by the Iraqi authorities	Baghdad rejected Erbil's separate deal with Rosneft
The claim about the extremely high cost of the NPP	Nuclear energy	Jordan	May 2018	Failed negotiation on Rosatom's NPP construction	Jordan offered to build the small modular nuclear reactors
Pashinyan's aggressive position toward Gazprom	Natural gas	Armenia	July 2018	Gazprom's tax violation revealed in Armenia	Gazprom denied the tax-related accusations
Technical and political reasons triggered a disruption	Oil	Latvia	November 2018	Total stop of oil supplies via Ventspils-Rosneft	Russia had energy-related problems with Baltic states
Belarus discovered a high concentration of chlorides in the oil	Oil	Belarus	April 2019	Total stop of oil delivery	Belarus demanded compensation for the oil supply disruption
Armenia refused to pay the high price and fined Gazprom	Natural gas	Armenia	June 2019	Russia raised the gas price for Armenia	Putin intervened directly in the energy conflict with Armenia
Russia aimed to restrict the coal supply to Ukraine	Coal	Kazakhstan	October 2019	Russia restricted coal transit from Kazakhstan	Eurasian Economic Commission intervened in the energy conflict
Gazprom sacrificed prices to maintain its share of the EU gas market	Natural gas	EU	February 2020	Gazprom lowered gas prices via the electronic trading platform	Spot LNG suppliers from the USA failed to compete with Russia
Rosneft Trading actively traded the Venezuelan oil	Oil	USA	February 2020	The USA imposed some sanctions on Rosneft Trading	Rosneft Trading refused any violations of the US regulations
Rosneft decided to sell its oil business in Venezuela without consent	Oil	Venezuela	April 2020	Venezuelan Parliament launched an investigation against Rosneft	An unnamed Russian state-owned company played a central role

(Continued)

The cause of energy conflict and supply interruption	*Energy type*	*Country*	*Date*	*Type of energy conflict or supply interruption*	*Result*
Nord Stream-2 pipes posed a threat to US national security	Natural gas	USA	June 2020	Senate expanded sanctions against the Nord Stream-2	USA-Russia energy relations deteriorated further
Restrictions were aimed at preventing the Nord Stream-2 pipeline	Natural gas	USA	January 2021	USA imposed gas-related sanctions (CAATSA) toward Russia	Completion of the Nord Stream-2 pipelines had seriously delayed
The decision was politically motivated by the USA pressure	Nuclear energy	Czech Republic	April 2021	Rosatom was excluded from the tender related to the Dukovany NPP	Russia-Czech Republic energy relations further deteriorated
Colonial Pipeline was forced to stop after a cyber-attack	Oil products	USA	May 2021	The USA blamed Russia for the cyber-attack on the Colonial Pipeline	US President said that there is no evidence of Russia's involvement
Russia misused the open auctions platform for gas exports	Natural gas	EU	July 2021	Gazprom refused to book additional transit capacity via Poland & Ukraine	Spot gas prices in Europe continued to break new records
The timing of the action overlapped with political tension with the EU	Natural gas	EU	August 2021	Gazprom stopped pumping gas into UGS facilities in the EU	The level of filling of underground gas storage (UGS) facilities reduced
The fire broke out at the Gazprom plant near the Novy Urengoy region	Natural gas	EU	August 2021	Gazprom reduced the gas flows via the Yamal-Europe gas pipeline	The gas prices in the EU market (TTF) increased significantly
Gazprom argued that it was preventive maintenance	Natural gas	China	September 2021	Gas export via the Power of Siberia pipeline suspended	Gas flows to China was quickly restored.

References

AA Energy. (2017). Turkmenistan Halts Gas Exports to Iran. https://bit.ly/3A1G9sM. 13 September 2019.

Abay, G. (2020). Russia's Oil Export Revenue Falls 13.6% in 1Q20. Anadolu Agency. https://bit.ly/3OQdEml. 21 May 2020.

Accounts Chamber of Russia. (2020). Subsoil Use. *Bulletin*, 5(270): 3–24. https://ach.gov.ru/upload/iblock/3ef/3efad1d974fb096eff58368ba6a9fca1.pdf. 15 July 2021.

Acemoglu, D., & Robinson, J. (2012). *Why Nations Fail: The Origins of Power, Prosperity, and Poverty*, 1st ed. New York: Crown, 529.

Acharya, A., & Buzan, B. (2019). *The Making of Global International Relations*, Cambridge University Press, 2–3.

Ahlin, E. M. (2019). Semi-Structured Interviews with Expert Practitioners: Their Validity and Significant Contribution to Translational Research. In: *SAGE Research Methods Cases*. https://dx.doi.org/10.4135/9781526466037

Ahmadov, I., Mammadov, J., & Aslanli, K. (2013). Assessment of Institutional Quality in Resource-Rich Caspian Basin Countries. *Kurswechsel*, 3(2013): 18–41.

Akçapa, M. (2020). *Rus Dış Politikasında Etkili Bir Aktör: Gazprom. Putin Dönemi Rusya-Sırbistan İlişkilerinde Enerji Faktörü*, Bursa: Dora Basım Yayın, 38–54.

Akhtyrko, A. (2021). If Russia Uses Weapons, the End of the Nord Stream 2 Gas Pipeline. Gazeta.ru. https://www.gazeta.ru/politics/2021/12/05_a_14281645.shtml 05.12.2021

Akulov, A. (2021). Russia Showed a Mini-Nuclear Power Plant Project. Gazeta.ru. https://www.gazeta.ru/business/2021/11/30/14264041.shtml. 01 December 2021.

Alekperov, V. (2011). *Oil of Russia: Past, Present, and Future*, Moscow: Creative Economy, 370–432.

Aleksashenko, S. (2021). "Red Lines" and Structural Supports of Slow Growth. "Liberal Mission – Expertise" Series. https://liberal.ru/lm-ekspertiza/krasnye-linii-i-strukturnye-opory-vyalogo-rosta. 17 April 2021.

Alifirova, E. (2021). The Russian Fuel and Energy Complex in 2021 Will Exceed the Results of 2020. Neftegaz. https://bit.ly/3y0FVzK. 12 November 2021.

Alifirova, Y. (2022). Pravitelstvo RF rasshirilo programmu l'gotnogo kreditovaniya na sistemoobrazuyushchiye predpriyatiya TEK. Neftegaz.ru. https://bit.ly/3MmGut2. 06 April 2022.

Alksnis, I. (2019). Why Russia Is no Longer Called "a Raw Materials Appendage". RIA Novosti. https://ria.ru/20190325/1552067626.html. 14 June 2020.

Allenova, O. (2009). Yuzhnaya Osetiya voshla v sostav rossiyskogo gaza. Kommersant. https://www.kommersant.ru/doc/1226798. 15 March 2021.

Analytical Center (AC) for the Government of the Russian Federation. (2020a). Dynamics and Structure of Russia's GDP. *Bulletin on Current Trends in the Russian Economy*, 62: 3–10. https://ac.gov.ru/uploads/2-Publications/BRE_62.pdf. 15 February 2022.

Analytical Center (AC) for the Government of the Russian Federation. (2020b). Dynamics of Russia's Foreign Trade in the Context of a Pandemic COVID-19. *Bulletin on Current Trends in the Russian Economy*, 65: 9–15. https://bit.ly/3NTwb0d. 15 February 2022.

Analytical Center (AC) for the Government of the Russian Federation. (2020c). Fuel and Energy Complex (TEK) of Russia in 2019. Statistical Bulletin. https://ac.gov.ru/uploads/2-Publications/TEK_annual/TEK.2019.pdf. 30 June 2021.

Ansoff, H. I. (1975). Managing, Strategic Surprise by Response to Weak Signals. *California Management Review*, 18(2). https://doi.org/10.2307/41164635

Antonov, M. (2022). Dve tysyachi yevro za tysyachu kubometrov. Vesti.ru. https://www.vesti.ru/article/2681137. 24 February 2022.

Aslund, A. (2019). *Russia's Crony Capitalism*, Yale University Press.

Aslund, A. (2021). Putin's Last Gasp? Project Syndicate. https://bit.ly/3IVfzUa. 08 December 2021.

Auzan, A. (2021). Russian Field of Experiments. "Yeshyo Ne Pozner" YouTube channel. https://bit.ly/3ADIaZ6. 13 January 2022.

Averbukh, M. (2021a). Keep Your Oil for Yourself. Novaya Gazeta. https://novayagazeta.ru/articles/2021/04/23/a-neft-svoiu-ostavte-sebe. 28 April 2021.

Averbukh, M. (2021b). Oil, Gas, and Copper Pipes. Novaya Gazeta. https://novayagazeta.ru/articles/2021/04/27/neft-gaz-i-mednye-truby. 28 April 2021.

Bachmann, R. (2022). What if Germany Is Cut Off from Russian Energy? VoxEU, CEPR. https://voxeu.org/article/what-if-germany-cut-russian-energy. 25 March 2022.

Badmayeva, I. (2021). Stocks Are Running Out. How Many Years Will Russia Have Enough Oil and Gas? Ria Novosti. https://ria.ru/20210921/zapasy-1751002337.html. 22 September 2021.

Baev, P. (2020). Transformation of Russian Strategic Culture: Impacts from Local Wars and Global Confrontation. Ifri. *Russie Nei Visions*, 118: 10.

Baldwin, D. (2016). *Power and International Relations*, Princeton University Press, 50, 56.

Balmaceda, M. (2013). *The Politics of Energy Dependency: Ukraine, Belarus, and Lithuania between Domestic Oligarchs and Russian Pressure*, University of Toronto Press, 3–36.

Balmaceda, M. (2021). *Russian Energy Chains: The Remaking of Technopolitics from Siberia to Ukraine to the European Union*, New York: Columbia University Press, 25–27.

Balockaite, R. (2012). *Russian Energy Imperialism: The World Mapped Along the Gas Pipelines*, Vytautas Magnus University, 85–96.

Bank of Russia. (2021). Estimate of External Debt of the Russian Federation. https://www.cbr.ru/eng/statistics/macro_itm/svs/. 30 September 2021.

Bank of Russia. (2022). International Reserves of Russia. https://bit.ly/3LURihN. 30 March 2022.

Bank of Russia. (2023). International Reserves of the Russian Federation. https://www.cbr.ru/eng/hd_base/mrrf/. 11 February 2023.

Barkanov, B. (2018). Natural Gas. In: A. Tsygankov (Ed.). *Routledge Handbook of Russian Foreign Policy*, Routledge, 138–152.

Belkovsky S. A. (2007). Imperiya Vladimira Putina. *M: Algorithm*, 190–192.

Belogoryev, A. (2014). Russia – China's Energy Rear. Vestnik Kavkaza. https://bit.ly/3xXMPG2. 30 September 2019.

Belyi, A. (2022). Yamal-Europe Gas Pipeline Shows How EU Competition Rules Backfire during a Shortage. Energy Post. https://bit.ly/3rqAGXH. 12 January 2022.

Belyi, A. V., & Locatelli, C. (2015). State and Markets in Russia's Hydrocarbon Sectors: Domestic Specificities and Interrelations with the West. In: A. V. Belyi and K. Talus (Eds.). *States and Markets in Hydrocarbon Sectors*, Palgrave Macmillan, 3.

Bergin, T. (2008). Factbox: Russian Oil and Gas Export Interruptions. Reuters. https://www.reuters.com/article/instant-article/idUSLS57897220080828. 01 December 2019.

Bernard, H. R. (2013). *Social Research Methods. Qualitative and Quantitative Approaches*, 2nd ed. SAGE Publications, 12–13; 524–539.

Bilgin, M. (2011). Energy Security and Russia's Gas Strategy: The Symbiotic Relationship between the State and Firms. *Communist and Post-Communist Studies*, 44(2): 119–127.

Blaustein, A. (2022). How Ukraine Unplugged from Russia and Joined Europe's Power Grid with Unprecedented Speed. Scientific American. https://bit.ly/3uOdsgf. 24 March 2022.

Bloomberg News. (2022). Russia's Long-Term Oil Growth at Risk from Service Firms' Pullback. https://bloom.bg/370WmCL. 22 March 2022.

Bobrov A. (2019). The Role and Place of the Post-Soviet Space in the Concepts of Foreign Policy of Russia: History, Current State and Development Prospects. MGIMO MFA of Russia.

Bobylev, S. (2021). Putin Said Russia Does not Use Energy as a Weapon. TASS. https://tass.ru/politika/12651419. 23 October 2021.

Bogaturov, A. (2007). Three Generations of Foreign Policy Doctrines of Russia. *International Processes*, 5(1): 54–69.

Bogaturov, A. D. (2017). *Contemporary International Relations and Russia's Foreign Policy*, Moscow: Aspect Press, 264.

Bordoff, J. (2022). Don't Blame Putin for Europe's Energy Crisis. Foreign Policy. https://bit.ly/3B6rATi. 02 February 2022.

Bordoff, J., & O'Sullivan, M. L. (2022). Green Upheaval. The New Geopolitics of Energy. Foreign Affairs. https://fam.ag/3QSdhcu. 13 May 2022.

Borovskiy, Y. V. (2018). *Energy Security Problem*, Moscow: MGIMO Universitet, 110–134.

Bouzarovski, S., & Bassin, M. (2011). Energy and Identity: Imagining Russia as a Hydrocarbon Superpower. *Annals of the Association of American Geographers*, 101(4): 783–794.

Bowen, M., & Dabbar, P. (2022). Reducing Russian Involvement in Western Nuclear Power Markets. The Center on Global Energy Policy. Columbia University, SIPA. https://bit.ly/3z7GIAT. 24 May 2022.

Boyko, B. (1996). Rabotat' zhestko, tverdo i pragmatichno. Kommersant Newspaper, 115: 2. https://www.kommersant.ru/doc/236025. 14 October 2021.

Boykov, S. S. (2020). Evolution of Russian Foreign Policy Towards the Baltic States at the Present Stage. *Post-Soviet Issues*, 7(3): 389–406.

BP. (2021). Statistical Review of World Energy 2020. https://on.bp.com/3np9V3s. 13 August 2021.

Braterskiy, M. V. (2018). Russia's National Security: The Evolution of Approaches. In: A. V. Lukin (Ed.). *New International Relations*, Moscow: International Relations, 106–109.

Bremmer, I., & Johnston, R. (2009). The Rise and Fall of Resource Nationalism. *Survival*, 51(2): 149–158.

Brezkun, S. (2015). Rossii nuzhna "lestnitsa" ne eskalatsii, a deeskalatsii. Nezavisimaya Gazeta. https://nvo.ng.ru/concepts/2015-11-27/1_stairway.html. 23 February 2020.

Brzezinski, Z. (1998). *The Grand Chessboard - American Primacy and Its Geostrategic Imperatives*, Basic Books, 64.

Brzezinski, Z. (2000). *The Geostrategic Triad - Living with China, Europe, and Russia*, Center for Strategic & International Studies (CSIS).

Burmistrova, E. (2021). Gazprom on Foreign Markets. Gazprom Group. https://bit.ly/3OZRuxX. 06 September 2021.

Burton, J. (1972). *World Society*, Cambridge: Cambridge University Press, 35–45.

Busygina, I., & Filippov, M. (2013). "Resource Curse" and Foreign Policy: Explaining Russia's Approach Towards the EU. In: J. M. Godzimirski (Ed.). *Russian Energy in a Changing World: What Is the Outlook for the Hydrocarbons Superpower*, F: Ashgate, 91–109.

Buzan, B., & Waever, O. (2004). *Regions and Powers: The Structure of International Security*, Cambridge University Press, 3–4.

Caselli F., Morelli, M., & Rohner, D. (2013). The Geography of Inter-State Resource Wars. *NBER Working Paper Series*, 41.

Casinge, E. (2014). Gazprom monopoly was broken in Moldova. EurActiv. https://bit.ly/3bD0cnx. 01 December 2019.

Caspian Barrel. (2021). Na rynke gaza zafiksirovan novyy mirovoy rekord. https://bit.ly/3fdxIzg. 22 December 2021.

Center for Army, Conversion and Disarmament Studies (CACDS). (2020). Peaceful Atom in "Hybrid" Wars. Materials of Expert Discussion. https://cacds.org.ua/en/?p=9704. 10 September 2020.

CenterPolit. (2020). Russia's Energy Strategy for The Period Up To 2030. Government Decree (13/11/2009). https://bit.ly/3OvI4KO. 16 April 2020.

Central Bank of Russia (CBR). (2021). Export of Natural Gas from Russia. https://www.cbr.ru/vfs/statistics/credit_statistics/trade/gas.xls. 20 November 2021.

Central Dispatch Office of the Fuel and Energy Complex (CDU TEK). (2021). Russia's Fuel and Energy Complex, and Oil Export Data. https://www.cdu.ru. 30 June 2021.

Cerny, P. G. (2010). *Rethinking World Politics: A Theory of Transnational Neopluralism*, Oxford: Oxford University Press, 22–85.

Cesnakas, G., & Juozaitis, J. (2017). Nuclear Geopolitics in the Baltic Sea Region: Exposing Russian Strategic Interests Behind Ostrovets NPP. Issue Brief. Atlantic Council. https://bit.ly/37lo6Sr. 12 January 2020.

Charap, S., Massicot, D., Priebe, M., Demus, A., Reach, C., Stalczynski, M., Han, E., & Davis, L. E. (2021). Russian Grand Strategy Rhetoric and Reality. RAND Corporation. Research Report. https://bit.ly/3OsL62N. 09 January 2022.

Chatham House. (2021). Myths and Misconceptions in the Debate on Russia. Russia and Eurasia Programme Report, 7–10. https://www.chathamhouse.org/2021/05/myths-and-misconceptions-debate-russia. 14 May 2021.

Chebakova, D., Tkachev, I., & Skobelev, V. (2021). Fifth Echelon Leadership. RBK. https://www.rbc.ru/newspaper/2021/04/14/607478fc9a794731d03611ab. 15 April 2022.

Chernenko, E., & Petrovich-Belkin, O. (2019). Soviet and Russian Foreign Energy Policy: Comparative Analysis. *Journal of Economic Cooperation and Development*, 40(4): 89–118.

CIA. (2021). Ethnic Groups. https://www.cia.gov/the-world-factbook/field/ethnic-groups/. 06 February 2021.

Claes, D. H. (2001). *The Politics of Oil-Producer Cooperation*, Westview, 81.

Clark, J. R. (2019). Russia's Indirect Grand Strategy. *Orbis*, 63(2): 225–239.

Cohen, A. (2009). Russia: The Flawed Energy Superpower. In: G. Luft and A. Korin (Eds.). *Energy Security Challenges for the 21st Century A Reference Handbook*, Praeger Security Inter., 92–105.

Colgan, J. D. (2013). *Petro-Aggression: When Oil Causes War*, Cambridge University Press.

Consultant Plus. (2005). Decree of the President of Russian (14.09.1995. No. 940) "On Approval of the Strategic Course of Russia with the Member States of the CIS". https://bit.ly/3Nr2gfy. 13 August 2021.

Consultant Plus. (2021). Resolution of the Supreme Soviet of the RSFSR (12.12.1991) "On the Ratification of the Agreement on the Establishment of the CIS". http://www.consultant.ru/document/cons_doc_LAW_30726/. 12 March 2021.

Cordell, J. (2021). Russia Faces $2T in Stranded Hydrocarbon Assets in Net Zero World. The Moscow Times. https://bit.ly/3KiYJQa. 06 November 2021.

Coşkun, C. (2021). Avrupa'nın enerji sınavı. BloombergHT. https://www.bloomberght.com/avrupanin-enerji-sinavi-2295127. 23 December 2021.

Council of Security. (2008). Fundamentals of the State Policy of Russia in the Arctic for 2020. http://www.scrf.gov.ru/security/economic/document98/. 10 February 2020.

Cox, R., (1996). Social Forces, States, and World Orders: Beyond International Relations Theory. In: R. Cox and T. Sinclair (Eds.). *Approaches to the World Order*, Cambridge University Press, 174–188.

Crandall, M. (2011). The Role of Central Asian Gas: Is It Possible to Bypass Russia? In: A. Dellecker and T. Gomart (Eds). *Russian Energy Security and Foreign Policy*, London: Routledge, 74–86.

Danielyan, E. (2003). Russia Tightens Grip on Armenia with Debt Agreements. Eurasianet. http://www.eurasianet.org/departments/business/articles/eav050703.shtml. 27 May 2020.

Dannreuther, R. (2013). Geopolitics and International Relations of Resources. In: R. Dannreuther and W. Ostrowski (Eds.). *Global Resources. Conflict and Cooperation*, Palgrave Macmillan, 79–97.

Dannreuther, R., & Ostrowski, W. (2013). *Global Resources. Conflict and Cooperation*, Palgrave Macmillan, 6–8, 232–237.

Degotkova, I. (2022). The Industry Has Become a Vulnerable Spot in the Regions. RBC. https://www.rbc.ru/newspaper/2022/04/21/625fe5be9a79470dc4d53c55. 22 April 2022.

Degterev, D. (2020). Multipolarity or "New Bipolarity"? Russian Council for International Affairs.

Dellecker, A., & Gomart, T. (Eds.). (2011). *Russian Energy Security and Foreign Policy*, London: Routledge, 206.

Deloitte. (2015). Sostoyaniye i perspektivy razvitiya nefteservisnogo rynka Rossii 2015. https://bit.ly/3bwzQTP. 17 May 2019.

De Vaus, D. (2001). *Research Design in Social Research*, SAGE Publications, 5–6.

Devetak, R., George, J., & Percy, S. (2017). *An Introduction to International Relations*, 3rd ed. Cambridge University Press, 92–93.

Dmitrieva, A. (2021). Lukoil cuts stake purchase in Azerbaijan's Shah Deniz gas field after BP boost. S&P Global Platts. https://bit.ly/3DN2TuU. 11 December 2021.

Domjan, P., & Stone, M. (2010). A Comparative Study of Resource Nationalism in Russia and Kazakhstan 2004–2008. *Europe-Asia Studies*, 62(1): 35–62.

Dorofeev, V., Solovev, A., & Bashkirova V. (2018). *Russia 2000: Putin and Others*, Moscow: ANF.

Doyle, M. W. (1983). Kant, Liberal Legacies and Foreign Affairs. Parts 1–2. *Philosophy and Public Affairs,* 12(3): 205–235; 12(4): 323–354.

Dugin, A. G. (2011). *Geopolitika*, Moscow: Akademicheskiy Proyekt. Gaudeamus, 583.

Dugin, A. G. (2015). *Last War of the World-Island. The Geopolitics of Contemporary Russia*, London: Arktos.

Dulneva, M. (2022). Yevrosoyuz utverdil otkaz ot rossiyskogo uglya s avgusta. Forbes.ru. https://bit.ly/3vz7Hlt. 12 April 2022.

Dyer, H., & Trombetta, M. J. (Eds.). (2013). The Concept of Energy Security: Broadening, Deepening, Transforming. In: *International Handbook of Energy Security*, Edward Elgar Publish, 3–18.

Dymarsky, V., & Ryzhkov, V. (2012). *26 Myths about Russia. Lies and Secrets of the Country*, Moscow: Astrel.

Dynkin, A., & Burrows, M. (Eds.). (2016). *Global System on the Brink: Pathways toward a New Normal*, Moscow, IMEMO, 32.

Dzhumaylo, A., Fomicheva, A., Barabanov, I., Galliamova, Y., & Popov, E. (2014). Rossiya ne greyet Ukrainu. *Kommersant*, 215: 9. https://www.kommersant.ru/doc/2619730. 25 March 2019.

Dzyadko, T. (2022). Rossiya perevela raschety za gaz v rubli. RBC. https://www.rbc.ru/business/31/03/2022/6245b6c39a7947e7182a7ff2. 01 April 2022.

Dzyadko, T., Tkachev, I., Sintsova, N., & Sukhorukova, E. (2022). Yevrosoyuz vvel pyatyy paket sanktsiy. RBC. https://bit.ly/3uyfH7g. 12 April 2022.

Egmond, C., Jonkers, R., & Kok, G. (2006). One Size Fits All? Policy Instruments Should Fit the Segments of Target Groups. *Energy Policy*, 34(18): 3464–3474.

EIA. (2017). Russia: Country Profile Overview. https://www.eia.gov/international/analysis/country/RUS. 25 April 2021.

Elliott, S. (2021). No Russian Gas Auctions Scheduled on Gazprom Export's ESP for Nov. 8–12. S&P Global Platts. https://bit.ly/3EjMKxl. 15 December 2021.

Elliott, S. (2022). EC President Warns of 'High Risk' for Companies Agreeing to Russian Gas Payment Demands. S&P Global Commodity Insights. https://bit.ly/3rWYAdy. 28 April 2022.

Energy Intelligence Group. (2022). Russian Energy Industry to Resist EU Sanctions. https://bit.ly/3xJ5vuj. 14 April 2022.

Energy Security Doctrine of the Russian Federation. (2019). Decree of the President of Russia. https://base.garant.ru/72240884/#friends. 15 May 2019.

Ershov, Y. A. (2004). Energy Strategy of Russia for the Period up to 2020: Pros and Cons of the New Energy Policy of Russia. *Foreign Economic Bulletin*, 3(4). https://iq.hse.ru/news/177844267.html. 16 April 2019.

Esakova, N. (2012). *European Energy Security: Analysing the EU-Russia Energy Security Regime in Terms of Interdependence Theory*, VS Verlag für Sozialwissenschaften, 16–53.

Eurostat. (2020). From Where Do We Import Energy? https://bit.ly/3KB7Tr4. 26 January 2022.

Eurostat. (2021a). Energy Imports Dependency. https://bit.ly/3CIVjkk. 26 January 2022.

Eurostat. (2021b). Renewable Energy Statistics. https://bit.ly/3qRXcZt. 09 October 2021.

Eurostat. (2022). EU Imports of Energy Products. https://bit.ly/33GIuLy. 03 April 2022.

Eurostat. (2023). Crude Oil Imports and Prices: changes in 2022. https://bit.ly/3IiJMy0. 29 March 2023.

Expert interview with Dr. Martin Jirusek (Masaryk University of Czech Republic). Date of interview: 08.08.2019. Place of interview: Telc, Czech Republic (Masaryk University's Energy Summer School).

Expert interview with Giorgi Mukhigulishvili (Lead researcher in energy studies at World Experience for Georgia, WEG). Date: 17.07.2018. Place: Tbilisi, Georgia.

Expert interview with Ilham Shaban (Director of the Oil Research Center). Date of interview: 19.08.2018. Place of interview: Baku, Azerbaijan.

Exxon Neftegas Limited. (2021). Sakhalin-1 Project. https://www.sakhalin-1.com/en-RU/Company/Who-we-are/25-years-anniversary. 29 December 2021.

Fabrichnaya, Y. (2008). Russia Says the Czech Oil Supply Cut "Not Political". Reuters. https://www.reuters.com/article/czech-russia-oil-idUSL1451616820080714. 21 November 2019.

Fadeeva, A., & Tkachev, I. (2020). Russia Becomes the Second Largest Energy Supplier to the United States. RBC. https://bit.ly/3qvGmPX. 07 February 2020.

Farrell, H., & Newman, A. L. (2019). Weaponized Interdependence. *International Security*, 44(1): 42–79. https://doi.org/10.1162/ISEC_a_00351

Federal Agency for Subsoil Use. (2016). Strategy for the Development of the Mineral Resource Base of Russia until 2030. http://www.rosnedra.gov.ru/article/8743.html. 15 April 2021.

Federal Customs Service of Russia. (2020a). Bulletin "Customs Statistics of Foreign Trade of the Russian Federation for 2019". http://stat.customs.gov.ru/documents. 01 January 2021.

Federal Customs Service of Russia. (2020b). Bulletin "Customs statistics of Foreign Trade of the Russian Federation". http://stat.customs.gov.ru/documents. 24 April 2021.

Federal Customs Service of Russia. (2021). Foreign Trade of Russia and Oil Export Statistics. https://customs.gov.ru/statistic. 01 January 2022.

Federal State Statistics Service. (2021). National Accounts. https://rosstat.gov.ru/accounts. 13 December 2021.

Federation Council. (2021). Current State and Prospects of Socio-Economic Development of the Nenets Autonomous Okrug. *Analytical Bulletin*, 1(744): 5–41.

Feklyunina, V. (2018). International Norms and Identity. In: A. Tsygankov (Ed.). *Routledge Handbook of Russian Foreign Policy*, Routledge, 5–21.

Ferraro, V. (2008). Dependency Theory: An Introduction. In: G. Secondi (Ed.). *The Development Economics Reader*, London: Routledge, 58–64.

Fettweis, C. J. (2009). No Blood for Oil: Why Resource Wars Are Obsolete? In: G. Luft and A. Korin (Eds.). *Energy Security Challenges for the 21st Century a Reference Handbook*, Praeger Security International, 66–77.

Finmarket. (2022). Oil Production in Russia in 2021 Increased by 2.2%, gas – by 10%. http://www.finmarket.ru/news/5623122. 11 January 2022.

Fishman, E., & Miller, C. (2022). The Right Way to Sanction Russian Energy. Foreign Affairs. https://fam.ag/3xiY4Iw. 18 May 2022.

Focus Group Discussion. (2018). World Experience for Georgia (WEG). Tbilisi, Georgia.

Foreign Policy Concept of Russia. (2000). http://www.ng.ru/world/2000-07-11/1_concept.html. 13 August 2021.

Foreign Policy Concept of Russia. (2008). http://kremlin.ru/acts/news/785. 15 August 2021.

Foreign Policy Concept of Russia. (2013). http://www.consultant.ru/document/cons_doc_LAW_142236/. 10 February 2020.

Frankfort-Nachmias, C., Nachmias, D., & DeWaard, J. (2015). *Research Methods in the Social Sciences,* 8th ed. Worth Publishers, 276–278.

Freedom House. (2020). Freedom in the World. https://freedomhouse.org/report/freedom-world. 30 May 2021.

Frieden, J. (1991). Invested Interests: The Politics of National Economic Policies in a World of Global Finance. *International Organization*, 43: 31–71.

Friedman, T. L. (2009). The First Law of Petropolitics. Foreign Policy. https://foreignpolicy.com/2009/10/16/the-first-law-of-petropolitics/. 06 February 2021.

Fuel and Energy Complex (FEC). (2019). Neftegaz.ru. https://bit.ly/3rKwMYR. 20 March 2020.

G8. (2006). Vladimir Putin's speech at Meeting with the G8 Energy Ministers. Moscow. http://www.g8.utoronto.ca/energy/energy_putin060316.html. 19 July 2020.

Gaidar, Y. (1997). *State and Evolution*, Moscow: Evraziya Publishing House, 46.
Gaydar, Y., & Chubais, A. (2011). *Razvilki Noveyshey Istorii Rossii*, Moscow: OGI, 32.
Gazprom. (2013). 40 years on the German market. https://www.gazprom.ru/about/history/events/germany40/. 14 January 2021.
Gazprom. (2020). Yamal-Europe: Russian Gas Supplies to Western Europe. https://www.gazprom.com/projects/yamal-europe/. 30 May 2021.
Gazprom. (2021a). Electronic Sales Platform. http://www.gazpromexport.ru/en/esp/. 30 November 2021.
Gazprom. (2021b). Gas & Oil Reserves. https://www.gazprom.ru/about/production/reserves/. 30 April 2021.
Gazprom. (2021c). About Gazprom's History in Detail for 1989–1995. https://www.gazprom.ru/about/history/chronicle/1989-1995/. 06 September 2021.
Gazprom. (2021d). About the Company. https://www.gazprom.ru/about/. 06 September 2021.
Gazprom. (2021e). Gazprom in Figures 2020 Handbook. https://www.gazprom.ru/investors/. 06 September 2021.
Gazprom. (2021f). How Is Natural Gas Transported? https://www.gazprominfo.ru/articles/natural-gas-transportation/. 06 September 2021.
Gazprom. (2021g). Gazprom in the Energy Sector of Russia and the World. https://bit.ly/3nn7yht. 06 September 2021.
Gazprom. (2021h). Annual Report for 2020, 28. https://bit.ly/3nCdbZq. 06 September 2021.
Gazprom. (2021i). Gazprom in Figures for 2016–2020, 59. https://bit.ly/3af8TE6. 06 September 2021.
Gazprom. (2021j). Alexey Miller. https://bit.ly/3Rasoy4. 06 September 2021.
Gazprom Export. (2020). Dynamics of Gas Sales to Europe. http://www.gazpromexport.ru/statistics/. 30 April 2021.
Gazprom Neft. (2021). Oil Routes. https://bit.ly/3GSTdBA. 25 December 2021.
Gelovani, V. A., Britkov, V. B., & Dubovskiy, S. V. (2009). *SSSR i Rossiya v globalnoy sisteme (1985–2030). Rezultaty globalnogo modelirovaniya*, Moscow: URSS, 169.
Geography of Russia. (2021). Fuel and Energy Complex of Russia. https://geographyofrussia.com/toplivno-energeticheskij-kompleks-rossii/. 22 February 2022.
Gerasimov, V. (2013). The Value of Science in Foresight. New Challenges Require Rethinking the Forms and Methods of Warfare. *"Military-Industrial Courier" (VPK) Newspaper*, 8(476).
Germanovich, A. (1999). Party Money. Vedomosti. https://www.vedomosti.ru/newspaper/articles/1999/09/14/dengi-partij. 15 October 2021.
Gilpin, R. (1975). *US Power and the Multinational Corporation*, New York: Basic Books.
Gilpin, R. (1987). *The Political Economy of International Relations*, Princeton University Press, 36.
Global Commission on the Geopolitics of Energy Transformation. (2019). A New World: The Geopolitics of the Energy Transformation, 29. https://bit.ly/3uTYuFh. 10 September 2021.
Godzimirski, J. (2021). Russian Grand Strategy and Energy Resources: The Asian Dimension. In: E. Buchanan (Ed.). *Russian Energy Strategy in the Asia-Pacific: Implications for Australia*, ANU Press, 57–83.
Goldthau, A., & Witte, J. M. (2009). Back to the Future or Forward to the Past? Strengthening Markets and Rules for Effective Global Energy Governance. *International Affairs*, 85(2): 373–390.

Goldthau, A., & Witte, J. M. (Eds.). (2010). *Global Energy Governance: The New Rules of the Game*, Brookings Institution & Global Public Policy Institute, 2–12.

Gonchar, M. (2022). The US Has a Unique Chance to Form a Powerful Response to Russia's Actions in the EU Market. The Center for Global Studies "Strategy XXI". https://bit.ly/3rHSUUp. 10 February 2022.

Gonchar, M., Chubyk, A., & Ishchuk, O. (2015). Energy Component in New Generation Warfare. Case of Russia's Hybrid Aggression against Ukraine. Centre for Global Studies "Strategy XXI", 9–13.

Graaf, T., & Sovacool, B. K. (2020). *Global Energy Politics*, Polity Press, 284–286; 349–359.

Graaf, T. V., Sovacool, B. K., Ghosh, A., Kern, F., & Klare, M. T. (2016). States, Markets, and Institutions: Integrating International Political Economy and Global Energy Politics. In: Thijs Van de Graaf, Benjamin K. Sovacool, Arunabha Ghosh, Florian Kern, Michael T. Klare (eds.). *The Palgrave Handbook of the International Political Economy of Energy*, Palgrave Macmillan, 3–44.

Graham, T. (2010). The Sources of Russia's Insecurity. *Survival*, 52(1): 55–74.

Graham, T. (2021). The Future of Russia. Pairagraph. https://pairagraph.com/the-future-of-russia. 13 January 2022.

Grib, N. (2003). Lukashenko Named Enemies of Integration. Kommersant. No. 196, p. 1. https://www.kommersant.ru/doc/422972. 16 November 2021.

Grigas, A. (2017). *The New Geopolitics of Gas*, Harvard University Press, 19–20.

Grigoriev, A. (2013). Fuel and Energy Complex of Russia: Key Risks and Prospects. The Fuel and Energy Complex Research Department of IPEM. http://www.ipem.ru/files/files/research/20_03_2013_mef_tek.pdf. 20 May 2019.

Grivach, A., & Denisov, A. (2008). The Successes and Failures of the "Energy Superpower". *Global Affairs*, (2) (March/April). https://globalaffairs.ru/articles/uspehi-i-neudachi-energeticheskoj-sverhderzhavy/. 14 June 2020.

Guillet, J. (2011). How to Get a Pipeline Built: Myth and Reality? In: A. Dellecker and T. Gomart (Eds.). *Russian Energy Security and Foreign Policy*, London: Routledge, 58–73.

Güler, M. Ç., & Teke, M. A. (2021). Resmi Belgeler Işığında Rusya'nın Dış Politika Eğilimi. SETA Rapor, 27. https://bit.ly/3bosAcI. 01 August 2021.

Güney, N. A., & Korkmaz, V. (2014). The Energy Interdependence Model between Russia and Europe: An Evaluation of Expectations for Change. *SAM Perceptions*, XIX(3): 35–59.

Gurkov, A. (2021). Gazprom Loses Gas Monopoly as Southeast European Market Advances. Deutsche Welle. https://bit.ly/3nNAMGH. 09 January 2021.

Gustafson, T. (2020). *The Bridge: Natural Gas in a Redivided Europe*, Harvard University Press, 9.

Haas, P. (1992). Knowledge, Power, and International Policy. *International Organization*, 46: 187–224.

Hashim, S. M. (2010). Power-Loss or Power Transition? Assessing the Limits of Using the Energy Sector in Reviving Russia's Geopolitical Stature. *Communist and Post-Communist Studies*, 43(3): 263–274.

Haucke, M., Hoekstra, R., & Ravenzwaaij, D. (2021). When Numbers Fail: Do Researchers Agree on the Operationalization of Published Research? *Royal Society Open Science*, 8(9): 191–354.

Hedlund, S. (2005). *Russian Path Dependence*, Routledge, 282–305.

Heikka, H. (2000). *The Evolution of Russian Grand Strategy – Implications for Europe's North*. University of Birmingham, POLSIS, 4–34.

Heinrich, A. (2014). Introduction: Export Pipelines in Eurasia. In: A. Heinrich and H. Pleines (Eds.). *Export Pipelines from the CIS Region*, Ibidem-Verlag, 13–76.
Henderson, J. (2016). Does Russia Have a Potent Gas Weapon? In: T. Van de Graaf et al. (Eds.). *The Palgrave Handbook of the International Political Economy of Energy*, Palgrave Macmillan, 461–483.
Hickin, P., Coleman, N., & Perkins, R. (2022). EU ban on Russian Seaborne Oil to Intensify Shifts in Trade Flows. S&P Global Commodity Insights. https://bit.ly/3lZkGZt. 31 May 2022.
Hill, F., & Gaddy, C. G. (2013). *Mr. Putin: Operative in the Kremlin*, Brookings Institution Press, 154.
Historical and Bibliographic Reference. (1999). State Power of the USSR. The Highest Authorities and Management and Their Leaders for 1923–1991. Moscow.
Högselius, P. (2013). *Red Gas. Russia and the Origins of European Energy Dependence*, Palgrave Macmillan, 218–224.
Högselius, P. (2019). *Energy and Geopolitics*, Routledge, 68–154.
Humpert, M. (2023). Norway Now Germany's Largest Gas Supplier, Future Supply from Arctic To Support Exports. High North News. https://www.highnorthnews.com/en/norway-now-germanys-largest-gas-supplier-future-supply-arctic-support-exports. 12 January 2023.
Hurska, A. (2019). Russia's "Coal Weapon": Hampering Kazakhstani Exports to Ukraine. *Eurasia Daily Monitor*, 16(154). https://bit.ly/35iIouH. 06 November 2019.
IEA (International Energy Agency). (2022a). Russia's War on Ukraine. https://www.iea.org/topics/russia-s-war-on-ukraine. 01 May 2022.
IEA. (2022b). Reliance on Russian Fossil Fuels Data Explorer. https://www.iea.org/reports/reliance-on-russian-fossil-fuels-data-explorer. 19 May 2022.
IEA. (2022c). Gas Market Report for Q2–2022, 6–18. https://www.iea.org/reports/gas-market-report-q2-2022. 16 May 2022.
IEA. (2022d). A 10-Point Plan to Reduce the European Union's Reliance on Russian Natural Gas. https://bit.ly/3jTBz6E. 30 April 2022.
Ikenberry, G. J. (2004). Liberalism and Empire: Logics of Order in American Unipolar Age. *Review of International Studies*, 30(4): 609–630.
Imyarekov, S. V., & Kevbrina, O. (2017). *Foreign and Domestic Policy of Russia at the Beginning of the XXI Century*, Moscow: Academic Project, 17–18.
Inozemtsev, V. (2015). Russia's Choice: An Energy Superpower or a Losing Country. Republic "Mneniya". https://republic.ru/posts/53541. 19 June 2020.
Inozemtsev, V. (2019). *Nesovremennaya Strana.* Rossiya v Mire XXI veka. Alpina Pablisher, 54–55.
Institute of Energy Security. (2003). Russia's Energy Strategy for the Period up to 2020, 4, 12–13. http://www.energystrategy.ru/projects/ES-28_08_2003.pdf. 15 April 2019.
Interfax. (2008). Putin: Rossiya ne dopustit kolonial'nogo ispol'zovaniya svoikh resursov. https://www.interfax.ru/russia/15508. 29 December 2021.
Interfax. (2020a). Russian GDP Growth in 2019 Slowed Down to 1.3%. https://www.interfax.ru/business/693841. 04 February 2020.
Interfax. (2020b). Oil Exports from Russia to non-CIS Countries Increased by 3.7% in 2019. https://www.interfax.ru/business/690116. 04 January 2020.
Interfax. (2022a). Rosstat podtverdil otsenku rosta VVP Rossii v 2021 godu na urovne 4.7%. https://www.interfax.ru/business/833994. 09 April 2022.
Interfax. (2022b). Transit of "Gazprom" through Ukraine on Saturday Remains at a Maximum. https://www.interfax.ru/business/824733. 27 February 2022.
Interfax. (2022c). ES vvel sanktsii na postavku v RF oborudovaniya dlya SPG i neftepererabotki. https://www.interfax.ru/world/834231. 14 April 2022.

International Association of Oil Transporters (IAOT). (2021). Druzhba Pipeline. https://bit.ly/3GTTzaS. 25 February 2021.

International Gas Union (IGU). (2022). Global Gas Report 2022, 20–41. https://www.igu.org/resources/global-gas-report-2022/. 09 March 2021.

Inter RAO Group. (2021a). About Company. https://www.interrao.ru/company/. 19 December 2021.

Inter RAO UES. (2021b). Export/Import Structure for 9M2021. https://www.interrao.ru/upload/iblock/675/IFRS_9m2021_rus_final_2.pdf. 19 December 2021.

Inter RAO UES. (2021c). Commercial Export and Import of Electricity by the Inter RAO. https://www.interrao.ru/activity/. 19 December 2021.

Inter RAO UES. (2021d). Overseas Business. https://www.interrao.ru/activity/foreignact/. 19 December 2021.

Inter RAO UES. (2021e). Annual Report 2020. Sustainability and Environmental Responsibility Report, 256–257. https://www.interrao.ru/upload/InterRAO_AR2020_RUSF_2.pdf. 19 December 2021.

Inter RAO Group. (2021f). Development Strategy for 2025–2030. https://strategyday2020.interrao.ru/ru/. 19 December 2021.

İpek, P. (2019). Presentation at the "Energy Security and Foreign Policy" Course. Energy Economics, Policy, and Security (EEPS) Master Program. Bilkent University.

IPEM. (2019a). Coal Export and Social and Economic Development of Russia. http://www.ipem.ru/research/fuel/fuel_presentations/206.html. 20 March 2020.

IPEM. (2019b). Large TPPs in Russia: Prospects for Modernization. http://www.ipem.ru/research/power/power_works/192.html. 20 March 2020.

ITC (International Trade Centre). (2020a). Major Import and Export Partner. https://bit.ly/3wmKdjC. 14 April 2021.

ITC. (2020b). Market Diversification. https://bit.ly/3BVttky. 18 September 2021.

ITC. (2021). Export Potential Map for Russia by Countries. https://bit.ly/3wlltZ8. 12 January 2022.

Ivanov, I. (2002). *Russian Foreign Policy in the Age of Globalization Articles and Statements*, Moscow: Olma-Press, 8–72.

Jackson, P. T., & Jones, J. S. (2017). Constructivism. In: R. Devetak, A. Burke, and J. George (Eds.). *An Introduction to International Relations*, Cambridge University Press, 256–258.

Jackson, R., & Sorensen, G. (2013). *Introduction to International Relations: Theories and Approaches*, 5th ed. Oxford University Press, 105.

Jirušek, M. (2017). *Politicization in the Natural Gas Sector in South-Eastern Europe: Thing of the Past or Vivid Present?* Masaryk University, Monographs Series, MUNI Press, 67. 177–188, 229.

Jirušek, M., Vlček, T., Koďousková, H., Robinson, R. W., Leshchenko, A., Černoch, F., Lehotský, L., & Zapletalová, V. (2015). *Energy Security in Central and Eastern Europe and the Operations of Russian State-Owned Energy Enterprises*. Masaryk University, 424.

Jiznin, S. (2013). *Energeticheskaya diplomatiya. Mezhdunarodnaya energeticheskaya bezopasnost*, (Russian), Moscow: MGIMO Universitet, 7–42.

Kaczmarski, M. (2014). Domestic Power Relations and Russia's Foreign Policy. Demokratizatsiya. *Journal of Post-Soviet Democratization*, 22(3): 383–409.

Kalantzakos, S. (2019). The Geopolitics of Critical Minerals. *IAI Papers*, 19(27): 7.

Kalyuzhnova, Y., Nygaard, C. A., Omarov, Y., & Saparbayev, A. (2016). *Local Content Policies in Resource-Rich Countries*, Palgrave Macmillan, 120.

Kandiyoti, R. (2015). *Powering Europe: Russia, Ukraine, and Energy Squeeze*, Palgrave Macmillan, 2–9.

Kapitonov, S. (2020). Rossiya na global'nykh rynkakh gaza. Neftegazovaya Vertikal. http://www.ngv.ru/magazines/article/rossiya-na-globalnykh-rynkakh-gaza/. 19 May 2021.

Kaplan, R. D. (2013). *The Revenge of Geography: What the Map Tells Us about Coming Conflicts and the Battle against Fate*, Random House Trade Paperbacks.

Karaganov, S. A. (2018). *International Trends and Russian Foreign Policy*, Moscow: International Relations, 15–29.

Karaganov, S. A. (2020). The Military Underpinning of the Geopolitical Revolution. In: G. Diesen and A. Lukin (Eds.). *Russia in a Changing World*, Palgrave Macmillan, 1–22.

Kasaev, E. (2009). Iraq: Investment Climate and Russian Interests. *Security Index*, 1(88), 15. http://www.pircenter.org/media/content/files/0/13408834720.pdf. 18 October 2021.

Katz, M. N. (2006). Policy Watch: Is Russia strong or weak? United Press International. https://bit.ly/3g8RSLj. 22 September 2019.

Kauppi, M. V., & Viotti, P. R. (2020). *International Relations Theory*, Rowman & Littlefield, 2.

Keohane, R. O., & Nye, J. S. (2011). *Power and interdependence*, 4th ed. Longman, 3–31.

Khylko, M. (2021). Russia Has Been Using Gas as a Weapon against the EU. The Foreign Policy Council "Ukrainian Prism". http://prismua.org/en/24-09-2021/. 24 September 2021.

Kindleberger, C. P. (1973). *The World in Depression: 1929–39*, University of California Press.

Klare, M. T. (2008). *Rising Powers, Shrinking Planet. How Scarce Energy Is Creating a New World Order*? One-World Publications, 7–259.

Klare, M. T. (2002). *Resource Wars. The New Landscape of Global Conflict*, Henry Holt, 208.

Klasson, M., & Bushueva, Y. (1999). Chechnya Is Under Energy Blockade. Vedomosti. https://bit.ly/3Ntj5WW. 17 May 2020.

Kobzeva, O., & Soldatkin, V. (2021a). Gazprom Books Fraction of Gas Transit Capacity via Poland Ignores Ukraine. Reuters. https://reut.rs/3pjA7hn. 19 October 2021.

Kobzeva, O., & Soldatkin, V. (2021b). Gas Prices Surge in Europe as Russian Yamal Pipeline Exports Fall. Reuters. https://reut.rs/33T7vDZ. 21 December 2021.

Kofman, M. (2019). Drivers of Russian Grand Strategy. Stockholm Free World Forum. https://bit.ly/3qQO2wl. 15 September 2020.

Kolesnikov, A., Gevorgyan, N., & Timakova, N. (2000). *From the First Person. Conversations with Vladimir Putin*. Vagrius Publishing House.

Kommersant. (2001). Zagranichnyye rodstvenniki "Gazproma", 6. https://bit.ly/3nA0dvB. 06 September 2021.

Kommersant. (2006). Dezaktivatsiya Yevropy. Gazprom predyavil ES ultimatum, 70: 1. https://www.kommersant.ru/doc/668168. 19 July 2020.

Kommersant. (2018). History of Soviet and Russian Gas Supplies to Europe. https://www.kommersant.ru/doc/3650812. 11 January 2021.

Kommersant. (2021). Rosnedra: Profitable Oil Reserves in Russia Will Last for 21 years. https://www.kommersant.ru/doc/4986885. 16 September 2021.

Korteweg, R. (2018). Energy as a Tool of the Foreign Policy of Authoritarian States, in Particular Russia. *European Parliament's Committee on Foreign Affairs*, 4–6.

Kortunov, S. V. (2010). Will Russia Join the Top Five World Leaders? Research Project "Russia in World Politics after the Crisis" (No. 09-01-0010), Supported by the Higher School of Economics.

Krasner, S. (1996). Accomplishments of International Political Economy. In: S. Smith, K. Booth, and M. Zalewski (Eds.). *International Theory: Positivism & Beyond*, Cambridge University Press, 108–127.

Kremlin. (1995). The Strategic Course of Russia towards Member States of the Commonwealth Independent States (CIS)", 14.09.1995. № 940. Clause No. 2.7. http://kremlin.ru/acts/bank/8307. 13 August 2021.
Kremlin. (2006). Speech at a Meeting with Ambassadors and Permanent Representatives of the Russian Federation. 27 June, Moscow. http://www.kremlin.ru/events/president/transcripts/23669. 20 October 2021.
Kremlin. (2007). Speech and discussion at the Munich Security Conference. Munich. http://kremlin.ru/events/president/transcripts/24034. 20 October 2021.
Kremlin. (2009a). The Crisis Has Demonstrated the Total Interdependence of the Economies of Different Countries. http://kremlin.ru/events/president/news/5989. 30 May 2019.
Kremlin. (2009b). National Security Strategy of the Russian Federation until 2020. Article 11. http://kremlin.ru/supplement/424. 23 February 2020.
Kremlin. (2012). Measures to Implement the Foreign Policy Course. http://kremlin.ru/events/president/news/15256. 10 February 2020.
Kremlin. (2014a). Meeting of the Valdai International Discussion Club. http://kremlin.ru/events/president/news/46860. 11 April 2019.
Kremlin. (2014b). Sessiya "Neftegazovyye kompanii – "dvigatel izmeneniy" mirovoy ekonomiki". http://kremlin.ru/events/president/news/21088. 11 April 2019.
Kremlin. (2014c). Meeting with Representatives of the Business Community. http://www.kremlin.ru/events/president/news/47263. 21 July 2020.
Kremlin. (2017). Meeting of the Valdai International Discussion Club. http://kremlin.ru/events/president/news/55882. 11 April 2019.
Kremlin.ru. (2021). Plenary Session of the International Forum "Russian Energy Week". http://kremlin.ru/events/president/news/66916. 19 January 2022.
Kremlin.ru. (2022). Soveshchaniye o tekushchey situatsii v neftegazovom sektore. http://kremlin.ru/events/president/news/68191. 14 April 2022.
Kroenig, M. (2020). *The Return of Great Power Rivalry: Democracy versus Autocracy from the Ancient World to the U.S. and China*, Oxford University Press, 162–163.
Krugley, I. (2022). Foreign assets in Russian oil and gas. Neft i Kapital. https://bit.ly/3vtqEpG. 12 March 2022.
Küçük, M. (2019). Uluslararası İlişkilerde Sosyal İnşacılık. İçinde: R. Gözen (Editör). *Uluslararası İlişkiler Teorileri*, İletişim Yayıncılık, 365.
Kudiyarov, S. (2022). Razvod Ponaroshku. Ekspert. https://expert.ru/expert/2022/19/razvod-ponaroshku/. 26 January 2022.
Kurdin, A. A. (2020). Energy in World Politics. In: G. Diesen and A. Lukin (Eds.). *Russia in a Changing World*, Palgrave Macmillan, 152–159.
Kurdin, A. A. (2018). Russia and the World Energy Market. In: A. V Lukin (Ed.). *New International Relations*, Moscow: International Relations, 135–159.
Kurze, K. (2010). The Changing Discourse of Energy Security. A New Impetus for Energy Policy Integration in the European Union. University of Osnabrueck. *TraPES* (2).
Kutuzova, M. (2021). In Deep Stock. Kommersant. "Oil and Gas" Appendix, 98: 4. https://www.kommersant.ru/doc/4848118. 10 June 2021.
Lamont, C. (2015). *Research Methods in International Relations*, SAGE Publications, 119.
Larchenko, L. V. (2015). Oil of Russia: Use of Income and the Reproduction of Raw-Materials Base. *Regional Economics: Theory and Practice*, 41: 2–12.
Larsson, R. (2006). *Russia's Energy Policy: Security Dimensions and Russia's Reliability as an Energy Supplier*, Swedish Defense Research Agency, Defence Analysis, 5, 177.
Lasswell, H. D., & Kaplan, A. (2013). *Power and Society: A Framework for Political Inquiry*, New Haven, CT: Yale University Press, 97.

Latynina, Y. (2009). Petrocracy. Ejednevniy Jurnal. http://www.ej.ru/?a=note&id=9339. 29 July 2020.

Latynina, Y. (2014). Potok soznaniya prirastayet «Siloy Sibiri». Novaya Gazeta No. 142. https://bit.ly/3yvHlUo. 02 October 2020.

Legvold, R. (2008). Russia's Strategic Vision and the Role of Energy. *NBR Analysis*, 19(2): 10–22.

Leijonhielm, J., & Larsson, R. (2004). Russia's Strategic Commodities: Energy and Metals as Security Levers. Swedish Defence Research Agency. *Totalförsvarets Forskningsinstitut (FOI)*, 12–30: 136–137.

Lin, C. Y. (2009). The Prince of Rosh: Russian Energy Imperialism and the Emerging Eurasian Military Alliance of the SCO. ISPSW Institut für Strategie-Politik-Sicherheits-und Wirtschaftsberatung. Berlin, 2.

Lipsky, A. (2021). Cold world. The Kremlin's Foreign Policy as a Tool for Maintaining Power. Novaya Gazeta. https://novayagazeta.ru/articles/2021/01/12/88660-holodnyy-mir. 12 December 2021.

Litova, E. (2021). How to Record US Inflation Will Affect Russia. Vedomosti. https://bit.ly/3A70g9g. 12 November 2021.

Liuhto, K. (2010). Energy in Russia's foreign policy. *PEI Electronic Publications*, 10: 51–52.

Lkhaajav, B. (2021). Can Russia and Mongolia Replace Australia's Coal Supply to China? *The Diplomat*. https://bit.ly/3bmz240. 30 October 2021.

Lo, B. (2002). *Russian Foreign Policy in the Post-Soviet Era: Reality, Illusion, and Myth-making*, Palgrave Macmillan, 114–158.

Lo, B. (2015). *Russia and the New World Order*, Chatham House and Brookings Institution Press, 19–213.

Lo, B. (2019). Greater Eurasia: The Emperor's New Clothes or an Idea whose Time Has Come? Russie. Ifri. *Nei Reports*, 27: 19.

Lobell, S., Ripsman, N., & Taliaferro, J. (Eds.). (2009). *Neoclassical Realism, the State, and Foreign Policy*, Cambridge University Press.

Lomagin, N. (2015). Foreign Policy Preferences of Russia's Energy Sector: A Shift to Asia? In: M. Sussex and R. E. Kanet (Eds.). *Russia, Eurasia, and New Geopolitics of Energy. Confrontation and Consolidation*, Palgrave Macmillan, 6, 16–18.

Lomagin, N. (2019). Energy Dimension of Russian Foreign Policy. European University at St. Petersburg (EUSP). ENERPO Series of Open Lectures "The Month of Energy". 06 March 2019.

Lukin, A. V. (2015). *Vozvyshayushchiysya Kitay i budushcheye Rossii*, Moscow: International Relationships, 377–548.

Lukin, A. (2020). Russia and the Changing World Order: In Search of Multipolarity. In: G. Diesen and A. Lukin (Eds.). *Russia in a Changing World*, Palgrave Macmillan, 67–69.

Lukoil. (2021a). History. https://lukoil.ru/Company/history. 12 December 2021.

Lukoil. (2021b). Alekperov Vagit Yusufovich. https://bit.ly/3tPyU4k. 12 December 2021.

Lukoil. (2021c). History for 1999. https://lukoil.ru/Company/history/History1999. 12 December 2021.

Lukoil. (2021d). Corporate Profile. https://lukoil.ru/Company/CorporateProfile. 12 December 2021.

Lukoil. (2021e). Geography of Presence. https://csr2020.lukoil.ru/about/geography. 13 December 2021.

Lukoil. (2021f). Annual Report for 2020. https://lukoil.ru/FileSystem/9/551394.pdf. 13 December 2021.

Lyutova, M. (2021). Why Gazprom will not be able to help Europe? TV Rain. https://bit.ly/3C4z2hs. 20 October 2021.

Makarova, Y. (2021). From Drilling to Hydrogen: How the Oil and Gas Cluster Works in Russia. RBK Trends. https://bit.ly/3buKNFA. 18 September 2021.

Mankoff, J. (2009). *Russian Foreign Policy: The Return of Great Power Politics*, Rowman & Littlefield Publishers, 5–42.

Marange, C. (2019). Russia. In: T. Balzacq, P. Dombrowski, and S. Reich (Eds.). *Comparative Grand Strategy: A Framework and Cases*, Oxford University Press, 50–69.

Marcinkevich, B. (2020). Russia Is an Energy Superpower. Geoenergetics. https://geoenergetics.ru/2020/03/06/rossiya-energeticheskaya-sverxderzhava/. 14 June 2020.

Marin, D. (2022). What If Germany Boycotts Russian Energy? Project Syndicate. https://bit.ly/3EwoxFX. 15 April 2022.

Markov, S. (1997). Lukoil Is Stronger than the Foreign Ministry. *Newspaper "Kommersant"*, 116: 4. https://www.kommersant.ru/doc/181410. 06 November 2021.

Marsh, C. (2019). Russia Sees Its Future in China and Eurasia. National Interest. https://bit.ly/3rySwqA. 29 April 2019.

Martinez-Vela, C. A. (2001). World Systems Theory. MIT, *ESD*, 83: 4.

Martsinkevich, B. (2018). Geoenergy as the Foundation of the Second Cold War. Geoenergetika. https://bit.ly/3a6YfPF. 30 July 2021.

McKinsey & Company. (2021). Snapshot of Gas and LNG Flows and Market Dynamics: Q3 2021. https://mck.co/3nua9GQ. 20 March 2022.

Mearsheimer, J. (2013). Structural Realism. In: T. Dunne, M. Kurki, and S. Smith (Eds.). *International Relations Theories: Discipline and Diversity*, 3rd ed. Oxford University Press, 78.

Mearsheimer, J. (2014). *The Tragedy of Great Power Politics*, W. W. Norton & Company, 21–146.

Medvedev, O. (1993). Kyiv Is Forced to Adjust Its Political Course. Kommersant. https://www.kommersant.ru/doc/51857. 13 August 2021.

Message of the President of the Russian Federation to the Federal Assembly. (1994). Yeltsin Center. https://yeltsin.ru/archive/paperwork/12590/. 18 April 2020.

Message of the President of the Russian Federation to the Federal Assembly. (1995). Kremlin. http://kremlin.ru/acts/bank/7521/page/10. 18 April 2020.

Message of the President of the Russian Federation to the Federal Assembly. (1996). Kremlin. http://www.kremlin.ru/acts/bank/36349. 18 April 2020.

Message of the President of the Russian Federation to the Federal Assembly. (1997). Kremlin. http://kremlin.ru/acts/bank/36355/page/6. 18 April 2020.

Message of the President of the Russian Federation to the Federal Assembly. (1998). Kremlin. http://kremlin.ru/acts/bank/20941/page/7. 18 April 2020.

Message of the President of the Russian Federation to the Federal Assembly. (1999). Kremlin. http://kremlin.ru/acts/bank/22400/page/1. 18 April 2020.

Message of the President of the Russian Federation to the Federal Assembly. (2000). Kremlin. http://kremlin.ru/events/president/transcripts/21480. 21 April 2020.

Message of the President of the Russian Federation to the Federal Assembly. (2001). Kremlin. http://kremlin.ru/events/president/transcripts/21216. 21 April 2020.

Message of the President of the Russian Federation to the Federal Assembly. (2002). Kremlin. http://kremlin.ru/events/president/transcripts/21567. 21 April 2020.

Message of the President of the Russian Federation to the Federal Assembly. (2003). Kremlin. http://kremlin.ru/events/president/transcripts/21998. 21 April 2020.

Message of the President of the Russian Federation to the Federal Assembly. (2004). Kremlin. http://kremlin.ru/events/president/transcripts/22494. 21 April 2020.
Message of the President of the Russian Federation to the Federal Assembly. (2005). Kremlin. http://kremlin.ru/events/president/transcripts/22931. 21 April 2020.
Message of the President of the Russian Federation to the Federal Assembly. (2006). Kremlin. http://kremlin.ru/events/president/transcripts/23577. 21 April 2020.
Message of the President of the Russian Federation to the Federal Assembly. (2007). Kremlin. http://kremlin.ru/events/president/transcripts/24203. 21 April 2020.
Message of the President of the Russian Federation to the Federal Assembly. (2008). Kremlin. http://www.kremlin.ru/events/president/transcripts/messages/1968. 21.04.2020.
Message of the President of the Russian Federation to the Federal Assembly. (2009). Kremlin. http://www.kremlin.ru/events/president/transcripts/messages/5979. 22 April 2020.
Message of the President of the Russian Federation to the Federal Assembly. (2010). Kremlin. http://www.kremlin.ru/events/president/transcripts/messages/9637. 22 April 2020.
Message of the President of the Russian Federation to the Federal Assembly. 2012. Kremlin. http://www.kremlin.ru/events/president/transcripts/messages/17118. 22 April 2020.
Message of the President of the Russian Federation to the Federal Assembly. 2013. Kremlin. http://www.kremlin.ru/events/president/transcripts/messages/19825. 22 April 2020.
Message of the President of the Russian Federation to the Federal Assembly. 2014. Kremlin. http://www.kremlin.ru/events/president/transcripts/messages/47173. 22 April 2020.
Message of the President of the Russian Federation to the Federal Assembly. 2015. Kremlin. http://www.kremlin.ru/events/president/transcripts/messages/50864. 22 April 2020.
Message of the President of the Russian Federation to the Federal Assembly. 2016. Kremlin. http://www.kremlin.ru/events/president/transcripts/messages/53379. 24 April 2020.
Message of the President of the Russian Federation to the Federal Assembly. 2018. Kremlin. http://www.kremlin.ru/events/president/transcripts/messages/56957. 24 April 2020.
Message of the President of the Russian Federation to the Federal Assembly. 2019. Kremlin. http://www.kremlin.ru/events/president/transcripts/messages/59863. 24 April 2020.
Message of the President of the Russian Federation to the Federal Assembly. 2020. Kremlin. http://www.kremlin.ru/events/president/transcripts/messages/62582. 16 January 2021.
Message of the President of the Russian Federation to the Federal Assembly. 2021. Kremlin. http://www.kremlin.ru/events/president/transcripts/messages/65418. 22 April 2021.
Milov, V. (2006). The Use of Energy as a Political Tool. EU-Russia Centre, *EU-Russia Review*, Issue 1 (May).
Milov, V. (2020). Departure Quota. Novaya Gazeta. https://novayagazeta.ru/articles/2020/04/24/85086-kvota-na-vylet. 28 April 2020.
Milov, V. (2021). Manchu President. How did Russia Become a Raw Materials Appendage of Beijing? The Insider. https://theins.ru/opinions/vladimir-milov/242390. 30 September 2019.
Milov, V., Coburn, L., & Danchenko, I. (2006). Russia's Energy Policy, 1992–2005. *Eurasian Geography and Economics*, 47(3): 285–313.
Mingst, K. A., Mckibben, H. E., & Arreguín-Toft, I. M. (2019). *Essentials of International Relations*, W. W. Norton & Company, 210.
Ministry of Economic Development of Russia. (2019). Forecast of the Socio-Economic Development of Russia for the Period up to 2024, 19. https://bit.ly/3ItVDHk. 01 June 2021.
Ministry of Economic Development of Russia. (2020a). Results of Foreign Economic Activity of the Russian Federation in 2019, 3–43. https://bit.ly/3QTyh2S. 14 August 2020.

Ministry of Economic Development of Russia. (2020b). Forecast of the Socio-Economic Development of Russia for 2021 and for the Planning Period of 2022 and 2023, 33–89. https://bit.ly/38B7Z3v. 14 February 2022.

Ministry of Economic Development of Russia. (2021). Forecast of the Socio-Economic Development of the Russia for 2022 and for the Planned Period of 2023 and 2024, 30–94. https://bit.ly/2ZRCxJQ. 14 February 2022.

Ministry of Energy of Russia. (2019). Energy Security Doctrine of Russia. https://base.garant.ru/72240884/. 16 April 2020.

Ministry of Energy of Russia. (2020a). Energy strategy of Russia for the Period up to 2035. https://minenergo.gov.ru/node/1026. 12 November 2021.

Ministry of Energy of Russia. (2020b). Energy Strategy of Russia for the Period of 2035. http://static.government.ru/media/files/w4sigFOiDjGVDYT4IgsApssm6mZRb7wx.pdf. 17 April 2021.

Ministry of Foreign Affairs of Belarus. (2019). http://mfa.gov.by/en/courtiers/russia/. 02 December 2021.

Ministry of Foreign Affairs of Russia. (2016). The Concept of Foreign Policy of Russia. https://www.mid.ru/ru/foreign_policy/official_documents/1538901/. 15 April 2019.

Ministry of Natural Resources and Environment of Russia and UNECE. (2016). Classification of Oil and Combustible Gas Reserves and Resources of Russia. https://bit.ly/3ypx4ZP. 03 March 2021.

Ministry of Natural Resources and Environment of Russia. (2020). On the State and Use of Mineral and Raw Materials of Russia in 2019. State Report. Moscow. http://www.mnr.gov.ru/docs/gosudarstvennye_doklady/?special_version=Y. 30 June 2021.

Mironov, N. V. (2003). *Mezhdunarodnaya Energeticheskaya Bezopasnost*, Moscow: MGIMO, 165.

Mishchenko, V. (2020). Neft' razdoraMneniye. NANGS. https://nangs.org/news/business/nefty-razdoramnenie. 28 January 2020.

Mitrova, T. (2021). The Notorious Resource Rent Is Practically Disappearing. Environmental Investment Center. https://bit.ly/31oalPz. 20 December 2021.

Mitrova, T., Grushevenko, E., & Malov, A. (2018). Prospects for Russian Oil Production: Life Under Sanctions. Energy Research Center of the SKOLKOVO Business School, 24–25. https://bit.ly/3nMfHg7. 29 June 2021.

Molnar, A. (2014). Russian Foreign Energy Policy under Vladimir Putin. In: A. Heinrich and H. Pleines (Eds.). *Export Pipelines from the CIS Region*, Ibidem-Verlag, 77–90.

Moravcsik, A. (1997). Taking Preferences Seriously: A Liberal Theory of International Politics. *International Organization*, 51(4): 513–553.

Moravcsik, A. (2019). Power of Connection: Why the Russia - Europe Gas Trade Is Strangely Untouched by Politics. *Nature*, 576: 30–31. https://www.nature.com/articles/d41586-019-03694-y. 13 December 2020.

Mordyushenko, O. (2021). All Paths Lead to the Arctic. State Resource Management Ecology. *Kommersant Appendix*, 1: 4. https://www.kommersant.ru/doc/4955127. 03 September 2021.

Morozov, V. (2018). Global (Post)Structural Conditions. In: A. Tsygankov (Ed.). *Routledge Handbook of Russian Foreign* Policy, Routledge, 22–42.

Movchan, A. (2019). *Russia in the Post-Truth Era*, Alpina Publisher, 495.

National Energy Security Fund. (2015). Russian Oil and Gas under Sanctions: Major Threats to the Industry. https://bit.ly/3xXQ4Nt. 16 May 2019.

NATO. (2021). Energy Security. Centre for Excellence. https://www.enseccoe.org/en. 13 November 2021.

NATO. (2002). Prague Summit Declaration. https://www.nato.int/cps/en/natolive/official_texts_19552.htm#ipap. 30 July 2021.
NATO. (2004). Istanbul Summit Declaration. https://www.nato.int/cps/en/natolive/official_texts_21023.htm#ipap. 30 July 2021.
NATO. (2006). Riga Summit Declaration. https://www.nato.int/cps/en/natolive/official_texts_37920.htm#ipap. 30 July 2021.
NATO. (2008). Bucharest Summit Declaration. https://www.nato.int/cps/en/natolive/official_texts_8443.htm#ipap. 30 July 2021.
NATO. (2009). Strasbourg/Kehl Summit Declaration. https://www.nato.int/cps/en/natolive/news_52837.htm#ipap. 30 July 2021.
NATO. (2021). Information on Summits. www.nato.int. 02 December 2021.
NBusiness. (2022). Nearly Half of Russia's Gold and Forex Reserves Were Frozen Due to Sanctions. https://bit.ly/3rDub3V. 14 March 2022.
Neft i Kapital. (2022). Gazprom: Gaz na eksport podayetsya shtatno. https://bit.ly/38RQJah. 16 April 2022.
Neftianka. (2020). Chubais and Kudrin against the "Energy Superpower". http://neftianka.ru/chubajs-i-kudrin-protiv-energeticheskoj-sverxderzhavy/. 14 June 2020.
Nemtsov, B., & Milov, V. (2008). *Putin and Gazprom*, Independent Expert Report, Moscow, RID Novaya Gazeta, 11–14.
Neskuchnaya Ekonomika. (2021). Kakiye kompanii i v kakikh regionakh dobyvayut neft' v Rossii?. https://bit.ly/3y4YhzI. 05 April 2020.
Neskuchnaya Ekonomika. (2022). V Rossii rekordnaya ubyl naseleniya za 75 let. https://notboringeconomy.ru/v-rossii-rekordnaja-ubyl-naselenija-za-75-let/. 11 December 2021.
Neuman, W. L. (2014). *Social Research Methods: Qualitative and Quantitative Approaches*, 7th ed. Pearson Education Limited, 38.
New York Times. (2007). Gazprom Completes Sakhalin-2 Takeover. https://nyti.ms/3Fe63Zo. 29 December 2021.
New York Times. (2022). Here's How Much It Is Costing Companies to Leave Russia. Daily Business Briefing. https://nyti.ms/3L62VCL. 12 April 2022.
Nodia, G. (2009). Reading Russia: The Wounds of Lost Empire. *Journal of Democracy*, 20(2): 34–38.
Nord Stream Pipeline. (2020). https://www.nord-stream.com/the-project/pipeline/. 14 July 2020.
Novak, A. (2022). Rossiyskiy i mirovoy TEK: vyzovy i perspektivy. Energeticheskaya Politika. https://bit.ly/3voz01S. 16 April 2021.
O'Sullivan, M. L. (2013). The Entanglement of Energy, Grand Strategy, and International Security. In: A. Goldthau (Ed.). *The Handbook of Global Energy Policy*, London: Wiley-Blackwell, 30–47.
Oatley, T. (2019). *International Political Economy*, 6th ed. Routledge, 25, 258–455.
Obayashi, Y., Chow, E., & Bousso, R. (2022). Russia Seizes Control of Sakhalin Gas Project, Raises Stakes with West. Reuters. https://reut.rs/3R4Q4Ee. 02 July 2022.
Office of the Historian (US DoS). (2021). Oil Embargo 1973–1974. https://history.state.gov/milestones/1969-1976/oil-embargo. 14 February 2021.
Oil & Gas Journal (2021). Worldwide Refining Survey 2020, 12–13.
Oil and Gas Information Agency (ANGI). (2022). Gas Production in Russia in 2021. https://bit.ly/3ttetK6. 11 January 2022.
OPEC (Organization of the Petroleum Exporting Countries). (2021). Brief History. https://www.opec.org/opec_web/en/about_us/24.htm. 14 February 2021.
OPEC. (2022). Brief History. https://www.opec.org/opec_web/en/about_us/24.htm. 01 March 2022.

Orban, A. (2008). *Power, Energy, and the New Russian Imperialism*, Praeger Security International Press.

Orlov, A., Topalov, A., & Todorov, V. (2015). 130 Budgets of Russia Underground. Gazeta. https://www.gazeta.ru/business/2015/01/26/6327017.shtml. 13 June 2020.

Orlova, N. (2021). Redistribution Model: Short Stature as a Conscious Choice. "Liberal Mission - Expertise" Series. https://liberal.ru/lm-ekspertiza/model-pereraspredeleniya-nizkij-rost-kak-soznatelnyj-vybor. 17 April 2021.

Orttung, R. W., & Overland, I. (2011). A Limited Toolbox: Explaining the Constraints on Russia's Foreign Energy Policy. *Journal of Eurasian Studies*, 2: 74–85.

Ostrowski, W. (2013). The Political Economy of Global Resources. In: R. Dannreuther and W. Ostrowski (Eds.). *Global Resources. Conflict and Cooperation*, Palgrave Macmillan, 98–115.

Overland, I. (2017). *The Hunter Becomes the Hunted: Gazprom Encounters EU Regulation*, Energy Union, 115–130.

Overland, I., & Poussenkova, N. (2020). *Russian Oil Companies in an Evolving World. The Challenge of Change*, Edward Elgar Publishing, 2.

Pain, E. (2013). The Future of the Post-Imperial Societies of the XXI Century. *Global Affairs Journal*, Special Issue, 3(1).

Pain, E. (2019). Post-imperial Situation: Citizenship and Nationalism Lost Powerfulness. Liberal Mission Fund. https://bit.ly/33DBsYa. 02 September 2020.

Pannier, B. (2017). Turkmen Cut-off of Iran Leaves Dwindling Gas Options for Ashgabat. Radio Free Europe/Radio Liberty. https://bit.ly/3by1CQa. 17 July 2020.

Parfitt, T., & Rushe, D. (2011). ExxonMobil Clinches Arctic Oil Deal with Rosneft. *The Guardian*. https://www.theguardian.com/business/2011/aug/30/exxon-rosneft-oil-arctic. 14 July 2020.

Pascual, C., & Elkind, J. (2009). *Energy Security: Economics, Politics, Strategies, and Implications*. Brookings Institution Press, 2–23.

Pastukhov, V. (2021). "Fourth Phase Regime. How Long Does Putin Have to Rule?" Republic. https://republic.ru/posts/99541. 03 January 2022.

Perkins, R., Kumagai, T., & Wang, H. (2022). EU Agrees Compromise Deal to Ban 90% of Russian Oil Imports by Year-End. S&P Global Commodity Insights. https://bit.ly/3GxxLCP. 31 May 2022.

Person, R. (2019). Russian Grand Strategy in the 21st Century. West Point: US Military Academy. NSI Team. https://nsiteam.com/russian-grand-strategy-in-the-21st-century/. 13 May 2019.

Petlevoy, V., & Toporkov, A. (2019). Kak gosudarstvo za 20 let vernulo sebe kontrol' nad neftegazovoy otrasl'yu. Vedomostey and Eksport. https://bit.ly/33AiOpa. 16.10.2019.

Petrov, K., & Gelman, V. (2019). Do Elites Matter in Russian Foreign Policy? The Gap between Self-Perception and Influence. *Post-Soviet Affairs*, 1–11.

Piontkovsky, A. (2020). Without Drawing a Sword. "Pompeo Doctrine". Svoboda. https://bit.ly/32GBJJx. 23 February 2020.

Pirani, S. (2010). *Change in Putin's Russia Power, Money, and People*, Pluto Press, 84–86.

Podlipsky, N. (1995). In 15 years, Russia Must Learn to Turn Off the Lights. Kommersant Newspaper. https://www.kommersant.ru/doc/108714. 15 April 2019.

Poltoranin, K., Chelnokov, A., & Postavnin, V. (2012). *How Russia is Being Killed. "Golden Horde" of the XXI Century*, Yauza Press, 13.

Popkostova, Y. (2022). Europe's Energy Crisis Conundrum. Origins, Impacts, and Way Forward. EUISS Brief No.2.

Portal of Foreign Economic Information (VED). (2021). Media Review on Foreign Economic Topics. http://www.ved.gov.ru/news/30071.html?type=media_review. 19 November 2021.

Poussenkova, N., & Overland, I. (2018). Russia: Public Debate and the Petroleum Sector. In: I. Overland (Ed.). *Public Brainpower*, Palgrave Macmillan, Cham.

Pravosudov, S. A. (2017). *Neft i gaz. Dengi i vlast*, Moscow: KMK, 17–144.

Presidential Library of the Office of the President of the Republic of Azerbaijan. (2020). Transportation of Azerbaijani Oil to World Markets. Chapter III. https://files.preslib.az/site/10il/gl3.pdf. 18 October 2021.

Primakov, E. (2009). *A World Without Russia*?, Moscow: Russian Newspaper, 23–141.

Primakov, E. (2015). *Russia. Hopes and Worries*, Moscow: Centerpolygraph, 4–69.

Primakov, E. (2018). *Russia in the Modern World*, Centerpolygraph, 319–341.

Prokopieva, Z. (2020). The Accounts Chamber Recognized a Significant Part of Oil and Gas Reserves in Russia as Fake. Economy and Life. https://www.eg-online.ru/news/420788/. 30 May 2020.

Protopopov, A. S., Kozmenko, V. M., Shpakovskaya, M. A., & Petrovic-Belkin. (2018). *Istoriya Mezhdunarodnykh Otnosheniy i Vneshney Politiki Rossii 1648–2017*, Moscow: Aspekt Press, 448.

Pusenkova, N. N. (2010). Rossiyskiy "Gazprom" v gazpromovskoy Rossii. Istoriya novoy Rossii. http://www.ru-90.ru/node/1320#_ftn44. 06 March 2019.

Putin, V. (1997). Strategic Planning for the Reproduction of the Region's Mineral Resource Base in the Context of the Formation of Market Relations. PhD thesis. Saint Petersburg. RusNEB Catalog. https://rusneb.ru/catalog/000199_000009_000168916/. 29 July 2020.

Putin, V. (2021). Being Open Despite the Past. Die Zeit - the German Weekly Newspaper. http://kremlin.ru/events/president/news/65899. 25 June 2021.

Pylin, A. (2012). Foreign Trade Relations of Russia with the Countries of the "Neighbourhood Belt". *Russia and the New States of Eurasia*, 1: 5–15. https://bit.ly/3ENsLaO. 09.09.2019.

Radio Sputnik. (2022). Medvedev perechislil "luchshiye sposoby" ostavit' Yevropu bez gaza. https://radiosputnik.ria.ru/20220330/medvedev-1780971401.html. 30 March 2022.

RAO Nordic. (2021). Cross-Border Trading. https://www.raonordic.com/trading. 19 December 2021.

RBK. (2021). Russian Lithium-Out Into the World. https://marketing.rbc.ru/articles/12651/. 06 July 2021.

RBK. (2022). Rossiya reshila priznat nezavisimost DNR i LNR. https://bit.ly/3HrCYLb. 22 February 2022.

RCC.ru. (2020). Rossiya riskuyet ostatsya bez nefti. http://rcc.ru/article/rossiya-riskuet-ostatsya-bez-nefti-74245. 02 June 2020.

Repyeuskaya, O. (2010). Energy as a Foreign Policy Tool: Assessing Russian Energy. Strategy towards the European Countries, Master Thesis, Department of Political Science, Central European University, Budapest.

Reuters Staff. (2021). Gazprom Exports by Country in 2021. https://reut.rs/3Gzusdk. 18 May 2021.

RIA Novosti. (2018). Dependence of European Countries on Russian Gas. https://ria.ru/20180426/1519454083.html?in=t. 26 April 2019.

RIA Novosti. (2022). Sholts: Germaniya snizit zavisimost ot rossiyskogo gaza "bystreye grafika". https://ria.ru/20220419/gaz-1784378915.html. 20 April 2022.

Rich, R. C., Brians, C. L., Manheim, J. B., & Willnat, L. (2018). *Empirical Political Analysis: Quantitative and Qualitative Research* Methods, 9th ed. Routledge, 70.

Ridder, M. (2013). The Geopolitics of Mineral Resources for Renewable Energy Technologies. *The Hague Centre for Strategic Studies*, 12–16.

Rogov, K. (2020). Is Russia a Trigger? Foreign Policy Problems and Risks. Liberal Mission. Reports and Analytics. http://liberal.ru/reports/rossiya--trigger-problemy-i-riski-vneshnepoliticheskogo-kursa. 27 March 2020.

Rogov, K. (2021). "Stagnation -2": Consequences, Risks, and Alternatives for the Russian Economy. "Liberal Mission - Expertise" Series. https://bit.ly/3fNFRdO. 17 April 2021.

Rosatom. (2020a). Performance of State Atomic Energy Corporation Rosatom in 2019. https://rosatom.ru/upload/iblock/0c1/0c106b40899f365fd8c2a6be935b092b.pdf. 09 January 2022.

Rosatom. (2020b). Supervisory Board. https://rosatom.ru/about/management/supervisory-board/. 09 January 2022.

Rosatom. (2021a). About the Company. https://rosatom.ru/about/. 09 January 2022.

Rosatom. (2021b). Results of Activities for 2020, 16–17; 18–19; 28–29. https://rosatom.ru/upload/iblock/f4a/f4a45a35f729df5e2ca8cfabe7a75fb2.pdf. 09 January 2022.

Rosatom. (2021c). NPPs Construction. https://www.rosatom.ru/production/design/stroyashchiesya-aes/. 09 January 2022.

Rosenau, J. N. (1990). *Turbulence in World Politics: A Theory of Change and Continuity*, Princeton University Press, 36–250.

Rosenergoatom. (2021). NPP Construction Abroad. https://bit.ly/3EMgpRQ. 09 January 2022.

Rosneft. (2020). IFRS Results for Q4 and 12 Months of 2019, 20. https://bit.ly/3OGQkXO. 07 September 2021.

Rosneft. (2021a). History of the Company. https://www.rosneft.ru/about/history/. 07 September 2021.

Rosneft. (2021b). Rosneft Today. https://www.rosneft.ru/about/Glance/. 07 September 2021.

Rosneft. (2021c). Board of Directors. https://www.rosneft.ru/governance/corpboard/. 07 September 2021.

Rosneft. (2021d). Reserves and Resources. https://www.rosneft.ru/business/Upstream/Reserves/. 07 September 2021.

Rosneft. (2021e). IFRS Results for Q2–2020, 18. https://bit.ly/3FOP7Jh. 03 December 2021.

Rosneft. (2021f). Rosneft Signed a Contract with Indian Oil to Supply up to 2 Million Tons of Oil to India. https://www.rosneft.ru/press/releases/item/208725/. 07 December 2021.

Rosneft. (2021g). Annual Report for 2020, 4–97. https://www.rosneft.ru/upload/site1/document_file/a_report_2020.pdf. 07 December 2021.

Rossiyskoy Gazety. (2014). Military Doctrine of Russia. https://rg.ru/documents/2014/12/30/doktrina-dok.html. 01 December 2021

Rosstat. (2021). Determination of the Share of the Oil and Gas Sector in the Gross Domestic Product of Russia. https://rosstat.gov.ru/storage/mediabank/1b5RpebS/Maximov-tezisy.pdf. 22 July 2021.

Rudakov, V. (2019). Doctrina Brezhnev. Istorik. https://xn--h1aagokeh.xn--p1ai/journal/42/doktrina-brezhneva-e5.html. 15 May 2020.

Rühl, C., & Erker, T. (2021). Oil Intensity: The Curiously Steady Decline of Oil in GDP. Columbia Center on Global Energy Policy. https://bit.ly/3jQryqQ. 10 September 2021.

Rumer, E. B., & Wallander, C. A. (2003). Russia: Power in Weakness? *Washington Quarterly*, 27(1): 57–73.

Russia Matters. (2021). Foreign Policy Principles Russian Federation for 1993. https://bit.ly/3AbbdV3. 13 August 2021.

Russian Federal Geological Fund. (2021). State Balance of Minerals of the Russian Federation. https://rfgf.ru/bal/index.php. 03 March 2021.

Rutland, P. (2016). The Place of Economics in Russian National Identity Debates. In: P. Kolsto and H. Blakkisrud (Eds.). *The New Russian Nationalism: Imperialism, Ethnicity and Authoritarianism 2000–15*, Edinburgh University Press, 343–360.

Sakhalin Energy. (2021). Sakhalin-2 PSA. http://www.sakhalinenergy.ru/en/company/overview/. 29 December 2021.

Saltanova, V. (2021). You Can't Lag Behind. IQ HSE RU. https://iq.hse.ru/news/463561256.html. 24 April 2021.

Santander Trade. (2021). Russian Foreign Trade in Figures. https://bit.ly/3QRPv0s. 23 April 2022.

Saradzhyan, S., & Abdullaev, N. (2018). Measuring National Power: Is Vladimir Putin's Russia in Decline? Russia Matters, Harvard University.

Sarı, B. (2021). Güç. İçinde: B. Sarı ve İ.E. Sula (Editörler). Kuramsal Perspektiften Temel *Uluslararası İlişkiler Kavramları*, Nobel Yayıncılık, 107–130.

Sascha, M. K. (2008). *Energy Security: Re-Measuring the World*, Routledge, 25–26.

Savin, L. (2012). Energy Geopolitics. Geopolitika.ru. https://www.geopolitica.ru/article/energeticheskaya-geopolitika. 17 July 2020.

Security Council of the Russian Federation. (2010). Meeting on the State and Measures to Ensure the Energy Security of Russia. http://www.scrf.gov.ru/council/session/2049/. 15 May 2020.

Sergeeva, M. (1996). Strana silna provintsiyey. Kommersant. https://www.kommersant.ru/doc/234387. 03 September 2020.

Shaban, I. (2018). History of Soviet and Russian Gas Supplies to Europe. Caspian Barrel. https://bit.ly/3QKRN1e. 12 January 2021.

Shaban, I. (2021). Putin Responded to Accusations of Europe and Ukraine against Gazprom. Caspian Barrel. https://bit.ly/3Jg6ZzK. 24 December 2021.

Shaffer, B. (2009). *Energy Politics*, University of Pennsylvania Press, 28–29, 93.

Shafranik, Y. K. (1996). Russia Needs a Unified Foreign Energy Policy. The Newspaper "Financial News". M. https://bit.ly/3Ajq7Ll. 15 February 2021.

Shafranik, Y. K. (2005). Mnogopolyarnyy energeticheskiy mir i Rossiya. http://shafranik.ru/publikatsii/-mnogopolyarnyi-energeticheskii-mir-i-rossiya-. 04 April 2019.

Shevtsova, L. (2009). Reading Russia: The Return of Personalized Power. *Journal of Democracy*, 20(2): 61–65.

Shevtsova, L. (2010). *Lonely Power: Why Russia Has Not Become the West and Why Russia Has Difficulty with the West*. Moscow Carnegie Center. ROSSPEN, 67.

Shevtsova, L. (2015). The Authoritarian Resurgence: Forward to the Past in Russia. *Journal of Democracy*, 26(2): 22–36.

Shmal, G. I. (2016). The Problem of Developing Oil Difficult to Recover in Russia and Solution Approaches. *Georesources*, 18(4): 256–260.

Shnyrov, A. B. (2004). *Russia's Foreign Policy and the Problem of Ensuring Energy Security*, Russia Diplomatic Academy of the Ministry of Foreign Affairs, 4, 62.

Siddi, M. (2021). Energy Transition Geopolitics: Key Challenges and Consequences for the EU and Russia. Valdai Club. https://bit.ly/3y2M1iP. 06 November 2021.

Sikri, R. (2010). Resource Competition, Nationalism, Security Implications. *South Asia Survey*, 17(1): 7–17.

Simachev, Y.V. (Ed.). (2021). *Russia in the Markets of Advanced Production*, The Publishing House of the Higher School of Economics, 6–47.

Simola, H., & Solanko, L. (2021). Russia's Oil & Gas Sector in The Global Energy Transition. *BOFIT Policy Brief*, 7: 6–8.

Simonov, K. (2006). *An Energy Superpower*, Moscow: Eksmo, 272.

Simonov, K. (2018). A Gas Bridge between Socialism and Capitalism. Vedomosti. https://www.vedomosti.ru/opinion/columns/2018/06/05/771800-gazovii-most. 15 January 2021.

Simonov, K. (2020). The Case Is a Pipe: How Does the Conflict in Karabakh Threaten the Gas Projects of Russia and Turkey. Forbes. https://bit.ly/3Fhcbjs. 02 October 2020.

Slavkina, M. (2016). Sharp Edges of "Black Gold". The History of the "Oil Needle" in the Soviet Union. *Rodina*, 4 (416). https://rg.ru/2016/04/25/rodina-neft.html. 15 February 2021.

Smil, V. (2020). Peak Oil: A Retrospective. Crosstalk. Spectrum. IEEE. http://vaclavsmil.com/wp-content/uploads/2020/06/OIL.pdf. 30 July 2021.

Smirnov, V. (2021). Drones over the Arctic. "Military-Industrial Courier" (VPK) Newspaper, 34 (897).

Socor, V. (2008). Czech Republic Offsetting Russian Oil Supply Cuts from Alternative Sources. *Eurasia Daily Monitor*, 5 (144).

Sokolov, V., & Meredith, E. (2022). IEA's Birol Blames Russia for European Gas Crisis. Energy Intelligence Group. https://www.energyintel.com/0000017e-4ef0-df72-a97f-eef48a300000. 13 January 2022.

Soldatkin, V. (2021). Russian Gas Pipeline Exports to Europe. Reuters. https://reut.rs/3rGTJw8. 18 February 2022.

Soldatkin, V., Gamal, R. E., & Lawler, A. (2016). OPEC, Non-OPEC Agree First Global Oil Pact Since 2001. Reuters. https://www.reuters.com/article/us-opec-meeting-idUSKBN13Z0J8. 13 April 2019.

Solovieva, O. (2021). The Standard of Living of Russians Returned to the Indicators of 2010. Nezavisimaya Gazeta. https://bit.ly/3Ictq91. 14 April 2021.

Sonin, K. (2021). Model without Growth and Development. "Liberal Mission - Expertise" Series. https://liberal.ru/lm-ekspertiza/model-bez-rosta-i-razvitiya. 17 April 2021.

Spencer, S. (2022). Global Energy Security Concerns Likely Drive Supply Expansion, Diversification: Schlumberger CEO. S&P Global Commodity Insights. https://bit.ly/3MsiNzD. 23 April 2022.

Stanford Encyclopedia of Philosophy. (2021). Fuzzy Logic. https://plato.stanford.edu/entries/logic-fuzzy/. 15 November 2021.

Starr, S. F., & Cornell, S. E. (2014). Tactics and Instruments in Putin's Grand Strategy. In: *Putin's Grand Strategy: The Eurasian Union and Its Discontents*, Central Asia-Caucasus Institute and Silk Road Studies Program, 59–81.

State Duma Committee on Energy of Russia. (2017). Nuclear Energy Technologies of the New Generation: Legislative Aspect. https://bit.ly/3OvLg92. 30 January 2021.

State Duma Committee on Energy. (2021a). The Energy Committee discussed the General Scheme for the Development of the Oil Industry until 2035. http://www.komitet2-13.km.duma.gov.ru/Novosti-Komiteta/item/26061159/. 14 April 2021.

State Duma Committee on Energy. (2021b). The Strategy for Low-Carbon Development of Russia Until 2050, Its Impact on the Energy Balance and Energy Development. http://www.komitet2-13.km.duma.gov.ru/Novosti-Komiteta/item/26049219/. 15 April 2021.

State Statistics Service of Ukraine. (2021). Energy Consumption from Renewable Sources for 2007–2019. https://ukrstat.org/en/operativ/menu/menu_e/energ.htm. 24 December 2021.

Stegen, K. S. (2011). Deconstructing the "Energy Weapon": Russia's Threat to Europe as a Case Study. *Energy Policy*, 39(10): 6505–6513.

Stoddard, E. (2013). Reconsidering the Ontological Foundations of International Energy Affairs: Realist Geopolitics, Market Liberalism, and a Politico-Economic Alternative. *European Security*, 22(4): 437–463.

Strange, S. (1988). *States and Markets*, London: Continuum, 195–197.
Strange, S. (1992). States, Firms, and Diplomacy. *International Affairs*, 68(1): 1–15.
Strange, S., (1995). The Defective State. *Daedalus*, 124(2): 55–74.
Strange, S. (2000). *States, Firms, and Diplomacy in International Political Economy: Perspectives on Global Power and Wealth*, 4th ed. Abingdon: Routledge, 60.
Strüver, G., & Wegenast, T. (2018). The Hard Power of Natural Resources: Oil and the Outbreak of Militarized Interstate Disputes. *Foreign Policy Analysis*, 14(1): 86–106.
Stulberg, A. N. (2008). *Well-Oiled Diplomacy: Strategic Manipulation and Russia's Energy Statecraft in Eurasia*, State University of New York Press, 354.
Talbott, S. (2007). *The Russia Hand*, A Memoir of Presidential Diplomacy, Random House, 232–379.
Taleb, N. (2007). *The Black Swan: The Impact Of The Highly Improbable*, New York: Random House Publishing.
TASS. (2020). Dobycha nefti v Rossii v 2019 godu vyrosla do 560,2 mln tonn. https://tass.ru/ekonomika/7458697. 03 January 2020.
TASS. (2021a). The Share of the Oil and Gas Sector in Russia's GDP May Continue to Decline. https://tass.ru/ekonomika/11894437. 14 July 2021.
TASS. (2021b). Security Guarantees Are Needed Immediately. https://tass.ru/politika/13284101. 24 December 2021.
TASS. (2022). Putin Said that Russia Remains Part of the Global Economy and Will not Harm It. https://tass.ru/ekonomika/13844823. 27 February 2022.
Taylor, A. (2014). The Failure of the U.S.–Russia Reset in 9 Photos. *The Washington Post*. https://wapo.st/3yfLJ9T. 15 May 2020.
Tereshin, A. (2021). Russia Faces the Danger of Falling Behind in Technology Forever. Secretmag. https://bit.ly/3ERWYFT. 14 April 2021.
The Coal Hub. (2022). Russia to boost coal exports to China. https://thecoalhub.com/russia-to-boost-coal-exports-to-china.html
The Council of Security. (2015). National Security Strategy of the Russian Federation. http://www.scrf.gov.ru/security/docs/document133/. 30 July 2021.
The Economist. (2022). How Would an Energy Embargo Affect Germany's Economy? Finance & Economics. Free Exchange. https://econ.st/3NN9ZVS. 30 April 2022.
The Observatory of Economic Complexity (OEC). (2021). Russia's Trade Profile. https://oec.world/en/profile/country/rus. 19 November 2021.
The Office of the United States Trade Representative (USTR). (2021). U.S.-Russia Trade Facts. https://ustr.gov/countries-regions/europe-middle-east/russia-and-eurasia/russia. 01 December 2021.
The University of Denver. (2020). Measuring Influence in the International System. Josef Korbel School of International Studies. https://korbel.du.edu/fbic. 07 February 2021.
The University of Würzburg. (2022). Democracy Matrix. https://www.democracymatrix.com/conception/democracy-matrix#c525. 06 February 2022.
The White House. (2010). U.S.–Russia Relations: "Reset" Fact Sheet. https://bit.ly/39TTIzT. 15 May 2020.
The World Inequality Database (WID). (2021). Income Inequality, Russian Federation, 1988–2021. https://wid.world/country/russian-federation/. 16 December 2021.
Thorun, C. (2009). *Explaining Change in Russian Foreign Policy: The Role of Ideas in Post-Soviet Russia's Conduct Towards The West*, Palgrave Macmillan, 1–12; 137–151.
Tikhonova, N. E., Lezhnina, Yu. P., Mareeva, S. V., Anikin, V. A., Karavay, A. V., & Slobodenyuk, E. D. (2019). Model of Income Stratification of Russian Society, Institute for Social Policy of HSE.

Tkachev, I., & Kotchenko, K. (2021). Rosstat for the First Time Calculated the Share of Oil and Gas in Russian GDP. RBK. https://bit.ly/3a10Muy. 14 July 2021.

Topol, S. (2019). What Does Putin Really Want? *New York Times Magazine*. https://nyti.ms/2xo0wzb. 16 April 2020.

Total Energies. (2021). Kharyaga PSA. https://bit.ly/3zZFczc. 29 December 2021.

Trade Map. (2021). List of Supplying Markets for a Product Imported by Moldova. https://bit.ly/3oWGuHq. 08 January 2022.

Trading Economics. (2021). Russia GDP. https://tradingeconomics.com/russia/gdp. 14 December 2021.

Transneft. (2021a). History of the Company. https://www.transneft.ru/about/story/. 15 December 2021.

Transneft. (2021b). Annual Report for 2020, 38–55. https://bit.ly/3nlIp6H. 15 December 2021.

Transneft. (2021c). Presentation for Investors for 9 Months of 2021, 3. https://www.transneft.ru/u/section_file/60871/prezentaciya_rus.pdf. 25 December 2021.

Travin, D. (2016). *Will Putin's System Last until 2042*? Saint Petersburg, Norma, 104–105.

Travin, D., Gelman, V., & Zaostrovtsev, A. (2018). *The Russian Way: Ideas, Interests, Institutions, Illusions*, The European University in St. Petersburg, 30–272.

Trenin, D. (2011). Post-imperium: a Eurasian Story. Carnegie Endowment for International Peace. https://carnegieendowment.org/pdf/book/post-imperium.pdf. 04 April 2019.

Trenin, D. (2012). *Russia's Foreign Policy Prospects. Russia-2020: Scenarios for the Future*. Carnegie Moscow Center. Russian Political Encyclopedia ROSSPEN, 59.

Tsygankov, A. (2011). Preserving Influence in a Changing World. *Problems of Post-Communism*, 58(2): 28–44.

Tsygankov, A. (2012). *Russia and the West from Alexander to Putin: Honor in International Relations*, Cambridge University Press, 2–4.

Tsygankov, A. (2016). *Russia's Foreign Policy: Change and Continuity in National Identity*, Rowman & Littlefield, 1–28; 193; 261–269.

Tsygankov, A. P. (Ed.). (2018). *Routledge Handbook of Russian Foreign Policy*, Routledge, 15.

Tumakova, I. (2021). Ansambl' ritual'noy plyaski. Interview with Andrey Movchan. Novaya Gazeta, №44. https://novayagazeta.ru/articles/2021/04/20/ansambl-ritualnoi-pliaski. 30 April 2021.

Umbach, F. (2011). Energy Security in Eurasia: Clashing Interests. In: A. Dellecker and T. Gomart (Eds.). *Russian Energy Security and Foreign Policy*, London: Routledge, 23–38

UNCTAD. (2021a). General Profile: Russian Federation. https://bit.ly/3Iu9I7p. 14.12.2021.

UNCTAD. (2021b). Handbook of Statistics 2020. Economic Trends. Fact sheet 9: Foreign Direct Investment. https://bit.ly/3Oq6KEf. 12 November 2021.

UNCTAD. (2021c). The World Investment Report 2021, 6. https://bit.ly/3ngFYSW. 16 November 2021.

UNCTAD. (2021d). Handbook of Statistics 2020. International Merchandise Trade. Fact Sheet 2: Trade Structure by the Partner. https://bit.ly/3A6wFwo. 12 November 2021.

UNCTAD. (2021e). RCA Radar. https://unctadstat.unctad.org/EN/RcaRadar.html. 29 November 2021.

UNCTAD. (2021f). Trade Openness Index 2019. https://stats.unctad.org/handbook/MerchandiseTrade/Indicators.html. 06 February 2021.

UNEP & IRP. (2020). Mineral Resource Governance in the 21st Century. https://bit.ly/3GSeU4I. 29 June 2021.

Vakhlachev, S. (2019). Why Is Russia so Lagging Behind? Nezavisimaya Gazeta. https://www.ng.ru/stsenarii/2019-11-25/10_7735_expert.html. 26 November 2019.

Valckx, N. (2022). Lower Oil Reliance Insulates World From 1970s-Style Crude Shock. IMF Blog. https://bit.ly/3NdVd9H. 07 May 2022.

Varol, T. (2013). The Russian Foreign Energy Policy. European Scientific Institute. *Egalite*, 20–397.

Vedomosti. (2000). Gas in Exchange for Friendship. https://bit.ly/3ytGWBC. 21 November 2019.

Vesti. (2021). Ministry of Natural Resources Assessed Oil and Gas Reserves in Russia. https://www.vesti.ru/finance/article/2560512. 12 May 2021.

Vladimir Milov's Personal Website. http://milov.org/. 10 October 2020.

Volchek, G. (2020). Road to the Ocean. Neftyanka. http://neftianka.ru/doroga-na-okean/#more-16532. 15 February 2021.

Wallerstein, I. (1974). *The Modern World-System I*, New York: Academic Press.

Waltz, K. (1979). *Theory of International Politics*, Addison-Wesley, 99–157.

Weber, Y. (2018). Petropolitics. In: A. Tsygankov (Ed.). *Routledge Handbook of Russian Foreign Policy*, Routledge, 99–113.

Webometrics. (2022). Countries Arranged by Number of Universities in Top Rank. http://www.webometrics.info/en/distribution_by_country. 30 March 2022.

Wendt, A. (1999). *Social Theory of International Politics*, Cambridge University Press, 82–148.

World Bank. (2019). Research and Development Expenditure (% of GDP). https://data.worldbank.org/indicator/GB.XPD.RSDV.GD.ZS. 30 November 2021.

World Bank. (2020a). Gini Index for Russia. https://data.worldbank.org/indicator/SI.POV.GINI?locations=RU. 16 December 2021.

World Bank. (2020b). Patent Applications by Residents. https://data.worldbank.org/indicator/IP.PAT.RESD. 30 November 2021.

World Bank. (2020c). Researchers in R&D per Million People. https://data.worldbank.org/indicator/SP.POP.SCIE.RD.P6. 30 November 2021.

World Bank. (2021a). Metadata. https://data.worldbank.org/. 27 February 2022.

World Bank. (2021b). The Changing Wealth of Nations. https://bit.ly/3rK5pyf. 12 June 2021.

World Bank. (2021c). Russia's Economic Recovery Gathers Pace. Russia Economic Report, 45: 7. https://bit.ly/3CDNzkq. 15 July 2021.

World Bank. (2021d). World Development Indicators. https://data.worldbank.org/. 23 November 2021.

World Bank. (2021e). Seven Countries Account for Two-Thirds of Global Gas Flaring. https://bit.ly/3nO9e43. 29 April 2021.

World Bank. (2022). Open Data. GDP growth. https://data.worldbank.org/indicator/NY.GDP.MKTP.KD.ZG?view=chart

World Integrated Trade Solution (WITS). (2021). Trade Summary for World 2019 and Trade Summary for Russia. https://bit.ly/3yGnjXo. 19 November 2021.

World Intellectual Property Organization (WIPO). (2021a). Global Brand Database. https://www3.wipo.int/branddb/en/. 30 November 2021.

World Intellectual Property Organization (WIPO). (2021b). Global Innovation Index 2021, 4. https://www.wipo.int/edocs/pubdocs/en/wipo_pub_gii_2021.pdf. 25 December 2021.

Yanovsky, A.B. (2018). Foreign Energy Policy of Russia: Challenges of the Time and Vector of Development. *Energeticheskaya Politika*, 6: 4–6.

Yavlinskiy, G. A. (2017). *Periferiynyy avtoritarizm. Kak i kuda prishla Rossiya*. Medium, 101.

Yavlinsky, G. (2015). Peripheral Authoritarianism. How and Where Did Russia Come?, Moscow: Medium Publishing House, 30–61.

Yavlinsky, G. (2020). The Political Situation in Russia. Partiya Yabloko. https://www.yabloko.ru/publikatsii/2020/08/31. 01 September 2020.

Yergin, D. (2006). Ensuring Energy Security. *Foreign Affairs*, 85: 2.

Yergin, D. (2011). *The Quest Energy, Security, and the Remaking of the Modern World*, The Penguin Press, 508–528.

Yergin, D. (2020). The New Geopolitics of Energy. *The Wall Street Journal*. https://www.wsj.com/articles/the-new-geopolitics-of-energy-11599836521. 12 September 2020.

Zapivalov, N. P. (2020). Oil of the XXI Century: A New Paradigm. *Georesources (Special Issue)*, 15–18. https://geors.ru/media/pdf/04_Zapivalov.pdf

Zaslavsky, A. (2011). Inostrannyye kompanii i Rossiyskaya neft. Carnegie Endowment Moscow. http://carnegieendowment.org/files/ProEtContra_53_40-50.pdf. 29 December 2021.

Zelensky, M. (2009). Changing the Energy Security Balance in the Baltic Sea Region. Nord Stream Gas Pipeline Case Study.

Zevelev, I. (2011). NATO's Enlargement and Russian Perceptions of Eurasian Political Frontiers. George Marshall European Center for Security Studies. https://www.nato.int/acad/fellow/98-00/zevelev.pdf. 01 December 2021.

Zhikharev, S. (1995). Gazprom chut bylo ne polomal bolshuyu diplomaticheskuyu igru. https://www.kommersant.ru/doc/119536. 13 September 2019.

Ziegler, C. E. (2016). Bringing Order Out of Chaos: Russia's Aspirations to Greatness. *Asia Policy*, 22: 230–234.

Ziegler, C. E. (2018). Principles, Style, and Conditions of Russian Diplomacy. In: A. Tsygankov (Ed.). *Routledge Handbook of Russian Foreign Policy*, Routledge, 126.

Zubarevich, N. (2021a). Dve treti regionov RF ne imeyut yavnykh konkurentnykh preimushchestv dlya razvitiya. Rosbalt. https://bit.ly/3OWmlLR. 25 December 2021.

Zubarevich, N. (2021b). There Will Be Much Less of Us. The Bell. https://bit.ly/3FJxw5y. 18 September 2021.

Zubarevich, N. (2022). New Economic Reality: A Regional Perspective. Association of Russian Banks (ARB). https://bit.ly/3k9dEjH. 22 April 2022.

Zygar, M., & Panyushkin, V. (2008). *Gazprom: New Russian Weapon*, Moscow: Zakharov, 2–3.

Index

Note: **Bold** page numbers refer to tables; *Italic* page numbers refer to figures and page numbers followed by "n" denote endnotes.

FSC
www.fsc.org
MIX
Papier | Fördert gute Waldnutzung
FSC® C083411

Kolibri 360 GmbH
Ferdinand-Jühlke-Straße 7
99095 Erfurt, Deutschland
produktsicherheit@kolibri360.de